Volume 2

EDUCATIONAL THERAPY

Jerome Hellmuth, Editor

SPECIAL CHILD PUBLICATIONS, INC.

SPECIAL CHILD PUBLICATIONS, INC.
4535 Union Bay Place N. E.
Seattle, Washington 98105

Library of Congress Catalog Card Number: 67-8807

Standard Book Number: 87562-011-6

Printed in the United States of America

CONTENTS

PREFACE   7
James J. Gallagher, Ph.D.

INSTRUCTIONAL MATERIAL CENTERS IN SPECIAL EDUCATION   13
James J. McCarthy, Ph.D.

CYBERNETICS AND AUTOMATION: THEIR IMPACT ON EDUCATION   33
Watson Klincewicz

CURRICULUM DEVELOPMENT AND THE DIMENSIONS OF EDUCABILITY   79
Bluma B. Weiner, Ed.D.

STUDIES IN SHORT TERM RETENTION OF EDUCABLE RETARDATES   87
Robert M. Allen, Ph.D.

RESEARCH AND DEVELOPMENT OF THE
PEABODY LANGUAGE DEVELOPMENT KITS   153
James O. Smith, Ed. D.
W. Mueller, Ph.D.

THE PRINCIPLES AND DYNAMICS OF THERAPEUTIC TUTORING   173
Bessie Sperry, Ph.D.
Robert G. Templeton, Ed. D.

READING, LOGIC, AND PERCEPTION:
AN APPROACH TO READING INSTRUCTION   195
David Elkind, Ph.D.

REINFORCEMENT THERAPY: A SYMPTOMATIC APPROACH
TO TEACHING EMOTIONALLY DISTURBED CHILDREN   209
Levi Lathen

**UNTAPPED LEARNING ABILITY IN TRAINABLE
MENTALLY RETARDED CHILDREN**   275
David Rothenberg, Ph.D.

**THE TEAM APPROACH IN THERAPEUTIC EDUCATION:
SUCCESSES AND FAILURES**   311
Harold Esterson, Ph.D.
Mattie Cook, M. A.
Muriel Mendlowitz, M. A.

THE DOMAN-DELACATO RATIONALE: A CRITICAL ANALYSIS   321
Melvyn P. Robbins, Ph.D.
Gene V. Glass, Ph.D.

TESTS INCARNATE: THE GAP BETWEEN TEACHING AND TESTING   379
Frank Garfunkel, Ph.D.

**TEACHER-CHILD RELATIONSHIPS IN PSYCHOEDUCATIONAL
PROGRAMMING FOR EMOTIONALLY DISTURBED CHILDREN**   391
Peter Knoblock, Ph.D.
Ralph A. Garcea, M. S. S.

**TREATMENT METHODS AND THEIR EVALUATION IN
EDUCATIONAL THERAPY**   413
Marianne Frostig, Ph.D.
Phyllis Maslow, M. A.

**AN ENGINEERED CLASSROOM DESIGN
FOR EMOTIONALLY DISTURBED CHILDREN**   433
Frank M. Hewett, Ph.D.

**THE STATUS OF RECENT AND CURRENT BEHAVIORAL RESEARCH
WITH IMPLICATIONS FOR NEW EDUCATIONAL PROGRAMS
FOR THE RETARDED**   463
Max G. Frankel, Ph.D.

**AN EVALUATION OF THE EDUCATIONALLY HANDICAPPED PROGRAM:
THE MEASURABLES AND THE UNMEASURABLES AFTER TWO YEARS**   479
Mary Meeker, Ed. D.

INDEX FOR VOLUME 1   498

INDEX FOR VOLUME 2   502

PREFACE

The writing of this preface for the second volume of EDUCATIONAL THERAPY is a source of great satisfaction to me. The articles in this volume represent the cutting edge of a new optimism and challenge for the special educator, and possibly the source of generation of new theories regarding children in educational trouble.

There seems to be a drawing together, or integration of two different professional approaches to help children in need of special care. The first represents the mental health approach, which places a great deal of emphasis on the self-image and ego structure of a youngster and emphasizes how defects in that structure could have unfortunate effects on the child's learning processes. Doubtless, there are a number of children whose case histories can provide examples of that position.

The second approach could be labeled psycho - educational, which focuses on the learning problem that might stem from a variety of reasons, including inadequate sociocultural experience, mild neurological injury, poor early education, and other factors. A child with such a learning difficulty or disability would not respond effectively to the ordinary educational program. Certainly there are many children that could be used as case studies for this approach.

Similarly, there are other youngsters who could be cited as examples of a combination of mental health and psycho - educational problems. Emotional problems might initially cause the youngster to be unresponsive to the educational program, and this unresponsiveness can lead to learning difficulties. The child then can have very real problems and difficulties in both the emotional and the psycho—educational spheres.

These two approaches imply different remedial measures to cope with the problem. The mental health approach attacks the problem of the personal relationship of the individual to his world, the significance of others around him to himself. The therapeutic philosophy is that if these problems were solved, the child would be free to respond to the learning tasks that he would meet in the school environment.

The psycho-educational approach hypothesizes that most of the emotional difficulties of the youngster extend from his failure in his society symbolized by the school—through his inability to learn. If educational tasks were sequenced in such a way to allow him to learn effectively, then the emotional adjustment problems would disappear. The articles in this issue such as those by Sperry & Templeton, and Knoblock & Garcea reflect an attempt to blend these two approaches, and to suggest that it is possible to include the best aspect of both approaches into the training of a new breed of psycho–educational specialists who are capable of dealing with most of the problems, regardless of the type of difficulty of the handicapped child. A variation on this theme is to construct a team that, in its composition, has the variety of mental health and psycho–educational resources to deal with whatever particular problem the child may manifest.

This volume is appropriately entitled EDUCATIONAL THERAPY as an indication that the educator is, or should be, specifically trained and equipped as a key element in the educational therapeutic team. More and more in the future the educational therapist will become the core of the therapeutic educational experience and he will call upon many different professional specialties to provide dimension and depth to the educational therapy provided for the child. His role is similar to the physician who has the crucial face–to–face therapeutic responsibility for medical treatment, and has surrounded himself with paramedical specialties each providing their own expert knowledge to enhance his therapeutic program.

This is a significant advance over the era when a variety of experts such as speech pathologists, social workers, clinical psychologists, and other specialists came into the school and each provided their own professional perspective as to what was needed by the child. Their diagnosis and prescriptions often had little meaning to the educator who had to carry them out, and in some cases, were more mischievous than helpful. In a psychological sense the profusion of experts seemed to result in an unintended downgrading of the teacher and the teacher's own role in direct contact with the child. The teacher became less and less confident in his own ability to deal with the problem, and was encouraged by implication, or by direct suggestion, not to deal with special problems of the child, but to leave them to "someone who really knew how." That someone was supposed to be the visiting expert. What we need now is a program to enhance the skills of the educational specialists–rather than constricting and reducing them.

Another of the more optimistic approaches to this problem can be seen in the growing tendency to involve developmental theory, and to rely less and less on the atomistic and fragmentary approaches to remedial problems. The articles of Elkind using Piagetian concepts and by Kass on the Illinois Test of Psycholinguistic Abilities built on a theoretical model from Osgood, clearly suggest a trend toward a more systematic theoretical framework as the basis for design of remedial programs. The most persuasive testimony to the effectiveness of this approach lies in the ability to design therapeutic models and sets of materials which fit into a common theoretical design. The article by Smith and Mueller on the Development of the Peabody Language Development Kits indicate clearly this trend. The Frostig development tests of visual perception also indicates a trend in this direction.

The article of Mary Meeker illustrates clearly the importance of long—range observation and evaluation of the therapeutic effort needed in order to provide a more adequate estimate of the ultimate value of therapeutic programs. In her article, the data shown supports the observations of the many persons in the therapeutic area, that whenever change starts to take place in the youngster who has been in substantial trouble, it often takes place first in the social and behavioral dimension. Then it occurs in the academic or achievement dimension. A program that is reduced to evaluating its effectiveness solely upon *immediate* changes in academic achievement as a result of the therapy appears to me as being unsound. As the Meeker article points out, achievement gains took place *only after* the behavioral gains were identified.

As Dr. William Rhodes pointed out in his preface of Volume I of EDUCATIONAL THERAPY, there is a climate of excitement and optimism in these fields that has been a long time coming. In some ways this new atmosphere represents the greater commitment to the learning ability potential of the youngster, rather than to a long range estimate of unyielding and unchanging potentials, as represented by the intelligence test and the biological medical model used in special education. At the same time, care has to be taken to provide a balanced view of both opportunities and limitations. Short term training programs such as presented by Allen & Elkind and by Frostig & Maslow may give greater hope than in fact is justified.

Unfortunately, the rules of genetics have not been repealed. Perhaps, we will eventually modify them with more experience and data. However, we have yet to find the ultimate training devices that will modify the trainable retarded child into an intellectually superior child. In most cases therapeutic attention results in a major initial shift or movement forward. This movement is then followed by a leveling off in performance to a rather consistent learning curve. For the therapeutic professional to suggest unlimited potential for the child may be a disservice as it might be to suggest that the child's performance in learning is biologically fixed, and nothing can be done to improve it. The true situation is probably somewhere in the middle range. That middle range allows the therapeutic educator room to seek meaningful changes and improvement in the youngster, without expecting or hoping for magical transformations.

One of the newer and most interesting trends revealed in this current volume is represented by the article by McCarthy on the Special Education Instructional Materials Centers. Teachers who have been involved in educational therapeutic responsibilities have long bemoaned the fact that they have not had the tools or resources to do the job correctly. Often they were reduced to constructing therapeutic materials on their own, with little assistance of any organized type. These Special Education Instructional Materials Centers represent a major effort by the Division of Research, Bureau of Education for the Handicapped, of the U.S. Office of Education, to provide a nation wide system of centers where teachers could readily obtain the latest in materials and media, and provide a resource center for the evaluation of such materials, as well as offering special short-term training to help teachers learn how to utilize the new materials effectively.

The Instructional Materials Centers are one of the more visible indicators of the greatly expanded Federal interest in educating handicapped children, and providing the educational resources necessary to achieve a program of excellence for them. An indication of the trend of the government's commitment to educate the nation's more than 5,000,000 children can be seen by comparing a commitment of less than $1 million in 1957 with a commitment of $78 million in the area of research, training and services in 1967 for purposes of providing special education for handicapped children. The establishment at the highest administrative level of units such as the Bureau of Education for the Handicapped in the U. S. Office of Education, represents another trend to provide special resources to local schools and the state educational agencies to supplement the efforts already under way at these two levels.

In the collection of articles in this volume concerned with issues of therapeutic education there is an important dimension that is left out. However, as the field develops, one may safely predict that it will appear with increasing frequency. This dimension involves the whole nature of the social milieu surrounding the child. The child's social and emotional problems are often more than his own internal misperceptions. In fact these problems may represent a sickness in his social group. Similarly, problems of motivation and special learning troubles may be the core of difficulty in the social group rather than in the individual. Educational therapy needs to be enlarged to conceptualize the social group as total problem needing remedial service. In this regard, the article by Hewett on the engineered classroom would represent a design of a viable educational experience on a group basis.

Above all, what this volume seems to suggest is that special education and remedial education are coming of age. This is reflected in the growing effort to provide a conceptual theory or framwork around which diagnosis and treatment can be designed. Further, other theoretical contributions in psychology and education should be involved to strengthen the therapeutic program. We don't need to apologize for pursuing alternative models of treatment and training in our present state of the art. As we learn more, these programs will find their conjunctions. Such ardent diversity as we now see is a mark of our vigorous progress as well as our therapeutic immaturity.

It is with a sense of enthusiam for future advances of knowledge in the area discussed by the contributors, and the potential of this knowledge to advance the goals of special education, that this preface is presented.

James J. Gallagher, Ph.D,
Associate Commissioner,
Bureau of Education for
the Handicapped,
Washington, D. C.

INSTRUCTIONAL MATERIAL CENTERS IN SPECIAL EDUCATION

James J. McCarthy, Ph.D., Director
Special Education Instructional Materials Center,
University of Wisconsin, School of Education,
Department of Counseling and Behavioral Studies,
Madison, Wisconsin

JAMES J. MC CARTHY, Ph. D.

The special educator of tomorrow will not have to build and/or modify her instructional materials to accommodate the needs of her pupils. At her local Special Education Instructional Materials Center she will find (1) a wide variety of instructional materials that have proven useful for use with handicapped children; (2) "Consumer Report" type publications which tell, in plain language, how effective given materials have shown to be under given field conditions; (3) a mechanical "search" system which will comb through existing instructional materials in special education, extract all materials on a given topic and print out the names of such materials together with vendor, cost, and address; and (4) expert consultation on problems relating to instructional materials. The tomorrow I speak of is almost here. In fact, some of these services are available now to special educators in some parts of the country.

Most chapters in this volume are concerned with **methods** of instruction; this chapter is concerned with the problems which are leading to a quiet revolution in concepts about instructional **materials** in special education, where the revolution has gone, and where it seems to be going.

Seldom does special education have the opportunity to make deliberate and calculated changes in its basic operations. However, Federal funds have been supporting programatic efforts which promise a genuine breakthrough for special education and, eventually, for education generally. The ideas involved are not new; the reader will find a ring of practical familiarity throughout. But the combination of ideas, and more particularly, their implementation, is novel and may ultimately affect the professional lives of every special educator in the country.

INTRODUCTION

One of the most persistent, major problems associated with special education is the lack of an adequate supply of effective instructional materials. It is difficult to explain this phenomenon. In a country which leads the world in production capacity, which is rich in research and innovative talent, and whose literacy rate is testament to the value and effort placed on education, how could this problem continue to exist for over a half century without serious effort at resolve?

Perhaps the quantity and effectiveness of instructional materials in special education was never actually viewed as a problem. Those being prepared to teach exceptional children are told to be creative and innovative in developing and adapting materials for use with their children because the commercial market contains so little that is directly useful. Having been thus instructed, perhaps the naked king still appears royally clothed. More probably, the problem is visible to all, but is one of such magnitude that it seems to defy solution and, therefore, becomes one we have learned to live with.

Clearly, no profession can continue to exist indefinitely on a patchwork of borrowed, modified, intuitive, untested and homemade materials. The special education enterprise, in the training of its practitioners and in the teaching of its exceptional children, must accept a basic responsibility; it must recognize and cope with the problem of instructional materials.

Teachers typically know more about the characteristics of the children they wish to instruct than they do about the characteristics of the materials they wish to instruct them with. The essence of special education lies in the matching of instructional materials to the learning characteristics of the child. Obviously this cannot be done unless the performance characteristics of the materials are also known (e.g., Has this type of material been used successfully with this type of child in the past? How many repetitions were necessary? What was the period of retention? Exactly what method of instruction was employed in achieving the stated results? How does it compare with similar material from another producer?). Given that special educators (or educational therapists) do not have a sufficient supply of effective instructional materials **and** that such materials are germane to their professional mission, what might be done about it?

First, let us reject the notion that teachers can produce such materials by simply using them to greater creativity and innovation. Learning is a complex phenomenon. It is error to believe that educators can predict and control such behavior simply because it occurs in their presence. It is arrogant to assume that the preparation special educators receive qualifies them for the task of preparing instructional materials that will lead to desired results. Considering the complex findings of psychology to date, one must conclude that much of what children learn in school is fortuitous and depends, not so much on the excellence of the educational process as upon the wondrous plasticity of the human central nervous system. Typically, the children seen by special educators have not been so fortunate.

One searches in vain to find teacher preparation programs in special education that contain courses dealing with the psychological principles underlying the design of instructional materials, or the testing of the effectiveness of instructional materials, or even the determination of the performance characteristics of instructional materials. One finds, in current teacher preparation programs, practically no evidence of courses in practical workshop and basic electricity that are needed for the **construction** of many of today's instructional materials. Thus, how can it be argued that the teacher is an apt designer and constructor of instructional materials? Frankly, I do not believe a special educator's preparation should include the above courses. This belief springs from the view that a special educator's expertise lies in the act of arranging the environment so that optimal learning will occur, not in constructing that environment. But, regardless of one's philosophy on the role of the educator, the fact remains that special educators are not prepared to design and construct instructional materials. Who should? The problem is even more complex than this, for it goes to the ability of special educators to properly choose and utilize appropriately prepared instructional materials, to the universities and colleges that train special educational personnel, and to the producers of instructional materials. Perhaps the best approach would be to begin with the **ideal** situation and then attempt to suggest how such a state might be achieved.

THE IDEAL STATE OF AFFAIRS

Ideally, the schools would engage in applied and action research, the colleges and universities would alter their training of special education personnel to account for the needs of the schools, and plentiful production of instructional materials would be assured through either providing markets or aids to commercial producers and/or by utilizing sheltered workshops for this purpose. These points, and their implications, are developed in the following paragraphs: Basic, Applied and Action Research.*

I understand research to mean careful, systematic study undertaken to establish principles or facts. Basic researchers seek to establish valid and generalizable principles of behavior. Their research strategy is to complete small bits of precise research which one day can be welded into a unified body of behavioral laws for the prediction and control of behavior, including learning behavior.

Basic research takes time and money; it absorbs much research talent and does not promise immediate, applicable results. From the school's standpoint, basic research is not of great immediate value for the results are often not relevant to the school's problems and are hardly ever applicable without further refinement. In addition, the school is placed in a position of having to compete for research talent.

*Portions of this chapter have been reprinted from the WINNOWER, Vol. II, Nos. 3 & 4, 1966, a quarterly publication of the SEIMC at the University of Wisconsin.

The demands of good applied research are no less strenuous than the demands of good basic research. Applied researchers are looking for answers to specific questions. They are often unconcerned with generating principles of behavior. Leaving aside these encumbrances allows the applied researcher to move ahead quickly and obtains answers to specific problems today, knowing that new problems and new answers will have to be sought tomorrow. It is precisely the characteristics of speed and specificity that suit applied research so ideally to today's schools. Traditionally, the differences between basic and applied research have been played down on the assumption that, at base, there is really very little difference between the two. Yet, there seems to be a tacit status distinction between basic and applied researchers themselves, favoring the former. The opposite should be true. The characteristics of each type of research should be made explicit so behavioral research can be put to optimal advantage. Nor should status distinctions be made between basic and applied researchers, for such imponderables have a way of influencing career choices and making fact of fancy.

"Action research" is a name applied to the efforts of practitioners at answering some of their questions through the use of elemental research design and statistics. It is premised on the fact that these tools can be learned fairly rapidly by practitioners and on the faith the validity of answers thus obtained exceeds that of solutions obtained via reference to tradition, administrative fiat, coin flipping, asking other teachers, and so on. In the realm of human behavior, where valid general answers or specific directions are typically not available, some viable means of obtaining answers must be supplied the practitioner. Consequently, elements of research are seen, by the present author, as an essential ingredient of pre-service and in-service teacher preparation, particularly in special education.

The School System

There are two facts of life school systems must face. First, a host of professional education problems exist which can be solved most effectively through research. Second, the schools themselves will have to take the responsibility for the conduct of this research.

How does a teacher, a school, or a school system decide which books to buy, whether to employ phonics or not, which of the several proposed methods of teaching spelling should be used, whether modern math is really superior to the regular math, or if teaching French in the fourth grade is the most effective time for such a venture? Should one trust the publisher's literature, ask another school or teacher, consult an "expert" on these topics, appoint a teacher's panel or a parent's panel to evaluate the alternative in question, or perhaps, flip a coin? I will not dwell on the faults of our past; this has been overdone. Many actions of the past have been quite reasonable and logical if judged in their historical context. But education has been mandated a new and vital status; society has begun to acknowledge the value of education in terms of adjustment, competition, and survival. Decisions on the professional aspects of education are vital; today's urgency demands our best efforts.

A most reasonable way of evaluating materials and methods is to try them on the children for which they have been designed and evaluate progress. I refer to this process as "applied research". It is, I think, an optimal means for making decisions about professional educational methods and materials. It is fairly fast, inexpensive, and objective; it typically adds to our store of information about education, and raises other relevant questions. Applied research, as a professional education method, should be a regular part of school routine. Unfortunately, schools have traditionally looked to non-school behavioral researchers for answers and we have all decried the twenty-five year gap existing between the laboratory and the school.

Underlying the "research gap" explanation of the school's inability to apply basic research findings is an assumption which is largely questionable, namely, that the research produced in the laboratory is directly applicable to the school situation. Here is the root problem. The basic behavioral scientist does not consult the schools about the research he should undertake. He does not construct his hypotheses to answer questions the schools ask. **Nor should he.** His aims are different than those of the schools and his professional rewards do not come from the schools. Indeed, it is surprising that such research can be applied in the school at all, even that done twenty-five years ago. If the schools are interested in obtaining applied research on **their** students and on **their** problems, **they** will have to conduct such research themselves. And when they do, the research gap will become as obsolete as the horse-drawn carriage.

To the degree that schools undertake applied and action research, the teacher will be involved as a researcher. As a minimum requirement, teachers—under the guidance of professional researchers—will have to be good data collectors. Schools, generally, have not realized their research potential in this regard. Within the nation's schools, hundreds of studies could be carried on simultaneously, each involving thousands of children. I do not think it is entirely irrelevant to remark that research of this magnitude, for extended periods of time, could enhance, enormously, the operation of the educational enterprise. But, at base, such efforts rest on the ability of the teacher to collect objective, psychological data. Thus, the role of the teacher, as a novice researcher, is wholly compatible with the school as a research agency.

Moreover, a teacher versed in the elements of research can do more than collect data for professional basic and applied researchers. She can initiate research studies on her own professional problems. Also, she is in a better position to understand the professional journals and to implement and evaluate some of the leads suggested in them. Of course, there are many practical difficulties in transforming a school system into a research agency and its teachers into action researchers, but the results of such efforts should be most rewarding.

The availability of Federal funds has made more than one school administrator wish fervently that he had a researcher on his team. Researchers, by training, have learned to identify problems and to state them clearly, together with suggested solutions and methods for evaluating the latter. These talents are critically required if school systems are to attract Federal monies and to spend them with optimal effectiveness within the intent of the funding legislation. It is disappointing that this staffing gap only becomes visible in the spotlight of fiscal incentive; however, it is good that it is becoming visible regardless of the circumstances.

Even prior to the onset of current Federal funds, however, a good staff researcher would have increased the efficacy of the educational programs and probably saved money doing so. Today, there should be no problem about **where the money for applied research comes from**. From the professional point of view, the question should never have been asked. In my view, the researcher is of the same unquestioned value as the school engineer, the principal, and even the teacher.

The Colleges and Universities

The recent willingness of some school systems to engage applied researchers has highlighted the critical shortage of applied behavioral researchers. Basic behavioral researchers were sometimes available, as consultants, to prepare proposals for funds but in so doing, they have frequently confirmed the school's view (right or wrong) that these people were excessively academic and really did not appreciate the practical problems facing the schools. Clinicians and teachers appreciated the practical problems facing the schools, but with a sometimes exception, could not prepare acceptable grant proposals. There were, and are, few persons with solid talent for both tasks. This is not due solely to the innate difficulty of such a role; few persons have been trained in both roles. Typically, Ed.D.'s in special education gravitate to administration and Ph.D.'s to graduate training and research; and the research these latter usually do is typically basic research for this is regarded as essential in the training of doctoral students. Now, whether high level applied researchers have not been trained because there was little previous demand or whether there was little previous demand because there were so few existing applied specialists, is a moot question. The point seems to be that such personnel are needed and the schools are increasingly willing to employ them. The universities, it would seem, have an obligation to prepare such personnel.

But, even if the schools were anxious to employ applied researchers and even if these researchers were available in adequate numbers, little or no applied research could be carried out unless the teachers in the system were adequate data collectors and had attitudes at least not unfavorable to research. Just as the teacher cannot carry out very adequate research without the support of the administration, the administration cannot carry out adequate research without the assistance of the teacher.

It is hoped, of course, that the teacher could be an independent action researcher; the minimum requirement is that she be capable of assisting knowledgeably in the research process. The skills and attitudes necessary for action research are not terribly difficult to acquire. While they should be acquired at the pre-service stage, Barnes (1964) has shown these same skills and attitudes can be successfully taught at the in-service level and taught in a fairly short time (less than a semester).

Any realistic attempt to incorporate efficient, school-related research into the schools requires that they accept their role as research agencies as well as service agencies. The view that the educational act and applied research are incompatible is no longer tolerable; these activities are mutually enhancing. Moreover, universities must make more deliberate efforts at producing high caliber, applied researchers at the doctoral level. The amount and nature of change required of present doctoral programs to accomplish this aim is a question to be dealt with by the universities; at first blush, it would appear that sweeping changes would not be required. And, of course, teachers pre-service preparation must include training in elemental research skills.

It was probably my concern with the questionable quality of many instructional materials used in special education that started me thinking about how the vast amount of applied research needed to evaluate our instructional materials might be accomplished. Clearly the laboratories would have to be abandoned; our great needs could only be met in the field where the children are, and through the large group of people who daily work with these children. It becomes clear, too, that the questions asked by the teachers and the questions asked by the university-based researchers were usually quite different. Thus, the inevitable conclusion emerges, namely, practicing professionals must have the capacity to implement and conduct their own research. Given this premise, the school's acceptance of a research role **and** the pre-service training modification (at both the pre and post bachelor's level) follow naturally.

Materials Production

It is becoming increasingly clear that materials shortages exist in special education because, among other reasons, few commercial producers are interested in this market. The persistent problem of limited markets, lack of materials research, and needs for special modification, will plague even the most altruistic of commercial enterprises. However, technical advances make limited scale specialty production possible today

providing the factor of profit competition need not be a paramount consideration. Ideally, Federal aid could be available to producers evidencing a willingness and a capacity to produce special education instructional materials.

From both a logical and social point of view, the sheltered workshop is suggested as an optimum type of limited producer for such materials. It is not guided solely by the profit-competition motive and it has the capacity for limited production. Coincidentally, the workshop support strategy of subcontracting work has increasingly been called into question because: (1) it is an erratic form of support, and (2) it usually does not provide the range of skill requirements that offer clients the optimum rehabilitative advantage. In brief, not only is this facility optimally suited to fill a special education materials need, but it should be, at this point in time, most disposed to cooperate in such an effort in behalf of its own ends. Of such substance does the ideal state of affairs consist.

THE RISE OF THE INSTRUCTIONAL MATERIALS CENTER IN SPECIAL EDUCATION

It is not difficult to suggest how things might be and how others must change to accomplish this millennium; the real difficulty lies in effecting the desired change. Such a change may have begun when, in 1964, two Special Education Instructional Materials Centers (SEIMC)* were established, under funds from the U. S. Office of Education.

The SEIMC at the University of Wisconsin was established to demonstrate how the chronic problem of effective instructional materials in special education might be met. It aimed to (1) provide direct service to special educators in the State of Wisconsin, (2) to stimulate the establishment of similar centers in states surrounding Wisconsin, and (3) to serve as an operational model for interested persons from around the country. Its specific aims included (1) serving as a depository for existing instructional materials in special education, (2) serving as a free loan library to professional personnel in special education in Wisconsin, (3) engaging in the evaluation of existing materials and disseminating these findings to practitioners, (4) providing individual consultation and in-service training on instructional materials for special educators in the state, (5) providing regional consultation to those wishing to establish similar centers, (6) assisting, by consultation, commercial and non-commercial producers of instructional materials, and (7) creating or adapting and evaluating instructional materials.

Within the first year of SEIMC's existence, much material had been acquired and cataloged; a library established; a system for borrowing, including loans through the mail, instituted; and an automated library search scheme established. Initially, materials on the retarded were acquired, followed by materials on the emotionally disturbed, and the physically handicapped and neurologically impaired. Much interest was evidenced

*At the University of Wisconsin and the University of Southern California.

22

by the national field and SEIMC's staff was constantly consulting with interested persons around the country. In time, Centers were established under Federal grants*, in Kentucky, Florida, Texas, Illinois, Michigan, Oregon, and Colorado, to join the existing Centers in Wisconsin and California. Though modes of operation and organization differ, the goals of all the special education Centers are the same.

Since most of the Centers were established at universities, within ongoing programs of teacher preparation in special education, the commitment of these institutions was assured. However, each Center, in its own way, sensed a lack of involvement among its constituent school systems. In the Wisconsin SEIMC, where copious records of borrowing and Center usage were kept, it became clear that only a small portion of eligible special educators were using the services of the Center, despite heroic efforts at publicity. In time, it became clear that unless "branch" or "satellite" Centers were established in local school systems, the desired involvement might never be achieved. Thus began the job of establishing branch Centers around the state by assisting local school systems in the preparation of grant proposals and by guaranteeing to them, from the Wisconsin SEIMC, as many of the technical and exotic services as their respective proposed Centers could not provide. The ultimate aim is to establish sufficient branches so that every special educator in the state is within the operational radius of a branch Center, and through that, the SEIMC. This, indeed, is achieving the involvement of the local school systems.

THE INSTRUCTIONAL MATERIALS CENTER NETWORK
FOR
HANDICAPPED CHILDREN AND YOUTH

The benefits of tying the SEIMC's into a national organization were too great to ignore. Every function of a given SEIMC could be done even more adequately by a national network of SEIMC's (e.g., searching for new materials, sophisticated cataloging and retrieval of materials, materials evaluation, publication, materials design, encouraging production of given materials, in-service and pre-service training in materials selection and evaluation, etc.). Moreover, if each SEIMC could establish a system of branches, then each special educator in the country could, ultimately, share the benefits of a **national** effort. The by-products of such a merger would include a valuable communication system beginning with the Federal Office of Education, through SEIMC's and their branch centers, and terminating with the individual special educators.

Accordingly, in 1966, a federation of the existing SEIMC's was formed and called the

*Centers are supported by grants from the U.S. Department of Health, Education and Welfare Office of Education, Division of Handicapped Children and Youth.

Instructional Materials Center Network for Handicapped Children and Youth (IMCNHCY). Thus, less than two years after the founding of the two original SEIMC's, a federation of ten such centers was formed with its own officers and by-laws. Each SEIMC is strengthening its ties within the IMCNHCY against the time when many of its tasks will be fully coordinated with the similar efforts of other centers. Centers are now being established in those regions of the country not yet under the service mantle of existing Network facilities; these centers, too, will join the IMCNHCY. While not all SEIMC's are restricted to a service region ending at the boundaries of a single state; it is most likely that each state in the union will have a major branch center or SEIMC before the development of the IMCNHCY is completed. A complete and functional "Network" by 1970 would seem a realistic expectation.

The primary professional goal of the "Network" is to enhance the quality and quantity of instructional materials in special education. To do this, it must look to the evaluation of materials and to realistic means for encouraging producers to provide the same in adequate quantities. Thus, **evaluation** and **production** are the principal concerns.

Evaluation

The two principal forms of evaluation that concern a SEIMC are evaluation of its own efforts and evaluation of instructional materials. In evaluating its own efforts, both the quantitative and qualitative aspects of a Center's operation must be scrutinized. The former includes the collection of data on number of loans, consultations, persons using the center, items processed and the like. The latter consists of determining, through interviews and questionnaires, the impact of the Center on the professional activities of the special educators in its service region. For various reasons, it is probably useful to have the qualitative evaluation done by a competent independent research agency.

There are many approaches to the evaluation of instructional materials. Williams (1966) has identified three major approaches as the (1) experimental method, (2) the psychometric method, and (3) the panel method, in order of sophistication.

The experimental method involves the use of competing materials under controlled conditions. Ideally, methodology is held constant and materials varied. The problems associated with this approach include control of pertinent variables, appropriate statistical analyses, and the cost of such efforts.

The problem of variable control is central to the evaluation efforts. The variables which can influence learning are so numerous that it is presently the practice to do such experiments in laboratory situations where many variables can be controlled. This approach, however, is not adequate to our needs because the sheer amount of materials to be evaluated would preclude the use of such limited facilities. To catch up with and keep abreast of instructional materials production, evaluation must be conducted in a coordinated manner, over hundreds of classrooms, with teachers collecting the data. Clearly, anything but "in-situ" assessment is out of the question; accordingly, techniques must be found to accomplish this. The key problem is to identify those variables which are significant for given learning situations and those which are not, so the researcher may control the former and ignore the latter. The researcher can usually apply some form of control (counter balance, elimination, etc.) to a given variable; the question is WHICH variables to control.

Statistical techniques must be capable of handling several variables simultaneously. Logically, and empirically (Sadek, 1966), intercorrelation, factor analysis, and step-wise regression are suggested; the last is, perhaps, the most suitable **single** technique of the three while the most effective approach is probably the step-wise regression FOLLOW-ING factor analysis. Sadek's results, though tentative, are promising and suggest that statistical techniques will probably be a minor problem in contrast to the identification of significant variables for control. Clearly, the experimental method will consume much time and effort; the generation of data could cover a period of several years in some instances. Therefore, a priority of techniques must be established, based upon the immediate and long range evaluation needs. In many instances, for example, it may be more desirable to have less precise information quickly than to have precise information for which one has to wait.

A less precise, but considerably faster method of evaluating materials is in the Psychometric Method. This consists of obtaining useful quantitative indices of instructional materials. For example, in reading materials, the mean sentence length, ratio of repetition, readability index, and similar types of indices may be obtained in a rather objective and straightforward manner (see McCarthy, 1966; 1967). Experience has shown that special educators are capable of computing such indices with a minimum of difficulty and utilizing them, in a comparative manner, for the selection among alternatives, of the most appropriate materials for given types of handicapped children. The adaption of index formulae to special education, and the creation of new formulae, has begun in the area of reading materials (Everson, 1967) but much work will be required to expand this work and extend it to other areas (e.g., arithmetic).

The concept of quantitative indices is not new; it has been used in education since at least the early 1920's. Publishers often supply useful quantitative information with their educational materials; however, recomputations are usually required since the diverse methods used by producers in obtaining these indices does not permit direct comparisons of products. Utilizing the coordinated efforts of the IMCNHCY, a rather substantial indexing of instructional materials could be accomplished in a relatively short time and act as a sort of "first approximation" to the more precise experimental data.

The third evaluation method, "panels", could perhaps be better regarded as "expert opinion" for it need not be limited to the collective opinions of teacher panels about given materials. "Trial usage" reports, expert reviews, and questionnaires and interviews are other common techniques for collecting such data. Such techniques are already in widespread use but often lack utility because there is no common source reference in which one can find all reports; clearly, such a reference could be generated by the IMCNHCY in a reasonably short time. Even here, however, groundwork is required. The traditional questionnaire may lack validity and reliability. Coloma (1967) is attempting the development of a valid and reliable questionnaire on reading materials for handicapped children; her techniques may be applicable to the development of similar devices. It is probable that panels and reviewers will have to be provided with guides so that all pertinent aspects of given materials will be considered and so that several reviews of the same materials can be directly compared from panel to panel and reviewer to reviewer. At this level of rather "intuitive" evaluation it is probably critical to require the consensus of replicated reports from representative panels before accepting outcome statements. Thus, the simple founding phrase, giving purpose to SEIMC's "to assure an adequate supply of **effective** instructional materials", appears to be a complex task. Assuring the production of such instructional materials, in adequate amounts, may be equally complex.

Production

Let us begin with the realistic premise that neither teachers nor SEIMC's are apt producers of instructional materials. Let us further assume that special educators should have available to them all needed major materials and should not have to construct or modify materials beyond the simple cutting and pasting stage. Neither teachers nor materials centers have the production, marketing, or distribution facilities for adequate materials production. Accordingly, those who do have such facilities must be encouraged to produce instructional materials. Ideally, teachers could approach SEIMC's with ideas for instructional materials; centers could produce prototypes and field test the same. In my judgment, those who produce, market and distribute materials AS A BUSINESS should be utilized at this point. If there are market possibilities, it would be a rare producer, commercial or non-profit, who would turn away from the task when it begins with a tested prototype; this is what I mean by "encouraging producers". Moreover, copyright assignment should be obtained by the materials designer (e.g., teacher) prior to the intervention of an SEIMC so the designer may reap whatever financial benefits might accrue. Though there might be some ethical and legal resolve needed on this last point, such procedures would assure the continued flow of materials design ideas in the best free enterprise tradition.

We have previously alluded to other methods of encouraging production (Federal subsidies to commercial producers and cooperation with sheltered workshops). Any and all legitimate avenues of production must be tapped to assure the supply of materials needed. For the special educator, the pedestrian processes of production, marketing, and distribution are equally as critical as evaluation efforts. No matter how much development and testing have gone into a material, its simple physical presence is still required before any of this groundwork has meaning.

Network Development

Looking to the future, the IMCNHCY might consist of a primary university-based network interwoven with a secondary school-based network. The primary network would consist of perhaps fifteen to twenty SEIMC's, each associated with a given region of the country and which, collectively, would include all of the country. Each region, in turn, would have one or more major service centers in each of its component states, each associated with its own network of branch centers. This concept is premised on the notion that MOST SEIMC's will stimulate the development of branch centers in local schools and state departments for direct service to special educators, reserving to themselves the kinds of tasks shown in Figure 1.

One could envision hundreds of branch and state department service centers if each special educator in the country is to have egress to the network system.

One cannot forecast development beyond this level at this time. Centers will probably be used for a wide variety of tasks not directly related to materials since the mere "communication" aspects of such a system could be invaluable in many ventures. Moreover, the influence of regional laboratories, research and development centers, and other projects and agencies, has not been incorporated into these predictions. Minus these elaborations, the scheme might look something like Figure 2.

	University-Based Network	School-Based Network
Funding	Federal, University	Federal, State Dept., Local
Primary Tasks:	Surveillance & influence of pre-service training, materials evaluation, Materials design, encourage materials production, search and retrieval.	Acquisition, cataloging, and loaning of materials, consultation, in-service training

FIGURE 1

Predictions of Network Development[a]

[a]Underlined tasks require the highest degree of coordination between the primary and secondary networks.

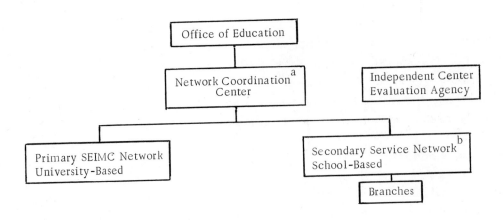

FIGURE 2
Predicted Network Organization

[a]It would seem that a specific coordination operation would be required.

[b]Large metropolitan branches, state departments of public instruction, and some SEIMC's will probably constitute the service network.

National events, professional apathy, and many other factors could thwart the development of a network similar to the one described herein. Yet, a beginning has been made; the primary network has been established and some elements of the secondary network have appeared, all in three years (1964-1967). Moreover, the needed Federal support for continued development seems inherent in existing and proposed legislation. Thus, acknowledged needs, and resources for their solution, seem to be in favorable juxtaposition.

THE IMCNHCY AND THE EDUCATIONAL THERAPIST

The value of SEIMC's for the educational therapist are apparent. These organizations offer, perhaps, the first full-time, massive and continuing assistance to the educational therapist (or special educator) in her professional role. They offer, in substance, **immediate** and appropriate assistance with **present** professional problems in special education.

University-based SEIMC's are currently developing service-based programs, many of which will later be transferred to local schools and state departments. Special educators may find services available, or soon to be available, in various regions of the country. Figure 3 indicates the existing SEIMC's, address, region served, and areas of handicapping in which given centers specialize.

Material loans to special educators within the immediate regions, material searches by category, various center publications, and professional consultations are among the services offered, or soon to be offered, by these centers.

CENTER – DIRECTOR	REGION SERVED	SERVICES

California
    Robert B. McIntyre
    Calvin C. Nelson
    17 Chester Place
    Univ. So. California
    Los Angeles, Calif. 90007
	Nevada
	Arizona
		M.R.
		Visually Handicapped
		Hard of Hearing

Colorado
    William Reid
    Colorado State College
    Greeley, Colorado 80631
	Montana
	Wyoming
	New Mexico
	Utah
		Physically Handicapped
		M.R.
		Emotionally Disturbed

Florida
    Leonard J. Lucito
    Engineering Bldg.
    Univ. So. Florida
    Tampa, Florida 33620
	Alabama
	Georgia
	Mississippi
	So. Carolina
		M.R.
		Emotionally Disturbed
		Speech Impaired

Illinois (State of)
    Mrs. Lenore E. Powell
    Miss Gloria Calovina
       (Center)
    410 S. Michigan Blvd.
    Chicago, Illinois
       (Admin)
    316 S. Second St.
    Springfield, Illinois
	State Center	M.R.
		Visually Handicapped
		Hard of Hearing

Kentucky (Regional)
    William Tisdall
    Univ. of Kentucky
    641 S. Limestone St.
    Lexington, Kentucky 40506
	Tennessee
	N. Carolina
	Virginia
	W. Virginia
		M.R.
		Speech Impaired
		Physically Handicapped
		Neuro. Impaired

Kentucky (Printing House)
    Carl W. Lappin
    1839 Frankfort Ave.
    Louisville, Kentucky 40206
	Non-Regional	Blind

Michigan
    Lou Alonso
    218 Erickson Hall
    Michigan State Univ.
    East Lansing, Mich. 48823
	Ohio
	Indiana
		Visually Handicapped

Oregon
    Melton Martinson
    Univ. of Oregon
    1676 Columbia St.
    Eugene, Oregon 97403
	Idaho
	Washington
	Alaska
	Hawaii
		Physically Handicapped
		Neuro. Impaired
		M.R.
		Emotionally Disturbed
		Speech Impaired

Texas
    William G. Wolfe
    Univ. of Texas
    304 West 15th St.
    Austin, Texas 78701
	Louisiana
	Arkansas
	Oklahoma
		Physically Handicapped
		Neuro. Impaired
		M.R.
		Hard of Hearing

Wisconsin
    James J. McCarthy
    2570 University Ave.
    Univ. of Wisconsin
    Madison, Wis. 53706
	Wisconsin	Physically Handicapped
		M.R.
		Emotionally Disturbed

**Special Education Instructional Materials Centers
as of June, 1966**

FIGURE 3

SUMMARY

A massive problem requires a massive solution. The chronic lack of a sufficient supply of effective instructional materials in special education may have been engaged during the Kennedy era, for it was reports from the Presidential Task Forces on Mental Retardation that led ultimately to the funding of the first two SEIMC's. As these centers became operational prototypes, the Federal Government funded a series of such centers. Organization is now proceeding in two directions. Upward, these centers have united into a network chiefly for the purpose of mutual enhancement of their efforts; downward, each center is encouraging the development of local branch centers so that service functions (e.g., materials loan, search and retrieval, consultation) can be directly available to special educators everywhere.

It appears that eventually, service tasks will be assimilated largely by branch centers, freeing the SEIMC's for materials evaluation and other applied research, encouragement of production of needed materials, advanced and massive retrieval and storage systems, and so forth. Even now, many basic services are available, or will be available, shortly, through regional SEIMC's; in time, such services should be available locally. The impact of this development on special education (and ultimately on education, generally) could be substantial. Since ultimate success depends upon a massive effort, it would be premature to forecast the success or even the eventual direction of this **development,** but if one extrapolates the future from the past, success is indeed indicated for the entire history of the SEIMC development, to date, spans only three years.

References

1. Barnes, Fred B. RESEARCH FOR THE PRACTITIONER IN EDUCATION. Department of Elementary Principals, National Education Association, Washington, D. C., 1964.

2. Coloma, Rita. Doctoral dissertation, in preparation. University of Wisconsin, 1967.

3. Everson, Elenor. Master's thesis, in preparation. University of Wisconsin, 1967.

4. McCarthy, James J. THE TEACHER AS A RESEARCHER. THE WINNOWER, 3 (1), 1966.

5. McCarthy, James J. THE TEACHER AS A RESEARCHER. THE WINNOWER, 3 (2), 1967.

6. Sadek, Farouk M. EVALUATION OF CERTAIN STATISTICAL TECHNIQUES IN THE ASSESSMENT OF MATERIALS IN SPECIAL EDUCATION. Doctoral dissertation. University of Wisconsin, 1966.

7. Williams, Phillip. THE EVALUATION OF EDUCATIONAL MATERIALS FOR EDUCAT-ING SUBNORMAL CHILDREN. Education and Training of the Mentally Retarded, I, 4, 1966.

CYBERNETICS AND AUTOMATION: THEIR IMPACT ON EDUCATION

Watson Klincewicz, Director,
The Vanguard School, Career Guidance Center,
Valley Forge Industrial Park,
Haverford, Pennsylvania

WATSON KLINCEWICZ

INTRODUCTION

At some future time, perhaps aeons from now, historians from an advanced civilization will be retrieving data concerning our age. Their computers, programmed to disgorge prolific facts about our habits, traditions, events, and discoveries, may be frustrated in the interminable test of characterizing this era. Initial trends may favor an atomic age label while subsequent ones will shift from the space age, the automation age, the electronic age, and the micro-biological age. Eventually, a synthesis of the full information processed by a newer generation, unimaginably lightning-swift, ultimately infallible machine, will be rendered.

Because of the sweeping lack of perspective and due to the incomplete course of present history, our generation will remain unenlightened about the influence it will have upon future civilizations.

We may gain some insight by examining other ancient cultures such as the Hellenistic society in the second and first centuries B.C. When it was no longer supported by an integrated culture, we find that it became cynical, anxious, and insecure. Gilbert Murray called this period "failure of nerve," a social period of change and disintegration. The medieval age was similarly characterized. With the coming of the Renaissance, Western man's confidence improved as he learned that he could predict and thereby control physical nature to some degree. There was increased faith in man as an individual.

As the nineteenth century approached we see again an undermining of the individual. O. Herbert Mowrer (1953) states that "it was as though the citizen of the nineteenth century was trying to solve his personal psychological problems by the same methods which had been so effective in mastering physical nature and so successful in the industrial world." All of us are interdependent and our lives are shaped and determined by the products, services and institutions of the industrial system.

"Western man has become industrial man," says Peter F. Drucker (1942), "but Western society is still fundamentally preindustrial in its social beliefs and values, its social institutions, and economic instruments. It is in the last analysis a mercantile society evolved at the close of the eighteenth century." He claims that a society cannot function unless it gives the individual member social status and function, and unless its socially decisive power is legitimate power.

George Orwell, in his novel **1984**, projected a chilling portrait of a future society in which dehumanized man suffered a totally controlled existence. "Halfway to 1984," claims John Lukacs (1966), "we can say fortunately, that most of Orwell's visions have proved wrong." He insists, however, that rather than warfare, torrents of automobiles, and mass tourism that threaten to destroy entire landscapes and cityscapes will emerge. "We are facing the erosion of privacy," says Lukacs, "of property, and yes, even of liberty. It has nothing to do with creeping socialism. It has very much to do with booming technology."

The key consideration is that 20th century technology is effecting social changes in a vastly different way than the technology of the first industrial revolution.

"Today's crop of machines is a far more powerful agent for social change," says John Diebold (1942). "Today's machines result from a new found ability to build systems which process and communicate information, translate from one language to another, respond to the human voice, and devise their own route to goals that are presented to them; machine systems which improve their performance as a result of encountering the environment; in short, machine systems which deal with the very core of society — with information and its communication and use."

The comparison often made between the industrial revolution in the nineteenth century and the present one is that formerly the machine substituted for human muscle power, while it is now taking over some functions of the human brain and sensory system. Technology is developing certain capabilities which are duplicating man or even outstripping him in other instances. The very nature of this technology will force us to reconsider our whole approach to work, to society, and to life itself.

The hypothesis is advanced that computers will aid in crystalizing future historians' thinking and the resultant description of our era will become "the Transitional age." The essential notion is that we must not necessarily focus upon the type or kind of technology which is evolving but rather upon the revolutionary nature of the rapidly developing technology and its social effects. The quickening pace of invention will result in the creation of a compression along the linear scale of history. As technology reaches a kind of "critical mass" in manufacturing, communications, transportation, business and agriculture, it will carry tremendous impact. It will demand enormous adjustments by the individual in his society. Man lived on earth for fifty thousand years without technology. In every century since 1650 man has roughly doubled his knowledge and this has been accelerating at a phenomenal rate ever since. The gap between theory and application was to 100 years in the Renaissance while in the late 1950's it is down to a decade. As we move into the 70's it may become half or less.

What will the effects of this acceleration be upon man and his institutions when we reach the point that knowledge and technology coincide?

While we do not intend to draw a perfect analogy from the following concept it will, nevertheless, stimulate the formation of further notions. One of the ideas introduced by Einstein in his Special Theory of Relativity was that the speed of light in a vacuum never varied, regardless of the motion of its source. He reasoned that increases in velocity would not only affect dimension and increase mass but also slow the pace of time.

In his General Theory of Relativity, Einstein offered proof that a strong gravitational field slows down time processes. He viewed gravitation as a property of space rather than a force between bodies. As the result of the presence of matter, space became curved, so to speak. The gravitational bending of light waves postulated by Einstein was subsequently verified, although differing slightly from the 1.75 seconds of arc predicted.

It is sometimes useful to study natural phenomena for the purpose of establishing a model which may then be transposed to another set of ideas. In this instance we applied the principles suggested by Einstein of the uniform speed of light and the bending or displacement of light due to gravitational forces, to the accelerating technology reaching its maximum pace when any invention can be feasibly produced. This will have a profound influence upon society with the consequent result that there will be a bending of the linear course of history. Simultaneously, there should occur an apparent slowing of the time dimension. For example, ever since the dawn of civilization there has been a continuity in inventions. The wheel has endured through the jet racing car moving at 500 m.p.h. Now, the hover-craft moves on a series of jets diverted toward the earth or sea surfaces to reduce forward frictional forces. This breaks the continuity of invention and although primitive, it is in the vanguard of a whole new series of surface vehicles perhaps culminating in an anti-gravity device substituting for the jets.

Microelectronics, laser devices, atomic and ion space propulsion, truly intelligent machines which reproduce themselves, and other fantastic technological developments are forecast by Arthur C. Clarke (1963) who was the first to predict communication satellites.

Clarke states "that ours is the first generation, since balance wheels and pendulums started oscillating, to realize that time is neither absolute nor inexorable, and that the tyranny of the clock may not last forever."

Because of the logarithmic progression of technology it may be that as we approach the period when any idea conceived by man may be easily translated through advanced technology into reality, we may experience a phenomenon affecting time. Perhaps we are at the leading edge of an era, much like a supersonic plane about to break the sound barrier. There is a period of enormous stress as the sound waves pile up almost like a snow bank upon the surfaces of the plane. Then, with further acceleration, the jet slices through the barrier via the accompanying "sonic boom" leaving its own sound waves far behind.

Illustration No. 1 offers a crude graphic view of the effects of our transitional age upon the linear course of civilization. It may be shown as a bending, like the refraction of light in water. It will resume its course after the adjustment, but in a wholly different manner, and it will not resemble any other transitional periods experienced heretofore. The transitional age will produce multiple consequences. Its chief effects will cause society to re-organize its institutions. Thomas Jefferson once remarked that as new discoveries are made, new truths discovered, and manners and opinions change, institutions must advance also, to keep pace with the times.

Illustration 1   Technological Development and the Course of Civilization

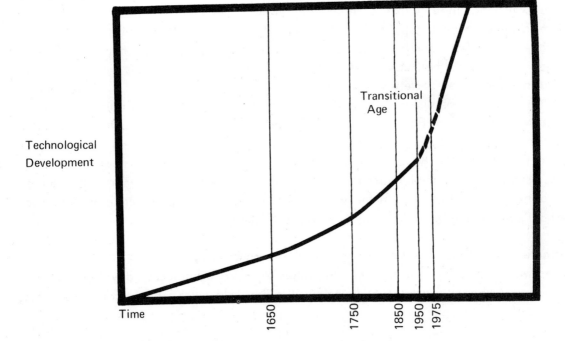

Man's experience in the emerging complex environment will undergo such a radical transformation that social engineers should be occupied in planning sessions this moment, if the lead time is to be met in the estimated decade and a half. Ironically, we cannot request budgets for non-existent agencies and unavailable disciplines. Nevertheless, there are forums for members belonging to established disciplines to carry on a dialogue in the community. While institutions may change drastically, the original American principles of freedom for the individual to find self-expression in a diverse society without undue restraints deserves to be preserved.

Thomas McHugh (1967) relates that ample documentation exists for showing that educational institutional thought throughout the ages has continued to lag behind its societies. The educational community must overcome its historic languor and approach the transitional age with a forward looking spirit, curiosity, enterprise and enthusiasm.

THE NEW EVALUATION AND CAREER GUIDANCE

Let's address ourselves more specifically to the issues which surround the overall field of education and the disciplines associated with special education and rehabilitation in the transitional age. Furthermore, let us assume that the extreme situation as posited by our theory, does not occur and also, that things will not remain as they are but some condition about mid-way develops. Even under these circumstances considerable adjustments in our society will need to be effected.

Speculating on emerging technology and innovation, the National Commission on Technology, Automation, and Economic Progress, made a forecast for the next decade: innovations will change from the lower school levels to higher education; these innovations will be institutionalized under the regional laboratories now being set up by the U.S. Office of Education; a new educational establishment will emerge that will focus upon science and technology to satisfy its purposes; and that giant new educational industries will develop who will contract not only with schools but with the military and industry. Some of these ventures will develop their own school systems.

"It is difficult to find any area in our society," states Col. Ofiesh in the same publication, "which has not had an exponential acceleration in its development—except for education and educational process. Our educational technology has fallen behind the rush of technological innovations in all other fields of individual and national endeavor." He proposes an organization patterned after the present Defense Research and Engineering office for education.

We are already witnessing some of the elements of the educational industry on the horizon with organizations such as General Learning, Westinghouse, IBM, and others established with capital outlays of millions of dollars. Yet, there are reports of internal struggles between the hardware and software people who are desperately vieing to place their own specialities in the vanguard of the new industry's program. Someday, after their conflicts are resolved, they may be surprised to learn that software development cannot be intelligently designed with the knowledge of the technical system with which it will be associated. It cannot be accomplished piecemeal.

Even more unfortunate is their reluctance to base the system development upon some known theoretical formulations or adaptations of a number of such patterns. Hilgard, (1956) discussed a few leading schools of educational research: Jerome Brunner's (1962) cognitive concepts, B.F. Skinner's (1961) operant reinforcement, ego therapy and the Gestalt approaches all have merit for study in actual application. Perhaps the chief fallacy of the educational industrialists' operations is their belief in a revolutionary rather than an evolutionary approach. They have staffed themselves with educational psychologists, and philosophers from their "think tanks"; while systems analysts and programmers come from operational centers; and learning resource people arrive from newly-acquired book publishing houses. It appears that a serious gap exists in the hiring of personnel who have recent experiences with youngsters and their educational and emotional problems.

In order to achieve success these industries will need to link up with school laboratory settings where theory, research, and development may be conducted on a system design basis. At the same time, public and private schools must eschew provincial practices and initiate and encourage research.

Some so-called realists will smugly assert that there exist too many political and economic factors which will deter cooperative research between public and private agencies. Their opportunity from the viewpoint of probability to be right is quite high. Yet, there sometimes arise certain fortuitous crossing of paths by persons representing rather circumscribed areas who have the vision and vigor to reach out from behind their enclaves. This is clearly evidenced by the recent announcement of a pioneering project to be initiated in September, 1967.

Dr. John W. O'Brien, Assistant Superintendent of the Ridley School District in Folsom, Pa., and Anthony Mannino, the Chief Psychologist of the District, who have long understood and advanced rehabilitation in their school system, proposed a unique project. They suggested that an "early warning" procedure of theirs can detect youngsters, ages 14 and 15, who will probably become drop-outs by their sophomore year. But special educational and rehabilitation facilities which might help intercept this almost inevitable chain of events are not available.

Discussions were held with Lee Wolf, District Administrator of the Pennsylvania Bureau of Vocational Rehabilitation who expressed a desire in exploring the possibilities of interesting some agency or institution to conduct such a pilot project. Subsequently, conversations with a private special education organization led to a formalization of an agreement to provide a prevocational program to these potential drop outs. Its focus will be to re-motivate, to evaluate the vocational potential, and to refer these children back to their home school district for specific programs, either in the educational main stream or the vocational-technical school.

Here is an example of a public school district, an official state rehabilitation agency and a private special educational facility—Vanguard School—operating in concert toward a common cause.

The Vanguard School, a private, non-profit institution which serves youngsters with learning problems is engaged in a wide range of special education and research. It deals with students from the elementary level through high school who, due to various neurological sensory, emotional or other disturbances, are unable to succeed in regular school. Standardized testing fails to differentiate these "interjacent" or in-between individuals with a normal potential, from the retardates. Staff psychologists at the school have developed techniques which offer a fine degree of reliability in screening interjacent children from the total referrals.

Seven years ago Henry D. Evans and Dr. Milton Brutten founded the Vanguard School with four youngsters. Now there are 450 children at the Lower School in Paoli, a Middle School in Wynnewood, and an Upper School in Haverford, Pa. A Florida branch is located in Lake Wales.

In July, 1966, the Career Guidance Center was established at the Valley Forge Industrial Park, Pa. Its objectives were to discover new methods in assisting interjacent young men and women, 16 through 20, to find appropriate careers in this age of transition. The population originates at the Upper School and consists of individuals who complete their high school certification but need vocational guidance or have residual emotional problems. Another group is composed of youngsters who do not respond to intensive educational remediation and are not likely to complete their secondary school requirements. They may also have concomitant emotional difficulties which may take a number of forms: delinquency, aggressive behavior, profound passivity or other adolescent manifestations.

More recently, a contract was consummated between the Center and the Pennsylvania Bureau of Vocational Rehabilitation to permit interjacent youngsters not attending the school to receive services.

The inappropriate behavior or emotional difficulty merely makes up the surface level of the interjacent individual. Underneath, we find various factors linked with learning problems, such as visual-perceptual distortions, language and conceptual disorders, reversals, and difficulties with immediate or delayed recall. A third level is associated with individualized phenomena such as tendencies for day-dreaming, and low attention-span, chronic lying and stealing, sadistic-like behavior and blocking in testing situations.

The goals of the Career Guidance Center are still not clearly understood by some parts of the community and what is even more unfortunate, by some members of the professions. We employ, though reluctantly, a rather archaic term—"vocational," collaterally with the career guidance concept in order not to lose whatever semblance of communication we possess with the broader community.

The Career Guidance Center notion transcends the rather stilted view of skill training as a solution to the satisfactory adjustment by young people to the adult responsibilities of citizenship. Assisting an adolescent merely to gain a specialized skill at an entry-level position will cease to be associated with the future guidance profession. Career Guidance implies a multidisciplinary approach which relies upon the counselor, psychologist, sociologist, economist, personnel specialist, systems analyst and others to help shape and prepare the student for the future.

The center has been designed as a transitional bridge—overlapping with the school experience and the employment experience. The youngster is aware that he is attending the Vanguard School but recognizes that he is at the same time practicing to participate successfully in the larger society. He knows this by virtue of the fact that the Career Guidance Center was expressly located in the Valley Forge Industrial Park to emphasize the Center's objectives in a concrete manner. The adolescent finds himself in the midst of a living and thriving industrial complex. He arrives at the Center along with the employees of Lee's Carpets data processing center. At lunch time he plays ball on a field adjacent to a large computer manufacturing plant—Control Data. He has the option to purchase his lunch from the same lunch truck which serves Railway Express employees next door. And he just manages to beat the monumental traffic rush before the General Electric Valley Forge Space Center's thousands of workers spill out on the highways at the close of the workday.

This concept is hardly novel. John Dewey (1916) said: "The school must avoid the trap of allowing techniques and representative forms to completely replace direct appreciations. These experiences must be of sufficient quality so that they can be connected with the symbolic material of instruction. Schools must always provide genuine situations involving personal participation on which to build the facts to be conveyed by symbols."

At that time, Dewey had not envisioned the future rapid pace of progress, and yesterday's genuine situation is quickly obsoleted by today's genuine situation. Teachers and counselors in their quest toward achieving certification and advanced degrees often become professional students with the consequent result that the reality of industrial and business life is rarely fully experienced. Perhaps, even worse, intermittent experience sometimes produces distorted perceptions of the real world with a failure to understand nuances of a true worker's role. "A little bit of learning is a dangerous thing," expresses the idea quite well. This type of individual might be characterized as the "hip-square." The consequences of the transitional age are that we must become attuned to change.

SOCIAL CHANGE, TRAINING, AND EDUCATION

There will be no safety behind the facade of skill. "Substantial numbers of the relatively skilled, including the middle-level manager and the middle-level engineer are going to be displaced," claims Donald N. Michael (1966).....*"the competences that have made these people economically valuable in the past will be made obsolete. Here we have members of a career-oriented, affluent segment of society, who were brought up to believe they possessed all the credentials for a lifetime of advancement, now forced to find another job, or go back to school and learn something new."

John Diebold (1964) suggests that a "whole new approach to business management will require retraining and expanded education for business executives. A world of accelerating change requires that educators not merely **train technicians**, but also **educate men** who can adapt to change."

We have incorporated Diebold's notion into the broad philosophy underlying the programs conducted at the Vanguard School Career Guidance Center. There is a dual emphasis upon training. One facet focuses upon the set of vertical skills which will result in realistic job entry while the other so-called "Core training" (horizontal) will serve to provide the individual with a sufficient background so that he will be prepared to make the re-training **transition** in the future.

As we swiftly advance into the age of transition the social and human adjustments which accompany technological obsolescence will create a whole new dimension to life in the latter part of the 20th and the emerging 21st Century.

Take anxiety for example. Anxiety is the experience of tension that results from real or imagined threats to one's security. Severe anxiety can produce utter confusion and result in complete immobilization. Less severe forms can be informative and when aroused it motivates a person to do something. Paul Tillich says that anxiety is the existential awareness of non-being. Existential in this respect means that it is not the abstract knowledge of non-being which produces anxiety but the awareness that non-being is a part of one's own being. Kierkegaard described anxiety as a painful experience and how a person can learn from it. Encounters with anxiety offer opportunities to acquire greater self awareness.

Gabriel Marcel states that man's courageous choices will result in personal growth, fuller human stature and greater participation in being. Every person finds himself in a given situation which constitutes the person's existence, but it must be goal-directed. It also must be done realistically and concretely.

"The modern industrial economy," insists Walter Buckingham (1963), "combines insecurity with its high living standards, narrow specialization with its high output, new responsibilities with its freedom and individualism, anxieties and dangers with its seemingly limitless opportunities."

Another of the major consequences of the effects of the age of transition will be that our concepts of reality will be drastically altered. Perhaps the chief objectives of the total counseling process in the Career Guidance Center is the acceptance by the student that often his vocational aspirations are unrealistic, that he may not possess the aptitude to attend college, and that he must learn to perform and behave in another manner more consistent with the values established by society. But as we advance forward, revolutionary shifts may emerge in the reality system. Great myths once belonged to ancient cultures, but as science developed these were replaced by another set of realities.

Harvard sociologist, David Riesman, foresees a decline in manners and charm and a correspondingly increased emphasis on such personal qualities as tenacity and willingness to learn new things. "To compensate for increased tension," says Riesman, "it becomes more precarious, less relaxed, less arbitrary and corrupt, with fewer respites from competition."

Even more spectacular vision of things to come are expressed by Arthur C. Clark (1963) in his book **Profiles of the Future**. Tomorrow's reality will include machines that will have the capacity to out-think man (today's best computer is a retardate) and to create its own progeny. As medical science advances toward the sophisticated process of replacing human organs and parts we may find that the line of demarcation between life and death may become fuzzy. Physicians may have the technology to keep individuals alive indefinitely, although a 300-year-old individual may lack the vigor to ambulate and may need to be kept alive in a special chamber.

Present day realities are on the threshold of fantastic alterations. What the computer experts refer to as the man/machine interface—or the communication linkage between human beings and computers—should be in operation in two decades. It may be disillusioning to some but the limiting element is homo sapiens—not the computer. We must code data by punched cards in order to transfer it to the computer's memory. Present day solutions revolve around the improvement of programming language to shorten the interval between the posing of a problem and its solution. Ultimately, spoken language will serve as an input function to the computer with the computer offering the solution in the same spoken language. To a limited degree—some computers speak today, although with a rather curtailed vocabulary. The American Stock Exchange in New York has such an operational computer which renders up-dated market quotations by phone.

Karl U. Smith, (1965) a psychologist who utilizes cybernetic principles and information theory, has been in the forefront of research dealing with feedback and its relationship to learning and rehabilitation. He employed visual time displacement via video-tape years ago and at the present time is conducting verbal feedback research through the use of closed loop computer technology.

Some anthropologists claim that tools are the extension of man and that he has achieved his prominence on earth because he has learned to create tools. He has now reached the point in the course of history when his tools threaten to match or even exceed his muscles, senses and his brain. This does not imply that the machine will ever replace all men. Those who survive the computer revolution will possess the facility to establish a symbiotic man/machine relationship. Most others may face obsolescence as workers in the transitional age but leisure will become socially acceptable due to the invention of the guaranteed annual wage and negative income tax.

Cybernation—the application of automation to material processes and the application of computers to symbols—is a technology which is discussed by Donald N. Michael. He sees the relatively skilled, and the middle-manager and the middle-level engineer faced with a real threat. The semi-skilled and the unskilled so-called blue collar workers however, will suffer the most dislocation under automation and its effects. While some service area jobs will be altered by technology, these personnel should be capable of making the shifts with additional training.

According to many manpower experts, the professionals will comprise the most over-worked members of our future society. We may yet see the time when only a few will be privileged to work. It may become the era of a public-supported consumer class who will purchase the products produced by automated factories, while the elite will conduct research, plan, reflect, indulge in the higher art forms and govern benignly. If all this seems rather remote, one only need be reminded of the testimony before Congress proposing a negative income tax. Medicare will be extended to include not only the aging but the handicapped, and later, the unemployable. Labor is predicting that union members in the manufacture of automobiles someday will be earning $30,000 per year. They soft pedal the fact that only those members who acquire the skills of man/machine relationships in the Detroit-automation complex will share in the benefits.

Even within the ranks of the elite there will be a tendency to dichotomize. Lord Snow defined as one of the most distressing features of the age the failure of our humanistic and technological cultures to develop a productive dialogue.

Not all observers agree that automation will have such ominous portents for our society. Among the most impressive commentators is Charles E. Silberman, (1966) who in his book **The Myths of Automation**, makes these three main points: "(1) Automation is not a significant cause of unemployment in large part because there isn't much automation. (2) New technology is exerting far less impact than has been assumed on the kind of work that men do and the amount of education and skill they need to do; and (3) man is not losing control of his environment. Technology is not taking over nor is it effacing human will."

"We have actually entered a new era of evolutionary history, one in which rapid change is a dominant consequence," insists Jerome B. Wiesner (1966). "It will do no good to resent this, as many humanists do, or even blindly fear the future as some others may. Our only hope is to understand the forces at work and to take advantage of the knowledge we find to guide the evolutionary process."

From a global point of view we need to assess these forces somewhat akin to Professor Galbraith's phrase—the ever changing New Industrial State. It has a consumer-oriented economy and emphasizes rapid technological progress. "The New Industrial State," writes Joseph Kraft, "does far more than turn out in endless profusion the deadly military hardware that is the most direct expression of power. It also sweeps across national borders in its investment, production, and marketing practices to engage masses of people in a forward-thrusting progress toward higher levels of economic, technical and intellectual achievement." Such is but a portion of the backdrop against which education will have to erect its new structures to keep pace with the social effects of technological change.

SIMULATION AND CHANGING INSTITUTIONS

The Vanguard School Career Guidance Center may be a precursor to the eventual changed institutions for it is in part a school, an industrial setting, an occupational training facility, a psychological training laboratory, and rehabilitation center. Outwardly, it appears to most as one of the numerous light and modern industries in the Valley Forge Industrial Park. Almost half of the total 10,000 square feet is allocated to production activities. The remaining space is distributed among administration, teaching, evaluation, learning resources and a cafeteria.

The Center was designed purposely to simulate a number of variables which exist in a modern industrial world. It is described in systems engineering as (Chestnut, 1966), "simulation is the use of models/or the actual condition of the things being modeled and the environment in which it operates. The model or conditions may be in physical, mathematical or some other form. The purpose of the simulation is to explore the various results which might be obtained from the real system by subjecting the model to representative environments which are equivalent to or in some way representative of the situation it is desired to understand or investigate."

In the field of Management Science, Harry H. Harmon (1961) states that "simulation is conceived as the systematic abstraction and partial duplication of a phenomenon for the purposes of effecting (1) the transfer of training from a synthetic environment to a real environment; (2) The analysis of a specific phenomenon; or (3) the design of a specific system in terms of certain conditions, behavior and mechanisms."

Our adaptation of simulation at present is a much broader one and it consists of a number of components suggested by Guetzkow (1962): models, gaming, Monte Carlo techniques, role playing and simulation including human actors. The Career Guidance Center is a simulated environment representing the industrial and business world, "OUTSIDE." The workshop, where production line activities are carried out, forms the focus of the programs. A diverse number of assembly, packing, electronic soldering, and other jobs are sub-contracted from regular industry on a competitive basis. This provides the Center with real work, and income with which to remunerate the students based upon their actual work output.

Although the youngsters earn less than the minimum wage per hour this has served as an excellent motivational medium. In addition, we have the alternative to deny those who display inappropriate behavior, reduced opportunities to participate in income producing activities. We never imagined at first, that many of our students who came from upper middle and higher income groups would respond in such a fashion to these monetary rewards for working. Two things are operating here: (1) Many families, despite their relative affluence, condition their children to earn money and (2) the salary at the Center represents the child's own genuine demonstrated achievement.

Once a program is underway, the youngster at the Center is offered a diverse number of educational and work-related activities. He will receive a battery of achievement tests and undergo an individualized academic diagnostic period with one of our special education or remedial reading instructors. Then he will be assigned to a group which is operating at his academic level. Each group consists of four individuals or less and the selection process considers the compatibility of the members to function in the class-room.

But the classroom image has long been a source of tension and anxiety to the inter-jacent student and consequently, we altered the traditional arrangement of orderly rows of seats, blackboards, and strict procedures. The new configuration is patterned after a typical industrial training room. It is bright and intimate. Flip charts replace the blackboards; the mood is relaxed but businesslike; television and visual aids are used abundantly; and the teacher attempts to achieve a mood of encouragement rather than one sounding like interrogation.

We refer to these areas as learning labs rather than as classrooms. These strategies have markedly helped to alleviate the student's anxieties and memories of earlier fail-ures in other school settings.

A year ago we began with a rather idealized curriculum, aspiring to afford each young-ster a continual individual program of instruction. It was soon discovered that a system of classification needed to be introduced to make the program economically feasible. The initial step was a dichotomization of the group from the standpoint of those who might eventually qualify to take the high school equivalent examinations and those who could not. Following that, subgroups were constructed according to the data available (class records, teachers' meetings, psychological reports and our own diagnosis and observations) and they were arranged systematically from "those most likely to pass the high school exams" down through the low group: "academically at the third or fourth grade levels and extremely poor progress."

The subgroups comprising the lower end of the dichotomy are offered a totally different curriculum from the high school oriented students. Generally, it's an enrichment program aimed toward preparing the interjacent individual to become a functional worker-citizen in society. It consists of three levels: (1) a diagnostic remedial program (2) an applied program dealing with insurance, payroll deduction, budgeting and purchasing, etc., and (3) vocationally-related subject matter linked to each individual's realistic job training objectives.

The academic instructors are not solely confined to the learning lab but play a much larger role in the Center's programs. Their major function is to serve as an educational manager. The are not only concerned with lesson plans but teacher made materials, field problems, integration of academic subject matter with vocational areas of interest, producing and conducting television programming and participating in the total counsel-ing strategies.

Generally, our overall curriculum follows G. Orville Johnson's (1963) recommendations: "First, the curriculum must reflect the characteristics of the child or a group of children for whom it is designed. Second, the curriculum must take into consideration the educational, vocational, and social prognosis of the individuals....it means that he will have the necessary tools and skills to make appropriate adjustments as they are required, and third, the curriculum should reflect the environment of the individual in order that he may learn to live as effectively as possible within that environment."

Even more significant than the curriculum is the manner of its implementation. If we were to characterize our approach, it would be termed "permissive." This is not to immediately bring into mind a Summerhill approach. We provide opportunities for a student to experience a certain degree of freedom and expression consonant with prevailing industrial practices. The underlying theme is that if we entertain notions of the students eventually behaving like adults we should simulate conditions which approximate reality and offer them a chance to rehearse their eventual roles. Running a "tight ship" affords untold advantages toward recognition in the administrative areas but the consequent cost, all too frequently, is the loss of communication with the adolescent.

Commenting on the social impact of technology, Donald N. Michael says that "value conflicts, and tension between generations will very likely increase, especially between the new generation that is moving into political and professional power and is using new types of operational and substantive expertise, and the older generation already occupying the field. These conflicts and their various expressions in differing values and operating techniques will mean that both the pressures and the inhibitions to make the kind of social and technological changes that we are going to need are certain to be very great."

The instructors in the Career Guidance Center maintain a relationship with the students which is perhaps, less formal than in a standard classroom situation, but certainly not below the threshhold of normal industry. They are addressed by their last names, adult protocol is followed, and other businesslike conventions are in effect. However, the student is freer to move about. (This is significant for the interjacent child whose tolerance for concentrated attention is affected.) Assignments in the learning labs are often so arranged that the students move in and out of the lab into other areas of the setting at about forty minute intervals.

A detailed description of the specific educational programs in the Center will be compiled and published one day and therefore, we will not attempt to discuss them in depth at this time. From a general point of view, we agree with Robert Glaser (1966) on the things going on that will influence the shape of education tomorrow.

"One can be called," he says, "the increasing emphasis in our democratic society on the individualization of education and the individualization of instructors....but under the pressure of doing a lot of educating, classroom instructors have developed with large groups of individuals who are taught in some sort of mass fashion....with the increasing personalization of education, schools will undergo a change in procedures, tools, and techniques. These changes are going to reshape the classroom, reshape the way teachers are trained and reshape the way in which publishers and people that produce products for education have to build things for more individual adaptability."

If individualized instruction has become a goal for general education then it must become an intensely sought objective for special education. An individually differentiated program for students with learning problems based upon sound diagnosis will become a necessity. James D. Finn (1966) foresees the emergence of a new educational establishment in the coming decade; "the new establishment will orient American education more in the direction of science and technology as associated with its own process and will absorb only that part of the older establishment which will fit this overall scientific-technological pattern."

"As institutions produce and use the new technology," states Michael (1966), "they inevitably will have to change at a rate concomitant with the changes produced in the society by the very technologies they have encouraged and applied."

In **Measurement of Technological Change**, Solomon Fabricant (1965) insists that "the problem of measurement has not yet been solved....there are competing and widely differing measurements of technological change."

Harold C. Hazlip (1965) recently said in a congressional hearing, "the objectives of education are what you want to teach, described in terms that we can measure rather than in process terms." Most of us have some notions of the technological tools, or hardware intended for educational purposes which are still largely in the early developmental stages. One important means of distinguishing the sophisticated innovators from the "flash-in-the-pan" variety is to examine their approach. If they insist that they are engrossed in software (program) development and minimize the hardware they belong to the latter. Those who have the bare hardware can be discounted entirely (shades of the teaching machine era of the late 50's).

True innovation will produce a symbiotic or interdependent arrangement between program and machine. Even a higher order approach will follow system design.

THE SYSTEM DESIGN, COMPUTER, AND MULTI-MEDIA

A total system is one in which all levels and sub-systems are considered as a whole, rather than merely as a collection of separate units or parts.

The systems approach is a method of problem solving. It involves setting goals first and then viewing a system in three parts or phases: input, process, and output. There is a close parallel between the systems approach and programming the computer. Consequently, one will find that system analyists rely greatly upon the use of computers in processing the data in arriving at solutions of their problems.

We are fully convinced that the computer will form the central core of the future educational technology. A large time-sharing computer will serve a wide area and will in fact, become an information utility. Time-sharing implies the operation of a computer facility that permits many users to operate the facility (apparently) simultaneously, in such a way that each is or can be completely unaware of the use of the facility by the other.

In some instances, smaller satellite (buffer) computers will serve smaller regions on a real-time basis and then unload their significant data into the central computer for further processing. One can envision the development of a major test in one afternoon. Thousands of students all over the country connected with their I/O (input-output) consoles to the shared-time central computer may be able to take a test and obtain the results immediately. The psychologists can then process the data and establish norms based upon the sampling of individual scores.

A few paragraphs ago we alluded to the fact that the objectives of education are to measure what we teach. Once we have given thoughtful attention to a logical and systematic arrangement of information which can be handled by the computer and programmed to respond to the student in a closed-loop fashion then we are on the way toward reaching the goal of measurement. The piecemeal approach, utilized recently by the teaching machine industries, resulted in a debacle.

We are now used to the standard portrayal of the student seated at a console consisting of a teletypewriter and a television-like display screen. Some equipment has in addition a light sensing pen to circumvent a typewritten response, merely by touching a specific point on the screen. A lesser variation utilizes film strips which are rear-projected upon the screen face and accompanied by pre-recorded audio tapes. The computer acts as a simple stepping-switch and scorekeeper.

The multi-media approach, which is essentially a multi-path sensory program, will constitute the ultimate closed-loop system. It is interesting to find some contemporary pop-artists such as Andy Warhol experimenting with the simultaneous presentation of various media. His goal is merely to stimulate the viewer and eventually it will go the way of the hula-hoop. The presently simple I/O console will be expanded to include not only a single screen which displays computer generated letters, symbols, x.-y plots, and three-dimensional diagrams, but a whole array of display devices. Eventually, a genuinely 3-D color television screen will form part of the ensemble through the perfection and integration of two present-day inventions: the laser and holography.

The student will not be ensconced in a single I/O station as some educators now envision the man/machine interface. He will move about from one learning lab to another. He will experience a multitude of situations while interacting with varying learning environments. This will become a truly dynamic learning situation.

One important strategy, heuristics, the study of the processes of problem solving, will be employed in this future system design. Heuristics attempts to determine human problem-solving processes by isolating the steps used by people to arrive at solutions to various complex problems.

In a rather primitive fashion we are implementing some of these computer-assisted institutional strategies in the Career Guidance Center. The paradox in this instance is that the hardware is lagging behind the software.

Before leaving the area of the multi-media approach we will merely allude to the various sensory components which will ignite a series of chain-reactions within the student to help make the educational experience truly stimulating and a lasting one. At least two organizations, IBM and Cognitronics have devices which are computer activated and result in comprehensible simulated speech. Pre-recorded syllables are retrieved swiftly according to a programmed sequence to produce language.

It is our considered opinion that the combination of random access spoken language and the multi-sensory approach will form a breakthrough in assisting the youngster with learning problems. If an individual has a reading problem, perhaps due to visual distortion or poor tracking, then the computer will be programmed so that it is phasing in favor of the audio track and reinforced with optimized color-coded print on the screen. Synchronized tactile stimuli coming on another track will guide the student with respect to inflection and tempo. An earlier diagnostic program will explore the sources of the interjacent individual's integrative sensory problems. We know that some youngsters with reading difficulties experience an inability to suppress extraneous stimuli. For instance, an individual may be unable to enforce concentration on his reading if a competing steady or intermittent sound is occurring. Having total control of the environment in the various learning labs will allow the teacher/diagnostician to isolate the variables affecting the child's reading difficulties and a learning prescription will be noted on his record.

It is apparent that the present fixation of many so-called "modern" educators on the carrel concept will eventually dissipate and evaporate as quickly as the aforementioned teaching machine. The fault lies with the static nature of the carrel which requires a protracted sedentary period and the eventual development of passive responses on the part of the student.

The teacher's role will be dramatically altered in the age of transition. He will be called upon to help establish strategies concerned with the placement of individuals in various learning environments and then participate in the tactics of implementing the program. He will increasingly function as an educational manager.

Even today there are "hip squares" who voice the rather tired and worn issue that the machine poses a threat to the teacher. It is obvious that he will never be replaced. But he indeed will have to make rather marked adjustments, along with all other segments of working society, to function successfully in the age of transition.

"The very first casualty of the present-day school system," explain McLuhan and Leonard (1967), "may well be the whole business of teacher-led instruction as we now know it. Tomorrow's education will be able to set about the exciting task of creating a new kind of learning environment. Students will rove freely through this place of learning, be it contained in a room, a building, a cluster of buildings or an even larger schoolhouse..... Responsibility for effectiveness of learning will be shifted from student to teacher." The staff at the Career Guidance Center has committed itself to the exploration of the most propitious learning environments which will stimulate, motivate, and spark the interjacent individual into seeking knowledge, to view himself as a potentially useful member of society and yet, as a unique creation of nature enjoying the wondrous experience of life. An atmosphere of change is constantly in existence and the transitional sense is continuously felt and welcomed. The staff is exposed to television, videotape, computers, and teaching devices, not as technological entities alone, but as tools which facilitate the production of clearer instruction, the study of student behavior, automatic testing, and the gaining of occupational information. Being so intimately involved with this wide range of sophisticated equipment on a daily basis, the staff soon accepted the technology right along with the chalk and blackboard. "Education will be more concerned with training the senses and perceptions than with stuffing brains," say McLuhan and Leonard. (1967)

"Experience is not to be had directly and neatly," insists Brunner (1962), "but filters through the programmed readiness of our senses. This program is constructed with our expectations and these are derived from our models, our ideas about what exists and what follows what structures of knowledge, its connectedness and the derivations that make ones ideas follow another is a proper emphasis in education for it is structure."

We have adopted some of the above notions and incorporated them with other ideas to form a concept which we call "Programmed Experience." It utilizes computer programming flow-chart methodology to schematize each step in the Career Guidance process at Vanguard School. Each possible contingency is outlined in the model. Too, we made provisions for feedback loops which take a particular programmed step backward in the model structure if certain criteria of readiness are not met. Programmers use a term **iterative** which means that one searches for the best possible answer through a sort of trial and error method. But as more data is gathered the probabilities for the answer to become more accurate become better.

PROGRAMMED EXPERIENCE

The basic concept of "Programmed Experience" is simply that we must be capable of organizing a unique set of experiences physically, intellectually, and emotionally, so that subsequently perceived experiences can be integrated meaningfully if we are to mature successfully.

Kant is to have shown that the external world is known to us only as sensation and that the mind is no mere helpless tabula rasa, the inactive victim of sensation, but a positive agent, selecting and reconstructing experience as it arrives. Space and time are not things perceived, but modes of perception, ways of putting sense into sensation; space and time are organs of perception. Steinmetz (1923) claimed that modern physics has concluded that time and space are not the products of experience but are categories. He stressed that the relativity theory concluded that absolute time and absolute space have no existence but are organs of perception.

A number of studies have shown that subjective time for each person is more or less independent of objective time. John Cohen (1964) in an article called **Psychological Time**, discussed a number of subjective aspects of time. "One is a tendency of the individual's view of past events to change with the passage of years. Another is that conceptions of time differ between one nation or culture and another."

Cohen says "that Hoagland concluded that there are chemical pacemakers in the brain that govern the speed of its metabolism and thereby affect the rhythm of subjective time." Cohen suggests that there is an interrelation of inner clocks and sensory-motor activity. Each can influence the other. He inferred from some experiments that if two parts of a trip are of equal distance, the part traveled at a slower speed for a longer time will seem to have covered the greater distance. And further, that if two parts of a trip are traveled at the same speed, the part in which the distance and time are shorter will seem faster.

We believe that the Programmed Experience is an appropriate method of analysis and decision-making applied to special education and rehabilitation. Its very fabric shapes common threads with computer techniques and automation. As we undergo the phenomena which accompany the age of transition, particularly such an important factor as distortions of the time dimension, a conceptual and schematic framework like Programmed Experience may prove of immense value in planning the appropriate individual adjustments in education. Within this framework we have incorporated some guidelines from Kierkegaard's exisentialism and William James' pragmatism.

Existentialism studies the individual in the concrete actuality of his existence. Its fundamental characteristic is to remain close to the concrete and shun abstractions. Man is in a state of becoming. Kierkegaard preceded the field of social sciences and consequently, some of his thinking, such as when he speaks of becoming a self, a "being," and when he views the individual inwardly and ethically, appears to reject the behavioral theories. They too accept "becoming" but this involves the stimulus-response cycle of problem solving. To the existentialist, "reality is located not in objective reflection but in subjective decision. I do not live in the past, with which the reflecting philosopher has to do, but in the present, where decision and involvement are mandatory." (Brian & Hill – 1966)

"Man exists wholly in the unstable present," Lundberg (1963) says in **The Coming World Transformation**. "The present, literally and exactly viewed, is an affair of the moment, quickly gone. It is constantly crumbling and disintegrating. But by means of recollection and anticipation man gives himself an illusion of living in more than a rapidly transitory present. He mentally expands the actual present into....a specious present."

Man must act in order to live but few of his actions can be consummated in the fleeting present. "Man remembers earlier stages of his acts even as he is involved in present stages, and thus is made sensitively aware of temporal sequences and continuity. This experienced continuity he insensibly projects toward the anticipated completion of his act in comsumation and satisfaction hence arriving at the concept of the future," adds Lundberg.

In William James' world there is no absolute truth in the present. "Truth is only the expedient in the way of our thinking, just as 'the right' is only the expedient way in our acting. What is true during the present is what leads us to a useful manipulation of experience," comments Kohl, "What is right is what helps us in confronting experience.

A belief may be true so long as it is not contradicted by experience, which itself merely is."

James' pragmatic method implies that truths should have practical consequences. But how can one believe something to be true and acknowledge that it may change? The problem is with the definition of truth. "Perhaps," suggests Kohl, "he wanted to say that the best one can ever have in the present is a reasonably well justified belief or a deeply felt, non-contradictory opinion."

However, James said, "Reality is in general what truths have to take account of...."He defined reality as having three parts but the pertinent comment which is relevant to our discussion is that reality is the flux of our sensations. "Sensations are forced upon us," he said, "coming we know not whence. Over their nature, order and quantity we have as good as no control. They are neither true nor false; they simply are. It is only what we say about them, only the names we give them, our theories of their source and nature and remote relations, that may be true or not."

For pragmatism reality is in the making and awaits part of its completion from the future.

We have extracted some fragmentary elements from a number of older philosophers to form a basic foundation for our Programmed Experience notion that itself, is linked with the more future oriented information and network theories.

Our original assumption is that automation and technological change will tend to increase until in perhaps a decade—most ideas will become immediately translatable into reality because of our unbelievably advanced technological competency. The immediate consequences will result in an apparent time distortion by our society. There will be an apparent slowing down of time which after all is subjective. But the effects of the transitional age will rather uniformly create a climate that will influence most technologically advanced societies.

The paradox of the psychological slowing down of time by an individual will result in the increase of sensory stimulation. Man's education will consist of human contacts as it is now, but will require an increased adjustment on his part to an innundation of his sensory apparatus by the multi-media of the new educational institutions. His cognitive processes will be severely strained in order to process this multi-path information flow. The brain may be designed to handle data in parallel form but does it not culminate in an eventual series circuit (consciousness perhaps?) This is the **bit** in information theory.

While man may never be superseded in the ultimate control of the machine because his finger will always be close to the start, stop, or reset buttons, he will face another threat. The machine will probably outstrip him as a more efficient extension of his sensory apparatus. Inferiority generates anxiety. He will fear the future and begin to distort "reality" as his environment continues to undergo accelerating changes. The effects of demography, automation, pollution, and social ecology forming a closed loop upon homo sapiens may produce a new kind of being in the evolutionary scale of development.

Our purpose in these futuristic speculations is not to delve into science-fiction but to stimulate the educator to assess and analyze contemporary events from the standpoint of his own experience and to project forward. Whether our theories prove to be part of general reality is of little consequence but if they serve as a catalytic agent to the sober administration or the placid professional to plan for adjustment to a new age then a worthwhile purpose will have been served.

With respect to the Career Guidance Center's activities these notions have been useful in the organization of a new kind of institution. We spoke earlier of the need for institutions to adapt to social changes in the age of transition. The Center represents one such transformation of a vocational school setting for interjacent adolescents that blended with a rehabilitation center, a remedial education program, and a psychological laboratory.

We have already briefly described the rehabilitation workshop setting and its function. It will be useful to review some of the major terminal objectives of the Center and to discuss the crucial role that the workshop plays in the attainment of these goals.

STRATEGIES IN THE NEW CAREER GUIDANCE

The principal aim of this Center is to help properly prepare interjacent individuals for a useful place in the swiftly changing technological society. It is not oriented solely toward training individuals for jobs. We are critical of such programs because they fail to grapple with the multiple dimensions underlying human aspirations, aptitudes, needs, attitudes, and capabilities, and the stark realities of our complex modern industrial society. Job training along straight vocational and technical lines will become less and less useful as a tool in the solution of youngsters' life problems.

Basically, the leadership in many sensitive educational communities is failing to think and plan according to the emerging trends and realities. Their trap is that they are holding on to a set of values which were established through the puritan ethic: hard work, nose to the grindstone, and all that. They cannot adapt to the new realities of the transitional age. We are in a period where work and apparent leisure are often overlapping: such as the salesman and his client on the golf course. Or, take the case of a highly trained engineer in a modern continuous process chemical plant. He makes an initial adjustment in the complicated system and then is apparently idle during prolonged periods while the system is operating. One wag suggested that the job requirements ought to advertise for a chemical engineer with a Ph. D. and an I.Q. of 82.

It becomes apparent that with such a complex world emerging, our educational and re-habilitation techniques need to take a quantum jump over the traditional methods of providing guidance to adolescents with learning problems.

Much of the guidance structure of the Career Guidance Center rests upon the "pro-grammed experience" concept. On the one hand, we have a diagnostic framework which assesses the individual socially, emotionally, and mentally. On the other hand, we con-tinuously keep abreast of the true criteria of the needs of business and industry. We do not rely solely upon printed materials but carry an ongoing contact with personnel people, executives, training specialists, and trade unions. Our task is to identify the place where the youngster fits on the flow chart of programmed experience, determine the optimal contingencies which will result in his attaining the criterion variables, make de-cisions, and check the feedback loop on the amount of deviation from the original criteria.

We described simulation earlier. The overall premise is that our Center is a rehearsal for the eventual industrial realities awaiting the youngster who attends the Vanguard School. The setting itself is identical with modern light industry. In our first year we concentrated upon developing a number of production line activities because these serve as the principal vehicle in simulating the qualitative and quantitative aspect of the ma-jority of jobs which exist today and in the earlier phase of the transitional period. This is frequently misunderstood to mean that we are overtly attempting to train our students for unskilled and semi-skilled production jobs. In the end, in some few cases this is the practical result. However, the production line serves to fulfill the development of a wide repertoire of desired characteristics in the simulation model which represents that broad area we call work. To be acceptable in today's business and industry the basic worker must be capable of meeting certain minimum standards of output. Whether he works in the production of goods or services he is required to turn out so many "widgets" or handle so much volume of sales per month if he is to remain with the organization. In addition, he must meet a pre-set qualitative tolerance level in order to sustain employ-ment with the company or to receive promotions.

Translated into human behavior, it means that an individual must discipline himself to attain particular motor, intellectual, or social set of skills. Generally speaking, the quali-tative and quantitative demands are reciprocal; as the need for qualitative attention goes down the out-put requirement goes up. The smaller the cycle of work per unit time the more amenable the task is to becoming taken over by the human autonomic nervous system. But before this kind of conditioning can occur, the individual must enforce a certain amount of concentration upon the activity.

It is well known that youngsters with learning problems have a great amount of difficulty with attention span. We have observed that this quality has generalized from the classroom situation to many other activities. Consequently, one of the strategies in the Center is to intercept the causes of distractibility, and to systematically assist the individual in developing a repertoire of habit patterns that result in improved concentration.

This is largely accomplished in the simulated industrial workshop center. In order to overcome the lack of motivation we offer remuneration scaled to the work output of each individual. The students are given job assignments according to their abilities and levels of potential. Those who display unusual talents are upgraded to junior and senior supervisors. Not only do they receive additional compensation but they also derive satisfaction from their status in the group.

As they rise in the hierarchial structure their contacts with others increase correspondingly. A multitude of gratifiers serve to act as reinforcing agents to improve motivation.

This sounds remarkably similar to an interesting technique called variously "operant conditioning, behavior modification, or reinforcement therapy." This is true. We utilize a number of techniques in a complementary fashion and each strategic arm of our network is linked to the techniques which we find brings best results.

In reinforcement therapy, O.I. Lovas states that "the basic principle we all work with is this — that certain behaviors are a function of their consequences and, as a result of their consequences, can be either strengthened or weakened."

Harold L. Cohen (1967) suggests, "human behavior is the result of an interaction between stimulus events and an organism which already has a behavioral history; a given environment affects individuals differently because the individuals themselves have been differentially shaped and reinforced. The action of environmental stimuli upon individual behavior and the individual's reaction to these stimuli produce a change in the individual. This change is called learning." We must perceive of our controlled environment (the Guidance Center) not as an isolated thing but really as an **ecological system design**. Therefore, while we use the principles of behavior modification in certain specific instances, the ecology which supports learning is composed of a diverse number of strategies, counseling techniques, simulation, group dynamics, automated hardware and gaming.

Sarane S. Boocock and James S. Coleman (1966) put forward the view that the structure of education for adolescents may be as important as its content. They have overcome some of the structural defects of secondary education by introducing gaming in simulated environments. In these games features of the socio-economic environment are simulated and at various points in the game, players receive feedback on the consequences of their actions.

"Adolescents operate generally in an existential manner," Boocock and Coleman say. "The games bring the future into the present, allowing the child to play roles in a large differentiated society of which he otherwise gets hardly a glimpse. Thus, they surround a child with an environment which is artificial for the present, but realistic for the future."

"The games have a peculiarly valuable motivating theory. They are also far more self-disciplining than most other forms of learning. In games, the discipline arises internally, from the necessity to obey the rules if the game is to continue. Thus, children who have never been socialized into the need to obey rules can become socialized when the rules are not arbitrarily imposed, but arise from the game itself....games are self-judging, the outcome decides the winner, and a player knows that he has won or lost by his own actions."

Similarly, the structure of the Career Guidance Center is systemically designed so that it simulates real live industrial and business conditions. The students are involved in a situation where the consequences of their actions are experienced across a temporal range from immediately to a week's time forward. A poker chip token signifies the reinforcement of a social behavior observed by a counselor. He offers approval to the act, which may be helping a peer, and immediately hands the student the chip. This immediately links the act with the token. The chip is later turned in to the secretary for a dime. We have found this an extremely powerful device in shaping behavior.

As the distance between the event and the reward or reinforcement increases our techniques become less acceptable to the operant theoreticians. Our strategies then take on notions which resemble gaming. We do not apologize to the operant-oriented people however, because while they accuse the Freudians of orthodoxy, they themselves appear rather pale and sterile in light of Karl U. Smith's conceptualizations.

K.U. Smith (1965) is the exponent of a cybernetic theory of learning and rehabilitation. "We believe," he says, "that memory reflects the spatially organized biochemical characteristics of internuncial cells and has no significant binary or Time-Series charactieristics other than those mediated by the persisting directional specialization of components of the feedback loop."

Smith's delayed feedback research may be of great significance in learning science as it challenges association or S-R (and R-S) theories of learning. These theories assume that learning involves the temporal linking of stimuli and responses. Smith's criticism is that the requirement of "Temporal Contiguity" is not spelled out in precise terms but is satisfied by variable time relationships. His delayed feedback studies, claims Smith, "show that behavior is not a flexible temporal sequence of stimuli and responses but a closed-loop process with rigidly fixed temporal relationships." Smith asserts that his results "support our cybernetic view of the brain as a spatially organized control system which utilizes the immediate feedback of motion to guide and control continuous response."

While Smith's views are controversial, non-conventional and esoteric, they cannot be entirely discounted. Traditional psychological testing as developed by Thurstone, Cattell and others is based upon the time contiguity principle. We have administered hundreds of standardized tests to interjacent adolescents and these tests were poor predictors of success. One obvious factor is that the tests were standardized on a so-called "normal" population. Smith apparently feels that the temporal contiguity underlying test standardization is at fault.

H. J. Eysenck (1953), long an advocate of the highest degree of scientific rigor in the design of psychological experiments, claims, "On the purely cognitive side, speed of mental functioning emerges as the prime determinant of intellectual ability."

The swiftly moving events in the age of transition will require a thorough reassessment of our methods of scientific research. We will have an extremely powerful ally in the computer, videotape, the laser, holography and other sophisticated instrumentation, and the rather narrow constraints of presently accepted methodology are in need of diversification and re-evaluation.

"It is time to evaluate our research process," asserts Samuel Kirk (1966), "and to determine whether or not the research granting agencies are forcing a 'technique bound' type of research.....It is said that granting bodies accept more readily a rigorous statistical design of an irrelevant problem, than they do a relevant problem not amenable to rigid statistical controls."

Applied research has far less status among researchers than pure research. If we are to gather significantly related information in the transitional age we ought to have the personal alternative to dial our random access computer for all types of research data, rather than to be restricted to one type. This is the philosophy of the explorations at the Career Guidance Center.

Our simulated industrial and business environment at the Career Guidance Center operates as a social ecological system. This model will someday be amenable to thorough cybernetic analysis. While the primary objectives of the Center are to render service to its clients, we are however, gradually developing a number of useful constructs which may eventually prove useful toward implementing a full-scale research effort.

CYBERNETICS AND ALLIED TECHNIQUES

"The fundamental theme of cybernetics," explains Mervyn L. Cadwallader (1964), "is always regulation and control in open systems. It is concerned with homostasis in organisms and the study of social organizations.....From the point of view of cybernetics, any large scale formal social organization is a communication network. It is assumed that these can display learning and innovative behavior if they possess certain necessary facilities (structure) and certain necessary rules of operation (content)."

Amitai and Eva Etzioni (1964) add that "ultrastability, basic to cybernetics, refers to systems that have mechanisms of feedback that allow them not only to respond to the environment but also to change their pattern of response...." They are critical of cybernetics in that "expressive communication—in which symbols that carry normative and emotional meaning are transmitted—often might prove more vital....It may well be that one could construct a computer model that would take into account all factors, including emotional and rational behavior."

Because cybernetics refers to the science of communication and control we need to know that the lines which depict the network of our system are in fact, its communications. The state of the lines at any given moment reflects the amount of information in the system. The structure of the communications and the nature of the information which flows through them to one of the elements of the system will determine, at any given moment, whether this element is in a given state or not.

For example, if we say that a system consists of n elements we must also examine the relations between the elements. The formula is as follows n(n-1). If a system say, has only seven elements, it will then have forty-two relations within itself. And if we further stipulate that each one of these relations is either in being, that is—binary, then there will be 242 different states of the system. This means that the number adds up to more than four millions of millions.

Cybernetics uses binary notion invented by George Boole (1815-64) in which there are only two states: on and off, or 1 or 0. Qualitative information, such as is found in verbal arguments and quantitative information can be reduced into the form of binary statements. A machine is a set of states undergoing transformations. One of the marks of the science of cybernetics is that it accepts complexity in systems. It accepts "real life" as we find it and not as a perfectionist abstraction. Real machinery, in contrast with the blueprints of machinery, from the typewriter through the blast-furnace, is likely to go wrong. Errors are not accidental, they are natural and important parts of a system's permanent behavior. Von Neumann investigated the risks of these errors and proposed methods for keeping the errors under control.

A unit called entropy is used to describe the tendency of a system to settle down to a uniform distribution of its energy. It says that order is more natural than chaos and is drawn from the second law of thermodynamics. Thus, it is convenient to discuss cybernetic systems with their self-regulating tendencies to attain stability or orderliness, in terms of entropy. Sanford Beers (1959) defines his total system as: "Complex, probabilistic and self-regulatory."

Having just described some very broad aspects of cybernetic notions it will be useful to discuss how they are related to our programmed experience concept. The workshop setting in the Center forms the nucleus of our communication network. The workshop manager is responsible for the technical operation of the shop and the counselor (who functions as the foreman) determines the daily placement of each client at a particular spot in the setting. This strategy is established after each weekly meeting of the staff where all the disciplines exchange information. The tactical operations are then entrusted to the counselor who in effect serves as a theatrical director. He directs a number of plays which occur simultaneously in the workshop and other parts of the Center.

While there is a strong resemblance to the theatre in the techniques employed by the counselor, from a theatrical viewpoint the activity has a decided group dynamics basis. M. Smith (1945) defines a social group as "a unit consisting of a plural number of organisms (agents) who have collective perception of their unity and who have the power to act, or are acting, in a unitary manner towards the environment." Morton Deutsch (1958) defines a group as existing to the extent that the individuals comprising it are pursuing promotively interdependent goals."

Cartwright and Zander (1953) define group dynamics as "a field of inquiry dedicated to advancing knowledge about the nature of groups, the law of their development, and their interrelations with individuals, other groups, and larger institutions. It may be identified by its reliance upon empirical research for obtaining data of theoretical significance, its emphasis in research and theory upon the dynamic aspect of group life, its broad relevance to all the social sciences, and the potential applicability of its findings to the improvement of social practice."

In effect, the Center has adapted a number of useful methodologies to serve its broad purposes, but it utilizes certain components in various combinations and permutations in an effort to solve or investigate a particular problem. The peer pressures serve to influence most of the adolescent behavior in the Center to follow the basic rules. When an individual or small clique act out against the rules a strategy is formulated to achieve a goal. In some instances, a hired actor is used. He comes on the workshop floor masquerading as a new client and is placed with the misbehaving group. Acting as a "shill" he begins to misbehave way beyond the realm of acceptability. The usual misconduct by the worst offenders is rarely exerted enough to justify exclusion from the setting.

The "shill" continues his inappropriate behavior and at the same time attempts to get the members of the clique to join him. Our experience so far has shown that even the most flagrant and frequent violators are reluctant to escalate their misbehavior beyond a certain level. In fact, the positive effects gained from the role playing are that even the delinquently-inclined members disassociate from the inappropriate activities of the actor. Post-interviews reveal extremely critical attitudes about the actor's poor performance.

These exercises are primitive and exploratory but we are gaining some evidence about group interactions and modes of learning in an industrial setting.

A cybernetic laboratory was incorporated into the design of the Center so that it will be possible to obtain precise information about individuals and thereby gain more effective control of their behavior. The laboratory consists of a complete television production studio which includes 4 TV cameras, EIA synchronization, 2 videotape recorders, audio equipment, and a console with remote control capabilities. Complementing the television facilities is a full range of audio-visual equipment.

We videotaped an exercise with the actor in the workshop setting through a one-way mirror in the Cybernetic Laboratory. He wore a wireless FM microphone hidden on his person to obtain the students' audible responses. This has proved to be of enormous benefit to the staff because we had the opportunity to review the tapes many times. Certain events which we failed to observe earlier were discovered in subsequent viewings. Also, we found that a frequency count of hand-to-head gestures could be made as a function of time against a given subject. We are now learning to make base lines of each individual's normal behavior and then to simulate an anxiety provoking situation, videotape it, and then to make a plot of the client's unique mannerisms, or other distinctive reactions created by the anxiety situation.

Videotaped observations are not entirely novel but in too many instances they are merely used as a peeping device rather than an instrument of measurement. Haworth and Menolascino (1967) at the Nebraska Psychiatric Institute have utilized videotape recordings and emerged with three basic patterns in a sampling of children 2 to 6 years of age. Situational tests are another form of videotaping with which we have experimented and with further refinement, may serve as valuable devices to measure progress of an individual's program in the Career Guidance Center. Inspired by the training techniques of the OSS, the World II precursor of the CIA, we devised some simple situational tasks. One day, the usual foreman (counselor) did not appear in the Center but a stranger, attired in a smock, armed with a clip board, and in an aggressive manner, began shouting orders to the students. They obeyed, but were shaken because they were accustomed to the stern but just demeanor of the regular boss figure. The new individual represented a rather detached, highly authoritarian boss.

We videotaped a number of sequences and found that the responses of our recent students to the stimulus situations just described proved to be amenable to measurement. It was possible to view the tapes and to categorize the students who made gains from the workshop counseling program and those who made little or no progress. Various situations were used. In one case a young lady was soberly given an assignment to get some scuba gear and dive into a pickle barrel to sort good from bad pickles. While such a ludicrous assignment should have evoked laughter, this girl was so conditioned to authority figures that she could not satisfactorily process this order.

Other individuals who were more sensitive to the environment were given more subtle orders by the simulated boss. In one situation, the rude foreman unmercifully criticized the products manufactured by a student. The individual was originally described as being emotionally fragile and his armory was replete with a myriad of defense mechanisms. Interestingly, the young man validated the months of support by his counselor and exercised magnificent restraint. The actor was forced into placing further pressure but to little avail. The student proved to be in excellent control of his emotions.

The staff agreed, after viewing the videotape reruns, that the student passed the situational test. The use of theatrical and situational techniques differ from J.L. Moreno's psychodrama principally in that the students are not aware of participating in a play. Out of the five essential components, only the group, the subject, the protagonist, and the director are utilized. The auxiliary and egos are not used (Yablonsky and Enneis, 1965). The director (counselor) implements the basic strategy established at a staff meeting. A set of objectives are given and either one or two individuals are brought into a scene. Everything from that point is spontaneous. The counselor in the Center has had extensive training and vast experience in the theatre and in fact, served recently as an assistant professor of drama at a local university. We have found certain specific strategies to be especially successful and they include: reflection, where an actor portrays the individual selected for counseling; paradox, a case where an adult figure protrays the subject but in a highly accentuated manner (indecisiveness, fear of new situations, need for approval); unremitting authority in which the adult figure exerts excessive demands upon the student-worker.

The use of these strategies in the form of gaming combined with certain theatrical techniques is a powerful device to determine a client's response to counseling. Further research is needed so that more precise measurement can replace the present pass-fail, binary scale.

Prior to the admission to the workshop program, each individual is offered an opportunity to be assessed in a specially designed pre-vocational evaluation center. Our pre-vocational facility is located in the Vanguard Upper School and its program is geared to serve the seniors in the academic setting. The other pre-vocational program exists in the Career Guidance Center. These programs reflect another element in the innovative design of new educational institutions.

The transitional age will increasingly demand the development of techniques which will help to identify the skill potential of young people. The largely random approach now in use will gradually disappear because the new era will be unable to tolerate the loss of talent.

It is inevitable that there will be a drastic reshuffling in the future presidential cabinet posts. One major agency will be fashioned from the present Labor Department, the Commerce Department, and perhaps other minor sections and will be called the Department of Human Resources. With the ever-increasing minimum qualifications for job entry be influenced by automation and technology, more sophisticated selection methods will need to be developed.

The vocational guidance process as it now exists cannot possibly continue to aid youngsters in matching their individual aspirations with the rapidly changing realities of the emerging society. The information gap between job realities and the listings in the official governmental dictionary of occupational titles will become divergent more and more. Computer retrieval with continuous updating, will be needed to supersede the presently archaic methods. But transmission to the whole country will present some problems before the system becomes universally available.

Counselors in secondary schools and colleges will be obliged to develop a profound man/machine interface. If current prophecies prove to be correct — each working individual will be required to retrain perhaps as much as five times. While certain careers will retain more stability than others, all careers will necessitate constant monitoring to keep up to date with changing realities.

"The time available to educators for the teaching of new occupations or to update the old ones is being constantly reduced," says Jerry M. Rosenberg (1966),".....A student who has been taught a skill no longer needed will be starting on his career equipped with no more than a piece of parchment.....Workers will have to return to school from time to time to keep up with the new skill requirements."

Whole careers will be upset—perhaps in as short an interval as five years. Automation will have a profound influence in all of our lives despite cynical comments that it is the substitution of mechanical error for human error. Drucker claims that automation is a concept of the structure and order of economic life, the design of its basic patterns integrated into a harmonious, balanced and organic whole.

Buckingham (1963) offers a more analytical definition. "Automation," he says, "can best be defined as any continuous and integrated operation of a production system that uses electronic or other equipment to regulate and coordinate the quantity and quality of production.....It includes both manufacturing and administrative processes." These processes can be distilled into the following principles: mechanization, continuous process, automatic control, and rationalization.

While specialization will continue to constitute the prevailing characteristic of job requirements a cross-fertilization of skill areas will emerge. For example, numerical control will require workers who are trained in metal lathe work, electronics, and simple programming.

Experts in automation have established categories such as dead-end jobs, status quo jobs and bright future jobs. In the dead-end category are such examples as: appliance assembly work, mail clerk, and body and fender man; in the status quo group are: accountant, sheet metal worker, warehouseman, automobile mechanic; and in the bright future jobs are such jobs as: aerospace worker, computer programmer, electronic testing, and medical technician.

Unfortunately, an acquaintance with such listings is extremely misleading. Geographical patterns may contradict such generalizations. Also, even the most sophisticated equipment needs someone to dust it. Those committed to vocational guidance will have to become more mobile and at least half of their time will need to be spent in the field assessing the ever changing patterns of occupational realities.

The transitional age will place a whole host of demands upon the field of education. One area with which we are experimenting is concerned with the guidance of young people to discover their true capabilities and enlarge their scope of understanding about the newly evolving society. We foresee the establishment of a prevocational evolution center in every junior and senior high school which will provide the following major services: (1) To assess each student through tests, simulations, job samples, gaming and other work try out techniques so that his occupational interests and aptitudes will correspond, (2) to expose the youngster to the shifting patterns of occupations so that he may develop his interests in realistic areas and ones which will sustain growth, and (3) to provide a period of time in a setting during which he can discover appropriate social behaviors and learn about his immaturities or other emotional needs which will hinder his potential growth in life.

The prevocational diagnostic laboratory will be perhaps, the first insitutional change which educators will be challenged to accept in the age of transition. Staffing will initially pose a problem but eventually the new discipline will emerge and as the song goes, "This will be the start of something big!"

CONCLUSION

The central thesis that we are now within the transitional age was advanced and that we will be witnessing rather spectacular institutional changes which will influence every facet of modern society. Rapidly accelerating technology will ultimately become so advanced that most ideas conceived by now will be capable of fruition. The singlemost phenomenon accompanying this transition will be the effect of psychological time upon man. There will be an apparent slowing down of time and man's sensory apparatus will be strained to accept the diverse, paralleled flow of information.

Human concept of reality will undergo a significant modification. Threatened by his technological innovations which are in reality mechanized extensions of his own senses, limbs, and brain, man's anxieties will take on new forms.

Automation and cybernetics are but two elements of organized "system design" science which are beginning to create the atmosphere for fantastic social change. The education and rehabilitation communities will be affected even more profoundly than other segments of society and will need to incorporate new learning technologies such as computers, television, and other inventions in a wholly novel environment.

The Vanguard School Career Guidance Center in the Valley Forge Industrial Park (Pennsylvania) is one example of the introduction of new institutions which are making sweeping strategic changes to accommodate to the realities of the age of transition.

As an epilogue—if the preceding material takes on an aura of unreality or science fiction one might well refer to the summer (1967) issue of **Daedalus**, the Journal of the American Academy of Arts and Sciences. The first working papers and discussions of the

Commission on the year 2000 have just been published there and have been authored by some of the leading thinkers and scholars of our age.

Margaret Mead, the anthropologist, comments upon the possibility that many functions of the present family unit will be tranferred to wider groups, based on different combinations within and across sex lines. George A. Miller, a psychologist, warns that we may be nearing the limit of man's mind to absorb the present level and complexity of information. Others talk about the loss of individual privacy due to inventions which can follow one anywhere on earth, and of huge supercities stretching in three parts of the United States.

"Man always modifies his environment and is, in turn, modified by it," writes S.P.R. Charter (1962). He calls this process the Ecology of Man— "man is a relatively new phenomenon on earth. He has not yet learned to live with his environment and actually may never do so, but may become extinct long before the natural expiration of this planet, to be replaced by an organism that will learn to live with its environment."

"Each descending step man takes into the maze of dependence upon technical involvements hinders the simplicity of his recuperation;" continues Charter, "and the more materially complex a society becomes, the more complex are the recuperative processes, to the point where survival itself may become increasingly doubtful....When a society suffers attrition of its recuperative needs, the probability of extinction is accelerated."

The "Law of the Minimum" states that under ideal circumstances a chemical reaction will continue until restrained by exhaustion of whatever essential ingredient is present in least supply.

"Quite likely," insists Charter, "it may emerge that our essential ingredient in least supply is not water, land, food, or any other physical item, but our applied intelligence toward the totality of man on earth. If this is true, and his most essential ingredient continues in least supply, man may exhaust himself long before the exhaustion of other earth resources."

".....The energy available to man limits what he **can** do and influences what he **will** do," says Fred Cottrell (1955).

Man is an information processing animal. His ability to think makes him the unique organism on earth. Information is one form of energy in man. The other is that he is a chemical-energy machine and he can be measured like any other converter. "His efficiency can be measured in terms of the best value of the food he consumes as contrasted with the best value of the mechanical energy he can deliver," states Cottrell.

"Information is measured by the probability of passing of one particular message from a set of passable messages," insists F. H. George. ".....There is a direct relation between the information flow and the change of the state of the particles of the world and their distribution."

Entropy, or the measure of disorganization, is measured by the same means as organization.

The population explosion, pollution, megalopolia, thermonuclear bombs, automation, and other realities which face us in the future present a formidable challenge to man, and represent the incessant effects of entropy. "Halfway between and now and another 1,960 years there will be only one square foot of earth space available for every living human being," says Charter rather gloomily, ".....for various reasons, including gravitational mechanics — is the fact that under current rates of increase, there can be no population on earth in another 1,960 years."

We must exhibit a faith in the information processing qualities of man and that he will solve the array of the rather formidable problems in a manner unique to the species homo sapiens. As our older institutions undergo dramatic changes during the age of transition we must collaborate in a truly interdisciplinary manner to promote the evolution of vigorous, new institutions which can better serve mankind and counter the trends of entropy.

Engineers say that machines are multiple-input, multiple-output transducers. They define a transducer as a mode of transforming messages. For example, a microphone is a transducer because it transforms the sounds of human speech and codes them into electrical messages.

We propose that the fields of education and rehabilitation can meet the challenges of the age of transition by thoughtfully planning modifications in their institutions. If these new institutions are thought of as "Social Transducers"—forces designed to transform man so that he can achieve his highest potential—then we will have succeeded in preparing him for the enormous responsibilities of advancing human society as he launches out into the vast reaches of space.

References

1. Beers, Sanford   CYBERNETICS & MANAGEMENT, New York: Science Editions, John Wiley & Sons, 1959.

2. Boocock, Sarane S., & James S. Coleman   GAMES WITH SIMULATED ENVIRON-MENTS IN LEARNING, Sociology of Education, Vol. 39, No. 3, Summer, 1966.

3. Brunner, Jerome S.   ON KNOWING ESSAYS FOR THE LEFT HAND, Cambridge, Mass. Bellknap Press — Harvard University Press, 1962.

4. Buckingham, Walter   AUTOMATION, ITS IMPACT ON BUSINESS AND PEOPLE, New York: Harper & Row, 1963.

5. Cadwallader, Mervyn L.   THE CYBERNETIC ANALYSIS OF CHANGE, Social Change, ed. Etzioni, Amitai & Eva Etzioni, New York: Basic Books, Inc., 1964.

6. Cartwright, D., and Zander A. GROUP DYNAMICS, New York: Harper & Row, 1953.

7. Charter, S.P.R.   MAN ON EARTH, Sausalito, Calif.: Angel Island Publications, Inc., Contact Editors, 1962.

8. Chestnut, Harold   SYSTEMS ENGINEERING TOOLS, New York: John Wiley & Sons, 1966.

9. Clarke, Arthur C. PROFILES OF THE FUTURE, New York: Bantam Books, 1963.

10. Cohen, Harold L.   IRCD BULLETIN, New York: Yeshiva University, Vol. III, No. 3, May, 1967.

11. Cohen, John   PSYCHOLOGICAL TIME, Scientific American, Vol. 211, No. 5, Nov., 1964.

12. Cottrell, Fred   ENERGY AND SOCIETY, New York: McGraw-Hill Book Co., 1955.

13. Deutsch, M. IN HUMAN GROUPS, W. J. H. Scott, Balt. Md.: Penguin Books, 1958.

14. Dewey, John DEMOCRACY AND EDUCATION, New York: MacMillan Co., 1916.

15. Diebold, John BEYOND AUTOMATION, New York, McGraw Hill Book Co., 1964.

16. Drucker, Peter F. THE FUTURE OF INDUSTRIAL MAN, New York: The New American Library of World Literature, 1942.

17. Durant, William THE STORY OF PHILOSOPHY, New York: Pocket Books, Inc., 1954.

18. Etzioni, Amitai and Eva Etzioni, (ed.) SOCIAL CHANGE, New York: Basic Books, Inc., 1964.

19. Eysenck, H.J. USES AND ABUSES OF PSYCHOLOGY, Balt. Md.,: Penguin Books, 1953.

20. Fabricant, Solomon MEASUREMENT OF TECHNOLOGICAL CHANGE, Wash., D.C., Manpower Administration, U.S. Dept. of Labor, 1965.

21. Finn, James D. EDUCATIONAL IMPLICATIONS OF TECHNOLOGICAL CHANGE, Vol. IV, The Emerging Technology of Education, Wash., D.C. U.S. Government Printing Office, Feb., 1966.

22. George, F.H. AUTOMATION, CYBERNETICS AND SOCIETY, London, N.W., Leonard Hill Books, Ltd., 1959.

23. Harman, Harry H. SIMULATION: A SURVEY, Santa Monica, Calif.: System Development Corp., SP-260, 1961.

24. Haworth, Mary R., and Frank J. Menolascino VIDEOTAPE OBSERVATIONS OF DISTURBED YOUNG CHILDREN, Journal of Clinical Psychology, Vol. XXIII, No. 2, April, 1967.

25. Hazlip, Harold C. MEASUREMENT OF TECHNOLOGICAL CHANGE, Wash., D.C., Manpower Administration, U.S. Dept. of Labor, 1965.

26. Hazlip, Harold C. TECHNOLOGY IN EDUCATION, Wash., D.C., Congressional Hearings, U.S. Government Printing Office, 1966.

27. Hilgard, E.R. THEORIES OF LEARNING, New York: Appleton-Century-Crofts, 1956.

28. Hill, Brian V. SOREN KIERKEGAARD & EDUCATIONAL THEORY, Educational Theory, Vol. XVI, No. 4, Oct., 1966.

29. James, Henry PRAGMATISM & OTHER ASSAYS, New York: Washington Square Press, 1963.

30. James, William ESSAYS IN PRAGMATISM, New York: Hafner Publishing Co., 1948.

31. Kirk, Samuel EDUCATING THE HANDICAPPED. CONTEMPORARY ISSUES IN AMERI-CAN EDUCATION, Wash., D.C.: OE-10034, Bulletin, No. 3 U.S. Government Printing Office, 1966.

32. Kohl, Herbert THE AGE OF COMPLEXITY, New York: Mentor Books, 1965.

33. Kraft, Joseph THE PHILADELPHIA EVENING BULLETIN, Editorial Box, Tuesday, July 25, 1967.

34. Lovas, O.I. REINFORCEMENT THEORY, Phila.: Smith, Kline & French Labs., 1966.

35. Lukacs, John NEW YORK TIMES MAGAZINE, New York: January 2, Sec. 6, pages 8-32, 1966.

36. Lundberg, Ferdinand THE COMING WORLD TRANSFORMATION, Garden City, N.Y., Doubleday & Co., 1963.

37. McHugh, Thomas, Thomas Woody SCHOLAR, TEACHER, HUMANIST, Ph. D. Dissertation, unpublished, 1967.

38. McLuhan, Marshall B., & George B. Leonard THE FUTURE OF EDUCATION, The Class of 1989, Look Magazine, Vol. 31, No. 4, Feb. 21, 1967.

39. Michael, Donald TECHNOLOGICAL INNOVATION & SOCIETY, Aaron & Warner (Ed.), New York: Columbia University Press, 1966.

40. Morse, Dean & Aaron W. Warner, Editors TECHNOLOGICAL INNOVATION & SO-CIETY, New York: Columbia University Press, 1966.

41. Mowrer, O. Herbert PSYCHOTHERAPY THEORY AND RESEARCH, New York: Ronald Press, 1953.

42. Riesman, David TIME MAGAZINE, New York: Vol. 90, No. 3, July 21, 1967.

43. Rosenberg, Jerry M. AUTOMATION, MANPOWER AND EDUCATION, New York: Random House, 1966.

44. Silberman, Charles E. THE MYTHS OF AUTOMATION, New York: Harper & Row, 1966.

45. Smith, Karl U. CYBERNETIC FOUNDATIONS OF LEARNING SCIENCE SYMPOSIUM ON CYBERNETIC SYSTEMS OF LEARNING AND REHABILITATIVE TRAINING, Mimeographed—August, 1965.

46. Smith, Karl U., and Margaret Foltz Smith CYBERNETIC PRINCIPLES OF LEARNING AND EDUCATIONAL DESIGN, New York: Holt, Rinehart & Winston, 1966.

47. Smith, M. SOCIAL SITUATION, SOCIAL BEHAVIOR, SOCIAL GROUP, Psychological Review, Vol. 52, 1945.

48. Steinmetz, Charles P. ADDRESS ON THE UNITARIAN CHURCH, Schenectady, N. Y., 1923.

49. Wiesner, Jerome B. SOCIETY AS A LEARNING MACHINE, New York: The Computer & Society, New York Times, Sec. 11, Page 15, April 24, 1966.

50. Yablonsky, Lewis and James M. Enneis Mimeographed, 1965.

Above:
The Career Guidance Center
building in the
Valley Forge Industrial Park.

Upper right:
a young lady prepares
for her high school
equivalency exams.
Academics complement
the workshop activities.
Her book work is
supplemented by Videotape.

Lower right:
a young man is wiring
a specially designed
testing computer as
part of the
Career Guidance Center's
Research Program

A new worker being
initiated into its processes.

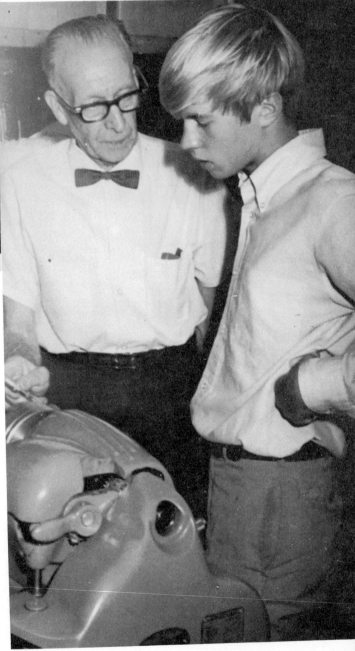

A young man
being informed of the
art of metal latheing
by the metal lathe instructor.

Above:

Young men begin
the search for jobs
in the help-wanted
columns of a newspaper.

Middle:

A view of the
graphic arts department.
This area provides
a refined area for the
evaluation of skill potential.
The two young men
are working at
the stripping table.

Bottom:

Included in the Career Guidance
Center's strategies of motivation
is a scheduled football game
with the Vanguard Upper School.

CURRICULUM DEVELOPMENT AND THE DIMENSIONS OF EDUCABILITY

Bluma B. Weiner, Ed. D., Associate Professor,
Department of Special Education,
Ferkauf Graduate School of Humanities and Social Sciences,
Yeshiva University, New York, New York

BLUMA B. WEINER, Ed. D.

The concept of **educability** is central to all programs of special education, but the term has never been adequately defined. The nearest approximation has been the differentiation made between "educable" and "trainable" mentally retarded children. This distinction is not completely satisfactory, but it has helped to focus attention upon certain facets of developmental progress, namely **level, rate,** and **range** of performance on educationally relevant tasks. These aspects of achievement are viewed here as "dimensions of educability." With the additional consideration of **efficiency** and **autonomy** they constitute bases for collecting and collating information on progress in appropriate curriculum experiences, and thus provide realistic foundations for appraising educability.

By **level** is meant the total amount of development or achievement. The notion of level is traditionally considered in terms of age or grade equivalences, but it can also be described in terms of degree of difficulty or complexity. The latter kind of description is of greater functional value, because it makes available substantive information for planning further instruction and opportunity.

Rate refers to the time required to attain a particular level or to achieve a specific amount of gain. It must be appreciated that rate may change from task to task and from circumstance to circumstance. We need to give closer attention to the activity rhythms of individual children and to their apparent peaks and plateaus in learning and in performance. We need also to understand that a child's rate of change may depend in part upon the behavior of the adult. To assume that rate is a fixed function of innate factors is to minimize the role of the educator as a manager of learning.

Range is used here in its territorial rather than in its statistical sense. We must be concerned with the array of learning opportunities that are provided as well as with the quality of the child's response to them. The important concern here is "educable in what functions?" This question is critical in our discussion of curriculum development, and we shall consider it more fully.

In observing for **efficiency,** we need to look for evidence of behavioral adequacy in terms of **accuracy** or **correctness,** and in terms of **availability** as it is expressed in economy and speed of performance. By **autonomy** we mean evidence of independent, self-actualizing activity. We need to observe not only how children approach and execute tasks which have been selected for them, but whether and how they initiate, select, and carry on tasks which they have chosen for themselves. We need to note whether our children perceive themselves as learners and doers, or whether they view themselves as non-learners and non-doers.

ANOTHER VIEW OF CURRICULUM

For the purpose of this discussion, the word curriculum denotes the scope and implies the sequence of the several instructional experiences which are commonly offered to children enrolled in school programs from the nursery or "preschool" period through grade six. Although nursery and kindergarten classes are not yet universally established features of American public school education, their potential contribution to the developmental environment of children has been increasingly acknowledged, especially for handicapped and other seriously disadvantaged children. Traditionally, school curriculum offerings are designated in terms of formal subject or content areas such as language arts, social studies, science, mathematics, physical education, art, music, and the like, although a less formal nomenclature is employed for nursery and kindergarten classes. In order to clarify the potential relevance of the common school curriculum to the **development** of children, and to make more explicit some of its possible and desirable applications to the education of mentally retarded children, a somewhat unorthodox formulation is used here.

Under the headings of **communication, behavioral tools, informational agenda, spatial and quantitative understandings and skills,** and **self-actualization,** reference points have been determined for the examination of curriculum content in terms of potential functional equivalence for several aspects of human growth and development. Specifically, attention is drawn to perceptual, motor, conceptual, and emotional and social learning. The present formulation is an invitation to look at and to devise fresh ways of employing stable features of the developmental environment.

Communication

The usual view of the language arts or **communication** areas embraces hearing and listening, speaking, reading, writing, and spelling. More elaborate achievements in spoken and written language depend upon their acquisition. But underpinning these foundations are even more primary processes: accurate and stable auditory, visual, tactile, and kinesthetic functions; reception, perception, integration, association, and retention; and dependable motor, visual-motor, and vocal coordinations. Difficulty with any of these processes or functions constitutes potential impediment to achievement in more complex school tasks, not only in the language arts as such, but in many other aspects of the school program. Especially serious and damaging are the obstructions to effective social interaction with parents and peers.

Behavioral Tools

Nursery and kindergarten teachers have understood for a long time that children have to learn how to become "school children." This observation is particularly applicable to the mentally retarded child. Certain behaviors must be established for effective participation, and when these responses are not already present at school entrance they should be considered a legitimate part of the curriculum. The young, or even the pre-adolescent or older, retarded child, may need some help in learning the **meaning** and acquiring the **motions** of behaviors which are often taken for granted: **looking at, listening to, waiting, taking turns, sharing, trying, helping,** and **working**. He may have to be guided by verbalizations, demonstrations, and going-through-the-motions in the development of meaning and reinforcement of positive valence toward such expectancies. Knowing how to behave under certain conditions provides the bases for establishing the inner controls needed to cope with one's labile impulses or low threshold of tolerance for competing attractions. The acquisition of such controls assists the retarded child, as well as other children, to assume and successfully carry out the role of school child.

The importance of this task should not be underestimated. The role of school child is fairly well defined and can be understood by children as young as three years. Expectations which are established for various maturational levels are reasonably stable and reasonable "reasonable." There is a progression in the role functions which is intrinsically rewarding for most children: the child who masters various tasks at one level moves on to the next task, group, room, or grade where he learns to do more complicated and potentially more interesting and more satisfying things. The development of competency in the use of various behavioral tools contributes not only to the effectiveness of achievement in the more traditional aspects of school curriculum, but also to the evolution of purpose or motivation for anticipated tasks.

Informational Agenda

All children require some kind of assistance in becoming aware of and in dealing with various natural and social phenomena. These conceptual aspects of experience are important "informational agenda" of nursery, kindergarten, and elementary school years. They are data to be acquired, understood, and incorporated into the expanding knowledge of one's self and of other persons and things. In more conventional terms such information is labelled "social studies" and "science." Retarded children need accurate information about many aspects of the physical world and the social groups in which they live. They need to know about visible and tangible things and about matters which are not visible or tangible: about thoughts and feelings, and about relationships between themselves and others. Such information is acquired gradually, often laboriously, and sometimes painfully. School is a place where these data may be augmented, corrected, and properly organized. The retarded child would be at great disadvantage if he were uninformed about commonly known events and relationships and acceptable ways of responding to them. Such know-that and know-how is not only a basis for social exchange; it is also a substructure for understanding and being at ease in the world of reality.

Spatial and Quantitative Understandings and Skills

Very careful attention needs to be given to processes which precede rote enumeration and computation. Awareness of one's self as a distinct entity, and of one's body members and digits and facial features has been advanced as necessary for the meaningful acquisition of more formal operations. Perception and discrimination of units, groups, mass, direction, and distance—and their comparative relationships—are the foundations upon which children learn how to locate and manipulate themselves and other persons and objects in space and in time. The many categories of spatial and quantitative percepts and concepts, and the verbal and visual symbols for their representation and functions are valid curriculum content, and the processes by which competencies are acquired are facilitated and verified by manual explorations and operations. Introduction of the "new mathematics" and the availability of several experimental systems suggest interesting possibilities as well as problems in the education of retarded children. Whatever "system" may be adopted, certain practical tasks of daily life will persist, and they will require spatial understanding and skill: rational counting and grouping, locating in space (**in, on, under, over, beside, before, behind**), reckoning (not simply "telling") time, and using money. These demands, as well as others of similar character, begin in early childhood and continue throughout life. Provision for systematic, rational instruction and appropriate reinforcement is viewed as an important part of the school curriculum for all children. Methods of instruction, especially for children who are handicapped, should insure perceptual accuracy, correct terminology, and frequent realistic social application.

Self Actualization

Many students of human development have been concerned with the infant's initial task of becoming aware of himself as a creature, separate from his surroundings, who is comprised of a variety of parts which stay put together in a dependable way and yet are capable of an exciting and satisfying repertoire of performances. But this achievement is just a prologue to the larger life-long drama of self realization and "actualization." The retarded child, like other children, participates in a continuous complexity of behaviors which increase and deepen his perceptions of himself as a **person**. Jersild has noted in simple, economical terminology that among the various aspects of "self" are **perceptual, conceptual,** and **attitudinal** components. Neglect of any of these phenomena in the educational management of the retarded child would distort our perspective of his problems and of our responsibilities, and would deprive him of a potential asset, a sense of being regarded as a person who is capable of growth and of active engagement in the promotion of that growth. In addition to those aspects of curriculum which have already been mentioned, there are others which offer fruitful opportunities for developing functions that contribute to general fitness, pride and pleasure in mastery, and social interaction. In particular, **physical education, arts and crafts,** and **music** have long been recognized not only as pleasant divertissements but as means for involving the "whole" person in powerful activity.

CONCLUSION

If we are to invest this word **educable** with functional meaning, a global and either-or viewpoint will not be sufficient. We need a construct that will help us to account for the continum of important characteristics which obtain from childhood through adulthood and which are translatable into functions that are accessible to educational manipulation. We have presented here a framework for such a model of educability. The aspects of **level, rate, range, efficiency,** and **autonomy** which have been discussed are observable at all ages and stages of development and in all social and cultural groups. The concept of curriculum is represented in this model by the term **range,** and the child's response to curriculum is noted in terms of **level, rate, efficiency,** and **autonomy**. Description of the child's response to his life and school experiences in terms of these multiple dimensions appears to be a better basis for assessing his educability than reliance upon a single numerical index.

*Presented at the Ninetieth Annual Meeting of the American Association on Mental Deficiency, Chicago, Illinois, May 10-14, 1966.

STUDIES IN SHORT TERM RETENTION OF EDUCABLE RETARDATES

Robert M. Allen, Ph.D.
Professor of Psychology,
Department of Psychology
University of Miami,
Coral Gables, Florida

ROBERT M. ALLEN, Ph.D.

Much effort, time, planning, and money are being channeled into programs for educating and training the educable mental retardate. The basic rationale for these projects is the firm belief that a child usually benefits from exposure to such programs.

The two studies, actually a pilot project and a redesigned investigation, discussed in this chapter revolve around the responses of groups of educable retardates to the presence and absence of specialized training in visual perceptual development. Certainly other perceptual modalities contribute to the intellectual growth of the child. This specific sense modality — vision — was selected because of its predominant importance to learning. Moreover, a specific remedial training program exists which emphasizes learning through this sense modality.

The retarded child is deficient in reading and writing, among other skills. More specifically, the retardate is lacking in word-perception ability, a skill that may be learned if the essential processes have been mastered to a sufficient degree.

Before discussing the studies which are central to this chapter, it would be well to consider visual perception and its role in learning. Visual perception is more than the reception of stimuli by the visual apparatus and the passage of neural impulses to the brain. This "pure" process is sensory stimulation. The organization of the visual stimuli into meaning for the perceiver is the additional ingredient that differentiates sensation from perception. Therefore, in order for the organism to learn the reception of stimuli serves only to initiate a complex set of processes which culminate in the extraction of meaning from these sensory experiences.

Homo sapiens differs from the lower animals, with regard to learning, in that perception is **increasingly** influenced by prior learning experiences as the phylogenetic scale is ascended. Regardless of anatomical, neural and physiological makeup, perceptual ability (beyond sensory stimulation) is a function of development in cognition and of informa-tion-extraction based on the quality and quantity of the individual's experiences.

Thus, an inquiry into perceptual maturity is actually an investigation into the person's past experiences and to what extent he has gained from these experiences. More specif-ically, the manner in which the child reacts to, selects, and organizes the multiplicity of stimuli impinging upon him from his total environment is embedded in every ex-periential step from conception to the moment of observation and even beyond. The latter, "and even beyond," is added since projection into the future in terms of goals, aspirations, and fears is also a part of the currently functioning person.* From a phe-nomenological point of view, the observed reaction to stimuli (or response to a test item) is actually an observation of how the person copes with a problem in the immedi-ate foreground against the backdrop of life-experiences with his physical, physiological and neurological equipment. Furthermore, the uniqueness of the individual (foreground) is judged in terms of the baseline afforded by the performance of the general popula-tion (background or normative data).

It was indicated that the retarded child is usually deficient in reading and writing, i.e., he is lacking in word-perception ability. Since this ability is dependent upon learning,** the population of the two studies in this chapter was limited to educable mental retar-dates so that the results of exposure and non-exposure to learning could be evaluated. The testing instrument used in these studies was the DEVELOPMENTAL TEST OF VISUAL PERCEPTION by Frostig and her colleagues (Frostig, Maslow, Lefever and Whittlesey, 1963). The learning experiences were the Frostig and Horne (1964) materials from their TEACHER'S GUIDE FOR THE FROSTIG PROGRAM FOR THE DEVELOPMENT OF VISUAL PERCEPTION.

THE FROSTIG DEVELOPMENTAL TEST OF VISUAL PERCEPTION

In school and out, objects and persons must be identified. An accurate perception of the material to be learned and the problems to be solved require noting details, observing similarities and differences among events, and comprehending relationships. Difficulty with these skills may yield, for example, reading and writing impairments since the child is very likely to see letters and words as meaningless conglomerations of unrelated

---

* To paraphrase Lewin's topological model: $B = f(P)_{n+t,}^{n-t}$ or Behavior is a function of the Person's past (now minus time), present (now), and future (now plus time) with the Person as the one in whom all three time dimensions reside and by and in whom they are integrated.

** This statement does not apply as forcefully to the brain damaged retardate and to the severely and pro-foundly defective child who does not manifest overtly discoverable encephalopathy.

details. Early reading, involving only simple forms, may be noticeably affected by these perceptual difficulties. However, when visual discriminations depend on the detection of **small** differences in letter and word shapes then poor reading becomes evident if this is deficient.

Experience with children having learning difficulties has implicated disturbances in visual perception as a major etiologic element (Frostig, **et al.,** 1964). Children with writing difficulties displayed poor eye motor coordination. Those who could not recognize words were below par in figure-ground discriminations. Other youngsters showed poor form constancy in their decreased ability to recognize letters and words presented in varying sizes and colors, or in capital letters in contrast to the usual lower case print. Reversals and rotations in visual perception were characterized as faulty "position in space" appreciation. Finally, the interchange of letters within a word suggested impaired analysis and synthesis of spatial relationships. These symptoms and manifestations identified poor students and retarded readers.

The five major classes of difficulties: eye-motor coordination, figure-ground discrimination, figure constancy, position in space, and spatial relationships are the five areas probed by the Frostig (Developmental Test of Visual Perception) Test. These are also the names of the five subtests of the Frostig Test.

Subtest I, Eye-Motor Coordination, entails the recognition of the objects at both ends of each test item, as shown in Figure 1, so that the instructions to draw a line from the Mouse to the Cookie through the tunnel is meaningful as it sets limits to the testee's line-drawing behavior, Figure 1.

A second function tapped is eye-hand motor coordination. Items 6 and 7, 10 and 12, and 16, Figures 2, 3 and 4 respectively, disclose the different kinds of hand movements that are involved in the eye-motor coordination tasks. These include curvilinear sweeps, Figure 2; horizontal and vertical motion, Figure 3; and diagonally varied movements in Figure 4.

This subtest serves as an index to the rate of developmental change as the child grows in physical maturity. The period of most rapid development in the type of eye-motor coordination essential to the successful completion of Subtest I items is between 3 years, 6 months and 5 years, 6 months. Figure 5 presents the standardization (or average) and Q1 and Q3 curves for this subtest (Frostig, **et al.,** 1964, p. 482) with a normal population. The development slows down and becomes negatively accelerated. Since the norms accompanying the Frostig Test convert raw scores to perceptual age equivalents, the retarded testee's level of development for this activity may be compared with a normal child in the corresponding age group.

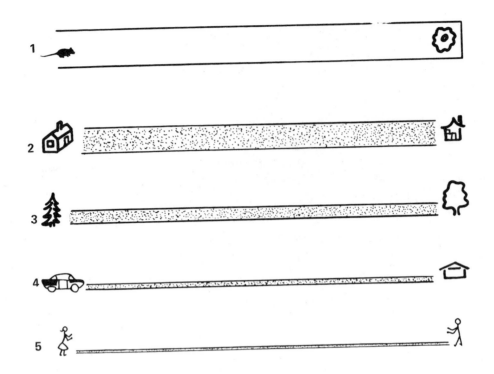

FIGURE 1

Items I through 5, Subtest I, Eye-Motor Coordination of the Developmental Test of Visual Perception. Reproduced by special permission from Frostig Developmental Test of Visual Perception of Marianne Frostig. Copyright 1963, published by Consulting Psychologists Press, Inc.

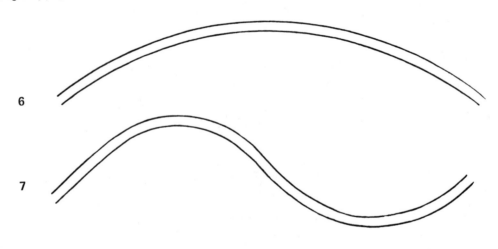

FIGURE 2

Items 6 and 7, Subtest I of the Frostig Test. Reproduced by special permission from Frostig Developmental Test of Visual Perception by Marianne Frostig, Copyright 1963, published by Consulting Psychologists Press, Inc.

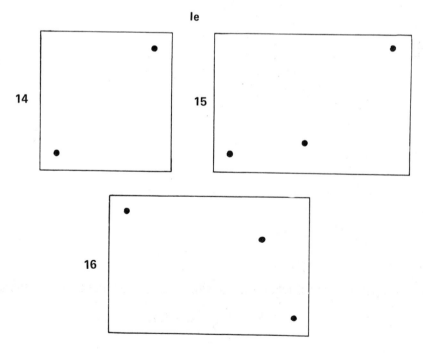

12

10

FIGURE 3

Items 10 and 12, Subtest I of the Frostig Test. Reproduced by special permission from Frostig Developmental Test of Visual Perception by Marianne Frostig. Copyright 1963, published by Consulting Psychologists Press, Inc.

le

14

15

16

FIGURE 4

Items 14 through 16, Subtest I, of the Frostig Test. Reproduced by special permission from Frostig Developmental Test of Visual Perception of Marianne Frostig. Copyright 1963, published by Consulting Psychologists Press, Inc.

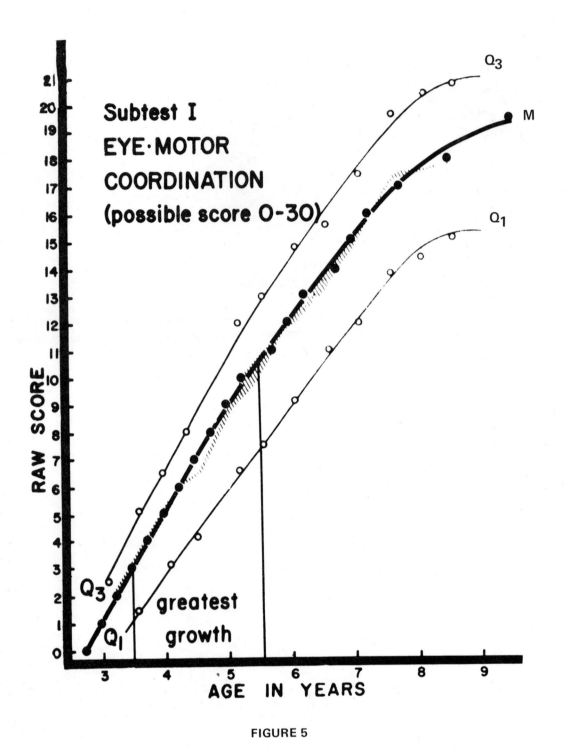

FIGURE 5

Standardization Curve and Q1, and Q3 Curves for Subtest I. Modified from Frostig, et al., 1964, Page 482. Reproduced by special permission from Frostig Developmental Test of Visual Perception by Marianne Frostig. Copyright 1963, published by Consulting Psychologists Press, Inc.

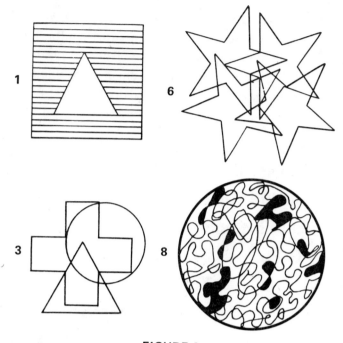

FIGURE 6

Items 1, 3, 6 and 8 of Subtest II, The Frostig Test. Reproduced by special permission from Frostig Developmental Test of Visual Perception by Marianne Frostig. Copyright 1963, published by Consulting Psychologists Press, Inc.

Corah and Powell (1963) have stated that the performance on Subtest I contributes to a "general intelligence" factor and to a second "developmental changes due to age" factor.

Subtest II, Figure-ground Discrimination, requires the ability to recognize shapes described orally and presented visually. The figures increase in shape and figure-ground complexity from Item 1 to 8, see Figure 6.

The child is asked to "outline" or "draw around" a specified shape or shapes with colored pencil(s). The triangle and cross of items 1 and 3 respectively are the "figure" shapes to be differentiated from the backgrounds in which each is embedded. In item 6 the child uses a different colored pencil to outline each of the four stars. The five ovals in item 8 are to be detected and outlined from the very complex and distracting background.

The development of the integrated skills culminating in figure-ground discrimination and motor coordination is rather slow to age 6 (as compared with the more "pure" motor activity of Subtest I). The period of greatest growth is between 4 years, 6 months and 6 years, followed by a slowing down to a ceiling shortly after 8 years*, see Figure 7. With maturity the child must learn to resist the visual distraction offered by the complex background and the easier flow of lines away from the specified form (the figure) and into a portion of the intruding design of a background figure. Figure 8 illustrates this: the child may follow the top straight line of the cross (see arrow) into the curving sweep of the imposed circle.

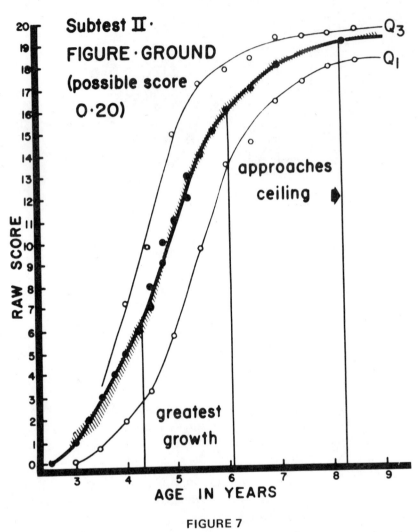

FIGURE 7

Standardization Curve and QI and Q3 curves for Subtest II. Modified from Frostig, et al., 1964, page 482. Reproduced by special permission from Frostig Developmental Test of Visual Perception by Marianne Frostig. Copyright 1963, published by Consulting Psycholotists Press, Inc.

The curves for Q1 and Q3 in this and in the other figures disclose the variance around the average growth curve.

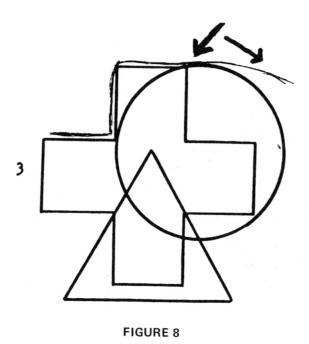

FIGURE 8

Item 3, Subtest II, showing interference of imposed Circle on outlining the Cross. Reproduced by special permission from Frostig Developmental Test of Visual Perception by Marianne Frostig. Copyright 1963, published by Consulting Psychologists Press, Inc.

Subtest II contributes to the "differentiation of developmental changes due to age" factor (Corah and Powell, 1963). Children who perform adequately on Subtest II have similar success with the items of Subtest I, Eye-Motor Coordination. Retardates have not developed the integrated skills necessary for dealing with figure-ground discriminations in visually perceived material. Much of their reading difficulty may be ascribed to this decelerated readiness for visual perceptual organization.

It was previously mentioned that the role of small differences in shapes is important for learning to read. Subtest III, Figure Constancy, evaluates the recognition of two-dimensional shape in different sizes and orientations. Figures 9 and 10 present the items in the two parts of Subtest III.

In Subtest IIIa the child will draw around all of the circles and squares only regardless of size, context (embeddedness) and angular position (orientation). The task for Subtest IIIb is exactly the same, to outline all squares and circles on the test page, Figure 10.

It should be noted that the recognition of shape is complicated by the presence of distractors such as size differences of the circles and squares and the discriminations between a circle and an oval on the one hand and a square and a rectangle on the other.

FIGURE 9

All items in Subtest IIIa of the Frostig Test. Reproduced by special permission from Frostig Developmental Test of Visual Perception by Marianne Frostig. Copyright 1963, published by Consulting Psychologists Press, Inc.

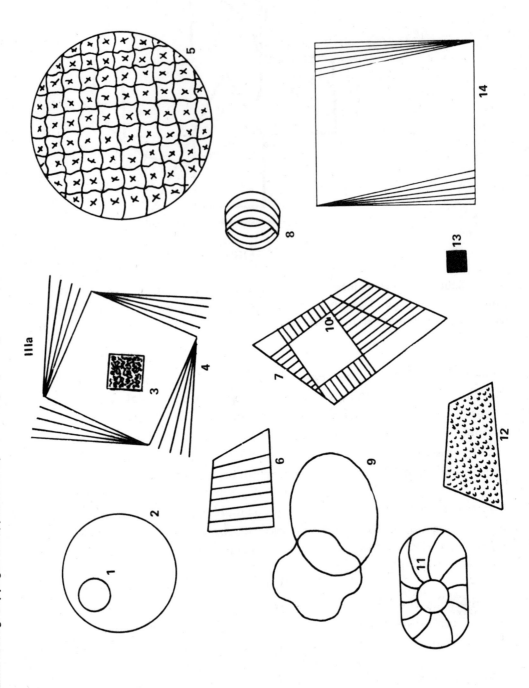

FIGURE 10

All items in Subtest IIIb of the Frostig Test. Reproduced by special permission from Frostig Developmental Test of Visual Perception of Marianne Frostig. Copyright 1963, published by Consulting Psychologists Press, Inc.

The process(es) labeled "form constancy" develop rather slowly, Figure 11, to 5 years, 9 months. A steep gradient thereafter between 5 and 7 years indicates a more rapid maturation followed by a deceleration. Figure-ground (Subtest II) discrimination develops earlier but the additional abilities for coping perceptually with complex distractors, angularity, and finer form discrimination appear to require physical maturation and experience.

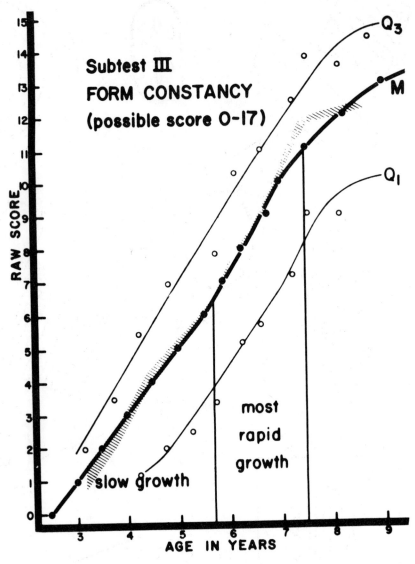

FIGURE 11

Standardization Curve and Q1 and Q3 Curves for Subtest III. Modified from Frostig, et al., 1964, page 483. Reproduced by special permission from Frostig Developmental Test of Visual Perception. Copyright 1963, published by Consulting Psychologists Press, Inc.

In Subtest IV, Position in Space, the task is to detect differences and similarities in the spatial orientation of designs. In Figure 12, items 1 and 4 of Subtest IVa are successfully completed by crossing out the one drawing different from the other four in each row. IVb, on the other hand, requires crossing out one of the four drawings identically oriented as the model figure in the box in each row. Recognition of form is essential. The ability to shift from a "different from" to a "similar to" ideational orientation is just as important as the recognition of spatial positions. The processes involved in this subtest are: form recognition, position in space discrimination, judgment, response to auditory instructions, and keeping the problem in mind. This subtest along with Subtest I (eye-motor coordination) and Subtest V (spatial relations) form an intelligence factor. Since this test is designed for young children (with norms between CA 4 years and 7 years, 11 months) this should not come as a surprise.*

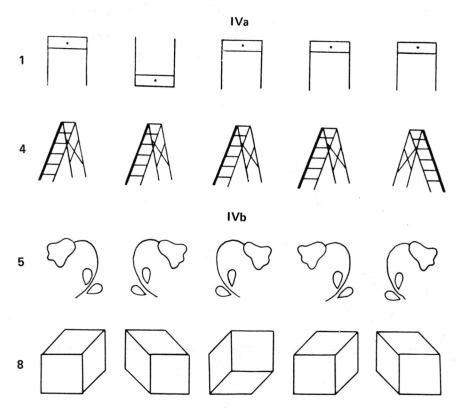

FIGURE 12

Subtest IVa, items 1 and 4; IVb, items 5 and 8, of the Frostig Test. Reproduced by special permission from Frostig Developmental Test of Visual Perception by Marianne Frostig. Copyright 1963, published by Consulting Psychologists Press, Inc.

*The so-called "baby tests" and pre-school evaluative procedures are predominantly non-verbal up to 6 years of age. The test items emphasize the reflections of neurological growth through manipulative tasks.

The developmental curve for the standardization population is given in Figure 13, note the slow maturation to 4 years, 6 months, followed by a spurt of more rapid growth to seven years, 6 months, the ceiling for this subtest. The development is quite rapid overall.*

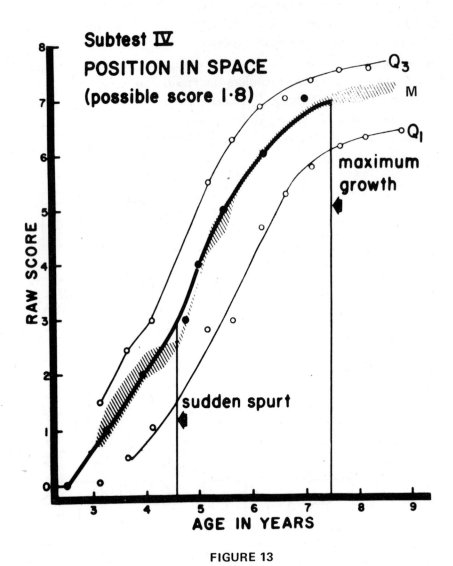

FIGURE 13

Standardization Curve and QI and Q3 Curves for Subtest IV. Modified from Frostig, et al., 1964, page 483. Reproduced by special permission from Frostig Developmental Test of Visual Perception by Marianne Frostig. Copyright 1963, published by Consulting Psychologists Press, Inc.

*Subtest IV differs from the other subtests in that it involves ideation more than the others. The first three subtests can be pantomimed, dry runs are permitted, demonstrations all but do the task for the child. In Subtest IV the child must grasp the core ideas involved in "similarity" and "difference."

Closely related to "position in space" is the content and rationale of Subtest V, spatial relations. The testee needs to analyze forms and patterns, as in Figure 14. The patterns increase in complexity from the single horizontal line of item Va to the extremely complex line-maze of item Vf. The task of analyzing and synthesizing **both** the model and the reproduction (on the right side of the page) requires a great deal of concentration and exclusion of intruding extraneous stimuli.

The actual eye-hand motor coordination activity reflects the degree of clarity or vagueness of the testee's analysis and synthesis of the visually perceived stimuli.

The integration or synthesis essential for the completion of the tasks beyond item 2 (reproducing a single diagonal line) is late in getting started (4 years of age) but is followed by a very rapid rise in the growth curve, Figure 15.

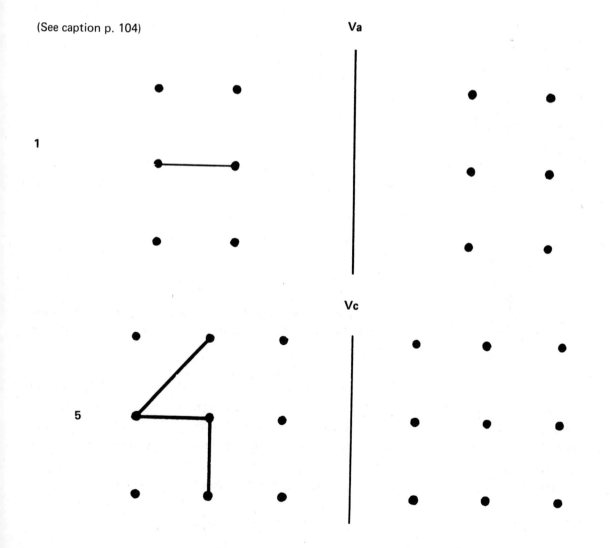

(See caption p. 104)

Va

Vc

1

5

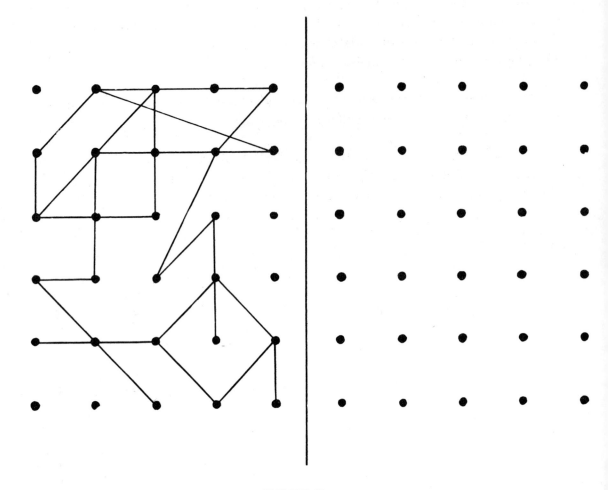

First Grade and up only

8

FIGURE 14

Items from Subtest Va, Vc, and Ve of the Frostig Test. Reproduced by special permission from Frostig Developmental Test of Visual Perception of Marianne Frostig. Copyright 1963, published by Consulting Psychologists Press, Inc.

The Frostig Test should be used with children between 3 and 9 years of age. In the present studies this was not feasible because retarded children within this chronological age range would tend to cluster at the very low end of the score-distribution. Thus, the decision to use children of MA 3 to 9 years with the complete understanding that two children, one a retardate with MA 5 and the other an intellectually average CA 5 year-old, are considered to be identical **only insofar as the MA score is concerned.**

The Frostig-Home Program for the Development of Visual Perception:

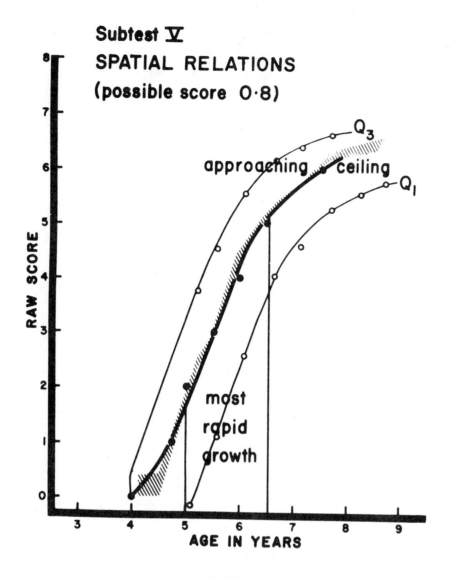

FIGURE 15

Standardization Curve and Q1 and Q3 Curves for Subtest V. Modified from Frostig, et al., 1964, page 484. Reproduced by special permission from Frostig Developmental Test of Visual Perception by Marianne Frostig. Copyright 1963, published by Consulting Psychologists Press, Inc.

Frostig and Horne (1964) have published a TEACHER'S GUIDE with this Preface: "The program described in this TEACHER'S GUIDE is intended to be both corrective and preventive. It is for use not only by specialists in the field of visual perception training, but also by regular primary-grade classroom teachers and by teachers of special classes for young children with learning difficulties...." (p. 3).

The GUIDE details methods of visual perception training by means of activity exercises and paper and pencil work sheets. The design of the current studies included learning with the work sheets only. The publisher distributes ditto stencils for the work sheets used with the graining group. There is a set of work sheets for each of the major areas of visual perceptual skills evaluated by the Frostig Test:

1. Eye-Motor Coordination (Subtest I), 90 exercises divided into worksheets for:

a.	Ex. 1-29	Drawing with Guidelines
b.	30-40	Tracing
c.	41-57	Drawing without Guidelines
d.	58-64	Drawing Slanting lines
e.	65-71	Joining Points
f.	72-74	Drawing Arcs
g.	75-77	Drawing Wavy Lines
h.	78-90	Coloring

Code Name VM.

2. Figure-Ground Discrimination (Subtest II), 78 work sheets for exercises in:

a.	Ex. 1-15	Intersecting Lines
b.	16-20	Intersecting Figures
c.	21-31	Hidden Figures
d.	32-44	Overlapping Figures
e.	45-57	Figure Completion
f.	58-59	Figure Assembly
g.	60-64	Similarities & Differences of Details
h.	65-69	Reversal of Figure-Ground

(14)

Code Name FG.

3. Figure Constancy (Subtest III), 70 exercises:

      a.   Ex. 1-37   Shape Constancy

      b.   38-70   Size Constancy

                                              Code Name PC.

4. Position in Space (Subtest IV), 36 worksheets for:

      a.   Ex. 1-11   Reversals and Rotations-Whole Figures

      b.   12-25   Position of Details

      c.   26-36   Mirror Patterns

                                            Code Name PS.

5. Spatial Relations (Subtest V), 85 exercises in:

      a.   Ex. 1-4   Related Positions of Two Objects

      b.   5-17   Similarities and Differences

      c.   18-24   Shortest Path to a Goal

      d.   25-40   Figure Completion

      e.   41-50   Connecting Dots

      f.   51-60   Recall of Motor Sequences

      g.   61-68   Spatial Sequences

      h.   69-85   Assembly of Parts

                                            Code Name SR.*

The work sheets are ordinarily used in conjunction with the perceptual impairment(s) as revealed by the Frostig Test. The purpose of the exercises is to provide remedial training for the child in the major area of poor visual perceptual function. Frostig and Horne

*The interested teacher should read Frostig, M. and Horne, D. TEACHER'S GUIDE. Chicago, Ill.: Follett Publishing Co., 1964. The stencils are also distributed by the Follett Company. Illustrations of the various exercises are not included in this chapter in the interests of saving space and the difficulty reproducing ditto'd material.

(1964, p. 14) write: "The work sheets are also appropriate for use with **mentally retarded children**. Many such children never develop the higher mental abilities—abstract thinking, concept formation, and the ability to draw logical conclusions. They therefore have to rely more fully on those abilities that develop mainly during the early childhood years. For these children, perceptual training is most important with regard to their later social and vocational adjustment, since employment opportunities can be open to them if they are perceptually proficient....Progress with the work sheets is slower, however, with these children than with children who are not mentally retarded."

Perceptual training during the period between three-and-one-half years and seven-and-one-half years is strategically timed. Prior to three years, six months sensory-motor growth takes place, thus preparing the child for visual perception maturation. After approximately seven years the cognitive processes blossom. Perception-training or re-mediation prepares the foundation for "....development in the cognitive realm of abstractions, thoughts, ideas...." (Frostig and Horne, 1964, p. 15). Herein lies the basic rationale for the investigations reported in this chapter.

The major question to be answered by both studies is: Does the educable mentally retarded child benefit from exposure to the Frostig-Horne training program for the development of visual perception? The investigators postulate an affirmative reply to this question.

PILOT STUDY

Subjects and Method

Educable day and resident students in the ungraded classes of the Hope School for Mentally Retarded Children (Miami, Florida) were administered the Frostig Test as the pre-training condition. Those with perceptual quotient scores below 35 and above 85 were eliminated. The former were dropped because their level of visual perception was below the arbitrary minimum for this pilot study. Those with PQs above 85 were chronologically older retardates. Their PQ scores indicated that they were close to, or at, the maximum level of visual perceptual maturation as measured by this test. If improvement did occur as a result of the training it would not be reflected in their post-training retest scores due to the test limitation.

During the one-semester training period 10 children of the randomly assigned experimental (E, or training) and control (C, or no-training) groups were lost to illness and excessive absences. The final stage of this study found 10 in the E and six in the C groups. The mean CAs for the E and C groups were 180 and 193 months respectively. Average MA and IQ data for the Ss in both groups indicated moderate to mild retardation. None of these had overt visual or motor impairments.

The experimental design consisted of pre-training testing with the Frostig Test (Condition—T), followed by intensive training for the E group with the Frostig-Horne materials by the special education teacher, and finally, post-training testing (Condition—RT), with the same test. The subjects in the C group were pre- and post-tested simultaneously with the E group. During the class periods of special training for the E group, the C group attended the regular academic, arts and crafts, and activities classes.

Results and Discussion

The scores discussed in this section are all **raw** scores. Transforming raw scores to standard scores, age-equivalents, or PQs would reduce the sensitivity of the five subtests by restricting the variability of achievement. Table 1 presents the mean raw scores for each of the five subtests and for the total test of both groups. Both groups show an increase in mean subtests and total scores from T to RT with the sole exception of the E group's scores on subtest I. The increase in the C group's RT scores suggests the influence of practice with the easier eye-motor tasks due to familiarity with the test material gained from the first administration of the Frostig Test. The differences between T and RT means are considerably larger for the E group than for the C group for Subtests II, III, V and Total Test scores. These differences in favor of the E group suggest, at most, the influence of the special training, or, at the least, a combined effect of training and practice.

Table I
Frostig Test (T) and Retest (RT) Mean Raw Scores for E & C Groups

Subtests	I		II		III		IV		V		Total	
Groups	T	RT	T	RT	T	RT	T	RT	T	RT	T	RT
E	11.6	11.3	8.5	13.5	2.6	5.4	3.4	3.8	1.0	3.0	27.1	35.2
C	7.8	8.5	7.8	9.0	2.5	3.5	2.1	2.5	2.1	2.6	22.6	26.0
Differences	3.8	4.8	0.7	4.5	0.1	1.9	1.3	1.3	-1.1	0.4	4.5	9.2

Five analyses of variance are considered in the order in which they appear in Tables 2 through 4. In the first of these three tables, Table 2, the variances of Frostig Test T and RT total scores for the E and C groups were analyzed. Since the RT scores on subtests II, III and V reflected the influence of the special training, the variances of the E and C groups' scores on each of these subtests were analyzed separately and presented in Table 3. Finally, the difference-scores, derived from the difference between the T and RT scores for each **S** on subtests II, III and V, were combined. Table 4 discloses

Table 2

Analysis of Variance of Frostig Test TEST and RETEST Total Test Raw Scores of the Experimental and Control Groups

Source	df	Sum of Squares	Mean Squares	F
Group (G)	1	365.7	365.7	.63
Trails (T)	1	331.5	331.5	13.20*
G x T	1	36.9	36.9	1.40
Ss/G	14	8067.8	576.2 (a)	22.90*
Ss x T/G	14	352.1	25.1 (b)	

Denominator is MS (b) for all F ratios except Group, which uses MS (a)
* p less than .01

Table 3

Analysis of Variance of Frostig Test TEST and RETEST Raw Scores for Subtests II, III, and V of the Experimental and Control Groups

Subtests Source	df	II Sum of Squares	II Mean Square	F	III Sum of Squares	III Mean Square	F	V Sum of Squares	V Mean Square	F
Group (G)	1	30.0	30.0	.69	7.5	7.5	.48	1.3	1.3	.14
Trial (T)	1	101.8	101.8	12.50*	36.0	36.0	6.90**	16.6	16.6	7.50**
G x T	1	47.3	47.3	5.84**	6.2	6.2	1.19	4.2	4.2	1.40
Ss/G	14	1166.5	43.2	5.33*	218.0	15.5	2.98**	122.5	8.7	3.90*
Ss x T/G	14	113.4	8.1		73.8	5.2		31.7		

Denominator is Ss x T/G for all F ratios except Group which uses Ss/G
* p less than .01
** p less than .05

Table 4

Analysis of Variance of Differences between Combined Raw Scores of Frostig Subtests II, III, and V

Source	df	Sum of Squares	Mean Square	F
E	9	307.6	34.18	11.1*
C	5	153.4	3.07	

p < .01

the variances of the E and C groups' scores when subtests II, III and V are treated as a single test (essentially the effect of combining the scores for these three subtests.

Table 2 shows the analysis of variance of the Frostig Test total scores. The F ratio of .63 is not statistically significant. In the analyses of variance of Subtests II, III and V scores, Table 3, the F ratios for Groups likewise did not reach statistical significance. This finding is further confirmed by the F ratios for the interaction effect of G x T in the analyses of total and subtest scores, Tables 2 and 3. These results suggest that the special training did not produce a significant change in total and subtest RT scores for the E group when compared with the C group scores. The only exception is subtest II in which the interaction G x T F ratio is significant beyond the .05 level. On the basis of these results alone it would be unwise to discount the influence of the special training upon the improvement in the abilities tapped by these subtests, particularly since this pilot study inadvertently employed a small N.

Several factors seem to have masked the importance of the training effects in subtests III and V and in the total test scores. With regard to the latter, it may be seen from Table 1 that subtest I contributes approximately one-third to the T and RT totals for both groups because the allotted raw points are higher for the easier items in this subtest than for the beginning items in the other subtests. Furthermore, not only does the RT mean of Subtest I show no increase due to training, but is actually lower than the T mean. Consequently the lack of increase in this RT score can be responsible for the non-significant results for total scores. This is confirmed by the data in Table 4. The combined difference-scores of subtests II, III and IV of the two groups were found to be significantly different. A second factor affecting subtest III and V and total scores is the significant variability of the subjects within groups. This is evident from F ratios for Ss/G.

In three of the four analyses of variances the ratios for Ss/G are significant beyond the .01 level and in the fourth beyond the .05 level. Significant variability is a characteristic both of the retarded children, used in these groups, and of the small N. These results emphasize the significant influence of the special training on improvement in figure-ground discrimination ability, subtest II.

The marked variability of the children within groups tends to obscure the actual value of the special training. The increase in RT means over the T means for the Total Test and for subtests III and V scores of the E group warrants this assumption of "masked" improvement as a result of the training. In addition to this conjecture is the evidence for practice effect that merits interpretation as learning by the educable retardate. The F ratio for Trials is significant beyond the .01 level for total and subtest II scores, and between the .05 and the .01 level for subtests III and V scores, Tables 2 and 3. These findings do point to a significant effect on RT scores by practice effect attributable to the familiarity with the test material gained from the first testing situation, a form of learning.

The more important finding of this study appears in the analysis of variance reported in Table 4. The scores utilized in this analysis reflect the differences between T and RT scores for subtests II, III and V treated as a single test. This procedure was deemed feasible because these three subtests have more in common with each other than with the other two subtests. In each of subtests II, III and V the testee is presented with a model figure to follow in performing the required task. Judgments have to be made with regard for the model and then motor execution must follow. In subtest I motor behavior is the most important element involved while in subtest IV the motor aspect is negligible. In each of the three subtests whose scores were combined for this analysis of variance the nature of the motor and judgmental tasks differed somewhat but both types of processes were required to solve the perceptual problems. The F ratio is significant beyond the .01 level. The assumption that the E and C groups would not differ in their T means is confirmed by the combined T mean scores of both groups for the three subtests of 12.1. The significant F ratio indicates that the means of the difference-scores between T and RT for the E and C groups are reliably different. Training, therefore, has had a significant influence, over and beyond practice effects, upon the RT scores.

Despite the limitations in this pilot study with a small N and unmatched pairs, the results are very encouraging. They indicate that special training can yield significantly better figure-ground discriminations by the educable mentally retarded youngster. Moreover, the results strongly suggest that the abilities tapped by subtest III (figure-constancy) and subtest V (spatial relations) may be improved through specific training, in this instance the Frostig-Horne method. This study should be repeated with more children and with several important educational, age, and intellectual controls which would be more feasible with a larger population.

With regard to the skills tapped by subtest I (eye-motor coordination) and subtest IV (position in space), the evidence does not support a favorable response to specific training and only a minor indication of a positive practice effect. Subtest IV involves not only visual perceptual development but also concept formation ability, i.e., understanding ideas implicated in detecting similarities and differences. Therefore the training program needs to include more direct verbal conceptual training as well as the exercises anchored in visual discrimination of likeness and difference. If the idea or principle involved in subtest IV could be established within the retardate's ability to comprehend, it could transfer more readily than the repeated series of concrete visual similarities and differences exercises.

Subtest I is a motor executive task related to physical development. The mean CAs of the Ss are 15 and 16 years for the E and C groups respectively. It is not likely that the training provided by these special exercises to retardates of this advanced chronological age could yield any, let alone significant, improvement. Both the better E group and the poorer C group Ss maintained their same relative levels of achievement from T to RT. This suggests that the training in eye-motor coordination is possibly more effective with the chronologically younger and/or the motor impaired child than with the kind of Ss included in this study. This is an area that should be investigated.

Summary for the Pilot Study

This pilot study attempted to ascertain the effectiveness of the Frostig-Horne program of training in visual perceptual skills. Events beyond the investigators' control (Allen, Dickman and Haupt, 1966) reduced the original study population to the point of small sample N design. The results are suggestive of the immediate benefit gained from the exposure to the visual perception training program in several of the major areas considered important for learning.

SECOND STUDY

It appeared that the immediate benefits to the training group was not in keeping with the time and effort put in by the special education teacher and the children. This led to an analysis of the experimental design. The first major and glaring error was the chronological age variable. The E and C groups of the pilot study averaged 15 and 16 years, 1 month respectively. The mean mental ages were within the range of the children for whom the test and training program were designed, 5 years, 4 months and 4 years, 5 months for the E and C groups. The CAs indicate that the children were most likely beyond the age period for maximum benefit from the Frostig-Horne training program for the development of visual perception.

The decision was made to repeat the pilot study with particular attention to greater homogeneity between the C and E groups and with chronologically younger children who fall more definitely in the educable (moderately to mildly retarded) range.

The method remains essentially the same as in the Pilot Study. Table 5 describes the 20 children in the Second Study. An inspection of the table reveals no significant differences between the 10 children in the E group and the 10 children in the C group with regard to CA, MA and Deviation IQ. Moreover, the children in the Second Study, were, as a group, 46 months (E group) and 62.2 months (C group) younger than their counterparts in the Pilot Study. These controls modify some of the serious defects in the Pilot Study but does not remove the experiment from the small—N category and has not brought the children within the CA limits of the Frostig Test norms. Exploring the possibilities available in regard to CA control: a mentally retarded population would yield Ss who are too low mentally if CA is constricted (Allen, Haupt and Jones, 1965), or too old chronologically if MA is the criterion (Allen, Jones and Haupt, 1965). The 20 children selected from among the day and residential students of the Hope School offered the best compromise.

Table 5
Mean Data for the E and C Groups

Group	N	CA (months)	MA (months)	Deviation IQ (Rev. S-B Scale)
E	10	134.0	63.7	50.5
C	10	130.8	61.1	50.5
Differences	0	3.2	2.6	0

Table 6
Frostig Test (T) and Retest (RT) Mean Raw Scores for E and C Groups

Group	I		II		III		IV		V		Total	
	T	R	T	R	T	R	T	R	T	R	T	R
E	7.5	11.3	8.6	13.4	2.6	5.3	3.5	4.0	1.0	2.8	23.2	36.8
C	7.5	7.5	8.0	8.7	1.8	3.5	3.0	2.3	2.1	2.5	22.4	24.5
Differences	0	3.8	.6	4.7	0.8	1.8	0.5	1.7	-1.1	0.3	0.8	12.3

As with the Pilot Study, the E (training) and C (no training) groups were pro- and post-tested (T and RT respectively) at the same times. The E group received one semester of training with the Frostig-Horne materials while the C group continued in its usual school activities.

The mean T (pre-training) and RT (post-training test for the E group and simply **retesting for the** C group) raw scores are presented in Table 6. The justification for the introduction of the various controls in the selection of the two groups is immediately evident from the non-significant differences in raw scores achieved by both groups of the Second Study in the T condition (pretest) for the five subtests and the total test score. This degree of homogeneity in pretest training test results was not achieved in the Pilot Study, see Table 7.

The differences between E and C groups' mean T and RT scores tell the story of the immediate effect of the training on the former group. Table 8 discloses that the mean raw scores for Subtests I, II, III and IV for the E group yielded significant score-differences between T and RT. The hypothesis that training immediately benefited the retardates exposed to special training in visual perception is supported for four areas. The effect of training advantage varied for the four subtests.

The most marked improvements were noted in Eye-motor coordination and Position in

Table 7

Mean Raw Subtests and Total Test Scores
for E and C Groups, Both Studies

	I				II				III				IV				V				TOTAL			
	T[1]		R[2]		T		R		T		R		T		R		T		R		T		R	
	P[3]	S[4]	P	S	P	S	P	S	P	S	P	S	P	S	P	S	P	S	P	S	P	S	P	S
E	11.6	7.5	11.3	11.3	8.5	8.6	13.5	13.4	2.6	2.6	5.4	5.3	3.4	3.5	3.8	4.0	1.0	1.0	3.0	2.8	27.1	23.2	35.2	36.8
C	7.8	7.5	8.5	7.5	7.8	8.0	9.0	8.7	2.5	1.8	3.5	3.5	2.0	3.0	2.5	2.3	2.1	2.1	2.6	2.5	22.6	22.4	26.0	24.5

1. Test
2. Retest
3. Pilot Study
4. Second Study

Table 8
Test of Significance

Between E Group T and RT Scores,
Univariate F Tests

Subtest	Mean Squares	F	P
I	103.937	19.308	.001
II	61.125	4.422	.056
III	15.450	4.397	.056
IV	6.571	7.400	.018
V	0.270	0.127	.728

Table 9
Mean Raw T and RT Scores for Subtest V,
Spatial Relations, of E and C Groups in Both Studies

Studies	Groups			
	E		C	
	T	RT	T	RT
Pilot	1.0	3.0	2.1	2.6
Second	1.0	2.8	2.1	2.5

space (Subtests I and IV) training. Figure-ground discrimination and Figure constancy (Subtests II and II) training also showed significant development from test to retest due to the intervening training. The ability to cope better with spatial relations did not respond to the training course. This lack of improvement was evidenced in the T and RT raw scores for the E group of the Pilot Study. Table 9 shows the raw scores for both groups under both conditions.

An analysis of the distributions of the Subtest V T and RT scores for both groups under both conditions reveals that 20 of the 36 pairs of scores are identical from T to RT. Thirteen children in the E and C groups increased their scores an average of 3.2 points. However, this is mitigated by the fact that two children (one each in the Pilot and Second Studies) increased their scores from 0 to 7 points. Three decreased in raw score for an average of 1 point. Table 9 further discloses that the extent of improvement for the training groups (e) in both studies were disappointingly similar.

In an effort to account for the lone training failure, the investigators reviewed the nature of the exercises in spatial relations—Subtest V. Only ten of the 85 exercises have work-sheets that present material to be learned that is similar to the items of Subtest V. It may be seen from page   of this chapter that the other exercises are in:

a. related positions of two objects—4 worksheets;

b. similarities and differences—131 work sheets;

c. shortest path to a goal—7 work sheets;

d. figure completion—16 work sheets;

e. recall of motor sequences—10 work sheets;

f. spatial sequences—8 work sheets; and

g. assembly of parts—17 work sheets

The point is that the contents of the exercises are valuable for the remedial training of the retardate but the retest situation assesses a small aspect of this training since the test items are of the dot-connecting variety only.[*]

The present author also suspects that another variable militating against improvement in spatial relations learning and test taking is the short attention span of the average retardate. Zeaman (1965) writes about the learning of the moderately retarded in these terms (p. 109): "1. Their discrimination learning is mediated, not by verbal behavior, but by attention....paying attention to relevant stimulus dimensions." The first four figures of Subtest V are simple, but beyond the fourth item the analysis and synthesis processes in breaking down and reassembling the parts are usually beyond the retardate's span

[*]It is not the purpose, nor within the competency, of the present author to be concerned with the specific contents of the Frostig-Horne training materials. As a psychologist the author has intended only to account for this one discrepancy from the general improvement picture of the Second Study group.

of attention. Very few of the retardates in both studies even attempted, let alone succeeded with, beyond Vd. They simply gave up, both at test and retest regardless of intervening training.

Using Wilk's lambda criterion as a test of significance for the Total test differences between T and RT raw scores obtained by E and C groups yields a probability less than 0.016 that the difference is a chance one. This supports the acceptance of the hypothesis of the study, that educable retarded children to respond favorably and are advantaged by exposure to the Frostig-Horne training program for visual perception development.

SUMMARY FOR THE SECOND STUDY

Several additional comments remain to be made. The introduction of important controls as CA, MA and IQ resulted in findings more pertinent to the evaluation of the training program. The homogeneity between and within groups yielded a more meaningful evaluation of the individual parts of the overall remedial program. While both studies show positive results for training, the Second Study strongly suggests that the chronologically younger educable retardate learns more effectively. The one remaining question is — how long will this learning remain with the child? This is being studied at the present time.

The final major consideration is to compare the performances of E and C groups of both studies. Table 7, page 115, depicts the entire story. Table 7 may be read as follows:

1. For Pilot Study intra-study comparison of E or C group T and RT raw scores read the P cells, alternately skipping the S cells. Thus, for group E in the Pilot Study the mean T and RT scores were 11.6 and 11.3 for Subtest I, 2.6 and 5.4 for Subtest III, and so on.

2. For Second Study intra-study comparison of E or C group T and RT raw scores read the S cells, alternately skipping the P cells. Thus, for Group C in the Second Study the mean T and RT scores were 7.5 and 7.5 for Subtest I, 1.8 and 3.5 for Subtest III, and so on.

3. For inter-groups comparisons with regard to either T or RT raw scores obtained by the E and C group members the cells should be read vertically. Thus, for Subtest II the mean raw T scores were 8.5 and 7.5 in the Pilot Study and 8.6 and 8.0 for the Second Study. The crucial comparison, however, would be the mean RT raw scores. Group E obtained 13.4 points on RT for Subtest II as against 8.7 points for the children in C group.

The pre-training test achievements of the E and C groups in both studies show that the Pilot Study group score-differences are greater than, equal to, and less than Second Study group score-differences in 4, 1 and 1 instances respectively. For the Pilot Study these differences ranged from 0.1 to 4.5 points. For the Second Study this range was from 0 to 1.1 points. The latter groups were more homogeneous with an average point score-difference of .63 as against 1.91 for the Pilot Study.

From Table 10 it may be seen that in the Second Study the RT score-differences were significantly higher than the E Group RT score-differences of the Pilot Study for Subtests I, II, IV and Total Score. Subtest V showed no significant difference while Subtest III was out of pattern with the other subtests. It could be postulated that unlike the more formal and less frequently encountered life experiences, such as are evaluated in Subtests I, II and IV,* figure-constancy problems constantly assail the child for solution since boxes, balls, figures and even people have to be recognized and dealt with not only daily but frequently during the day. Thus, the similar improvement of the children in both studies mirrored the improvement helped along not only by the prior testing experience but also by the training program.

Table 10
Mean RT-T Raw Score Differences
on the Frostig Test for Both Groups in Both Studies

Subtests	I		II		III		IV		V		Total	
	P	S	P	S	P	S	P	S	P	S	P	S
E RT-T	-0.3	3.8	5.0	4.8	2.8	2.7	0.4	0.5	2.0	1.8	8.1	13.6
C RT-T	0.7	0.0	1.2	0.7	1.0	1.7	0.5	-0.7	0.5	0.4	3.4	2.1
Differences (E-C)	1.0	3.8	3.8	4.1	1.8	1.0	-0.1	1.2	1.5	1.4	4.7	11.5

The final word—educable mental retardates are educable in the area of visual perception development. Where such maturation is deficient it should be subjected to remediation. Allen, Haupt and Jones (1965, p. 299) wrote:

> .....the retarded child with apparently intact visual perceptual abilities is generally more efficient than the retarded child with impaired perceptual development as measured by the WISC performance subtests. The high perceiving group superiority appears to result from the more

*In everyday experiences it is less usual for the retarded child to have to undergo limited drawing and figure-ground discrimination experiences. "Similarity" and "difference" concepts have to be taught and learned in formal learning situations.

meaningful organization of the environment and the better discrimination of important from irrelevant facets of the perceptual world.

Society owes the retarded child every opportunity to meet and deal with his milieu with every means developed to their maxima.

The study was supported in part by National Science Foundation Grants GU 728 and GU 1218 (1964-65, 1965-66) for the statistical work.

The author wishes to thank: Mrs. Judy Holland, Executive Director of the Hope School for Mentally Retarded Children, Miami, Florida, for the use of the physical facilities of the school and for making the children available; Mr. Israel Dickman and Mr. Thomas D. Haupt for working directly with the children; Dr. Dean Clyde for his aid with the computational design; and Dr. John D. Black of the Consulting Psychologists Press, Inc., for permission to reproduce the entire Frostig Developmental Test of Visual Perception.

References

1. Allen, R.M. and Allen, S.P. INTELLECTUAL EVALUATION OF THE MENTALLY RE-TARDED: A HANDBOOK. Beverly Hills, Calif.: Western Psychological Services, 1966.

2. Allen, R. M., Dickman, I. and Haupt, T.D. A PILOT STUDY OF THE IMMEDIATE EFFEC-TIVENESS OF THE FROSTIG-HORNE TRAINING PROGRAM WITH EDUCABLE RETARDATES. Except. Child., 33 (1); 41-42, 1966.

3. Allen, R.M., Haupt, T.D. and Jones, R.W. VISUAL PERCEPTUAL ABILITIES AND IN-TELLIGENCE IN MENTAL RETARDATION. J. Clin. Psychol., 21: 299-300, 1965.

4. Allen, R.M., Jones, R.W. and Haupt, T.D. NOTE OF CAUTION FOR THE RESEARCH USE OF THE FROSTIG TEST WITH MENTALLY RETARDED CHILDREN. Percept. Mot. Skills. 21: 237-238, 1965.

5. Corah, N.L. and Powell, B.J. A FACTOR ANALYTIC STUDY OF THE FROSTIG DEVEL-OPMENTAL TEST OF VISUAL PERCEPTION. Percept. Mot. Skills, 16: 59-63, 1963.

6. Frostig, M. and Horne, D. THE FROSTIG PROGRAM FOR DEVELOPMENT OF VISUAL PERCEPTION: TEACHER'S GUIDE. Chicago: Follett, 1964.

7. Frostig, M., Lefever, D. and Whittlesey, J.M.B. DEVELOPMENTAL TEST OF VISUAL PERCEPTION. Palo Alto, Calif.: 1964.

8. Osler, S.F. and Cooke, R.E. (eds.) THE BIOSOCIAL BASIS OF MENTAL RETARDA-TION. Baltimore, Md.: The Johns Hopkins Press, 1965.

9. Zeaman, D. LEARNING PROCESS OF THE MENTALLY RETARDED. In S.F. Osler and R.E. Cooke (eds.) The biosocial basis of mental retardation. Baltimore, Md.: The Johns Hopkins Press, Pp. 107-127, 1965.

APPENDIX A

In this section the author presents examples of pre-training and post-training protocols of a child 9 years of age, with a Wechsler Intelligence Scale for Children (WISC) deviation IQ of 64, who has had the benefit of special training with the Frostig-Horne Materials.

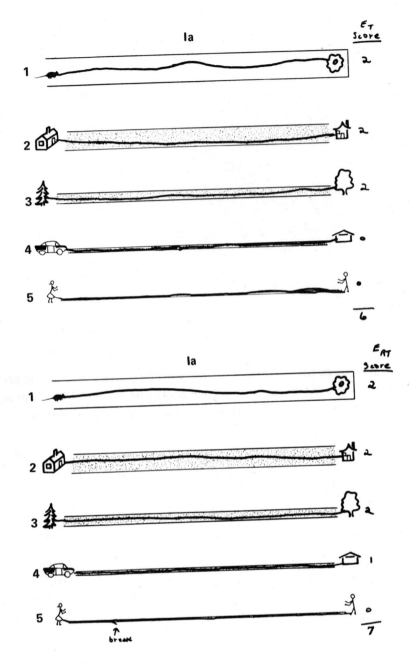

FIGURE 16

Examples of Pre-Training and Post-Training Performances of a 9-year Old Child; WISC Deviation IQ, 64; in the E group. (All of the test figures on which the child's performance appears are reproduced by special permission from Frostig Developmental Test of Visual Perception by Marianne Frostig. Copyright 1963, published by Consulting Psychologists Press, Inc.)

Subtest I. Items 1 - 5, 12 and 13. (Original pencil lines darkened and made heavier to facilitate reproduction.)

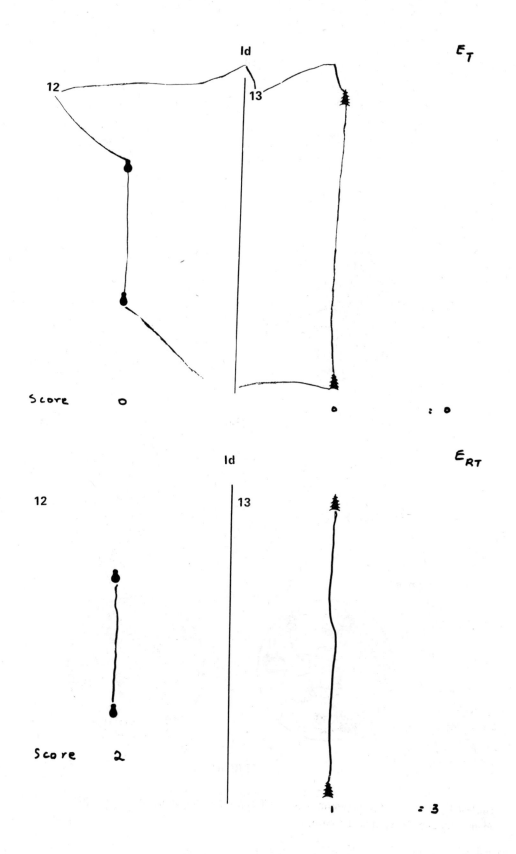

E_T

Id

12   13

Score 0   0   : 0

E_{RT}

Id

12   13

Score 2   1   : 3

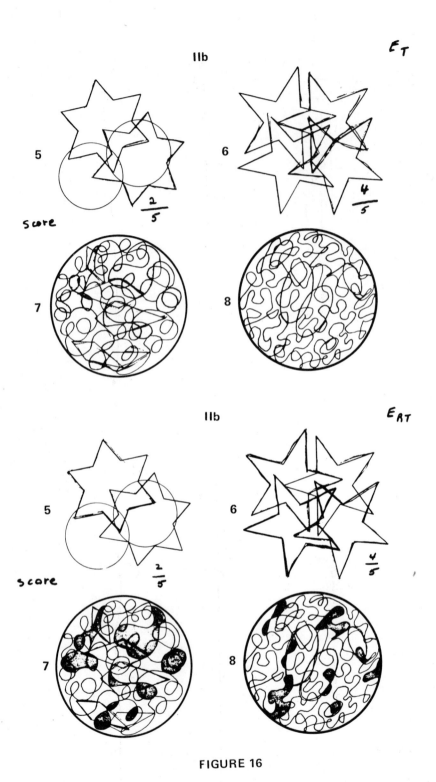

FIGURE 16

Subtest II. Items 5 - 8. (Maximum score on T and RT obtained by child, however RT figures outlined more adequately and firmly than T figures.)

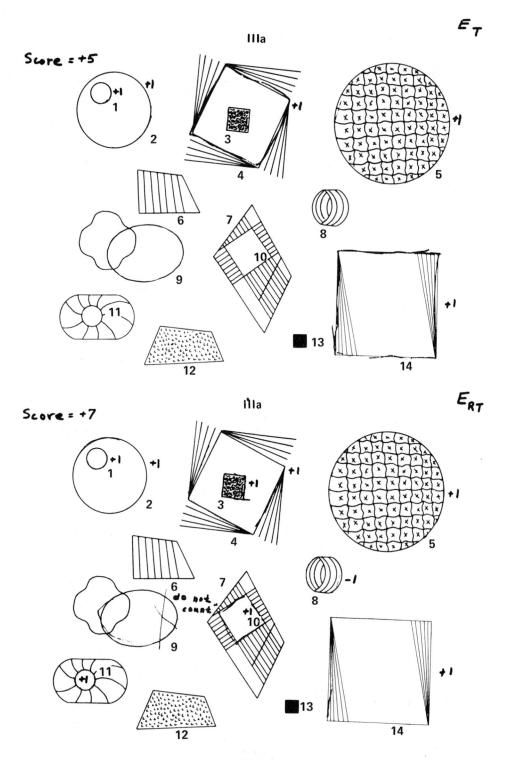

FIGURE 16

Subtest III. Items 1 - 14.

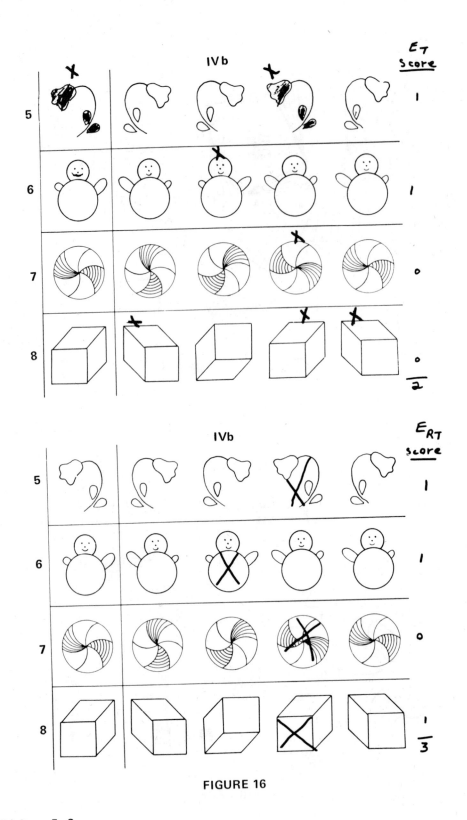

FIGURE 16

Subtest IV. Items 5 - 8.

126

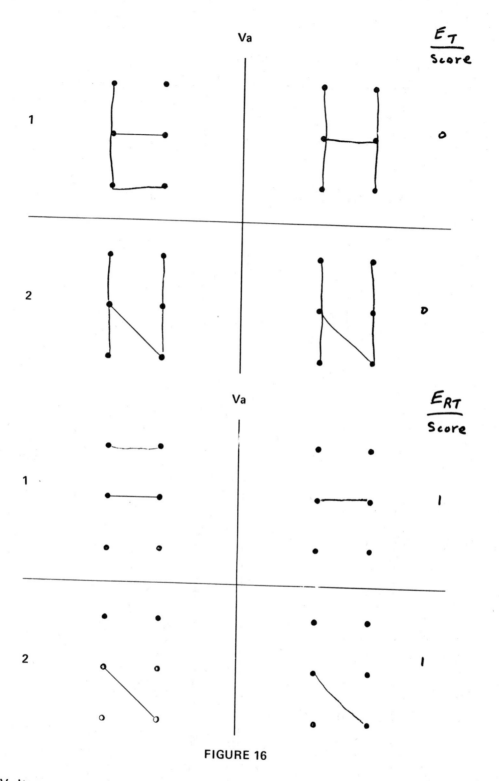

FIGURE 16

Subtest V. Items a - e, to show marked improvement of RT over T performances. (Note that this child attempted the five items, with elaborations.)

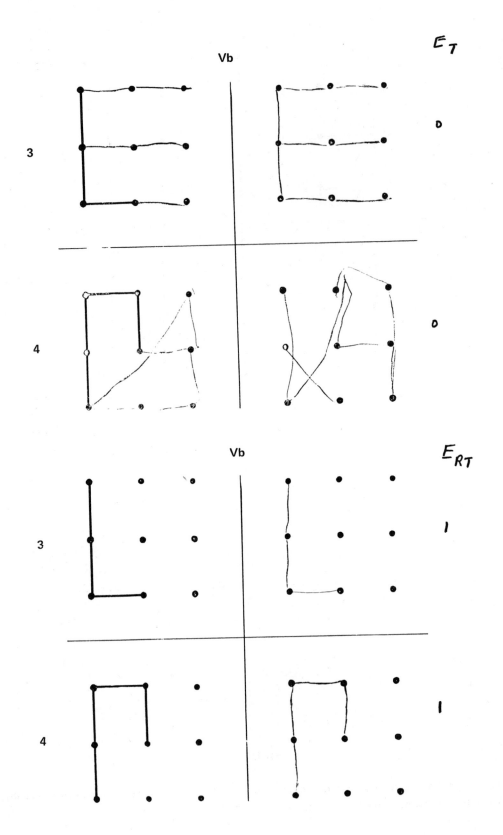

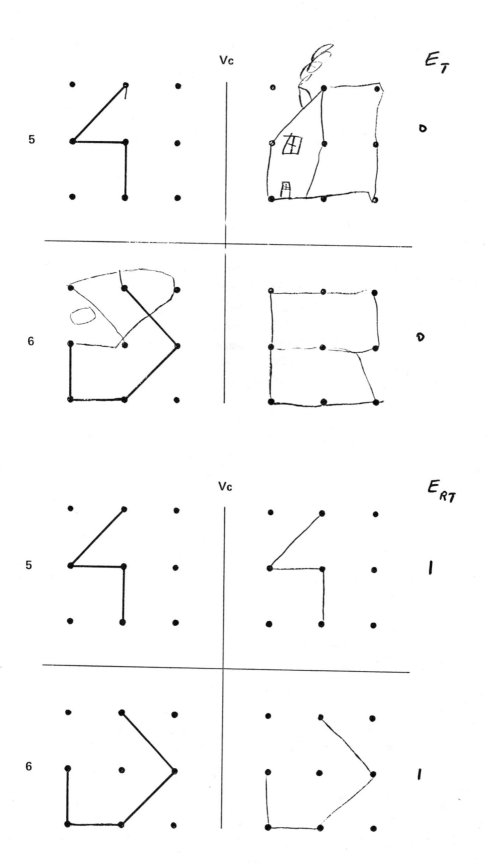

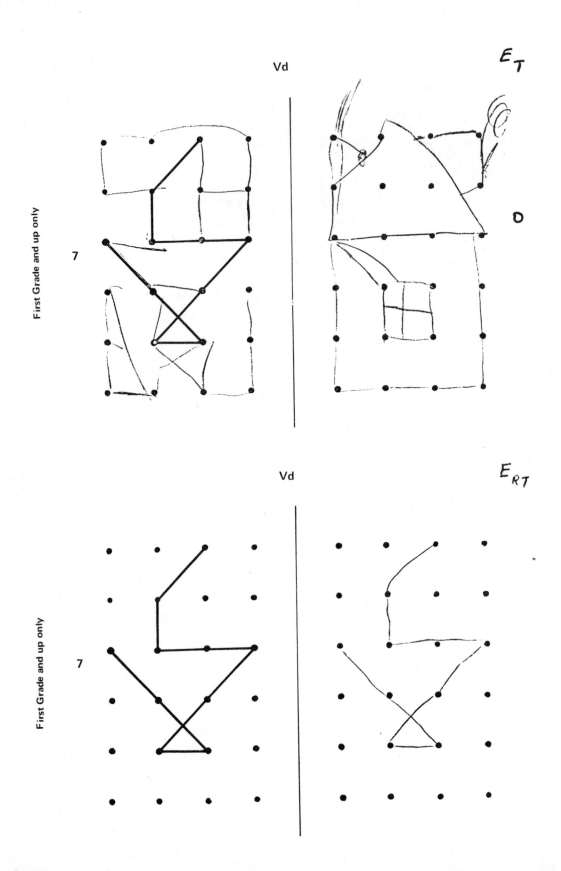

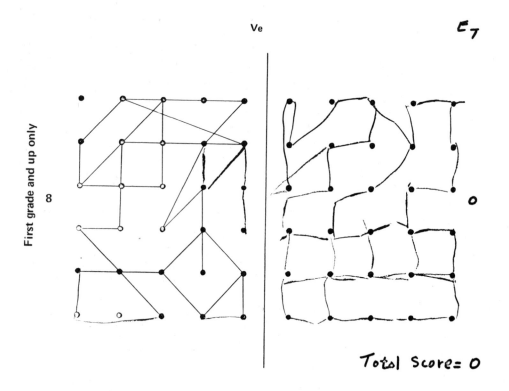

Ve

E_7

First grade and up only

8

0

Total Score = 0

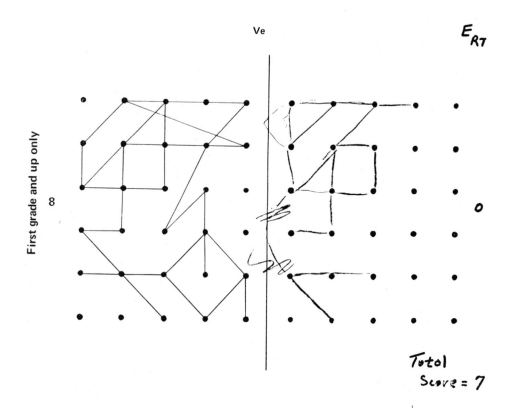

Ve

E_{R7}

First grade and up only

8

0

Total
Score = 7

Figure 16. Summary Of T and RT Raw Scores For This Child

Subtests	I		II		III		IV		V		Total	
	T	RT	T	RT	T	RT	T	RT	T	RT	T	RT
Raw Scores	10	14	20	19	5	8	6	7	0	7	41	55
RT−T	4		−1		3		1		7		14	

APPENDIX B

In this section the author presents examples of pre-training and post-training protocols of a child 8 years, 10 months of age with a WISC deviation IQ of 60, who has not had the benefit of special training with the Frostig-Horne materials.

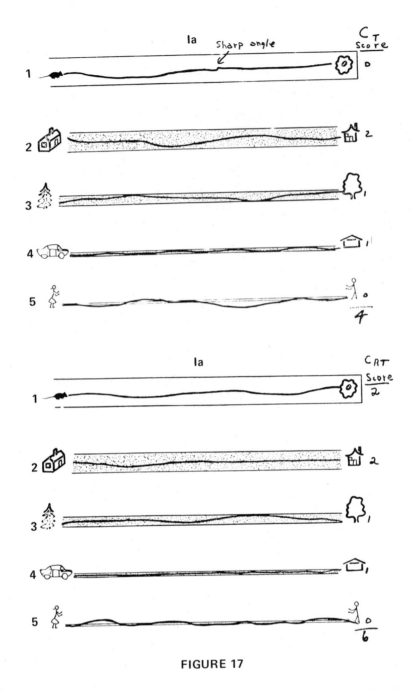

FIGURE 17

Examples of Pre-Training and Post-Training Performances of an 8 years, 10 month Old Child, WISC DIQ of 60, in the C Group (no training). (All of the test figures on which the child's performance appears are reproduced by special permission from Frostig Developmental Test of Visual Perception by Marianne Frostig. Copyright 1963, published by Consulting Psychologists Press, Inc.)

Subtest I. Items 1 - 5, 12, 13. (Original pencil lines darkened and made heavier for purpose of reproduction.)

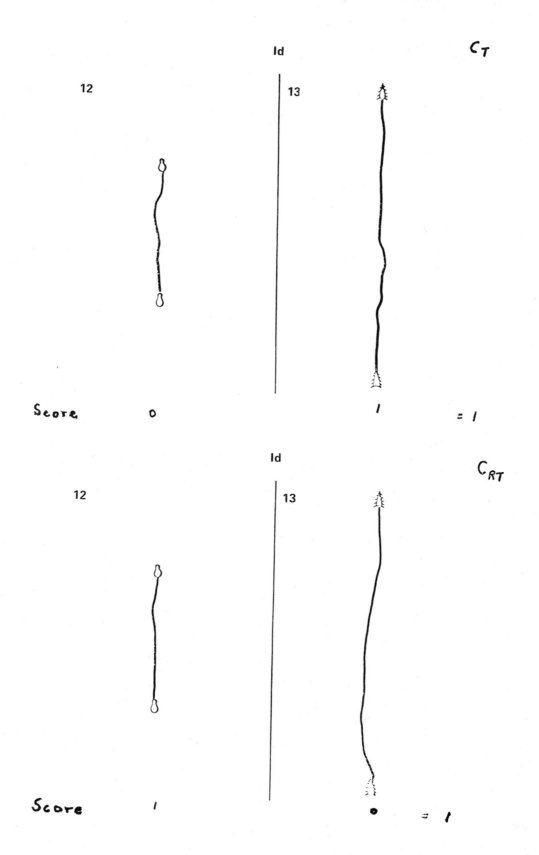

C_T

Id

12 13

Score 0 1 = 1

C_{RT}

Id

12 13

Score 1 0 = 1

135

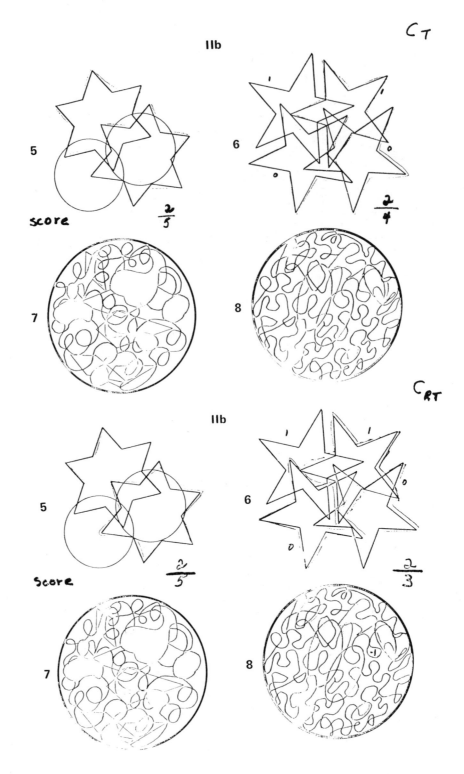

FIGURE 17

Subtest II. Items 5 - 8.

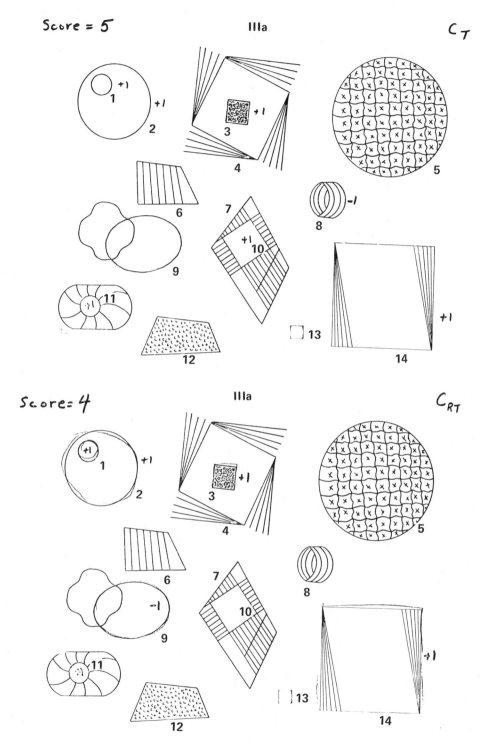

FIGURE 17

Subtest IIIa. Items 1 - 14.

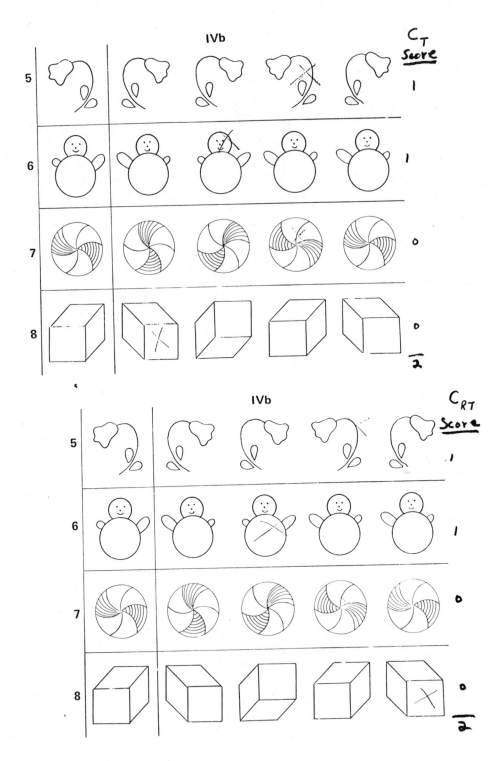

FIGURE 17

Subtest IVb. Items 5 - 8.

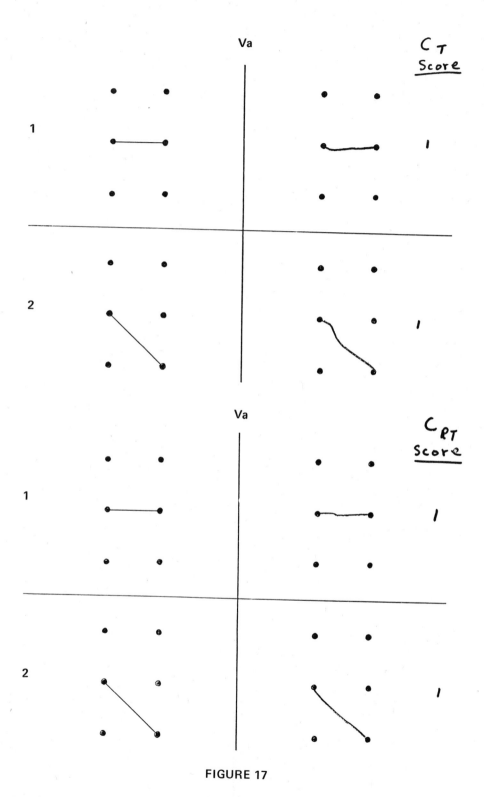

FIGURE 17

Subtest V. Items Va - Vc. (This child did not attempt to reproduce items Vd and Ve, despite urging to do so.)

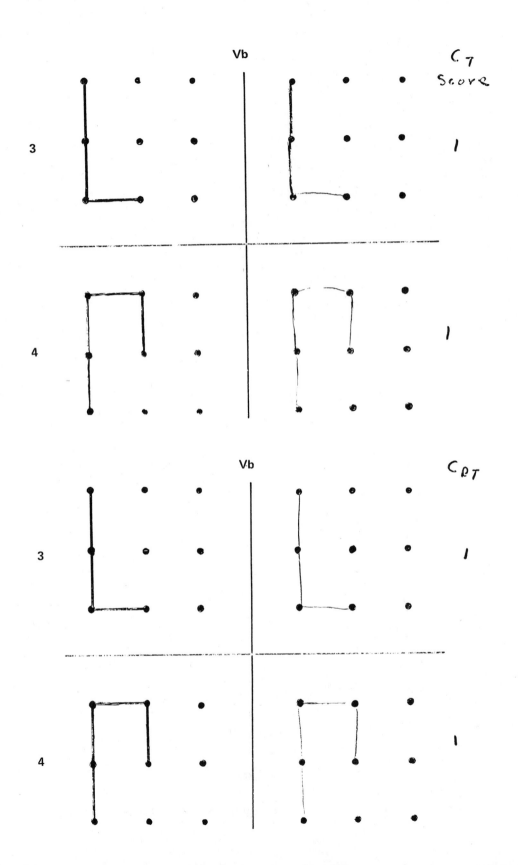

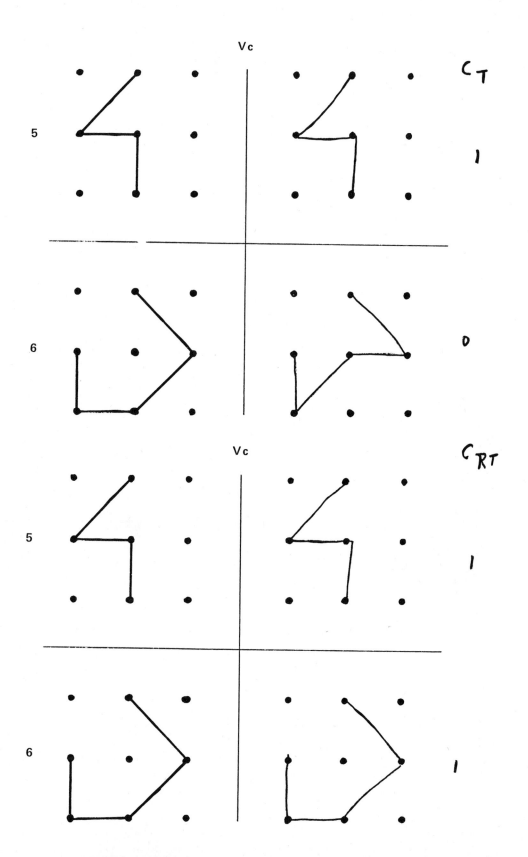

Figure 17. Summary Of T and RT Raw Scores for This Child

Subtests	I		II		III		IV		V		Total	
	T	RT	T	RT	T	RT	T	RT	T	RT	T	RT
Raw Scores	9	10	16	16	6	6	4	5	5	6	40	43
RT − T	1		0		0		1		1		3	

In this section the author presents selected items from the Frostig Test protocols of three girls of approximately the same chronological age (CA) but of differing mental age (MA), deviation intelligence quotients (DIQ) and levels of reading ability. The three girls are:

Name	CA	MA	DIQ	Raw Scores					
				I	II	III	IV	V	Total
Valerie (non-reader)	9-0*	4-11	53	7	3	4	0	0	14
Selma (1st grade) reader)	9-0	6-1	66	23	10	10	8	8	59
Ruth (accelerated reader)	8-7	10-3	117	24	10	17	8	8	67

*to be read 9 years, zero months

The differences in visual perceptual development and consequent performances on the test items are evident by inspection of Valerie's (non-reader) protocol on the one hand and the reproduction by Selma (first-grade reader) and Ruth (accelerated reader) on the other.

As between Selma and Ruth, the quality of the lines and the manner in which Ruth completed the tasks differentiate her from Selma. The latter aspect of test-taking, manner of performance, is an observational (in this instance by the author) factor that is not reflected in any particular score except insofar as it is mirrored in the firmer and straighter lines. Score-wise the difference between the two is not remarkable.

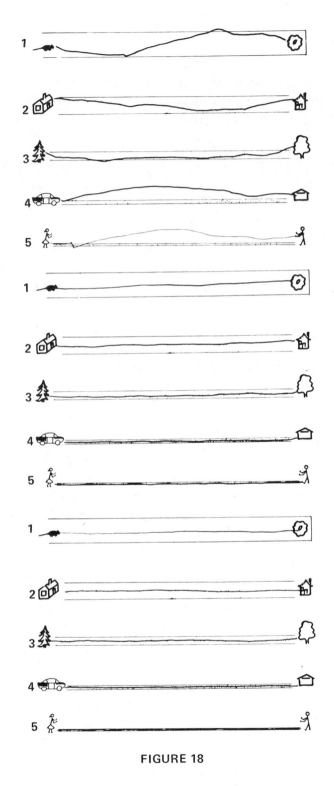

FIGURE 18

Subtest I. Items 1 - 9. In each instance the illustrations are presented in this order: first, Valerie, non-reader; second, Selma, first grade reader; and third, Ruth, accelerated reader.

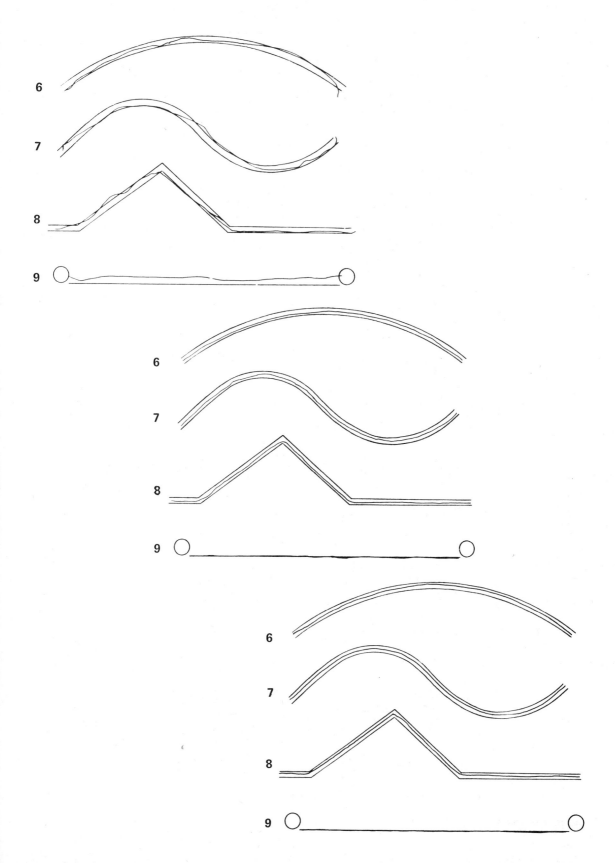

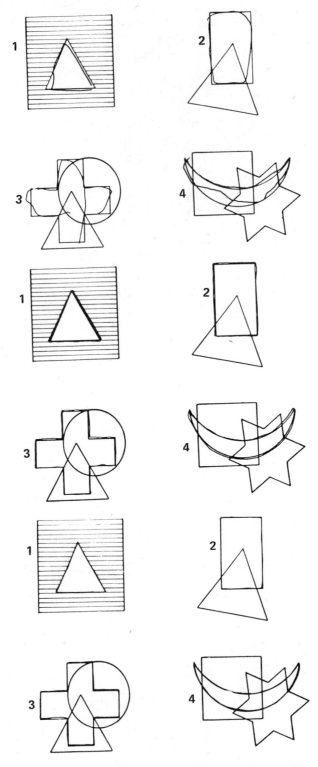

FIGURE 18

Subtest II. Items 1 - 8.

146

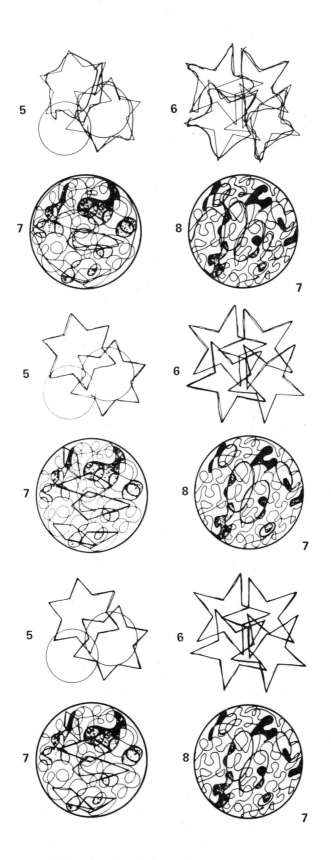

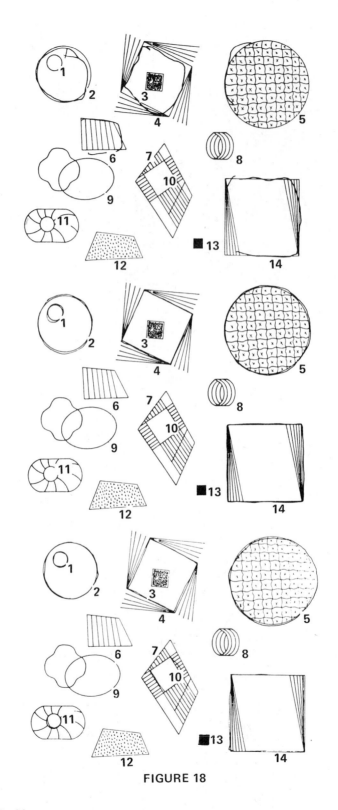

FIGURE 18

Subtest IIIa. Items 1 - 14.

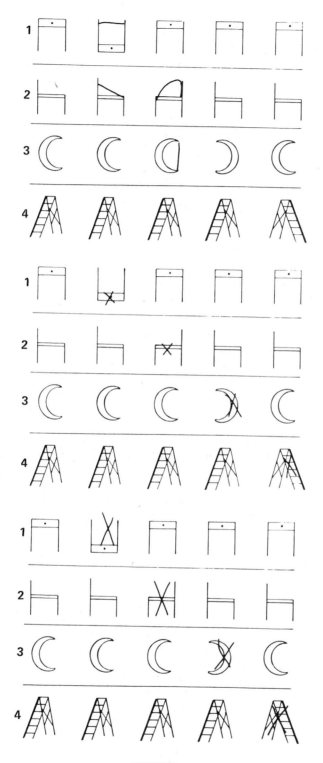

FIGURE 18

Subtest IV. Items 1 - 8.

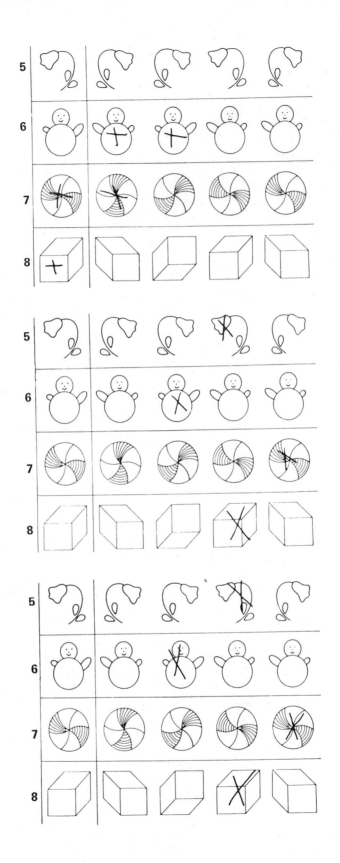

150

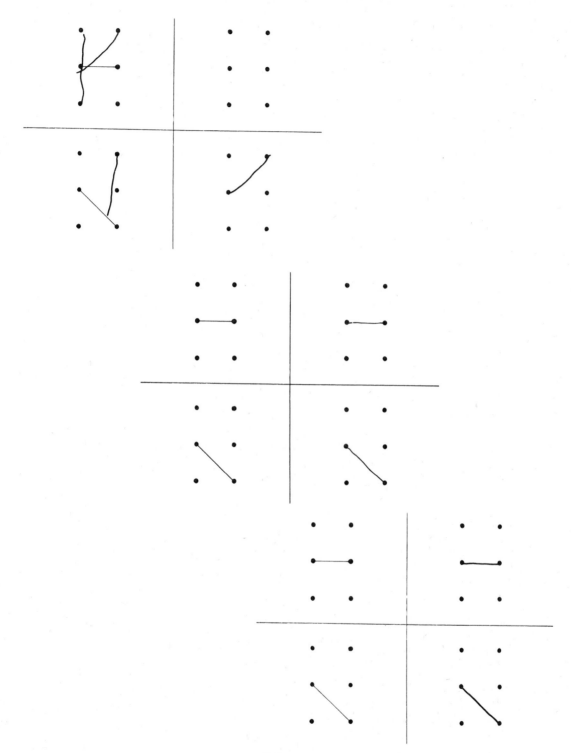

FIGURE 18

Subtest V. Items Va and Ve. All of the test figures on which the childrens' performances appear are reproduced by special permission from Frostig Developmental Test of Visual Perception by Marianne Frostig. Copyright 1963, published by Consulting Psychologists Press, Inc.

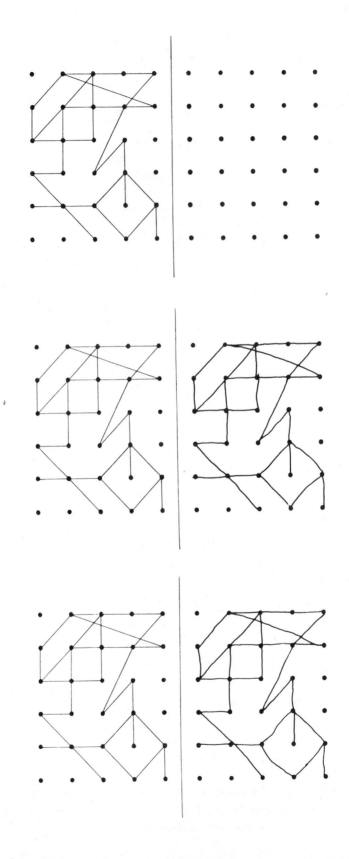

RESEARCH AND DEVELOPMENT OF THE PEABODY LANGUAGE DEVELOPMENT KITS

James O. Smith, Ed. D.,
Professor of Education,
College of Education
University of Missouri,
Columbia, Missouri

Max W. Mueller, Ph. D.,
Oxon Hill, Maryland

JAMES O. SMITH, Ed. D.   MAX W. MUELLER, Ph.D.

The Peabody Language Development Kits (PLDK) are a series of four sets of materials and lessons designed to stimulate oral language development. The program was designed for use primarily with disadvantaged and retarded children, though its utility is not necessarily limited to those groups. While the basic goal of this program is to enhance linguistic skills, secondary goals include improvement of verbal intelligence and school achievement. Each of the four kits (designated Level P, Horton, Dunn & Smith, 1967; Level 1, Dunn & Smith, 1965; Level 2, Dunn & Smith, 1966; Level 3, Dunn & Smith, 1967) provides lesson plans and materials necessary for daily instruction through one academic year. The instructional level of these kits corresponds roughly to ability levels which would be expected in a disadvantaged population in preschool through grade three.

The need for such programs grew out of the author's early experiences as a speech therapist in trying to provide more meaningful programs for the educable mentally retarded. Originally, planning for these populations moved from a traditional speech therapy to a more general speech improvement program. Emphases shifted from individual to group work and from phoneme centered to communication centered lessons. The derivation of early programming was intuitive and grew from feelings that mentally retarded children needed to **see more, hear more, associate more, talk more,** and **gesture more** than was possible in the half-hour sessions called speech therapy. The seeming success of such an approach caused a movement even further from "speech improvement" and "correctness of certain sounds" to a program stressing better reception (auditory and visual), associations, and expression. Here the necessity for continuing, planned, and intensive language development programs became apparent.

With these prior experiences and such an intuitive approach, the theoretical model advanced by McCarthy and Kirk (1961) emerged as an additional stimulus to the planning of language development lessons. Such a comprehensive theoretical model appeared most useful for generating a wider variety of language development lessons. Just as one could plan test items that appeared to sample decoding, it was possible to develop many similar lessons that require children to perform this **psycholinguistic process.** Just as test items were constructed to measure auditory input and vocal output, it was possible to develop numerous activities that gave the child opportunities to develop these channels of communication. Just as tests were developed to assess automatic-sequential and representational **levels of organization**, it appeared possible to develop items that appeared to stimulate practice and participation in similar ways.

Later attention to Guilford's (1959) structure of the intellect with its operations, products, and contents evoked renewed interest in lesson-planning. As Guilford and his associates discovered more and more facets of the intellect, it became of very real concern that lessons planned to develop language from the ITPA base did not include activities which seemed to stimulate all of these many "kinds of intellectual activities," did not deal with these "broad classes of information" or pay enough attention to the "forms that information takes in the person's processing of it" (Guilford & Hoepfner, 1963). A concrete example here would be the development of lessons to specifically enhance the retarded child's abilities to produce divergently. A review of earlier language development lessons found few, if any, exercises that caused children to generate information from given information where the emphasis was on variety and quantity of output.

The influence of reinforcement theory on this approach to language development must be mentioned. The praising of correct responses, the awarding of points for a child or team, the handing of a picture card to a child after an appropriate response, the awarding of color chips to individuals, all are intended to serve as stimuli that when presented strengthen the behavior they follow. This positive reinforcement of participation, i.e., looking, listening, touching, or supplying appropriate vocal or motor responses, is an important factor in language development. Generally, other aspects of reinforcement theory have permeated this program.

DEVELOPMENT

Beyond the basic theoretical developments discussed previously, the initial step in the development of the PLDK was the work of Smith (1962). For this investigation, a series of 33 lessons, each consisting of several brief exercises, was designed to stimulate language abilities of primary age, educable mental retardates. These lessons were developed largely along the lines of typical speech improvement and reading readiness programs. Lessons were planned on a week by week basis while the program was being administered to 16 young EMR's. This allowed for optimal flexibility of planning and individualization of the lessons. This program required a wide variety of materials; some commercially available, many made by the investigator. The resulting series of lessons plans provided an excellent model by which the energetic teacher could hope to replicate the language development program, given adequate time for modification of lessons and preparation of materials. However, several factors limited the generality and usefulness of these initial lessons.

Smith (1964) carried out a project designed to reduce these limitations in lessons and materials. Lessons were initially revised to eliminate seasonal material, tried out with an elementary EMR class, and revised again in consultation with the teacher **and pupils** in that class. Finally, a teacher's manual and standard set of materials were developed. This project resulted in the first "kit" consisting of 33 lessons plans and the materials necessary for presentation.

Though based upon the earlier lessons, this PEABODY ORAL LANGUAGE DEVELOPMENT KIT was considerably revised from the original program. An important innovation was the package concept. All materials needed to conduct the language development program were collected and assembled. Not only does this assure a level of standardization in this program, but it also relieves the user of the responsibility of preparing materials. In addition, the manual provides a complete description of all materials so that a teacher could collect her own "kit" with which to teach the program. In addition, the manual represents a significant improvement over the original lessons. Lesson plans were more fully developed with complete directions for presentation, and materials necessary for each lesson were listed.

Changes were also made in the program itself. Lessons were adapted and added to assure attention to aspects of language demonstrated to be especially difficult for retarded children, and to assure a reasonable balance of activities directed at all aspects of language development. The ITPA model of language behavior was the base from which the lessons were evaluated in terms of breadth of coverage. A second major modification was the extension of lessons to cover a wide range of interest, ability, and background. Finally, lessons were shortened to require approximately 30 minutes per session as opposed to the 45 minutes suggested originally.

Research conducted using these early lessons was sufficiently encouraging to stimulate further interest. It also served to identify a number of problems of particular concern in continued development efforts. First, it was clear that a comprehensive program of language stimulation required a far more extensive series of lessons. Second, though the early lessons and materials had been designed for use with small groups of children, it was considered desirable to develop a program which could be managed by a teacher working with her full class. In this respect, it was obvious that many of the materials were of insufficient size or clarity to adapt to such use. In addition, the number of sources required to collect these materials was prohibitive (as was obtaining permission from copyright holders). Third, other research efforts suggested that the language development program envisioned should be appropriate for other children as well as for the mentally retarded. Finally, it was apparent that the lessons in the initial kit were still of insufficient range in terms of content and difficulty. Therefore, a major project was mounted to develop a program which provided daily lessons for a full school year, paced to hold the attention of a total class, flexible enough to adapt to a fairly wide range of abilities and capable of being clearly communicated to teachers. In addition, this project resulted in a set of original materials for presentation of those lessons.

The developmental sequence described here is that used with Level 1 of the PLDK, but techniques used with other levels were essentially the same. Creation of the PLDK was largely a team effort. The team was made up of teachers, artists, and college staff and students. Teachers were chosen on the basis of experience with appropriate student populations (culturally disadvantaged and mentally retarded), and demonstrated excellence in teaching, especially creative use of materials and innovative lesson planning. Artists were selected on the basis of ability to translate the ideas of professional staff into clear, pictorial representations. Staff from the college was chosen for prior familiarity with the language development program and background in both psychology and special education.

After new personnel had been familiarized with the task at hand and previous developments, the team set about writing lessons plans. Each person's contributions to a pool of activities were then reviewed by other team members and in many cases tried out with small groups of representative subjects. Through these two techniques it was possible to estimate the appropriateness of given lessons in terms of difficulty level, interest, effectiveness, and consistency with the theoretical model; and to modify lessons that appeared weak. The editors then ordered lessons, clarified instructions, added general background information, and evaluated art work and other materials. The result of this editing was an experimental edition of the kit which was produced on a limited basis.

Experimental kits were field tested in a number of settings, under various degrees of experimental control, over a broad geographical area. In many of these field tests, controlled evaluation of the effectiveness of the language development was carried out, as will be discussed presently. However, in terms of the development of the PLDK, the most important aspect of these field tests was the feedback provided by teachers using the program. Each experimental kit provided for field testing was supplied with forms for the evaluation of each daily lesson. These forms were set up to facilitate the teachers' job of evaluating lessons in terms of interest, difficulty level, and general value. Teachers were asked to fill out these evaluation forms as soon as possible after each lesson was presented, and to return them periodically to the editors. These evaluations formed the basis for modification of materials, deletion of certain activities, revision of others, and placement of activities in the final plan. In addition, teachers field testing the materials were asked to suggest additional activities which they felt would fit into the program. These suggestions were reviewed by the editors and led to a number of important additions to the PLDK.

Some experimental data were also available to the editors by the time the final form of the PLDK was prepared. The primary advantage of these data was to identify certain language skills which appeared to be largely unaffected by experience with the language development program. This information enabled the editors to add certain activities to provide a more balanced program.

Thus, from a speech therapist's discomfort concerning the effectiveness of his work with the handicapped, through the efforts of a large number of professionals in education and related fields, a comprehensive language development curriculum has come into existence. The methods used in the development of the PLDK, and the attractiveness and utility of the final product assured a measure of acceptance among educators, especially those responsible for children with particular problems in the area of language. It remained for educational researchers to evaluate the effectiveness of the program.

RESEARCH

Throughout the period during which the PLDK was being developed, the various forms of language development programs were continually subjected to evaluation. Few commercially produced educational programs have been researched as broadly or as consistently as the PLDK.

Early Language Development Programs

As indicated previously, the PLDK grew out of an investigation (Smith, 1962) of the effects of an oral language development program used with primary age educable mental retardates. This investigation involved 16 experimental subjects taught in groups of eight by an itinerant language developmentalist. The language program consisted of 33 lessons, each approximately 45 minutes in length, taught three times per week over a period of 11 weeks. These subjects and a matched group of 16 control subjects were administered the Illinois Test of 'Psycholinguistic Abilities (ITPA, McCarthy & Kirk, 1961) at the beginning and end of the treatment period. Analysis of ITPA total scores indicated that the average improvement of the experimental group was significantly greater $(p < .01)$ than that of the control group. This sample of children (less three control subjects who could not be located) were retested one year after their experience with the language development program (Mueller & Smith, 1964). Though the experimental group was still distinctly superior to the control group in overall language ability (p. < .10), the difference was accounted for almost entirely by half of the experimental group which had continued to show an accelerated rate of linguistic growth. The other half of the experimental group evidenced virtually no growth. It was not possible to identify any characteristic of these subjects which might account for this marked difference in response to the experimental program. However, the authors were encouraged that the program appeared to have had a lasting effect on the development of half the experimental group, especially considering the relatively short treatment period.

Blue (1963) replicated Smith's study with a sample of trainable mental retardates. Experimental and control groups of 12 subjects each were matched on the basis of chronological age and total language age as measured by the ITPA. The language development program was administered by a speech therapist working with groups of six children at a time. Gains in linguistic skills were slightly greater in the experimental group, but this difference was not significant. A **post hoc** analysis revealed that the six youngest experimental subjects progressed much more than did older subjects during the course of the investigation. The author concluded that the program was of too short duration to have a significant effect on the behavior of these seriously handicapped children.

Rouse (1965) provided another dimension to the development of the PLDK. She demonstrated that the performance of mental retardates in productive thinking could be enhanced by training. In this investigation an experimental group of 47 EMR subjects from 7-16 years of age received a series of 30 lessons designed to enhance productive thinking. Scores from the Product Improvement Task and Circles Task of the Minnesota Tests of Creative Thinking (Torrance, 1962) indicated significantly greater growth in productive thinking over this period than was demonstrated by a control group of 31 comparable subjects. These findings led the PLDK editors toward a broader concept of the trainability of abilities. As a result, the PLDK was expanded to include activities designed to enhance a broader range of intellectual tasks.

CURRENT RESEARCH

More recent research related to the PLDK has been carried out with experimental editions of the kits. Generally speaking, the published editions of the PLDK are sufficiently similar to these experimental editions that the results reported can be expected to apply equally. In view of the fact that changes made in the published editions of the kit were based on experience and research with the experimental edition, it is reasonable to hope that the present version of the program may be even more effective.

Subjects

Personal communications with the authors indicate that the PLDK has been and is being used with a wide variety of student populations. Formal research efforts have included evaluations of the effectiveness of the PLDK with the mentally retarded (Forgnone, 1966; Gibson, 1966; Mueller & Dunn, 1966; Dunn, Pochanart, & Bransky, 1967), slow learners (Ensminger, 1966), culturally disadvantaged (Carter, 1966; Dunn, Neville, Bailey, Pochanart, and Pfost, 1967; Bailey, 1966; Dunn & Mueller, 1966; Dunn, Pochanart, & Pfost, 1967) and with normal kindergarten children (Milligan, 1966; Dunn & Ahlersmeyer, 1967). As might be expected, the majority of these research efforts have involved subjects demonstrated to have particular problems in the area of language: the retarded (McCarthy, 1964; Mueller & Weaver, 1965) and the culturally deprived (Weaver, 1965; Gray, 1965).

Procedures

Generally, the basic technique of instruction was to present the PLDK program to experimental subjects following the directions outlined in the manual. In most cases the investigators provided some additional guidance to teachers either in the form of preservice or inservice training. In contrast to earlier investigations of language development programs, most recent studies have presented the PLDK in a regular classroom setting with the lessons being taught by the regular teacher. Carter (1966) used itinerant teachers working with groups of eight children, but noted that these teachers were not specially trained. Keehner (1966) did not follow the PLDK program exactly, but drew heavily on PLDK lessons and materials in connection with other activities.

Considerable variability in the length of the treatment period is also seen among this group of studies. Dunn and Smith (1966) report on two investigations of a longitudinal nature, however, the majority of studies reported to date have involved a relatively short term treatment program. Table 1 includes data on duration of treatment and number of lessons presented.

Evaluation

The PLDK is intended specifically to enhance language development and verbal intelligence. Further, it is expected that this will lead to increased academic growth. Therefore, the efficacy of PLDK treatment programs has generally been evaluated in terms of tests of language, intelligence, and academic achievement. Language abilities have been measured by the Illinois Test of Psycholinguistic Abilities (ITPA), the Peabody Picture Vocabulary Test (PPVT), and by analysis of language samples obtained in response to still and moving pictures. Evaluations of intelligence have used the Stanford-Binet Intelligence Scale (S-B), the Wechsler Intelligence Scale for Children (WISC), and the Primary Mental Abilities Test (PMAT). Instruments used to measure achievement include the Metropolitan Achievement Test (MAT) and the Wide Range Achievement Test (WRAT). Specific tests used in various investigations are indicated in Table 1. In a majority of these studies, tests were administered both prior to and following the treatment period and the efficacy of the program evaluated in terms of increases in performance during that period. In all studies reported here a control or contrast group, or both, was used to provide data against which to evaluate gains made by experimental subjects.

Results

To date, results of investigations of the efficacy of the PLDK with culturally disadvantaged children have been highly encouraging. Carter (1966) investigated the effects of a PLDK program on the language ability (ITPA) and intelligence (S-B) of 32 disadvantaged first grade children as compared with 32 control subjects matched for CA, MA, IQ, and initial language age (LA). The first 40 lessons of Level 1 of the PLDK were taught over a period of 10 weeks by nonspecialized, itinerant teachers, while the control group received no special treatment. Analysis of ITPA and S-B scores indicated that the experimental group gained significantly more than the controls on LA ($D = 11.31$; $p < .001$), MA ($D = 5.97$; $p < .001$, and IQ ($D = 5.38$; $p < .01$).

A longitudinal study conducted by one of the editors of the PLDK (Dunn & Mueller, 1966; Dunn, Pochanart, & Pfost, 1967) provides further evidence of the effectiveness of the program. This investigation involved a total of almost 1,000 culturally disadvantaged children, though statistical treatment of data was based on smaller, selected samples. The investigation is scheduled to follow these children through their elementary school years, and reports are currently available over two years. Results at the end of first grade (Dunn & Mueller, 1966) indicated that the PLDK had a favorable effect on language development as measured by the ITPA and the Peabody Language Production Inventory (PLPI, Nelson, 1966) and intelligence as measured by the S-B. Scores from the PPVT failed to reveal any interpretable differences among experimental, contrast, and control groups. Administration of the MAT also failed to disclose any academic superiority which could be attributed to the PLDK program. Results at the end of second grade indicated that subjects having had experience with the PLDK for only one year (during first grade) no longer exhibited significant superiority in either language or intelligence. However, those who were continued on PLDK treatment were distinctly superior ($p < .10$) in LA to both the control group and the one-year experimental group. The PLDK program was significantly more effective for boys than girls. Again, achievement data failed to disclose differences among groups.

TABLE 1

SUMMARY OF PLDK RESEARCH STUDIES

Reference	Sample	Duration	Presentation	Evaluation
Carter, 1966	Disadvantaged	10 Weeks	Nonspecialized	ITPA
	32 Exp.	40 Lessons	Itinerant	S-B
	32 Control		Teachers	
Dunn & Mueller, 1966	Disadvantaged 108 Ext.	1 Year	Regular &	ITPA
		Level #1	Itinerant	PPVT
	54 Contrast		Teachers	Language Sample
	54 Control			
				S-B
				MAT
Dunn, Neville, Bailey, Pochanart, & Pfost, 1967	Disadvantaged	1 Year	Regular	ITPA
	352 Exp.	Level #1	Teachers	S-B
	185 Contrast			PLPI
	62 Control			MAT
Dunn, Pochanart & Pfost, 1967	Disadvantaged	2 Years	Regular &	ITPA
	281 Exp.	Level #1	Itinerant	S-B
	62 Contrast	Level #2	Teachers	MAT
	41 Control			
Stearns, 1966	Disadvantaged	3 1/2 Months	Regular	ITPA
	12 Exp.	67 Lessons	Teachers	
	9 Contrast			
	5 Control			
Dunn, Pochanart, & Branksy, 1967	EMR	1 Year	Regular	ITPA
		Level #1	Teachers	

Table 1 (Continued)

Reference	Sample	Duration	Presentation	Evaluation
Forgnone, 1966	EMR	3 Months	Regular	ITPA
	27 Exp.	58 Lessons	Teachers	PMAT
	29 Contrast			Word Recognition
	27 Control			
Gibson, 1966	EMR	6 Months	Regular	ITPA
	13 Exp.	45 Lessons	Teachers	PPVT
	13 Control			Language Sample
				WISC
				WRAT
Mueller, & Dunn 1966	EMR	4 1/2 Months	Regular	ITPA
	283 Exp.	90 Lessons	Teachers	
	85 Control			
Ensminger, 1966	Slow Learners	6 1/2 Months	Regular	ITPA
	29 Exp.	132 Lessons	Teachers	S-B
	33 Control			
Ahlersmeyer & Dunn, 1966	Normals	6 Months	Regular	ITPA
			Teachers	S-B
				MAT
Milligan, 1966	Normals	24 Weeks	Regular	ITPA
	97 Total		Teachers	Met. Readiness

Stearns (1966) presented 67 selected lessons from the PLDK with a group of 12 deprived kindergarten children in connection with an overall experimental program. Analysis of ITPA scores did not reveal improved language abilities which could be attributed specifically to the PLDK treatment, though the experimental group did make significant gains in language in response to the total experimental curriculum.

One major study (Dunn, Neville, Bailey, Pochanart, & Pfost, 1967) has been reported in which the published edition of the PLDK was used. A total of over 600 disadvantaged first graders took part in this investigation, though findings are based on analysis of scores of smaller selected samples. Regular teachers presented the Level 1 PLDK lessons daily through the first grade year. In comparison with a comparable control group, the experimental groups demonstrated significantly superior performance ($p < .05$) in language as measured by the ITPA and school achievement as measured by the MAT. Gains in mental age (S-B) also favored the experimental group ($p < .10$).

Results of studies with EMR subjects are less clear cut. A major longitudinal study (Mueller & Dunn, 1967; Dunn, Pochanart, & Bransky, 1967) is scheduled to carry a group of 283 special class, EMR subjects through levels 1 and 2 of the PLDK. Interim evaluations of development of language skills indicate favorable effects of the PDLK after 4-1/2 months of treatment (Mueller & Dunn, 1967) and still more favorable effects after one year. Final evaluation at the completion of two years of treatment will also include evaluation of intellectual and academic growth. A study by Keehner (1966) which included activities from the PLDK among other training activities also demonstrated significant growth in language abilities and intelligence.

Gibson (1966) provided a PLDK program to a group of 13 EMR children from 6-1/2 to 9 years of age. The program in this investigation was slightly modified in that only 45 lessons were taught in the course of 109, 40 minute, daily sessions. The effectiveness of this program was evaluated by 34 measures of oral language, intelligence, and academic achievement. On only five of these variables (four from a language sample and PPVT MA) was the experimental group superior to a matched control group. Scores from the ITPA, WISC, and WRAT did not differentiate between the groups. Overall, the author concluded that the PLDK treatment failed to significantly affect the development of this group. Forgnone (1966) found no significant differences among experimental, contrast and control groups when the effects of three months of PLDK treatment (58 lessons) were evaluated in terms of language, intelligence, visual perception, and word recognition.

Ensminger (1966) covered 132 lessons of Level 1 of the PLDK with a group of 29 children identified as slow-learning and borderline retarded. Evaluation of growth in overall language ability and intelligence revealed no difference between experimental and control subjects' performance. However, a **post hoc** analysis of gains made by the youngest 14 subjects (CA 6-5 and below) revealed a clear difference in language growth (D = 8.74; p < .07) in favor of the experimental group.

Two studies of kindergarten children of normal intelligence have been reported. Milligan (1966) evaluated the effects of 24 weeks of PLDK treatment in terms of scores on the ITPA and the Metropolitan Readiness Test. Experimental subjects proved to be significantly superior on total language age, but the control group was superior on the Metropolitan.

Dunn and Ahlersmeyer (1966) provided 6 months of PLDK training to a group of 27 normal children prior to first grade entrance. Scores on the ITPA, S-B, and MAT indicated that these children performed better in all these areas than comparable children receiving regular preschool and first grade experiences, and also better than children receiving a comparable training program beginning in first grade.

Several other studies dealing with questions other than the general efficacy of the PLDK bear mentioning. Several investigations (Dunn & Mueller, 1967) Ensminger, 1966; Milligan, 1966) have considered the differential effects of the PLDK in terms of its effect on ITPA subtest scores. All three studies indicate that scores on the Auditory-Vocal Association and Vocal Encoding tests are most sensitive to improvement as a result of PLDK treatment. The question of using itinerant or regular teaching personnel to administer the PLDK program was explored by Dunn and Mueller (1966). This study suggests that the program is equally effective regardless of type of teaching personnel.

Summary and Discussion

The editors of the PLDK have indicated (Dunn & Smith, 1965) that the program is intended to stimulate linguistic and intellectual development and therefore also to enhance academic ability. Though the evidence collected to date does not clearly indicate that the editors have achieved this goal, it does provide considerable support for their position.

The PLDK program would appear to bear most directly on language behavior. Studies of the PLDK with culturally disadvantaged children have consistently indicated that the program does enhance language ability, particularly skills in verbal association and expression. Similar results have been obtained in investigations of the PLDK with normal kindergarten children. Investigations with other populations (EMR and border-line retarded) have been less consistent. Several studies of relatively short duration have failed to demonstrate significant effects attributable to the PLDK. However, the one longitudinal study reported has demonstrated significant improvement in language at a point half way through and at the conclusion of presentation of Level 1 of the PLDK. Overall, it appears likely that the PLDK will prove to be an effective tool for working with the retarded, but it is clear that a more sustained program is necessary with retardates than with the disadvantaged. In view of the generally slower development exhibited by retardates, it is not surprising that more extensive programs are necessary to produce significant changes in their development. In summary, it appears that the available evidence clearly supports the efficacy of the PLDK in enhancing overall language ability when used with appropriate student populations over adequate periods of time.

An additional question has been raised regarding those aspects of language behavior which are affected by PLDK treatment. Unfortunately, most investigators have failed to report data on differential language behavior. Those studies which do provide this type of data suggest that the program is primarily effective in enhancing verbal associative ability (ITPA, Auditory-Vocal Association) and verbal expression (ITPA, Vocal Encoding and various measures of verbal production in response to pictures). One study (Keehner, 1966) did demonstrate fairly even growth across the various aspects of language sampled by the ITPA, but her program also included numerous activities, in addition to PLDK lessons. In this connection, it should be noted that available findings are based largely on the use of the experimental edition of Level 1 of the PLDK. Perhaps the single most important modification in the published edition, and in experimental editions other than Level 1, is the increased attention to providing a balanced program. It remains for further research to verify the success of this modification.

Evidence regarding the efficacy of the PLDK in enhancing intellectual development is somewhat more limited, but follows essentially the same pattern. Studies of culturally deprived children are fairly consistent in revealing increases in performance which are attributable to the PLDK. Data related to the effect of PLDK on intellectual growth in other populations reveal little evidence to support the efficacy of the program. However, these data are based on only a few studies of very short duration. The comments made previously regarding modification of the published editions of the PLDK may apply equally here. Overall, the available data suggest that the PLDK may be, as claimed, an effective tool for stimulating intellectual growth. However, its effectiveness in this modality has been less clearly demonstrated than its effectiveness in stimulating language development. Further investigation into this aspect of PLDK efficacy is clearly needed in view of the somewhat equivocal results to date.

Very few studies have explored the extent to which the effects of PLDK program generalize to academic growth. Of two major investigations incorporating this variable, one demonstrated positive effects and the other did not. Though the effectiveness of the program in a single study may be viewed as encouraging, it would be inappropriate to recommend the PLDK on this basis. In addition, it should be noted that the effects of the PLDK on academic areas are much less direct as compared with language and intelligence. Thus, it might be expected that changes in achievement would not be so immediately apparent. Longitudinal studies currently under way should eventually provide data to confirm or refute this supposition.

Research on the effectiveness of the PLDK with populations other than the culturally disadvantaged and the mentally retarded is still too limited to draw any firm conclusions. Clearly, the need for a program such as the PLDK is less critical with normal populations. Nevertheless, results of the few studies with normal and near normal populations are sufficiently encouraging to suggest that further study might be of value. Reports of studies with other populations were not available to the authors. However, it seems reasonable to assume that other groups might profit from the type of experience offered by the PLDK. It certainly appears that the programs should be adaptable to working with problems of speech impairment. In view of the severe problems in language development found in deaf and hearing impaired populations, it would appear that investigations of the PLDK with these populations are also warranted. Finally, it has been suggested that some of the academic problems experienced by the orthopedically handicapped are a result of a lack of breadth of experience. The broad range of content included in the PLDK program might also be of value to this handicapped group. On the basis of available data it is not possible to conclude that the PLDK has completely fulfilled the goals of its authors, nor that it has proven itself as an effective teaching aid. However, results of early studies appear extremely promising. Research into the efficacy of the PLDK is continuing, and as the total program becomes readily available, additional research can be expected. There is every reason to believe that interest in the PLDK and enthusiasm for language programs generally will result in sufficient research efforts to clearly identify those groups with which it is an effective tool, and the conditions under which it is most effective.

This chapter was co-authored by Dr. Mueller in his private capacity. No official support or endorsement by the Office of Education or the Department of Health, Education, and Welfare is intended or should be inferred.

References

1. Ahlersmeyer, D.E., & Dunn, L.M. THE EFFECTS OF EARLY READING INSTRUCTION AND LANGUAGE DEVELOPMENT WITH PRE-FIRST GRADERS. Unpublished abstract. Nashville, Tenn.: Peabody College, 1966. (Available from the Institute on Mental Retardation and Intellectual Development at Peabody College).

2. Bailey, Carolyn F. A COMPARISON OF THE EFFECTIVENESS OF TWO READING PROGRAMS WITH CULTURALLY DISADVANTAGED CHILDREN. Unpublished doctoral dissertation. Nashville, Tenn.: Peabody College, 1966.

3. Blessing, K.R. AN INVESTIGATION OF A PSYCHOLINGUISTIC DEFICIT IN EDUCABLE MENTALLY RETARDED CHILDREN. Unpublished doctoral dissertation, University of Wisconsin, 1964.

4. Blue, C.M. THE EFFECTIVENESS OF A GROUP LANGUAGE PROGRAM WITH TRAINABLE MENTAL RETARDATES. Unpublished manuscript, Appalachian State Teachers College, Boone, North Carolina, 1963.

5. Carter, J.L. THE EFFECT OF A LANGUAGE STIMULATION PROGRAM UPON FIRST GRADE EDUCATIONALLY DISADVANTAGED CHILDREN, Ed. and Trng. of Ment. Ret., 1:169-174, 1966.

6. Dunn, L.M., & Mueller, M. DIFFERENTIAL EFFECTS OF THE PEABODY LANGUAGE DEVELOPMENT KITS ON THE ITPA PROFILE. Nashville, Tenn.: Institute on Mental Retardation and Intellectual Development, Peabody College, (in preparation — A)

7. Dunn, L.M. & Mueller, M. THE EFFECTIVENESS OF THE PEABODY LANGUAGE DEVELOPMENT KITS AND THE INITIAL TEACHING ALPHABET WITH DISADVANTAGED CHILDREN IN THE PRIMARY GRADES: AFTER ONE YEAR. IMRID Monograph #2. Nashville, Tenn.: Peabody College, 1966.

8. Dunn, L.M. & Mueller, M. EFFECTS OF THE PEABODY LANGUAGE DEVELOPMENT PROGRAM WITH EDUCABLE MENTALLY RETARDED CHILDREN: AFTER 4-1/2 MONTHS. Nashville, Tenn.: Institute on Mental Retardation and Intellectual Development, Peabody College, (in preparation — B)

9. Dunn, L.M. & Pfost, P. THE EFFECTIVENESS OF THE PEABODY LANGUAGE DEVELOPMENT KITS AND THE INITIAL TEACHING ALPHABET WITH DISADVANTAGED CHILDREN IN THE PRIMARY GRADES: AFTER TWO YEARS. IMRID Monograph #6. Nashville, Tenn.: Peabody College, 1967.

10. Dunn, L.M., Pochanart, P. & Bransky, M. EFFECTS OF THE PEABODY LANGUAGE DEVELOPMENT PROGRAM WITH EDUCABLE MENTALLY RETARDED CHILDREN: AFTER ONE YEAR. Nashville, Tenn: Institute on Mental Retardation and Intellectual Development, Peabody College, (in preparation).

11. Dunn, L.M., Neville, D., Bailey, Carolyn F., Pochanart, P., & Pfost, P. THE EFFECTIVENESS OF THREE READING APPROACHES AND AN ORAL LANGUAGE STIMULATION PROGRAM WITH DISADVANTAGED CHILDREN IN THE PRIMARY GRADES: AFTER ONE YEAR. IMRID Monography #7. Nashville, Tenn.: Peabody College, 1967.

12. Dunn, L.M. & Smith, J.O. PEABODY LANGUAGE DEVELOPMENT KITS: Level #1. Circle Pines, Minn.: American Guidance Service, 1965.

13. Ensminger, E.E. THE EFFECTS OF A CLASSROOM LANGUAGE DEVELOPMENT PROGRAM ON PSYCHOLINGUISTIC ABILITIES AND INTELLECTUAL FUNCTIONING IN SLOW-LEARNING AND BORDERLINE RETARDED CHILDREN. Unpublished doctoral dissertation. Lawrence, Kansas: University of Kansas, 1966.

14. Foote, Elizabeth. AN EXPLORATION OF THE LANGUAGE ABILITIES OF YOUNG, CULTURALLY DEPRIVED CHILDREN USING THE ILLINOIS TEST OF PSYCHOLINGUISTIC ABILITIES. Unpublished M. Sc. thesis, Nashville, Tenn.: Vanderbilt University, 1966.

15. Forgnone, C. EFFECTS OF GROUP TRAINING IN VISUAL PERCEPTION AND LANGUAGE DEVELOPMENT UPON THE VISUAL PERCEPTION AND PSYCHOLINGUISTIC ABILITIES OF RETARDED CHILDREN. Unpublished doctoral dissertation. Nashville, Tenn.: Peabody College, 1966.

16. Gibson, R.C. EFFECTIVENESS OF A SUPPLEMENTAL LANGUAGE DEVELOPMENT PROGRAM WITH EDUCABLE MENTALLY RETARDED CHILDREN. Unpublished doctoral dissertation, University of Iowa, 1966.

17. Guilford, J.P. THREE FACES OF INTELLECT. Amer. Psychologist, 14:469-479, 1959.

18. Guilford, J.P. & Hoepfner, R. CURRENT SUMMARY OF STRUCTURE-OF-INTELLECT FACTORS AND SUGGESTED TESTS. Studies of aptitudes of high level personnel, Reports from Psycholology Laboratory. Los Angeles: University of Southern California, No. 30, 1963.

19. Keehner, U. A COMPARATIVE STUDY OF LINGUISTIC AND MENTAL ABILITIES BEFORE AND AFTER A DEVELOPMENTAL-REMEDIAL LANGUAGE PROGRAM WITH MENTALLY RETARDED CHILDREN, Unpublished masters thesis, University of Wisconsin, Madison, Wisconsin, 1966.

20. McCarthy, J.J. THE IMPORTANCE OF LINGUISTIC ABILITY IN THE MENTALLY RE-TARDED, Mental Retardation. 2:90-96, 1964.

21. McCarthy, J.J. & Kirk, S.A. THE ILLINOIS TEST OF PSYCHOLINGUISTIC ABILITIES — AN APPROACH TO DIFFERENTIAL DIAGNOSIS. Amer. J. Ment. Def., 66:399-412, 1961.

22. Milligan, J.L. A STUDY OF THE EFFECTS OF A GROUP LANGUAGE DEVELOPMENT PROGRAM UPON THE PSYCHOLINGUISTIC ABILITIES OF KINDERGARTEN CHILDREN. Unpublished doctoral dissertation. Lawrence, Kansas: University of Kansas, 1966.

23. Mueller, M. & Smith, J.O. THE STABILITY OF LANGUAGE AGE MODIFICATION OVER TIME. Amer. J. Ment. Defic., 68:537-539, 1964.

24. Mueller, M.W. & Weaver, S.J. PSYCHOLINGUISTIC ABILITIES OF INSTITUTIONAL-IZED AND NON-INSTITUTIONALIZED TRAINABLE MENTAL RETARDATES. Amer. J. Ment. Defic., 68:775-783, 1964.

25. Nelson, J.C. PEABODY SPEECH PRODUCTION INVENTORY. Nashville, Tenn.: George Peabody College for Teachers, 1964. (Available from the Institute on Mental Retardation and Intellectual Development at Peabody College).

26. Rouse, Sue T. EFFECTS OF A TRAINING PROGRAM ON THE PRODUCTIVE THINK-ING OF EDUCABLE MENTAL RETARDATES. Amer. J. Ment. Defic., 69:666-673, 1965.

27. Smith, Carolyn M. DEVELOPMENT OF A REVISED EXPERIMENTAL KIT FOR ORAL LANGUAGE STIMULATION. Unpublished Ed. S. thesis. Nashville, Tenn.: George Peabody College for Teachers, 1964.

28. Smith, J.O. EFFECTS OF A GROUP LANGUAGE DEVELOPMENT PROGRAM UPON THE PSYCHOLINGUISTIC ABILITIES OF EDUCABLE MENTAL RETARDATES. Peabody College Research Monograph Series in Special Education. No. 1. Nashville, Tenn.: George Peabody College for Teachers, 1962. (Available from the Peabody College Bookstore.)

29. Stearns, K.E. EXPERIMENTAL GROUP LANGUAGE DEVELOPMENT FOR PSYCHO-SOCIALLY DEPRIVED PRESCHOOL CHILDREN. Unpublished doctoral dissertation. Bloomington, Ind.: Indiana University, 1966.

30. Weaver, S.J. USE OF THE ITPA WITH EXCEPTIONAL CHILDREN. Unpublished paper. Nashville, Tenn.: Peabody College, 1965. (Available from the Institute on Mental Retardation and Intellectual Development at Peabody College.)

30. Torrance, E.P. GUIDING CREATIVE TALENT, Englewood-Cliffs, N.J.: Prentice-Hall, 1962.

31. Weaver, S.J. USE OF THE ITPA WITH EXCEPTIONAL CHILDREN. Unpublished paper. Nashville, Tenn.: Peabody College, 1965. (Available from the Institute on Mental Retardation and Intellectual Development at Peabody College.)

THE PRINCIPLES AND DYNAMICS OF THERAPEUTIC TUTORING

Bessie Sperry, Ph. D., Chief Psychologist,
Judge Baker Guidance Center,
Boston, Massachusetts

Robert G. Templeton, Ed. D.,
Judge Baker Guidance Center,
Boston, Massachusetts

BESSIE SPERRY, Ph.D.,   ROBERT G. TEMPLETON, Ed. D.

Children of normal intelligence, without perceptible sensory and neurological problems, who fail in the acquisition of the basic school skills have been studied by our research group at the Judge Baker Guidance Center and by several other clinical research teams with regard to their problems in motivation. This kind of investigation has been by no means fruitless; such children appear to have grown up in families with a higher incidence of trauma than have other children; they frequently occupy a subtly devalued role with regard to the family group, and they have complicated internal problems especially with the management of aggression. Around these motivational aspects of the child's problem the most careful therapeutic efforts are obviously indicated, both to relieve the manifest symptom and to alter the self-destructive tendencies with which the primary neurotic learning problem is associated.

In our experience the remedial teaching methods used with these children in their early school years is also of great importance. Once the learning difficulty has developed as an expressive channel for the child's conflicts, a collaborative approach involving both educational and therapeutic techniques is frequently necessary to deal effectively with the problem.

There are various forms of therapeutic tutoring and a variety of methods for putting to good use the tense and meaningful relationships that occur between the therapeutic tutor and the child with learning problems. The essential task of the tutor is to help the child proceed with the mastery of the symbolic tools of learning and simultaneously cope with the threatening intrusions of affect and fantasy that impinge directly on the learning activity. In this tutorial process action rather than introspection is the basic transaction. A perceptive knowledge of the dynamics of the situation is important; the tutor uses it in ways to enable the child to learn about the outside world rather than to engage in introspection about himself.

In this paper we shall discuss the following essential elements of the therapeutic tutoring process: 1) **the individual and collaborative aspects of therapeutic tutoring;** 2) **the basic cognitive and emotional difficulties of learning problem children;** 3) **some general principles, strategies, and materials of therapeutic tutoring along with** 4) **illustrative considerations of the process itself.**

INDIVIDUAL AND COLLABORATIVE ASPECTS OF THERAPEUTIC TUTORING

Therapeutic tutoring, as we conceive it, is essentially a kind of educational practice in which the knowledge available about the child's educational and emotional problems can be used in the interaction between the tutor and the child for the alleviation of the psychogenic learning problem. The therapeutic tutor adapts his knowledge of the child's dynamics to manipulate certain aspects of the relationship including the transference. He also uses his knowledge of the child's level of cognitive, emotional, and educational development to shape their style of communication.

To accomplish this the tutor utilizes two important aspects of the traditional psychotherapeutic process: the personal relationship with its transference quality, and educative aspects in their broader meanings. In contrast to the process of traditional psychotherapy the tutor and the child have a specific objective reality situation within which they are attempting to solve certain problems. In spite of the fact that the learning situation is a displacement of broader problems, it contains within its specificity a focus of activity. A second difference is that the therapeutic tutor allows only a limited amount of regression with frequent attempts to redirect the child's energy toward sublimatory types of activities.

The skilled use of transference in the tutoring situation requires that the tutor possess a sound knowledge of psychodynamics and an ability to make a good diagnosis or that he collaborate closely with someone who can provide this knowledge. In most situations sound tutorial progress is in no small measure contingent on developing techniques and procedures with reference to the original diagnosis as well as on making continuing evaluations of ego and transference shifts. So far in our experience this method has been successfully used by clinically trained psychologists or by other staff members supervised by them. This does not mean, however, that this work has not been done by tutors without clinical training, for occasionally there are exceptional people who appear to have an intuitive understanding of such children and their needs and who do exceptionally well with them. As a rule we have found that a knowledgeable manipulation of the tutorial situation has advantages over the intuitive one, though of course the ideal tutor would use both.

There are certain situations in which psychogenic learning problems can be reasonably well handled by therapeutic tutoring without concomitant psychotherapy: 1) when the child has mild neurotic difficulties with learning that have become exacerbated by relatively benign family or school crises; 2) when psychotherapy has already resolved some of the major psychological difficulties and a residual of the learning problem remains; and 3) when either parent or child is too resistant to traditional psychotherapy to achieve a favorable alliance with a psychotherapist. In this last situation though optimal results may not be achieved, there may be some partial mitigation of the child's learning difficulties — enough at least to make some continued learning possible in school.

When the child has been suffering from chronic and severe learning difficulties accompanied by serious emotional disturbances, both psychotherapy and therapeutic tutoring are usually the treatment of choice. When the diagnosis involves borderline ego functioning, severe character disorder, or entrenched masochistic neurosis, such a joint endeavor is particularly pertinent if there is to be a favorable prognosis.

For such a collaboration to be effective there must be a friendly, confidential relationship between therapist and tutor, since usually during the course of treatment some splits in the transference will occur. The child will often act out difficulties with his parents in the two clinical situations, and only a knowledgeable and objective view of the transference problems will prevent the child's two helpers from becoming unwitting participants in the neurotic struggle. As in any situation in which the clinical personnel acts out with the patient, the results are non-therapeutic, and progress can be brought to a sharp halt.

Since the transference relationship is one of the most powerful factors in both the therapy and the tutoring, only a careful and continuous appraisal will permit a really fruitful use of it. In many situations it is worth evaluating whether therapist and tutor of different sexes may not be the best choice. If they are too similar in their identities, this in itself can sometimes operate to promote difficult transference splits: that the one is good and the other bad, or the one liked and the other not liked. Such reactions may create transference difficulties of a sort that are almost impossible to manage in the best interests of the child's learning and growth in therapy. Transference manifestations can be useful in tutoring only when they are moderate rather than when they produce a continuous series of crises.

Usually it is not easy for the child to make two such relationships simultaneously. Since their timing is crucial to the success of the collaborative effort, the relationship with the therapist should usually be established first, particularly since the child very likely has had previous difficulties with teachers and less therapeutically oriented tutors. It is important that the negative feelings which the child more often than not brings to the clinical situation receive some amelioration in therapy prior to the introduction of the therapeutic tutor. On the other hand there are situations in which the child and his parents are afraid of psychotherapy and yet the child is suffering from severe learning difficulties. In such cases the psychologist may begin seeing the child for therapeutic tutoring as a way into psychotherapy when the child and parent become less threatened.

Usually, this will not be the case. During the initial stage of psychotherapy the therapist usually works first with the child's negative expectations about any kind of help. Before the tutor is introduced, the therapist will explain to the child why he needs to see a tutor for help with his schoolwork and explore any reservations the child may have about such an arrangement. It is a good rule of thumb to avoid getting into specific issues about what knowledge and information will be shared between the therapist and the tutor during the beginning period of the collaboration. It is important, however, to explain to the child that his helpers will communicate with each other about matters pertaining to the child's school progress.

Relevant communication between therapist and tutor is usually important to the success of the mutual understanding. In the early stages of the child's relationship with his therapist, he may from time to time become anxious lest the therapist communicate certain very intimate material he has shared with him. At such times the therapist will have to reassure him that there is absolute confidentiality about this, though as the therapy and tutoring progress such issues will diminish.

The problem of confidentiality may also arise with the tutor. The child may be ashamed of some of the things he does or says during the tutoring sessions and not wish the therapist to find out about them. Our usual rule about this is that the tutor will not guarantee to withhold important information from the therapist, since the therapeutic situation itself involves the child's understanding that he should communicate troublesome matters to his therapist. For this reason the tutor should refuse to become a collaborator with the child in the withholding maneuver.

Issues of confidentiality are bound to arise. Because basic problems around communication and sharing of knowledge can be crucial for children with learning problems, it is all the more pertinent that the two helping people use the sharing of information to foster rather than to hurt the relationships between them and the child, to make it a constructive instrument for relieving anxiety rather than producing it.

A child with chronic learning problems who has for several years endured a marginal existence in school frequently has little conscious wish to collaborate either with the therapist or with the tutor. Especially to the tutor he brings his previous experience with teachers and parents trying to help him who have not succeeded and who have in fact made him feel increasingly embarrassed, discouraged, and displeased with the whole learning process. The child has usually made certain adjustments at home and at school, and he has more often than not achieved secondary gains from his position as the slow learner. As one boy said about his situation, "My sisters can have their marks in school. I'll get my help."

Some of the child's present difficulties have often been the outcome of his way of mobilizing some kind of concern in his own behalf from parents who he thinks prefer the other siblings in his family. He does not have the same conscious anxiety as the school phobic child who is confronted with the daily experience of acute fear. Those who attempt to get him to look into the future to see how complicated and difficult his life situation will become if his problem is not alleviated usually experience little success. The child himself frequently does not think the future is that important largely because time means little to him and because he is just barely finding enough energy to make some kind of adaptation to his immediate environment.

Often the child is suffering from a chronic underlying depression which makes him feel that his own efforts and those of his therapist and tutor will come to nothing. In his more energetic moments he is likely to be openly negative toward the tutor and to express some of the hostility that he has accumulated through the years of failure toward the person who is trying to help him. Younger children who have not for so long experienced the frustration and humiliation of school failure frequently are more active in their efforts to circumvent tutorial help. They may, for example, possess an infantile attitude of omnipotent self-assertion and so may with some partial belief announce to the tutor that they don't need any help, that they know how to do it themselves. Sometimes such a child will refuse to demonstrate what he has learned or to look at proffered learning material. Occasionally he will pick out material that is much too difficult for him, look at it, do one small task, and stop, since his omnipotence has been threatened by the difficulty of the task. He may save face then by devaluating the particular book or complaining that the tutor does not have any of the right material. These are illustrative of a few of the attitudes and behaviors the tutor will observe in such children; indeed, they afford him clues to some of the very complicated and deep rooted cognitive and emotional difficulties such children are attempting to adjust to.

SOME ASPECTS OF THE COGNITIVE AND EMOTIONAL DIFFICULTIES COMMON TO LEARNING PROBLEM CHILDREN

Among the many difficulties these children try to cope with are immaturities in their cognitive development, immaturities that are not only intimately related to their emotional conflicts but also handicaps to effective learning. Although we shall explore these in more detail in connection with the tutorial process, we should like to touch on certain general aspects of their cognitive problems before looking briefly at some of their major emotional conflicts.

In a paper directed primarily to studying children's ideas about causality other members of our learning research group have reported differences in levels of cognitive maturity as measured by Piaget's tests between latency-age boys of normal intelligence with neurotic learning inhibitions and their matched controls. Described most generally their cognitive difficulties involve thinking that is either too vague and personalized or concrete and detail bound. These differences are differences in the apparent pattern of thinking and not necessarily the underlying motivational processes. We have observed shifts in patterning from one type to the other during the process of treating learning problem children, and we have also observed them to coexist. Their learning errors appear to have something in common with the subjective synthesis described by Piaget in his **Language** and **Thought of the Child**, though in much of their thinking they appear to be operating at a cognitively more mature level. When these children are confronted with the school learning situation, their thinking tends to become defensive, egocentric, and cognitively regressed. Much of the success of the tutorial undertaking will hinge on the strategies and techniques the tutor can devise to limit and control this regression, redirect the child's energies to the learning tasks, and work toward the gradual amelioration of these and other types of cognitive difficulties.

In addition to the problems these children have with their thinking, there are certain underlying emotional conflicts common to those with whom we have worked. Though their defenses and modes of dealing with them may vary according to their ages and idiosyncrasies of the family situations, denial of conflicts and avoidance of learning are present in all of them.

The first of these problems is related to the enormous amount of accumulated aggression we see in these children, much of which is deeply repressed. Learning activity is commonly poorly differentiated from expressions of hostility, and the child protects himself by relative immobilization. The common sources for this hostility lie in the excessive amount of trauma they have experienced earlier along with parental derogation and adverse learning experiences. Our research findings indicate that such children have in fact been much more heavily traumatized during the first seven years of life than their normal controls. Learning behaviors involving both helplessness and childish omnipotence are common manifestations.

The second problem involves the child's fear of assuming his own sex role or at least of expressing any active indication that he wishes to do so. Primarily these boys wish to take a more neuter position and to that end an immature social role. One of their common fantasies involves the motion that in order to be masculine and to grow up to be a man a boy must hurt or kill, and that similar things will happen to him in retaliation.

Their third major problem and related problem is the conflict between the wish for independence and the fear of abandonment. Since many of these children are afraid to seek out age appropriate gratifications, they cling to those of more infantile and regressed kind.

Clinicians are familiar with the variety of strategies these children will employ in an attempt to avoid some of these basic fears and to hold onto the secondary gains that are part of the security adaptation they have managed to achieve. Not only will the therapeutic tutor have to cope with some of their more indirect manifestations in the child's learning situation but also some of the attitudes and feelings that have developed as a result of the child's interactions with his parents around learning and achievement.

Specific parental attitudes and behaviors we have commonly seen operating in a negative and destructive way around the child's learning are as follows:

1. The parent does not give the child simple and direct information incidental to either academic or general learning experiences since the parent feels this will not help him to grow and function independently. This frequently occurs in a relationship in which the nurturant aspect was never mutually satisfying. For example, the child may want to know how to spell a word in the middle of trying to write a homework composition. His mother says, "Look it up in the dictionary." The child replies, "I can't. I don't know how to spell it."

2. The parent encourages the child to work independently, succeeds finally in getting him to do it, and then removes the pleasure of achievement by pointing out nothing but his mistakes and stressing the need for doing the work over to an excessive degree.

3. The parent uses his or her experience and superior knowledge and intellectual ability to prove the child is wrong in every discussion of his ideas relevant to schoolwork, general information and ability, and discipline at home.

4. The parent uses **stupid** or **dumb** as a general term of displeasure or in disciplining any behavior that does not meet with parental approval.

5. Parents fail to adapt their ways of communication to the child's level of understanding, leave out relevant information, or distort meanings. They use sarcasm and threats in ways that the child can either take literally and be frightened or be left confused.

6. The parents set the impossible task for the child or create conditions that guarantee he will have continuous experience with failure. For example, the parents buy the child such a complex model that

he cannot make it and asks for help. The father may attempt to teach the child how to build it, using the same derogatory techniques as he does around the schoolwork to make the child feel inept and stupid.

These are a few of the specific parental behaviors and attitudes towards the child's achievement and his achievement-oriented activities that the therapeutic tutor must anticipate and contradict in his teaching behavior and in his relationship toward the child. Ideally there are certain possibilities based on our previous clinical experience that the tutor should take into account in devising his strategies and materials if he wishes to maximize his chances of success.

PRINCIPLES, STRATEGIES, AND MATERIALS IN THERAPEUTIC TUTORING

In his general approach to teaching the tutor tries to behave in a manner which is opposite to or contradicts the negative and derogatory attitudes and behavior the child may have come to expect from adults toward his learning. If the tutor is not aware of the particular parental attitudes, he will rely on his previous experience with such children and watch for transference type behaviors for clues to the child's negative expectations. Since we know a good deal already about such expectations, some general principles and rules can be formulated to serve as guidelines for proceeding:

1) It is important that the tutor present himself as a warm, understanding, and receptive adult who wants to help the child with his learning but who will not use pressure, negative criticism, anger, or censure to get the child to learn. **He demonstrates from the beginning that he can be a sympathetic ally who has the power to help the child overcome his learning disabilities through action**. So he will explore at first, not the areas of the child's incompetence and learning deficits, but those in which the child already has gained some small degree of proficiency. He will try to help the child see for himself that despite his school problems he already knows and has learned many things and that there are some things the tutor can teach him.

The tutor may then demonstrate that he can teach the child one easy thing without too much effort or embarrassment on the child's part. For example, the child may come to the tutor while he is floundering in the middle of grade two, only able to read a few words or sentences at a time with his teacher by his side. He may be weak in phonetic and word recognition skills, and just average in arithmetic. He may print and spell only poorly, and his attention span may be unusually short for his age. The tutor suggests to him that like many boys he has trouble with his reading but "that doesn't mean you can't read any words." He then quickly prints three or four simple words, including the child's first name (**cat, man, hat, George**) on index cards using a magic marker.

He lays out the cards before the child, saying, "I'll bet you know some of these words already." Usually the child will be able to read them. The tutor praises him, and if he has missed a word, the tutor may add, "Guess that's a word you haven't had in school yet." He says the word for the child, asks the child to say it, and comments, "See, you know a new word. I can teach you other new words, too."

As a corollary to the above, it is important during the first few sessions that the tutor introduce only those learning tasks he feels fairly confident the child is either already familiar with or that he can easily master so that the new learning will be felt as easy and pleasurable. Using the same principle the tutor will gradually explore other areas of learning deficits with the child, making every effort to provide him with as many positive learning experiences as possible.

2) **The tutor should estimate the pacing of the learning activities so that permitted expressive periods can alternate with those involving school tasks before the point of fatigue or frustration is reached.** In other words, the tutor must determine the lengths of time the child can comfortably tolerate learning without becoming unduly anxious or restless. This means that what is done during each hour be structured and materials and activities introduced according to the capacity of the child to tolerate the learning confrontation. How the hour is paced, the amount of pressure the tutor can exert on the child to learn, and the ways he allows him to move from learning tasks to freer and more expressive activities and back to the learning tasks — these will determine in no small measure the success of the therapeutic venture.

3) **From time to time the tutor must deal with some fantasy material both in relation to the school work and to the intermittent expressive activity.** When the child is only mildly anxious about such material, the tutor may chose to make some brief comment about the child's feelings and safely wait to communicate this to the child's therapist. When the child is visibly anxious or upset, it will be necessary for the tutor not to retreat but to handle the conscious aspects of the fantasy with a recognition of its meaning and encouragement that the fear can be overcome.

4) **The tutor carefully demonstrates over a period of time that he can help the child recognize and correct errors and difficulties in his performance and teaches him to become a friendly critic of his own productions.** During the initial phases of the tutoring the tutor usually will point out only those things about the child's work that are good or praiseworthy and make no reference to minor mistakes and difficulties. As the child progresses and gains confidence, the tutor will then be in a position to help him look at his productions somewhat more critically, particularly when new learning is being consolidated before moving on to more difficult material. If, for example, the child has managed to do four out of five subtraction problems correctly, and it is apparent that the child understands the basic processes involved, the tutor may say,

"Good! You've done very well. They're almost all right except for a little trouble with that problem. Do you suppose you could look that problem over and fix it up?" Usually the child will be able to do this, sometimes not without considerable self-derogation when he realizes he has made a mistake. When this happens the tutor has an opportunity to recognize the child's feelings of inadequacy and to help him come to see that a performance does not need to be perfect to be good and praiseworthy.

These then represent some of the principles that the tutor should find useful in forming a sound relationship with the child and an effective style of communication around the learning. Before exploring certain aspects of the tutorial process in some detail, we should like to touch on the ways the tutor may introduce and use the learning materials.

In most instances young children with severe learning difficulties can profit more if the tutor introduces materials not from their current school situation but those that are specifically designed to meet their various educational and emotional needs.

1) Although it is important that the tutor introduce order and structure to the learning tasks as soon as possible, it is highly desirable that he learn to prepare many of the materials on the spot as they are needed. The early school readers, the workbooks, and previous teaching methods are usually negatively cathected as the properties of a situation of profound discouragement. Therefore fresh material, usually produced by the tutor himself, will be most effective in the initial phases of the therapeutic tutoring.

An imaginative tutor can produce interesting material with a pile of index cards, a supply of various colored typewriter paper, an assortment of magic markers, pencils and erasers, a ruler, and a large roll of Scotch tape. He may use the colored typewriter paper to print in magic marker "stories-to-be-continued-next-time" involving topics, persons, or events of particular interest to the child. He can choose words at first which the child may be mostly able to read, copying them off with a magic marker onto the index card for the child to study separately. Many children then like to have these cards taped in rows on the wall for later review, adding new words during each session.

2) Using such materials the tutor will not only take every advantage he can of their novelty but also their possibilities as constructive appeals to the child's fantasy life around the learning. Instead of mounting word cards on the wall, the child may prefer to "hoard" or collect his words and store them in a cardboard file box, alphabetizing them as they are filed, and reviewing them from time to time. The tutor will emphasize the positive aspects of the fantasy by saying that the words now belong to the child. Or the tutor may arrange words on the wall in an apex, encouraging the child to read up one side and down the other, sometimes under time.

Since the most common expectation about the learning situation is that the child will lose something rather than gain anything, the tutor may wish to offer the child points for doing his work, adding them up at the end of each hour, and recording them on a wall chart. This can be made of colored paper with either a thermometer, a ladder, or a rocket drawn on it and divided into squares for the progressive noting of points accumulated. After eight or ten sessions when the child has filled in all the squares, the points can be tallied and periodic prizes given for achievement. The periodic concrete reward system has been valuable in our experience in sustaining some minimal effort when other motivational problems are impeding the learning.

3) It is not possible for these children to maintain a high level of cognitive activity for very long periods without permission for relatively lower level activities to occur intermittently. Some children will be able to work for longer periods of time without a break than others, while some can only tolerate learning periods of extremely brief duration at first. In either case the tutor should have available certain play materials that allow a minimum of cognitive and emotional regression and at the same time provide pleasurable and perhaps even a little learning activity for the child when he is not directly involved in school tasks. The expressive material should not be so highly libidinized as to promote so much regression that the child becomes incapable of returning to the cognitive level of functioning necessary for the resumption of the learning activity. For this reason, although it may be possible for the clinician or highly skilled tutor to allow the child to use paints or modeling clay at times, it is best to avoid them. A child may enjoy playing a pinball game and letting the tutor help him add up the score, which may provide the tutor with a chance to do a little incidental teaching. Or the child may choose to build a house or a castle with blocks or pay a game of bingo or pickup sticks.

4) Finally as the tutoring progresses, the materials used during the advancing phases should gradually approach again more systematic and school-like forms to help the child overcome any remaining aversion to them and to provide him with more orderly ways of increasing his knowledge and skills. Hopefully as the child enters the terminal phases of his tutorial work, his tutor will have become less of a transference figure and more of a friend and coping helper.

THE PROCESS OF THERAPEUTIC TUTORING:
ILLUSTRATIONS

Though the thinking of these children has many qualities in common with that of normal children, there are differences that especially tend to occur in the learning confrontation and in crises in interpersonal relationships. Let us look a little more closely at what we mean by the concretization of thought so prevalent in these neurotic children and define more specifically the kinds of cognitive operations we have in mind.

Essentially the child focuses on the particular aspects of perception of meaningful material and fails to consider the whole. At the earlier levels of school learning this may result in the confused identification of letters or words, in a centering on part of a letter or certain letters of a word, or in a suppression of the perception of further relevant details. In trying to teach the child phonics the tutor may be confronted with a youngster who can sound all the letters of a word separately but be unable to combine the sounds into a recognizable word. Then when a child has acquired a fair reading knowledge of individual words, he still may block on the connectives. Even though he may know the connecting words like **and** and **for** as individual words, his real difficulty may lie in the perception of larger units of meaning.

At more advanced learning stages, when the child may have already acquired a fair knowledge of reading skills, the problem of centering on the concrete aspects of the reading material is still in evidence. For example, when a boy was asked to read material that was at the highest level of his reading skills, he tended to respond to questions about the content by centering on individual words or phrases rather than evaluating the question in terms of the general ideas contained in what he had read. This was in marked contrast to his superior performance on individual intelligence tests and the good level of abstraction reflected in his verbal and social exchanges.

This kind of centering on details and failure to deal with the whole can lead to blocking of the perception of meaning. At other times the focusing on negative detail of the child's own performance can result in the interruption of learning or an attempt to destroy either his own productions or the learning material itself. This obsession with detail appears most frequently to have a defensive use; that is, to prevent the intrusion of fantasy through the blocking of the perception of meaning. The child acts as if any meaning, if perceived, might be one that could lead to associations with fears he is trying to suppress.

On the other hand, there are times when such centering on detail appears to be related to the conflict itself rather than to the avoidance of it. This can result in repetitive omissions or additions of letters, or in the concentration on particular words or letter forms.

In the case of one little boy his repetitive omission of the letter "i" in his name, **Neil**, appears from the therapy material to be related to his wish to give up his own identity. With another child his frustrating overinvestment in printing perfect "m's" in his name, **Jimmy**, was related to an earlier time when he habitually printed his name as **Jinny**. Another child would gratuitously add an "e" or an "a" to certain words, saying, "They ought to be a little longer," while he was having great difficulty in forming the lower part of the letter "f." He contracted the lower part until the letter looked like a misformed "b" or "l." For the latter two children the association of masculinity as destructive was crucial in their repetitive malformations of letters and words. Such a concentration on details, which seems to be conflict expressive rather than defensive, illustrates the type of obsession with detail which may issue in interruptions of production when the pressure of conflicts becomes conscious.

For example, the child who printed his name **Jinny** instead of **Jimmy** did not seem to be disturbed by this spelling of his name during the time his main longings were for a more feminine resolution of his oedipal conflict. It was only as the wishes for masculinity became more active during therapy that his dissatisfactions with printing his name correctly became more pronounced.

Vague overgeneralization in thought and perception is also frequently seen in the learning situation and is a special handicap to precision learning. Used defensively it performs the function of reducing specificity of meaning which may be fantasy arousing. When it fails in its defensive functioning, it may result in conflict expression. At the early stages of learning it may give the appearance of a simple unwillingness to attend to details in contrast to the attitude of the child who appears to be laboring over specifics. The youngster using this defense frequently appears to be avoiding the task either by refusing to look at the learning material or seeming without sufficient energy to discriminate the details. The child, for example, may take a quick guess at what a word is in his reading, refusing to attend to anything more than the first letter or other minimal cues.

In a later stage of learning the defense may take the form of rapid, careless reading, involving a failure to attend to certain small words or to include others. Sometimes the meaning will nevertheless be approximated; at others, grossly distorted. One primary purpose here comes to be the immediate establishment of meaning and thereby the exclusion of any other possible meanings.

This kind of defensive operation serves several purposes: by an immediate apprehension of meaning, it shuts out fantasy-arousing alternatives; it re-enforces the sense of omnipotence; and it excludes the perception of effort. It is as if what had been seen as forbidden activity has hardly occurred at all.

We have observed this defensive use of vague overgeneralization in a number of situations. For example, a boy with certain phobic symptoms involving looking at words tended to substitute in his reading synonyms of varying degrees of preciseness, such as **watch** for **clock, evening** for **twilight,** and **very** for **every** for certain words he encountered. He also had difficulty in reading accurately small connective words crucial to the meaning of a sentence or a paragraph.

In an attempt to deal with these difficulties the tutor as an exercise for part of each session would place two vertically arranged series of word cards in parallel on the wall. One series contained difficult words; the other, small words like **each, every,** etc. The boy was asked to read from the bottom to the top of the series in a zigzag manner, from big word to little word and back to big word at a speed he found confortable. At first he read them slowly and haltingly while maintaining a stiff body posture, as if he were trying to inhibit aggressive muscular movement of limbs and hands. As time went on, he read such exercises with increased speed and varying degrees of accuracy as he jumped about excitedly and almost shadowboxed with the words. In the most general sense we inferred from this material that the accurate eye movements that were necessary for the concrete perception of the words were associated with aggressive tendencies to act in the muscles. If we were to cite more material, it would be possible to infer the more personal meanings that the task evoked.

This boy and others like him used a generalized vagueness for other purposes as well. He preserved a picture of his own impulse life and of the family activities as not deviant from those of other people and therefore not troublesome. Intense sadomasochistic involvement with a sibling can be concealed by viewing it as normal rivalry; social deviations in family behavior can retain their mask of normality if one does not examine them too closely.

There are also instances when the child, if he is threatened by certain fantasy-arousing alternatives, focuses on the immediate perception of the meaning of the parts of reading material to the exclusion of the whole. This way of centering on a part of the meaning gives the impression of vagueness and imprecision. It is only when the material is examined in detail that the combination of egocentricity with overemphasis on one detail to the exclusion of the whole becomes apparent.

An adolescent boy with long-standing reading problems who has now attained reasonably good skills read a paragraph from a story about Myra, the salesgirl. The main import of this paragraph was the efficiency of her role as a salesgirl. Additional information included was that she kept a true love magazine under her counter but made no flirtatious efforts to attract the men customers. When offered a choice from a series of alternative answers to a question having to do with the author's main attempt to characterize Myra, the adolescent boy ignored the main point of the paragraph—her good performance of the salesgirl role—and chose instead a statement saying that Myra was disillusioned with men.

He made this judgment regarding the main import of the paragraph rapidly, and it was difficult for his tutor to persuade him to take other statements into account. Our inference here was that sex was salient in his own concerns. In attempting to grasp the meaning he wished to close out rapidly the implication of sexual interest aroused by the reference to the salesgirl's magazine under the counter, and was unable to consider the author's point of view in describing her as a competent salesgirl. Rapid closure of meanings and an inability to take a variety of elements into account have hampered this boy at a later stage of his reading in the same way that some years before in his early school years he was handicapped in his accurate perception of words.

One of his major difficulties then was his tendency to guess at identifying a word using only the first letter as a cue and then whether there were letters extending about or below the line. The use of personally salient detail, rapid closure on meaning, and a quick guess have hampered the synthetic and organizing function of this boy's perception and thought in the reading situation, though in verbally administered tests and his conversation the more mature logic of thought is usually maintained.

Another pre-adolescent boy with phallic-aggressive concerns had, in the process of therapy and special tutoring, managed to achieve good reading skills. At times, however, he tended to substitute a personalized, specific meaning based on his own experience for a more general meaning in the reading material. For example, when trying to answer a question as to where lobster pots were said to be located in a paragraph about a fishing village, he replied, "On the docks," even though the writer of the paragraph had stated specifically that the pots were "everywhere." When the tutor challenged the accuracy of his answer, the boy complained defensively, "But that's where lobster pots are kept. I've seen them on docks." It was extremely difficult for him to discriminate between what the writer had said and his own pictorial imagery. It was as if the questions about the objective content of the reading matter had in reality been directed to his own knowledge of the subject. It looked as though this boy, who could only be secure if everything were concretely in place and immediately perceivable, could not tolerate the vagueness and ambiguities implied by "everywhere."

We should now like to turn our attention in somewhat more detail to the ways in which the cognitive immaturities of such children affect their learning of numbers and some of the coping devices that have proved useful to us in helping them move through the initial stages of learning. The situation of Jack will serve to illustrate our discussion.

Jack is a bright-eyed, well-formed, eight-year-old with dark hair, fine features, and a whimsical, elfish way of presenting himself. A severely neurotic child, suffering from preoccupations with death, annihilation, and destruction, learning for him is fraught with fantasies of castration and punishment related to his anxiety over exercising an active masculine role. Although his Binet performance was at a normal level, there was marked evidence of primitive and quite concrete pictorial thinking. On the similarities test, for example, his responses indicated that he focused on the descriptive details rather than on the properties of the objects to be compared. Further testing revealed no further evidence to raise the question of organicity. He had attended a public school for one year, and he was beginning his second year in a private school. He came to the psychologist for tutoring during his second year of psychotherapy. In school he was unable to attend longer than a few minutes to the simplest of learning tasks. He was unable to obtain even a scorable reading level, and his notion of numbers was extremely primitive.

Although similar tutorial methods were used to help him in reading, we shall discuss the ways in which the tutor attempted to effect the transition from pictorial thinking to a more mature way of dealing with numbers. During the initial stages of tutoring, Jack could count groups of like objects fairly accurately up to ten if he took his time and placed a finger on each object as he counted. He knew the number forms and could print the numbers from one to ten, usually making several reversals. His notion of number forms appeared to function separately from ideas of numbers of objects: for example, the number form "7" was not related to the idea of "7" blocks. In trying to do simple problems like 7-2, he therefore might print a random answer like "1." It was as if the numbers were separate pictures for him, known but not related to definite quantities.

There were various problems present to be dealt with in the tutorial situation. In the first place the association of the numbers with their appropriate quantities needed to be established. Obviously, this little boy had been in school for two years and had had the number work books that should have taught him this association. Therefore we assumed that he was blocked and that the tutor had to devise a method of dealing with this at the start.

Even in the giving interpersonal atmosphere that the tutor set up, the attempts to associate the number forms with blocks or ordinary pictures of objects, such as are used in work books, resulted in unstable associations of number forms and quantity. The presence of possible completing imagery associated with the number forms needed a conceptual system within which these could be taken into account. The tutor devised a way for the child to create his own work book for numbers in which the child did the drawings of what the numbers meant. What emerged shortly was a page of numbers, previously prepared by the tutor as simple problems, in addition to which the child added swords extending uniformly from each number regardless of which number was involved. These swords were actually stereotyped crosses that functioned not as pictures but as signs of the extended swords of a robber. Apparently the sign quality of the numbers was allocated to an impulse toward aggression rather than to an idea of quantity. The tutor in this situation did not take up the aggressive wishes but permitted further elaboration in drawings.

He next began to capitalize on whatever verbal exchanges involving numbers he could encourage. For example he might say, "If I had two chocolate bars, (or horses, or names of objects the child valued) and gave you two chocolate bars, how many would I have left?" Very basically he tried to oppose the pictorial imagery of the child, not by direct confrontation but by attempting to substitute its opposite. It was not long before the child began to apprehend the function of numbers as signs of quantity or related units. The child then was able to add correctly, and at the level of simple one-unit problems he was able to perceive that symbolically the combination of two horses and two candy bars meant he had received four things from his tutor.

Among others some of the important elements in such a tutorial situation have to do with its generally warm and accepting atmosphere, the eliciting of the competing association, and the substitution of opposite imagery that is sufficiently relevant to the child's learning situation to have some chance of attaining saliency over his negative imagery.

During succeeding hours the tutor allowed the child to play with clay and to draw pictures as he presented the child with verbal problems in arithmetic. While the child's phallic-aggressive concerns were being expressed in these media, he was able to give some of his attention to the numbers and their quantitative connotations, apart from the pictorial types of fusions that had earlier prevented their use as signs of quantity. The usual teaching methods involving number cards and explanations of the reversible properties of quantity were used simultaneously with devices that permitted the child to express accompanying fantasies. The gradual development of the child's freedom to use numbers did not proceed in compartmentalized stages. Rather, the tutor had to be sensitive to those times when attention to fantasy expression was most necessary and to the times the child had sufficient energy free to abandon pictorial imagery and deal with the somewhat more abstract aspects of numbers. He then modified his techniques and learning content accordingly. In this way the child was able to consolidate and re-enforce his deepening understanding of the notions of units, constancy and reversibility that are so crucial to the ultimate mastery of arithmetic.

CONCLUSION

In conclusion we should like to speculate briefly about certain problems and issues that have concerned us in the process of preparing this paper. When the psychologist acts as the tutor, he observes the details of an extraordinarily complex situation — one which is not readily explainable in terms of the separate frames of preference we have previously used to conveniently codify certain aspects of the learning process. It becomes apparent that the fundamental relationships within the triad of thought process, fantasy and effect are much more complex than the daily routine of clinical practice or the research in experimental psychology have made explicit. Obviously Piaget's work on syncretion and the part-whole problem in children's thought is relevant as are the psychoanalytic concepts about the operation of unconscious fantasy in producing inhibition. Presently we feel that the concept of association as used either in psychoanalysis or in psychological theory is not sufficiently explicit to be maximally useful. A more careful and intensive study of the particular nature of the associative process in different children in varying motivational states would amplify not only the theoretical frame of reference but also give the tutor a more effective way to intervene in furthering the development of logical thought and precision learning.

It has seemed to us in the course of our clinical observations that modes of thought that appear on first inspection to be dissimilar may in fact be evidences in some children of a determined fastening on detailed pictorial imagery that attemps to exclude more frightening and autistic elements of thought. That is, a more real and socialized pictorial image is being used to exclude motives less socialized and imagery much more primitive and frightening. It is also possible with some children that their imagery is essentially motoric in origin and that an opposed motoric reaction is being used to exclude motoric enervations to action.

We do not mean to be pessimistic about the possibilities of clinical improvement when the therapeutic tutor deals with one or another aspect of the child's total problem, whether it be motivational or cognitive. With some children there can be some symptom relief and some forward movement in their learning. However, when the child's learning difficulties do not yield to the manipulation of the most obvious aspects of his problem, a more exhaustive study of the thought processes and fantasy interaction is in order. Such studies have been of assistance to us in devising tutorial methods that in so far as possible take into account the idiosyncratic aspects of what we have been able to observe about the imagery, the logic, and the unconscious fantasies that have been manifested in the learning errors and difficulties.

Selected References

1. Korstvedt, Arne; Kuhlman, Clementina; Prentice, Norman M.; and Tessman, Ellen. CAUSAL THINKING IN LEARNING DISABILITIES IN LATENCY-AGED BOYS. American Journal of Orthopsychiatry, 1964, 34, 367-368. (No. 2, March). (Digest).

2. Prentice, Norman M. and Sperry, Bessie M. THERAPEUTICALLY ORIENTED TUTORING OF CHILDREN WITH PRIMARY NEUROTIC LEARNING INHIBITIONS. American Journal of Orthopsychiatry, 1965, 35, 521-530. (No. 3, April).

3. Sperry, Bessie M.; Staver, Nancy; and Mann, Harold E. DESTRUCTIVE FANTASIES IN CERTAIN LEARNING DIFFICULTIES. American Journal of Orthopsychiatry, 1952, 22, 356-365, (No. 2, April).

4. Sperry, Bessie M.; Staver, Nancy; Reiner, Beatrice S.; and Ulrich, David. RENUNCIATION AND DENIAL IN LEARNING DIFFICULTIES. American Journal of Orthopsychiatry, 1958, 28, 98-111 (No. 1, January).

5. Wallach, M.; Ulrich, D.; and Grunebaum, Margaret. RELATIONSHIP OF FAMILY DISTURBANCE TO COGNITIVE DIFFICULTIES IN A LEARNING PROBLEM CHILD. Journal of Consulting Psychology, 1960, 24, 355-360. (No. 4, August).

READING, LOGIC, AND PERCEPTION: AN APPROACH TO READING INSTRUCTION

David Elkind, Ph. D.,
Associate Professor of Psychology,
Department of Psychology,
University of Rochester,
Rochester, New York

DAVID ELKIND, Ph.D.

Within psychology, the perceptual aspects of reading are most frequently dealt with as problems in discrimination learning. Although this emphasis is most prominent in the work of Gibson (1965) and her colleagues it is also present in the work of those who have taken a more Skinnerian (e.g., Staats, et al, 1964) approach to reading instruction. This discriminative response orientation to the perceptual aspects of reading is not, however, unique to psychologists and appears to underly the major methods of reading instruction employed in the schools. Both the "Look Say" and the "Phonic" methods of reading instruction seem to be premised on the assumption that the perceptual task in reading is that of discrimination and association. The purpose of the present paper is to present a somewhat different version of the role of perception in reading —a version which derives from the developmental theory of perception propounded by Piaget (1961).

The plan of presentation is as follows: In the first section of the paper, Piaget's theory of perceptual development will be summarized together with research which has been generated by that theory. In the second section, the perceptual processes involved in reading will be analyzed and interpreted from the standpoint of the Piagetian theory and research. Then, in the final section, a method of reading instruction which has grown out of the theory, research and interpretation will be described. It should perhaps be said at this point, that Piaget himself has not been concerned with the problem of reading and that the interpretation of reading which is presented here is not necessarily the way in which he would approach the problem were he to attack it.

THE PIAGET THEORY OF PERCEPTUAL GROWTH

Although Jean Piaget is perhaps best known for his work on conceptual development, he has also elaborated a general theory of perceptual growth (Piaget, 1961). Piaget's theory of perception has two aspects —a psychometric aspect epitomized in the "law of relative centrations" and a qualitative aspect, expressed in the contention that perceptual processes are "partially isomorphic" with those of logic and intelligence (Piaget & Morf, 1958). While Piaget's qualitative theory of perceptual development would seem to have relevance for a wide range of perceptual phenomena, he and his colleagues have limited their research almost entirely to the psychometric aspects of his theory as these can be tested in the study of geometric illusions. The research and teaching procedures described in the present paper derive from an attempt to systematically explore some of the implications of Piaget's qualitative theory of perceptual growth for the perception of meaningful materials.

The qualitative aspect of Piaget's perceptual theory can be briefly summarized. According to Piaget (Piaget & Morf, 1958), the perception of the young child is **centered** in the sense that it is caught and held by the dominant aspects of the visual field. In each particular case, the dominant aspects of the field are determined by Gestalt-like features such as continuity, proximity and closure which Piaget speaks of as **field effects**. With increasing age, however, and the development of perceptual activities (internalized actions), the child's perception becomes increasingly **decentered** in the sense that it is progressively freed from its earlier domination by field effects. This theory can be put more succinctly by saying that, for Piaget, perception in the young child is primarily determined by peripheral sensory processes whereas in the older child and in the adult, central nervous processes come to play the leading role in what is perceived.

This brief sketch of Piaget's theory needs to be amplified somewhat to show its direct relevance to the research described below. First of all, for Piaget, perceptual activities are not all of a kind and include such diverse processes as exploration, reorganization, schematization, transport and anticipation (set). Furthermore, while all of these diverse activities are probably present from the start of life in some vestigial form, they do not apparently all develop at the same rate. That is to say, one and the same child may be more decentered with respect to exploration or transport than he may be with respect to reorganization or schematization. Finally, the degree to which a child is able to decenter in any given situation is always a joint function of the level of maturity of the perceptual activity in question and the strength of the field effects presented by the configuration. In short, decentration is never a once-and-for-all phenomenon but rather is always relative to the particular characteristics of the subject-object interaction.

While this sketch of Piaget's theory is necessarily schematic and incomplete it may nonetheless suffice as a rationale for the research on the various perceptual activities which is described below. The theme which dominates this research is that all perceptual processes can be seen as embodying a kind of logic.

Perceptual Reorganization

Perceptual reorganization has to do with the ability to mentally rearrange a stimulus pattern or array without acting physically upon it. A simple example of such reorganization is the unscrambling of scrambled words. The reader can, for example, identify the color word present in the scrambled letters **lube** by visually rearranging the letters. A similar process is involved in figure-ground reversal where, depending upon the visual arrangement of the elements, different forms are seen.

To assess the development of perceptual reorganization, we have devised a set of ambiguous pictures (Elkind, 1964; Elkind & Scott, 1962) which in theory require perceptual reorganization in order to perceive all the possible figures in the drawings. When these pictures were shown to children at different age levels, it was found that the ability to detect the hidden figures improved regularly with age. The results were thus in keeping with Piaget's theory which predicts that perceptual activities should improve with age (maturation) as well as with experience.

In order to make concrete the way in which logic is involved in perceptual reorganization, consider the "duck in the tree" depicted in figure 1. Let C = the contour line common to the duck and to the tree. Further, let W stand for the white area in the shape of a duck and B stand for the black area in the shape of a tree. Now the organizing activity which permits recognition of the duck can be expressed as follows: $C + W =$ Figure (tree) and $W - C =$ Ground. The reason that these activities are not entirely identical with the operations of logic and intelligence rests in the fact that a possible logical combination, namely, Figure $- B$ (or W) $= C$ is not at the same time a possible perception. A contour line can be conceived as independent of the surrounding areas but it cannot be **perceived** in isolation. Even with this reservation, however, it is clear that perceptual reorganization can be regarded as involving a kind of logic.

Perceptual Schematization

Perceptual schematization has to do with the ability to organize parts and wholes in such a way that both retain their unique identities without at the same time losing their independence. To assess this activity, we have devised a set of seven drawings in which whole figures are made of parts with independent meanings. In one drawing, for example, there is the shape of a man with an apple for a head, a pear for a body, bananas for legs and bunches of grapes for hands. When we presented these drawings to children at different age levels (Elkind, Koegler & Go, 1964) we found that the nursery school children saw only the parts, the kindergarten and first grade children saw only the wholes and the children in the second grade and beyond saw the wholes and parts in combination, e.g. they said, "a man made out of fruit."

On the logical plane, the relations between parts and wholes are frequently determined by logical multiplication. Logical multiplication occurs whenever we form a new class out of two classes which overlap with respect to their membership. The class "American Protestants" can, to illustrate, be thought of as the logical product of the multiplication of the class of Americans by the class of Protestants. Graphically portrayed, the logical product would correspond to the area shared in common by two overlapping circles when these circles represent the classes being multiplied. We know, from our work on religious concepts (Elkind, 1963) that the ability to logically multiply classes such as Protestant and American does not emerge until middle childhood.

Looked at from the standpoint of logic the ability to visually coordinate parts and wholes would also seem to involve a kind of logical multiplication. That is to say, to recognize that a given figure is a "man made out of fruit" the child must recognize that one and the same round form can represent **both** an apple and a head, that one and same pear shape can represent **both** a pear and a torso, etc. This is analogous, on the cognitive plane, to the recognition that a child can be both an American and a Protestant at the same time. In both cases we have the intersection of two classes and the corresponding recognition that an individual can be a member of both classes at the same time. Perceptual schematization, therefore, can also be conceived as a semi-logical process.

Perceptual Exploration

Perceptual exploration has to do with the ability to systematically scan an array or figure so as to note all of its particular features. In order to assess this ability we (Elkind & Weiss, 1967) employed cards upon which pictures of objects familiar to nursery school children were pasted. On one card, the pictures were pasted in a disordered array while on another they were pasted in the form of a triangle. Both cards were then shown to children at different age levels, from four to eight years, who were asked to name every picture on the cards. On the disordered array card there was a regular decrease with age in the number of errors of omission and commission (naming the same object twice). There was also a change in pattern of exploration with age and young children employed an unsystematic scattered pattern of exploration, while older children scanned the array systematically from left to right and from top to bottom.

With respect to the card upon which the objects were pasted in a triangular array, the results were surprising. While the young children and the oldest children followed the triangular pattern, the first grade children read the pictures from left to right. This suggested that in the course of learning the left to right swing required for reading, the first grade children spontaneously practiced it where it was not, at least from the adult point of view, appropriate. Among the older children, in whom the left-right pattern had become automatic, this spontaneous practice dropped out. These results suggest that even when older children and adults explore in a manner dictated by Gestalt principles, this is genotypically a different response than that of young children. Older children and adults follow the triangular pattern because they **choose to** while younger children follow it because **they have no alternative.**

It might seem, at first glance, that these patterns of exploration have nothing whatever to do with logic. To illustrate that logic-like processes are involved, consider the problem of scanning the disordered array card. To scan such an array in a systematic manner so as to avoid both errors of omission and of commission the child must, in effect, organize the various pictures into a **serial order.** Only if the child establishes such a serial order can he succeed on the task. But the establishment of a serial order is already a semi-logical process and corresponds to a rank ordering of events; A B C D... etc. Here again an apparently simple perceptual performance can be viewed as encompassing a much more complicated form of perceptual action.

Work on other perceptual activities such as transport and anticipation could be described, but the foregoing should suffice to illustrate the fact that many different types of perceptual performance can be viewed as involving a kind of logic. Indeed, as the following section will show, many of the simplest perceptual aspects of reading can be viewed as semi-logical problems.

PERCEPTUAL ACTIVITY AND READING

Once perception is regarded as involving its own form of logic, the perceptual hurdles in learning to read appear in an entirely new light. Consider, for example, the problem so prominent in English phonics, namely, that one and the same letter can represent more than one sound, while one and the same sound can be represented by more than one letter. This is a hard fact to deal with from the discriminative response point of view, since it requires an explanation of how the subject comes to make different responses to the same stimulus at different times. That the problem is not primarily one of discrimination has been clearly demonstrated by the success of the Pitman (cf. e.g., Downing, 1963) International Teaching Alphabet (ITA). From a purely discriminative response point of view, this alphabet should present the child with more difficulty than the English alphabet, first because it has 40 rather than twenty-six characters and second because all of the characters are unfamiliar. Yet children find the ITA easier than the English alphabet.

If the Pitman alphabet does not aid discrimination, how does it help the young reader? One answer to this question comes from looking at the ITA from the point of view of the logical problem it enables the child to avoid. Looked at logically, the recognition that the same letter can represent different sounds and that the same sound can be designated by different letters poses a problem of logical multiplication analagous to that previously described in the discussion of whole-part perception. Once the child can perform logical multiplications (i.e. schematizations) on the perceptual plane, he can arrive at all possible combinations of letters and sounds and, on the basis of experience, rule out those which do not occur in his language. Prior to this stage, however, the child should encounter all sorts of difficulties in dealing with the vicariousness of letter and sound combinations. In short, according to the analysis presented here, the Pitman ITA aids the young reader by eliminating the need for perceptual activities.

It should be said, however, that perceptual activities are important beyond the initial stages in the acquisition of reading skill. The ability to construct spatial seriations, for example, is clearly essential for comprehending the grammatical significance of word order. Reorganization, likewise, would seem to be important to the analysis and comprehension of new words. In the same way, schematization of part and whole would appear to play an important role in dealing with prefixes and suffixes and with the tense and pluralization transformations of words. Finally, effective rapid reading would seem to require the ability to quickly explore and correctly anticipate (infer) words and sentences.

At all levels of reading skill, therefore, whether at the level of letter and sound combinations or at the level of advanced reading and comprehension, perceptual activities seem to be involved. This is not a mere supposition. In one study (Elkind, Horn & Schneider, 1965) we gave children at different age levels a battery of tests which included measures of perceptual activity included, in addition to the figurative tests of reorganization and schematization already described, tests of the ability to read upside down and to unscramble words. A factor analysis of the data indicated that, at all age levels, there was a common factor which underlay performance on the various tests. That this common factor was not merely a general intelligence factor was shown by still another study. In this investigation (Elkind, Larson and Van Doorninck, 1965) slow and average readers, matched for intelligence, were pre-tested, trained and re-tested with respect to reorganizing activities. The results showed that the slow readers were deficient with respect to perceptual activity both initially and after training in comparison with the average readers. It seems reasonable to assume, then, that perceptual activity—in the generic sense—is an important factor in reading achievement.

TRAINING IN PERCEPTUAL ACTIVITY

The foregoing analysis of the role of perceptual activity in reading, together with the research data, suggests that such activities are involved in reading failure as well as in reading success. Good readers appear to have well developed perceptual activities whereas slow readers appear to be deficient in this regard. Accordingly, it seems reasonable to suppose that training in perceptual activity might be of benefit to at least some retarded readers. The exercises described below were specifically designed for such children but might be beneficial for all children at an early stage in the acquisition of reading skill.

Before presenting the exercises in detail, a few introductory remarks are in order. First of all, the exercises are by no means to be construed as a total reading program. Indeed, they are best thought of as comparable to playing scales when learning to play the piano. While the practice of such scales is essential for dexterity and control, such practice can in no way take the place of instruction in fingering, timing and expression. In the same way, the exercises described here would seem to be beneficial in limbering up the child's perceptual muscles, so to speak, but they do not eliminate the need for training, in phonics, vocabulary and comprehension.

In addition, the exercises are designed for classroom use and as an adjunct rather than as a replacement for other classroom procedures. The exercises are non-verbal so that children are forced to attend to the blackboard and to use their eyes. Finally, the exercises require no special training on the part of teachers nor do they require any special materials. Once the teachers grasp the principles involved, it should be easy for them to construct additional exercises along the same lines. In short, the exercises are designed as a readily utilizable tool which teachers can add to their existing storehouse of methods and which they can use whenever they feel such exercises are needed.

The exercises described here are specifically for second grade children but simpler exercises are available for younger age groups and more difficult exercises can be constructed for older age groups. Although the exercises are most effective with small groups, say of fifteen children, they can be used with an entire classroom. In general the exercises are designed to get children to explore, reorganize, schematize and anticipate perceptual figures and arrays. Furthermore, the exercises are designed so that the child's task is to find the nature of the problem as well as the solution. In these exercises, once the problem is known the solution usually follows as a matter of course.

To introduce the exercises, the teacher tells the children that "we are going to play a kind of game in which no one talks. I am going to put some things on the board and you have to figure out what should come next. If you think you know the answer raise your hand and I will call on you by pointing to you with the chalk. Then you come to the board and write the answer. Remember, the important part about this game is that you cannot ask questions and that I cannot tell you anything more than what is on the board."

An easy exercise with which to begin is a simple series such as the alphabet or number series. For example, it is helpful to begin a session with the following series A B C D E _____ on the board. After pointing to the vacant space with the chalk one or another child who has raised his hand can be called to the board. Most children get the idea immediately but it is useful to continue for a number of letters to insure that all the children understand the game. The same procedure can be used with number series. This exercise can be varied by moving backwards e.g., Z Y X W _____ or by putting down every other letter i.e., A C E G ____ . For younger children circle faces and stick figures can be used whereas for an older child more complex series can be employed (e.g., ABC BCD CDE DEF). Note that these exercises train children both in left to right exploration and in serial relationships.

The following is an exercise in visual reorganization. Several words are put on the board which are meaningful when written either forward or backward. For example:

WAS = SAW
TAR = RAT
PIT = ____

A whole series of words of this kind can be used. Similar to this exercise is another in which scrambled words are employed. Starting with a class of words (an orienting set is helpful) the following task can be presented:

ENT   = TEN
RUFO   = FOUR
OTW   = ____

Second grade children seldom have difficulty with such problems which provide good training in visual organization and reorganization. The scrambled word exercises can be repeated with other classes of words such as fruits, numbers, etc.

To train children in transport activities a coding exercise is entertaining as well as effective. On the top of the board one puts the following:

1 2 3 4 5 6 7 8
E T S H A P L I

and then:

482 = HIT
382 = SIT
452 = ___

Quite clearly, many different kinds of codes could be set up but this is an easy one that works well. These exercises train children both in transporting symbols across space and in vicarious symbolism and representation.

Still another class of exercises are designed to develop the child's schematizing abilities as well as his understanding of logical symbols and relations. An illustration of this type of exercise is as follows:

$$\triangle \;+\; \square \;=\; \text{⌂}$$
$$◇ \;+\; \text{∞}_{000} \;=\; ◇\text{-}_{0000}$$
$$\bigcirc \;+\; \text{人} \;=\; \underline{\hspace{2cm}}$$

In addition to whole part schematization one can also move from pictographic to verbal representation:

$$\bigcirc \;=\; \text{SUN}$$
$$\text{☽} \;=\; \text{MOON}$$
$$\text{◑} \;=\; \underline{\hspace{1.5cm}}$$

Note that in these exercises the left to right and top to bottom patterns of exploration are also reinforced.

Additional exercises can be used to provide training in tenses, pluralization and phonics as well as in perceptual activities. Here is an exercise in rhyming:

RAT	HAT
LIKE	BIKE
HIT	SIT
SUN	___

And another in pluralization:

HAT	HATS
TOE	TOES
BOOT	BOOTS
FOOT	_____

And still another in tenses:

HAS	HAD
DO	DID
IS	___

By making such exercises non-verbal one insures that the child is actually attending to the printed work and to the perceptual as well as grammatical relations involved.

Although many more exercises could be described, these should suffice to illustrate the method in a general way. Indeed, once teachers are given the underlying principles involved most can make up their own exercises as they go along. In this connection a couple of practical "tips" are perhaps in order. We have found that about one half hour of such exercises a day is sufficient to produce some effect and not so long as to produce boredom and disinterest. It is also well to vary the nature of the exercise frequently within allotted time period. Finally, once the children are accustomed to the exercises and the procedures, it is instructive to allow the children themselves to go to the board and act as teacher.

These then are the non-verbal exercises in perceptual activity. All of the exercises have value in the sense that they force the child to attend to the visual materials and to uncover the relations involved. In a very real sense, then, these exercises could be regarded as a **discovery** method of reading instruction.

CONCLUSION

The purpose of the present paper was threefold: a) to summarize the Piagetian theory of perceptual development and the research on that theory as it pertains to the response to figurative materials; b) to interpret the perceptual aspects of reading from the standpoint of the Piagetian theory and research; and c) to present a set of exercises for training children in perceptual activity which could be used in conjunction with established methods of reading instruction.

If the approach to reading described here has any unique feature, it is the emphasis upon the logical character of even the simplest perceptual processes involved in reading. At all levels of reading skill perceptual activities, which in their mode of operation resemble logical processes, seem to play a significant role. Training in such perceptual activities would, therefore, seem to be a beneficial adjunct to reading instruction.

It should be said, before closing, that the efficacy of the training procedures described here is currently being tested with large groups of children over a relatively long time period (12 weeks). In addition, the usefulness of the perceptual activity measures in diagnosing and predicting reading difficulties is also being explored on a large scale. In short, the present paper might be regarded as an interim report on an ongoing research program which hopes to detail still further the significance of Piaget's theory of perceptual growth for reading instruction and achievement.

References

1. Downing, J.A. THE AUGMENTED ROMAN ALPHABET FOR LEARNING TO READ. The Reading Teacher, 16:325-336, 1963.

2. Elkind, D. THE CHILD'S CONCEPTION OF HIS RELIGIOUS DENOMINATION III: THE PROTESTANT CHILD. Journal of Genetic Psychology, 103: 291-304, 1963.

3. Elkind, D. AMBIGUOUS PICTURES FOR THE STUDY OF PERCEPTUAL DEVELOPMENT AND LEARNING. Child Development, 35:1391-1396, 1964.

4. Elkind, D., Horn, J., & Schneider, Gerrie. MODIFIED WORD RECOGNITION, READING ACHIEVEMENT AND PERCEPTUAL DE-CENTRATION. Journal of Genetic Psychology, 107:235-251, 1965.

5. Elkind, D., Koegler, R.R., & Go, Elsie. STUDIES IN PERCEPTUAL DEVELOPMENT II: PART-WHOLE PERCEPTION. Child Development, 35:81-90, 1964.

6. Elkind, D., Larson, Margaret, E., & Van Doorninck, W. PERCEPTUAL LEARNING AND PERFORMANCE IN SLOW AND AVERAGE READERS. Journal of Educational Psychology, 56:no. 1. 50-56, 1965.

7. Elkind, D., & Weiss, Jutta. STUDIES IN PERCEPTUAL DEVELOPMENT III: CHILD DEVELOPMENT, (in press).

8. Gibson, Eleanor, J. LEARNING TO READ. Science, 148:1066-1072, 1965.

9. Piaget, J., & Morf, A. LES PREINFERENCES PERCEPTIVES ET LEURS RELATIONS AVEC LES SCHEMES SENSORI-MOTEURS ET OPERATOIRES. In J. Piaget (Ed.), Etudes d'epistemologie genetique, vol. VI. Paris: Presses Universitaires de France, 1958.

10. Piaget, J. LES MECANISMES PERCEPTIFS. Paris: Presses Universitaires de France, 1961.

11. Staats, A.W., Minke, K.A., Finley, J.R., Wolf, M., & Brooks, L. A REINFORCER SYSTEM AND EXPERIMENTAL PROCEDURE FOR THE LABORATORY STUDY OF READING ACQUISITION. Child Development, 35:209-231, 1964.

REINFORCEMENT THERAPY:
A SYMPTOMATIC APPROACH TO TEACHING
EMOTIONALLY DISTURBED CHILDREN

Levi Lathen,
formerly of Elgin Illinois Public Schools,
Elgin, Illinois

LEVI LATHEN

FORWARD

The role of special education as related to emotionally disturbed children is to many an ambiguous one. The ambiguity of this role too often leads some potentially good special teachers into formulation of unrealistic goals for themselves, to the extent of excluding the role for which they are trained and best qualified to assume (teaching). The value of successful school performance should not be ignored nor go unrecognized as a means of reconditioning behavior. School success, after a history of failure, can provide a common denominator for the reconditioning of attitudes toward school, peers, teachers, academics and oneself. Success in school generalizes to the home to symbolize success for parents. This success may alter parent's attitudes and lead to a greater degree of acceptance and recognition of desirable character traits formerly overshadowed by failure and defensiveness on the part of the child. Those teachers who downgrade or fail to recognize the value of success in academic performance as a medium through which behavior may be reconditioned, do themselves and their profession a disservice.

A recent interview with a teacher of emotionally disturbed children clearly indicated her confusion and ambiguity in role definition. Her confusion and indecisiveness of role leads her to view academics as a repulsive aspect of the child's present, past and future adjustment in which success should not be pursued. She states her objective as being that of teaching children to live, was not sure how she would accomplish this monumental task, but was sure that she would not attempt it through academics. She proceeded to describe herself as an expert who is unorthodox in her teaching methodism. When asked, "How do you teach children to live?" her reply was that it depends upon the child, and proceeded to state that she may teach a child to play a good game of poker, adding that she would see that he won. It was not difficult to agree that she was unorthodox in her approach, but was very difficult to understand how she could seriously consider such an all-encompassing objective of teaching children to live. Teaching a child to play poker may be therapeutic if intended to provide a success experience, but this does not constitute teaching one to live.

Without a doubt, this teacher who labels herself an expert is confused in her role. She is not a teacher, but a self-styled social worker, psychologist, psychiatrist, neurologist and pediatrician whose role it is to teach children to live. She assumes all of the responsibilities of home, church, community, character development agencies and professional organizations concerned with behavioral deviations in children. She completely ignores personal introaction, which does not include herself, as being important in "teaching children to live." This seems to be an omnipotent role for any one person to assume regardless as to how much of an expert he or she thinks herself to be. It is conversely idiotic to think that academics should be considered an unessential part of a child's life to be avoided because of unfavorable predisposition in this area. It would seem that a more therapeutic approach would be that of reconditioning attitudes toward school and academics in an effort to evolve a more positive response to a formerly threatening area of adjustment. This can most effectively be done by accepting a child at his level of achievement and planning success experiences of an academic nature for him. Planned success experiences in an area of inadequacy eliminates much of the threat that may exist in such unfavorably predisposed area of adjustment. The contributions of a teacher to a child's life adjustment can most effectively be made through the medium of academic success, which depends heavily upon the teacher's ability to establish rapport, recognize needs and plan successful reconditioning behavioral experiences.

The teacher who deprives a child of love and acceptance deprives him of an education. The child will surely rebel under such conditions. It is equally true that a teacher who deprives a child of successful academic experiences deprives him of those bits of knowledge that will permit him to form healthy attitudes about school and precipitated life situations. She too deprives the child of an education. Acceptance and planned successful educational experiences appear to be the major ingredients for re-enforced educational therapy.

When children are admitted to the special classes for emotionally disturbed the first concern is to get a good educational diagnosis. The educational diagnosis consists of five levels.

    I. Determination of capacity for learning which includes:
       1. Intelligence testing
       2. Personality evaluation

    II. Achievement evaluation

    III. Comparison of achievement and capacity for achievement

    IV. Analysis of diagnosis

    V. Plan for remediation based on an analysis of the diagnosis

At **Level I** an assessment of capacity for learning is made. Assessment of capacity for learning includes an evaluation of personality and determination of intellectual functioning. This information forms the basis for setting what is hoped to be attainable realistic behavioral and academic goals. **At Level II** an answer to the question, "Where to begin academically with the child?", is sought. An answer to this question requires an assessment of academic achievement. The concern, at this level, is limited to determination of **level of academic functioning** in reading, spelling and arithmetic. **At Level III** a comparison of achievement with potential for achievement is made to determine degree of academic retardation. Chronological age is insignificant at this level. Our concern is how does the child's achievement relate to his present capacity for achievement and what should we expect academically of him on the basis of this comparison.

Typically there is a discrepancy between achievement and intellectual functioning. **At Level IV** we make an analysis of this discrepancy in an effort to find defective skill areas that may be depressing achievement, and thus creating the existing deficit. This analysis consists of assessment of communication skills, diagnostic testing of reading, arithmetic and spelling, and evaluation of perceptual skills. Acquisition of guide lines for an objective plan of remediation is the end result of the analysis. **At Level V** an individualized plan for remediation based upon analysis of the diagnosis is devised. This outline (p. 51) is not limited to reading but provides guidelines for the remediation of behavior, linguistic disabilities and deficit academic skills.

BEHAVIORAL DEVIATIONS AND CLASSROOM CONTROLS

To this date no one has been able to supply us with a solution to the management and training of deviations in children. Many causes have been postulated, some of which are; cerebral dysfunction, perceptual disorder, cultural deprivation, emotional disturbance, minimal brain injury and a host of others. In all cases these terms imply causative factors relating to internal malfunctioning with an organic basis and/or external environmental conditioning encompassing, among other generalized conditions, those of neglect rejection, overprotection, inadequate conditioning and improper conditioning.

Indicated causation in the form of broad generalizations is difficult if not impossible to incorporate and use effectively in the practical application of school instruction; however, it appears to be a necessary and important first step. Diagnostic classification (which postulates causation for behavioral deviations and academic retardation) and generalizations relating to predisposed conditioning deficiencies (such as neglect, overprotection, etc.) create a basis from which an analysis of a diagnosis may emanate leading to detection and remediation of specific behavioral and academic deficiencies.

It is important that the educator define his role clearly and become proficient within the confines of these limitations. It is equally important and obvious that we cannot be all things to all children, nor can any discipline assume such an all-encompassing role. Though we are concerned with development of the whole child, it would seem that as educators we are properly trained and primarily concerned about the area of education, which encompasses management, training and remediation of behavioral and academic deviations as related to the school and as opposed to research endeavors which seek primarily to determine causation. Hopefully the influence of education will generalize to many activities and aspects of development outside of the educational setting. However, a job well done in the area of education is far better than a poor one attempted in both education and related areas.

Our (educators) overconcern about determination of causation often leads us into investigation of aspects of the child's development in which we are not properly trained to investigate. This overconcern and misdirected effort can be held in check when we are knowledgeable of the fact that other disciplines are equally concerned about different aspects of the child's development, some of whom are better trained to investigate causation such as the neurologist, psychiatrist, psychologist and pediatrician. There is need to consolidate the efforts of all disciplines working with separable aspects of **child development**, and to utilize this information for the welfare of the whole child. This cannot be done by a single person; but perhaps can be attempted by experts in all areas working as a team. Neurologists are attempting to correlate learning disabilities and are studying such constructs as motivation, attention, perception, sets and the like; educational psychologists are endeavoring to test and synthesize findings from neurology, psychiatry, pediatrics and psychology. While research is being conducted the educator is confronted with the problem, namely the child, and must make a determination as to what to do here and now on the basis of present evidence of malfunctioning. It would appear that out of necessity we (educators) must deal with psychological correlates until such time that information from the above disciplines can be compiled and synthesized to give us clearer indication of causation.

The purpose of this chapter is therefore not to postulate causation for emotional disturbance, as important as this may be, but to describe behavioral, intellectual, academic and linguistic disabilities of a group of diagnostically classified emotionally disturbed children; and to enumerate the controls and training procedures used to help them compensate for their emotional handicap.

Admittedly, the cause for emotional disturbance, except in broad general terms which are not unique to this diagnostic classification, is not known. However, psychological correlates or symptomatic behavior is probably directly related to **causations** or **etiology**. Through the reconditioning of deviant behavior and academic retardation we hope to indirectly but positively **alter the effect** of negatively predisposed factors in the child's past history of life striving, and to counterbalance present negative valances.

Existing Special Classes For Emotionally Disturbed Children In The Elgin Public Schools

The first class for emotionally disturbed children was opened in the fall of 1964. The children admitted to the class had not been able to make a desirable adjustment to regular class placement, but it was believed that they could profit from special class placement and a residential setting. It was generally agreed that these children would require placement outside of the home environment if they were to profit from that which was to be offered in the special class. Children in these classes are not physically handicapped, they are not mentally retarded, they are not delinquents and they do not have sensory handicaps such as blindness or deafness. These are children who are emotionally handicapped. They deviate in behavior and psychological development to such an extent that they have not been able to make a desirable adjustment at home or at school or learn in school by ordinary teaching methods. They have not learned to express their emotions effectively, flexibly and appropriately to achieve goals and solve problems.

In the special classes for emotionally disturbed children we have assumed the role of trying to determine the nature and extent of disabilities experienced. On the basis of this information we endeavor to construct a program of remediation to "train in" or "build in" skills which are deficient.

Behavioral Deviations and Environmental Controls

Based on psychological evaluations and controlled classroom observations, it appears that the most typical behavioral deviations of children in these classes emanate from their inability to solve problems directly. The result of this disability is that the children have learned to be defensive or they are in the process of learning to be defensive and guarded in their behavior. If a child cannot solve problems directly and make integrative substitute adjustments when direct problem solving is not possible, he then faces humiliation and self-devaluation by his peers, parents, teachers and all associates. A major objective of defensive behavior is to defend against humiliation and self-devaluation. A child who cannot read may use aggression as a mode of behavior to divert attention from this disability; another may use withdrawal to avoid becoming involved in situations that will reveal deficiencies; and still another may use dependency as a mode of behavior to gain strength from others and disguise his shortcomings.

A diagram of the social adjustment process will give indications of some of the behavioral deviations and deficiencies that prevail.

*THE SOCIAL ADJUSTMENT PROCESS

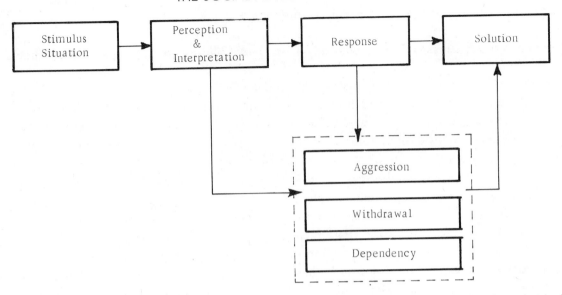

This diagram shows that a stimulus situation is created, it is perceived and interpreted by the individual; on the basis of his perception and interpretation he makes a response leading to a direct solution of the problem. If he is unable to make a response leading to a direct solution, he then (on the basis of perception and interpretation of the situation) selects to use aggression, withdrawal or dependency as a mode of behavior to overcome barriers and achieve a solution to the problem. On the basis of perception and interpretation of the situation he knows whether to use aggression, withdrawal or dependency and how much of which to use to achieve his objective.

The well adjusted individual has learned through a gradual process of conditioning how to solve numerous problematic situations at a direct level. He knows on the basis of past experiences when to use aggression, withdrawal and/or dependency. He also knows how much of which to use depending upon the situation. He can make integrative substitute adjustments and give up unattainable goals. This seems not to be true for emotionally disturbed children. They are unable to solve problems directly and they are unable to use aggression, withdrawal and dependency effectively to solve problems. Through a process of conditioning by way of failure experiences, lack of exposure and improper conditioning the children have learned to use a single pattern of behavior rigidly and often inappropriately to meet problematic situations. Threatening, problematic situations are frequently precipitated by generalized inadequacies.

Learning to be Emotionally Insecure

When a child is learning to be emotionally insecure he is learning to be threatened by many precipitated social situations, and to be defensive in many situations that would otherwise be viewed by him as non-threatening. It seems that the total objective of his behavior is not to solve specific problems but to defend against threatening situations.

*L. Lathen, CONCEPT OF SOCIAL ADJUSTMENT

He uses aggression to ward off people and divert attention from his shortcomings. Withdrawal is used to move away from people and avoid becoming involved in situations that reveal inadequacies; and he uses dependency to move toward people in effort to gain strength from them which he does not have, and to disguise his deficiencies. In all cases, behavior is intended to protect the self, rather than solve the problem. Socially acceptable solutions to problems is but one method of adjusting as the emotionally disturbed child has discovered. He may make adjustments that are socially unacceptable that succeed in avoiding or relieving tension. Substitute satisfaction can be derived from being the worst in the class, which may represent an adjustment if it reduces tension.

Stages of Defensiveness

During the process of learning to be insecure and to be defensive one passes through perhaps two stages. These stages are the **Varied Response Stage** and the **Fixed Response Stage**. A diagram of defensive behavior of emotionally disturbed children observed in Elgin's special classes is as follows:

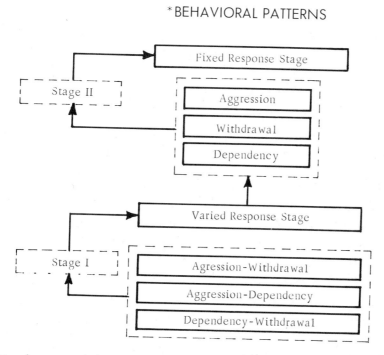

*BEHAVIORAL PATTERNS

Vacillation from one behavioral pattern to another in effort to find the mode of behavior that can effectively reduce tension and anxiety typifies the **varied response stage**. Without any abrupt change a **fixed response stage** evolves, at which a rigid pattern of behavior that seems to reduce tension most effectively is acquired.

*L. Lathen, DEFENSIVE BEHAVIOR PATTERNS

The pattern of behavior selected is used to meet most problematic situations and to defend against strong feelings of inadequacy and inferiority. Within the confines of overly developed patterns of behavior is to be found specific symptoms of strong feelings of inadequacy and inferiority: The child shows extreme sensitivity to criticism, he resents direct or implied evaluation of personal qualities, he finds it difficult to react constructively to criticism, he applies most criticism to himself, he reacts poorly to competition, and he has a tendency to be derogative of others. As sophistication in the use of a defense pattern is gained all signs of inferiority and inadequacy may become submerged under the pattern of behavior.

After working in a teaching capacity with emotionally disturbed children for some years, patterns of aggression, withdrawal and dependency are apparent without careful scrutiny and study of behavior. For the neophyte teacher and those who have not used this approach to reconditioning deviate behavior patterns it is necessary to define the patterns of behavior that have been discussed in this paper and to observe carefully for indicated symptoms. It should be pointed out that aggression, withdrawal and dependency are used to make substitute adjustment but are also used to overcome barriers and arrive at direct solutions to problems.

In the process of learning to read, a child is required to use aggression, withdrawal and dependency. To attack a reading task directly is an aggressive act; for the child to recognize that he does not know certain words and cannot sound them out is a with-drawing act, and to ask for help and assistance for those words not known is a dependent act. Learning to read requires that one use such behavior flexibly and appropriately. Because this behavior has long-term value for the child it is considered integrative. Integrative behavior encompasses appropriate expression of aggression, withdrawal and dependency.

Non-integrative aggression exhibited by emotionally disturbed children may generally be described as **unchecked expansion** of the basic and essential behavioral pattern of aggression. It is characterized by persistent and intense aggression directed against people in threatening situations (many situations are threatening for a disturbed child). It alienates and angers others and does not lead to a direct or integrative substitute solution to existing problems. It is characterized by overemotionalism and overt hyperactivity. A child who displays unchecked aggression is explosive, impulsive and wants immediate ego satisfaction. He must learn to postpone ego gratification.

Non-integrative withdrawal is considered an overexpansion of withdrawal or isolation tendencies that are persistent and intense. Such a child is thought of as shy, timid and otherwise constricted in social introactions; he is typically a fringer and fearful of becoming involved in situations. Unlike the aggressive child whose behavior is directed against people, the withdrawn child directs his behavior away from people. The expression of his emotions are directed inward, causing them to often be later expressed in the form of hypochondrical reactions with potentials for psychosomatic illnesses or psychosis. Such a child is in many instances more severely ill than the aggressive, acting-out child.

Non-integrative dependency is the overexpansion of a behavioral pattern which moves toward people. This pattern of behavior is persistent and intense. The major characteristic of the dependent child is the absence or near absence of aggression and withdrawal in his behavior. Often he is considered a "bother" because he is forever seeking support, assistance and reassurance from those around him. He eagerly and frequently becomes involved in academic and social situations, but is as frequently incapable of independently coping with the situations. He disguises his inadequacies by persistently asking for help and reinforcement in his endeavors, thus gaining strength and stability from others which he does not possess.

On the basis of behavioral patterns observed and supporting psychological evidence, the general diagnostic classification of Emotionally Disturbed may be sub-divided into six less general classifications or types:

Emotionally Disturbed Type A — **Aggression - withdrawal**

Emotionally Disturbed Type B — **Aggression - dependency**

Emotionally Disturbed Type C — **Withdrawal - dependency**

Emotionally Disturbed Type D — **Aggression**

Emotionally Disturbed Type E — **Withdrawal**

Emotionally Disturbed Type F — **Dependency**

L. Lathen — Types of emotional disturbances

APPROACH TO RECONDITIONING BEHAVIORAL PATTERNS

Theoretical knowledge of these disabilities, based upon observations and psychological evaluation, is but the first step in the direction of helping the children. The crucial question that remains unanswered is what do we do about it. Our approach to changing rigid, overly developed patterns of behavior is to evoke and reward underdeveloped patterns of behavior. However, our first objective is to teach basic academic skills that permit problem solving of an academic nature directly. If the child cannot read, we want to teach him to read. He will then not have the need to be defensive when called upon to read in the presence of his peers. Secondly, we endeavor to evoke and reward underdeveloped patterns of behavior in an effort to establish a delicate balance between aggression, withdrawal and dependency that permits the use of each behavioral pattern flexibility, effectively and appropriately to make substitute adjustments and to find socially accepted solutions to problems.

The behavioral objective for a child who vacillates from aggression to withdrawal is to evoke and reward dependency. Such a child should learn to ask for help and assistance when needed. It is our objective to teach him to do this. Children who vacillate from aggression to dependency should be taught to lower expectations and to give up unattainable goals, while we are teaching basic skills that will make the attainment of the goals possible at a later date. We must therefore, evoke and reward withdrawal. We want to evoke and reward responses of aggression for children who display a dependency-withdrawal pattern. Such a child requires assistance in finding integrative outlets for the expression of his emotions. The behavioral goal at the Fixed Response Stage (fig. 2) is the same as that of the Varied Response Stage. We try to teach basic academic skills and "build in" or "train in" behavioral responses that are not being utilized.

Specific Behavioral Characteristics Affecting Classroom Achievement

It is important to have knowledge of general patterns of behavior that negatively effect adjustment; it is equally important to have knowledge of specific behavioral characteristics found within these patterns that adversely affect classroom performance. Many of these characteristics are obvious to the objective observer. One such major characteristic is distractibility. Any visual, auditory or tactil stimuli is sufficient to distract many of the children, regardless as to how unrelated it may be to what they are doing. Distractable children must learn not to respond to unessential, extraneous stimuli. Though it appears that they are inattentive, the fact is they are overly attentive. They focus their attention on everything but on nothing long enough for learning to take place.

Distractibility may be displayed by way of **Motor Disinhibition**; which is an inability to refrain from responding to anything that can be pushed, pulled, folded, twisted or thrown. Manipulative objects automatically evoke a motor response from such a child. Distractibility may also be expressed in the form of **Dissociation** which is an inability to perceive and interpret situations as a whole or a unit. Such a child sees stimulus situations in part and therefore responds to such situations in part rather than as a whole. He has difficulty following instructions given by the teacher in the sequential order given. It is highly probable that he will hear the first part of the instructions and miss other parts. In his reading there is likely to be many reversals, omissions and substitutions. He typically is unable to screen out important information from his reading to answer related questions. Distractibility may be displayed in the form of **Figure Background Disturbances**. This disability can be most clearly understood only when we are cognizant of the fact that the brain can absorb only a small portion of the mass of visual stimuli it is "bombarded" with. That which we focus our attention on becomes the figure, while the mass of stimuli go to make up the background.

> i.e.
> When Mary is bouncing a ball on the playground, she focuses her attention on the ball which becomes the figure. The swing, sandbox and other playground apparatus she is only sufficiently aware of to avoid colliding with. This forms the background.

Many children have difficulty differentiating the figure from the background. They may reverse figure and background or they may be unable to change with ease from one figure to another or they may confuse figure and background. The distortions and confusions produced by this disturbance would make it difficult if not impossible for any child to learn in school regardless of how intelligent he may be.

Perseveration is a second major characteristic of emotionally disturbed children. One who perseverates is unable to change with ease from one psychological activity to another. The teacher and the class are always just a slight distance ahead of such a child in all activities. Typically he is one who requests that assignments be repeated. He is still concerned about reading after the class has been working on English the past ten minutes. He does not change sets rapidly and therefore reads sluggishly and slowly often repeating words. For such a child there is an overlap in time between the shift from an old to a new situation. A third characteristic is that of **Body Image Concept**. Poor body image concept is apparent when we look at the distorted figures drawn by the children, representing people. It is hypothesized by Cruickshank, Frostig and many others, that good body image is necessary before one can develop a good self concept and that until a good self concept is developed learning of all kind will be significantly retarded. Within the confines of these behavioral characteristics and behavioral patterns there is sufficient room for variability and individual differences. The characteristics thus far described and behavioral patterns discussed may be typical of emotionally disturbed children but they are not unique to this diagnostic classification.

Environmental Controls for Behavioral Characteristics

We cannot do anything about the internal workings of the children which causes them to feel inadequate and to be defensive when they enter the special classes, but we can manipulate the physical environment to the extent that it helps them to compensate for their disabilities. Since distractibility is a dominant characteristic, the children must learn not to respond to unessential environmental stimuli, and we must help them compensate for this disability by controlling, as much as possible, distraction in the classroom and immediate physical environment. If a child has poor sight and is diagnostically classified **partially seeing**, we provide him with glasses and large print, among other adjustments, to help him compensate for this disability. If he is hard of hearing we amplify sounds for him by way of hearing aids and make other environmental adjustments and allowances for his specific disability. It would seem logical that if a child is distractable there is a need to reduce unessential environmental stimuli. For this reason, the classroom is painted a neutral color, drapes are used at the windows to shut out unessential auditory and visual stimuli, carpeting is used to reduce the noise level in the study area.

As space increases the amount of stimuli within the space increases proportionately; as space decreases the amount of stimuli within the space decreases proportionately. It is then possible to reduce the amount of extraneous stimuli within a given physical setting by reducing space. To reduce space and decrease unessential stimuli within the learning environment we use 4 x 4 cubicles which we call offices. No instructional materials, toys, trinkets, pictures or other unrelated stimuli is kept in these offices. The children need a quiet, relaxed physical environment in which to function if they are to compensate for the disability that exists.

Since they have been unable to keep still long enough for learning to take place, we believe that the children need a highly structured school day. The class is initially completely teacher directed with a time and a place for all things considered essential. The teacher must therefore have knowledge of potential for achievement, level of achievement and rate of expected academic progress if she is to set attainable, realistic goals which lead to reconditioning success experiences.

The children are distracted by stimuli, therefore, it is logical to make the assumption that they can be attracted to stimuli that is purposely organized and increased in stimulus value. For this reason, into the dull, bleak, unstimulating physical setting of the cubicle which we call an office, we insert controlled stimulus instructional materials on which attention is to be focused. Since unessential stimuli has been decreased the probability that the child will focus his attention on the specially prepared stimulus material is increased proportionately.

We believe that we are helping children compensate for their disabilities, and that they are gradually internalizing the external controls that are being exerted. As they learn to attend to the routine of the day and experience academic success they are required to take a more active part in planning activities and making decisions that involve themselves. Before the year is over it is hopeful that they will be working in small groups and that the room will be filled with stimuli.

Learning of some kind takes place under all conditions. We believe that: a child learns to be emotionally insecure, that he learns to be emotionally secure, we believe that under conditions of persistent failure he is likely to learn defensiveness and rigidity in the expression of his emotions. And that under conditions of success he is likely to learn confidence, emotional security and flexibility in the expression of his emotions.

Children display basically the same emotions and behavior. It is not the emotion, but the intensity, persistence and relationship of emotions to situations and people that form the basis for classifying emotion and behavior as normal and abnormal. Normal emotional reactions are realistically related to the existing situation. Normal emotional reactions can be discharged or dissipated by the individual. Normal emotional reactions do not persist to make it impossible for the individual to respond to gratifications when the painful situation has passed. When a child has the capacity to move forward, let go of painful aspects of the past, look for new interests, learn from past experiences how to prevent unnecessary pain and how to get help when he needs it, his emotional reactions are within normal limits. Reconditioning, or reteaching of behavioral patterns and behavioral characteristics through environmental manipulations, behavioral controls and planned success experiences form the basis for our attempts at changing behavioral deviations in children assigned to classes for emotionally disturbed in Elgin.

COMMUNICATION SKILLS AND CLASSROOM LEARNING

Learning takes place as the result of exposure to stimulus situations and one's ability to receive and express ideas and concepts communicated. Classroom learning involves, among other processes: the intake, translation, and output of visual, auditory and tactual stimuli in an organized pattern. Work at the University of Illinois by Kirk and McCarthy, etc. assist us considerably in getting an assessment of communication skills or linguistic functioning of children in Elgin's special classes for emotionally disturbed. A model or a blueprint of the communication process as used by Kirk and McCarthy is as follows.

Explanation of Model

Based on the Illinois Test of Psycholinguistic Abilities (ITPA) the communication process is divided into two levels: (I) the automatic sequential level (II) and the representational level. Communication at the automatic sequential level involves rote learning or immediate recall of visual and auditory stimuli. At this level are three communication skills: 1) the ability to immediately recall that which is heard (auditory, vocal, sequential) in the sequential order heard. This ability may be appropriately thought of as auditory memory. 2) the ability to immediately recall that which is seen (visual motor sequential) in the sequential order seen. This ability may be appropriately thought of as visual memory. 3) and the ability to anticipate grammatical patterns on the basis of that which

MODEL OF COMMUNICATION
Representation Level II

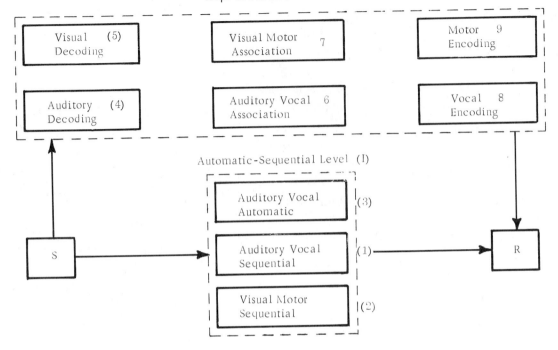

has been said (auditory vocal automatic). Resulting from exposure to the spoken word one learns to anticipate that which is going to be said on the basis of that which has been said.

> Example: Here is an apple. Here are 2 _____ . The anticipated word is apples. Here is a thief. Here are 2 _____ . The anticipated word is thieves.

The ability to anticipate grammatical responses is likely to be of great importance in moving along at a comfortable rate with the flow of ideas expressed. Inadequate development of this ability may be in part responsible for much of the perseveration seen in emotionally disturbed children, which depresses one's ability to receive, at an optimal level, that which is communicated to him.

It would appear that communication at a rote or automatic sequential level is prerequisite to communication at a representational or meaningful level. Based on this model (ITPA) the individual must first remember auditory and visual stimuli (fig. 1, #1 & 2) and be able to anticipate grammatical patterns (#3). He must then be able to understand (decode) that which is seen and heard (#4-5), internally relate (associate) that which is seen and heard (#6-7); and have at his disposal the skills to express vocally and/or by way of gestures that which is seen, heard and internally related (#8-9), if he is to communicate at an optimal level.

The channels for the reception of communication are visual and auditory. We see it or we hear it. The channels for the expression of that which is communicated are vocal and motor. We express that which we see or hear vocally or by way of gestures. A breakdown in any of the channels or processes at either the automatic sequential or the representational level can seriously depress communication and retard classroom learning. An analysis of this one aspect of the child's development (linguistic functioning) clearly illustrates that the disabilities of these children are not as apparent as those of children who are blind, deaf or mentally retarded but they are as real and can be as crippling academically as any of the more obvious disabilities of a physical nature. We need knowledge of specific disabilities if we are to develop an objective program of remediation.

Our experience has been that a global assessment of the child's ability and personality too often leads to broad generalizations about causation that has little practical application, in its global form, to classroom planning. This information, without being broken down, into smaller components, is too general to provide for the planning of an individual program of remediation. Our approach is to make an analysis of the general diagnosis of emotional disturbance in an effort to determine specific learning disabilities that may be responsible for the low intellectual functioning and academic deficits which we can observe. On the basis of this information we develop an individualized program of remediation to teach those skills which are deficient.

Linguistic abilities are so disguised, so molecular in structure and so camouflaged that the children are often unaware of their disabilities. When admitted to the special classes they know only in general terms why they are there, example: "I was bad," "why can't I read," "I don't like school," "I got into fights," etc. If we are to help such children we must determine specific deficits, make them aware of their disabilities, and teach them to discriminate their disabilities from others so they may help themselves. We must also select and develop instructional materials to train those skills which are underdeveloped. Finally we should help the children synthesize or relate new learning to that which is already known. We must therefore, provide numerous situations that will permit the application of new learning to familiar situations.

Our analysis of linguistic functioning based upon results from the Illinois Test of Psycholinguistic Abilities, revealed deficit language skills in many areas of linguistic functioning.

Test Summary	Raw Score	Language Age	Standard Score	Profile Test Numbers
Auditory-Vocal Automatic Test	14	6-10		7
Visual Decoding Test	19	A-N		2
Motor Encoding Test	22	A-N		6
Auditory-Vocal Association Test	22	8-3		3
Visual-Motor Sequencing Test	15	6-4		9
Vocal Encoding Test	16	6-4		5
Auditory-Vocal Sequencing Test	22	6-3		8
Visual-Motor Association Test	13	5-5		4
Auditory Decoding Test	27	7-11		1
ITPA Total	170	7-2		

Test Standardized to Age 9-5.

This boy is 11 years 1 month old and should be able to communicate at this level. However, his communication skills are generally like those of a child 7 years 2 months old. His ability to associate that which he sees is like that of a child 5 years 5 months of age. He expresses that which he sees and hears vocally like a child 6 years 4 months old.

CASE ILLUSTRATION #1 — T.M.

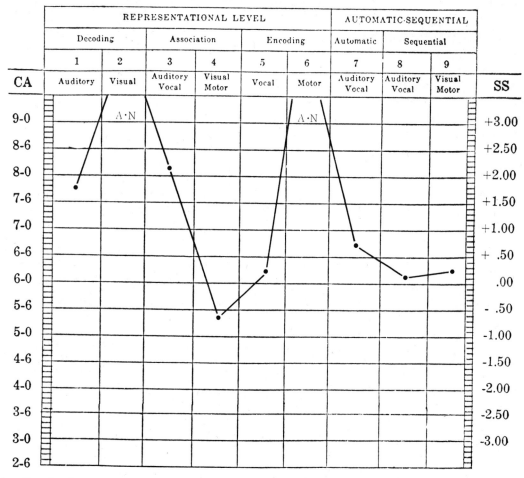

CA	REPRESENTATIONAL LEVEL						AUTOMATIC-SEQUENTIAL			SS
	Decoding		Association		Encoding		Automatic	Sequential		
	1	2	3	4	5	6	7	8	9	
	Auditory	Visual	Auditory Vocal	Visual Motor	Vocal	Motor	Auditory Vocal	Auditory Vocal	Visual Motor	
9-0		A·N				A·N				+3.00
8-6										+2.50
8-0										+2.00
7-6										+1.50
7-0										+1.00
6-6										+ .50
6-0										.00
5-6										- .50
5-0										-1.00
4-6										-1.50
4-0										-2.00
3-6										-2.50
3-0										-3.00
2-6										

Aided by a grant from the United Cerebral Palsy Research and Educational Foundation and the Grotto Humanitarian Foundation.

The lowest area of deficit is that of visual motor association. Visual motor association is the ability to internally relate that which is seen. Example: When a child sees a pencil he should be able to relate this to writing, paper, chalkboard, chalk, teacher and numerous other objects and situations based on past experiences. We must therefore provide him with repeated activities that require him to utilize this ability in an effort to train this basic skill.

Test Summary	Raw Score	Language Age	Standard Score	Profile Test Numbers
Auditory-Vocal Automatic Test	19	8-9		7
Visual Decoding Test	13	6-3		2
Motor Encoding Test	15	6-4		6
Auditory-Vocal Association Test	20	7-3		3
Visual-Motor Sequencing Test	11	5-1		9
Vocal Encoding Test	23	A·N		5
Auditory-Vocal Sequencing Test	24	7-0		8
Visual-Motor Association Test	15	6-1		4
Auditory Decoding Test	26	7-6		1
ITPA Total	166	7-0		

Test Standardized to Age 9-5

This girl is 10 years old. She remembers that which she sees like a child 5 years of age and she understands that which she sees like a child 6 years 3 months old. Her composite language functioning or language age is like that of a child 7 years of age.

CASE ILLUSTRATION #2 — J. W.

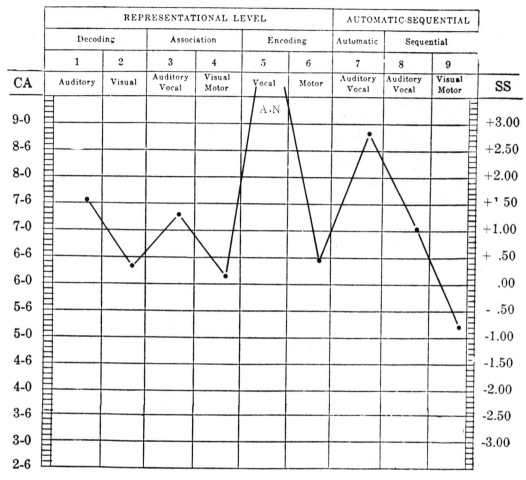

Aided by a grant from the United Cerebral Palsy Research and Educational Foundation and the Grotto Humanitarian Foundation.

The lowest area of linguistic functioning is visual motor sequential (visual memory). We should therefore attempt to train this disability area by way of repeated activities which require the utilization of visual memory.

CASE ILLUSTRATION #3 — M.B.

Test Summary	Raw Score	Language Age	Standard Score	Profile Test Numbers
Auditory-Vocal Automatic Test	17	8-0	*	7
Visual Decoding Test	22	A·N		2
Motor Encoding Test	15	6-4		6
Auditory-Vocal Association Test	24	A·N		3
Visual-Motor Sequencing Test	22	A·N		9
Vocal Encoding Test	19	7-4		5
Auditory-Vocal Sequencing Test	23	6-7		8
Visual-Motor Association Test	11	5-1		4
Auditory Decoding Test	23	6-5		1
ITPA Total	176	7-6		

*Test Standardized to age 9-5

This boy is 10 years of age. He is able to relate that which he sees like a child 5 years of age. His composite communication skills are like those of a child 7 years 6 months old. His communication skills generally are 2 years 6 months below that of his chronological age.

CASE ILLUSTRATION #3 — M. B.

CA	REPRESENTATIONAL LEVEL						AUTOMATIC-SEQUENTIAL			SS
	Decoding		Association		Encoding		Automatic	Sequential		
	1	2	3	4	5	6	7	8	9	
	Auditory	Visual	Auditory Vocal	Visual Motor	Vocal	Motor	Auditory Vocal	Auditory Vocal	Visual Motor	
9-0		A·N	A·N						A·N	+3.00
8-6										+2.50
8-0										+2.00
7-6										+1.50
7-0										+1.00
6-6										+ .50
6-0										.00
5-6										- .50
5-0										-1.00
4-6										-1.50
4-0										-2.00
3-6										-2.50
3-0										-3.00
2-6										

Aided by a grant from the United Cerebral Palsy Research and Educational Foundation and the Grotto Humanitarian Foundation.

The lowest area of linguistic functioning is that of visual motor association (internal relating of that which is seen). We will therefore plan activities that require him to repeatedly relate that which he sees.

CASE ILLUSTRATION #4 — W.B.

Test Summary	Raw Score	Language Age	Standard Score	Profile Test Numbers
Auditory-Vocal Automatic Test	15	7-3	-.10	7
Visual Decoding Test	13	6-3	-.86	2
Motor Encoding Test	12	5-0	-1.24	6
Auditory-Vocal Association Test	17	6-1	-1.76	3
Visual-Motor Sequencing Test	11	5-1	-1.55	9
Vocal Encoding Test	12	5-1	-1.35	5
Auditory-Vocal Sequencing Test	21	5-11	.87	8
Visual-Motor Association Test	13	5-5	-1.79	4
Auditory Decoding Test	29	A·N	.86	1
ITPA Total	143	6-0	-2.04	

This boy is 8 years old. He expresses that which he sees by way of gestures like a child 5 years old. He is able to remember that which is said like a child 5 years of age. He remembers that which is seen like a child 6 years of age. He expresses vocally that which he sees and hears like a child 5 years of age. His composite language functioning is like that of a child 6 years of age.

CASE ILLUSTRATION #4 — W. B.

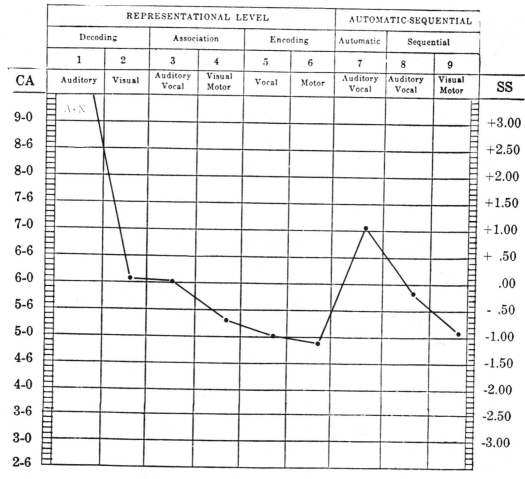

CA	REPRESENTATIONAL LEVEL						AUTOMATIC-SEQUENTIAL			SS
	Decoding		Association		Encoding		Automatic	Sequential		
	1	2	3	4	5	6	7	8	9	
	Auditory	Visual	Auditory Vocal	Visual Motor	Vocal	Motor	Auditory Vocal	Auditory Vocal	Visual Motor	

Aided by a grant from the United Cerebral Palsy Research and Educational Foundation and the Grotto Humanitarian Foundation.

Though W.B. is extremely low in all areas except auditory decoding (understanding that which is heard) and auditory vocal automatic (anticipcation of grammatical patterns), the lowest area of linguistic functioning is the encoding process (expression of that which is seen and heard vocally or by way of gestures). We will therefore plan activities to train this process; hopefully other disabilities will be corrected by the training of the encoding process.

Plan For Remediation

The following outline of remedial suggestions were followed in part or completely in developing a program of remediation for this aspect of child development.

I. **Auditory Decoding** (understanding of auditory symbols)

A. Awareness of language—through the use of finger plays and simple representative games.

B. Understanding of labels of actions, objects, and pictures.

C. Understanding of directions.

D. Concepts of spacial relationships; such as, on, under, big, little, etc.

E. Understanding of words (vocabulary).

II. **Visual Decoding** (understanding of visual symbols)

A. Awareness of visual symbols—through toys, pictures, books, etc.

B. Understanding of actions, objects, and pictures.

C. Likenesses and differences.

D. Understanding of printed words.

III. **Auditory-Vocal Association** (internal relating of auditory symbols)

A. Recall of familiar words.

B. Recognition of objects from its characteristics.

C. Retelling of stories in own words.

D. Antonyms and synonyms.

E. Classification exercises and word games.

IV. **Visual-Motor Association** (internal relating of visual symbols)

A. Sorting by color, size, shape, and function.

B. Relationships; for example, matching things that go together.

C. Classification of ideas which visual symbols evoke.

V. **Vocal Encoding** (vocal expression of ideas)

A. Verbal labels.

B. Telling of experiences.

C. Descriptions of situations, a picture, a story, etc.

VI. **Motor Encoding** (gestural expression of ideas)

A. Orientation and space (Kaphardt, N.C. the SLOW LEARNER IN THE CLASS-ROOM. Columbus, Ohio, Charles E. Merrill, 1960).

B. Acting out directions, stories, ideas (such as charades).

C. Writing ideas. **Automatic-Sequential Level.**

VII. **Auditory-Vocal Automatic** (the use of grammar)

A. Closure, such as sound blending.

B. Specific teaching of grammar.

VIII. **Auditory-Vocal Sequential** (auditory memory)

A. Concentration on what is heard.

B. Repeat words, sentences, nonsense syllables, numbers.

C. Exercises in inductive reasoning: for example; 1, 2, 3, 4, what comes next.

IX. **Visual-Motor Sequential** (visual memory)

A. Concentration on what is seen.

B. Imitation of what is seen, such as gestures, bead patterns, etc.

C. Story sequences.

D. Fernald method of tracing, writing from memory.

These last three abilities under the automatic-sequential level are probably the most related to learning problems in the classroom. Educators may well infer that perhaps more emphasis should be placed on the skill aspect of the three R's.

Results of Psycholinguistic Training and Program of Remediation

It should be emphasized that no remedial method works with economy for all children. Knowledge of many remedial techniques and understanding of specific disabilities combined with imaginative teaching form the basis for development of an objective and possibly productive individualized program of remediation. A program of remediation emphasizing level of intellectual functioning, specific linguistic abilities, achievement deficiencies and emotional stability (patterns of adjustment and behavioral characteristics) can be developed on the basis of a detailed analysis of the diagnosis. Such analysis yield information about specific disabilities. With an awareness of specific disabilities, a remedial program can be developed that presents instructions in a way that its didactic value is served while training the disability, for example: we may teach spelling at the child's level of achievement to train visual memory by:

1. Writing the word on the chalkboard.

2. Quickly erasing the word and asking the child to repeat the sequential order of letters in the word.

3. Then asking him to pronounce the word.

4. If he does not know the word — tell him and help him connect visual and auditory stimuli to learn the word.

Emphasis is placed upon remembering the sequential order of letters. This procedure permits one to teach in small steps to assure success and to train visual memory in the process of teaching essential spelling vocabulary.

Diagnosis without remediation is a waste of time, not to mention money and effort. On the basis of our educational diagnosis a plan for remediation was developed for each child resulting into the following linguistic and academic progress for students during the five-month test period between 11-25-65 and 5-3-66. The plan for remediation took into consideration: intellectual functioning, achievement level, linguistic functioning and specific deficits experienced in reading and other subject areas. In this section we will compare reading and linguistic progress to determine whether or not there is a correlation between the two for this group of children studied.

CASE ILLUSTRATION #1

Test Summary	Raw Score	Language Age		Standard Score	Profile Test Numbers
Auditory-Vocal Automatic Test	* 19-16 * *	8-9	7-7	———————	7
Visual Decoding Test	13-15	6-3	7-3	———————	2
Motor Encoding Test	15-20	6-4	A·N	———————	6
Auditory-Vocal Association Test	20-22	7-3	8-3	———————	3
Visual-Motor Sequencing Test	11-15	5-1	6-4	———————	9
Vocal Encoding Test	23-19	A·N	7-3	———————	5
Auditory-Vocal Sequencing Test	24-23	7-0	6-7	———————	8
Visual-Motor Association Test	15-15	6-1	6-1	———————	4
Auditory Decoding Test	26-31	7-6	A·N	———————	1
ITPA Total	166-176	7-0	7-6	———————	

* test score 11-23-65
* * test score 5-3-66
* * * Test Standardized to age 9

During the five-month period of school between 11-23-65 and 5-3-66 this child, who was 10 years 1 month old at the beginning of the test period, made six months progress linguistically. Her language age at the beginning of the period was 7.0, at the end of the period it was 7.6; showing a six month gain in overall communication ability. Five months progress was made in the area of reading for the same period which correlates favorably with linguistic progress.

CASE ILLUSTRATION #1

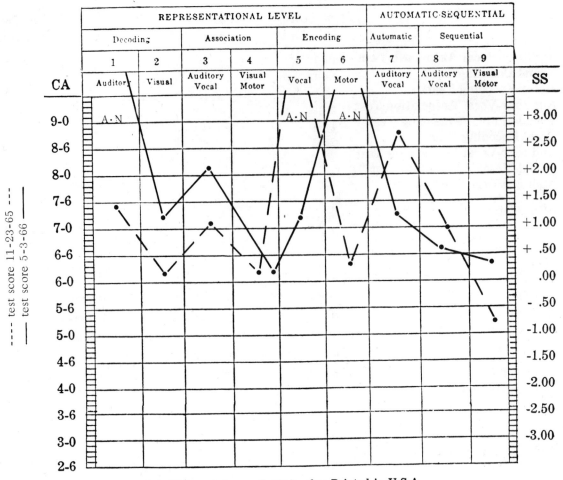

Aided by a grant from the United Cerebral Palsy Research and Educational Foundation and the Grotto Humanitarian Foundation.

The lowest area of linguistic functioning was visual motor association (visual memory). Substantial gain was made in this ability by providing repeated experiences, in every academic area possible requiring memory of that which is seen in the sequential order seen. A total of one year three months progress was made in ability to remember the sequential order of visual stimuli. Though progress was made in this ability, chronological age at the end of this period was 10.6, language age was 7-6 a total of 6 months gain was made for language age and 5 months gain was made in reading. The lowest area of language functioning remained that of visual memory at the 6 year 4 month level. Continued training of this disability area while teaching necessary academic skills is indicated.

CASE ILLUSTRATION #2

Test Summary	Raw Score	Language Age	Standard Score	Profile Test Numbers
Auditory-Vocal Automatic Test	14-18	6-10 84		7
Visual Decoding Test	15-13	7-3 6-3 *		2
Motor Encoding Test	10-7	4-2 3-2 *		6
Auditory-Vocal Association Test	15-18	5-6 6-6		3
Visual-Motor Sequencing Test	11-10	5-1 4-10 *		9
Vocal Encoding Test	10-11	4-5 4-9		5
Auditory-Vocal Sequencing Test	15-16	4-4 4-7		8
Visual-Motor Association Test	10-20	4-4 4-10		4
Auditory Decoding Test	26-30	7-6 A·N		1
ITPA Total	126-143	5-5 6-0		

*Areas in which child regressed

This girl, who was 9 years 11 months of age at the beginning of this test period (11-25-65) and 10 years 4 months of age at the end of this period (5-3-66) made 7 months progress in her total language functioning. Her language age at the beginning of this period was 5 years 5 months; at the end of the period it was 6-0. During the same period 6 months progress was made in the area of reading. Reading progress again correlates favorably with linguistic progress. It should be emphasized that though time was allowed for the training of specific linguistic skills; reading and language training were taught as much as possible as a single process. In all cases reading was taught emphasizing training of specific deficit language skills.

CASE ILLUSTRATION #2

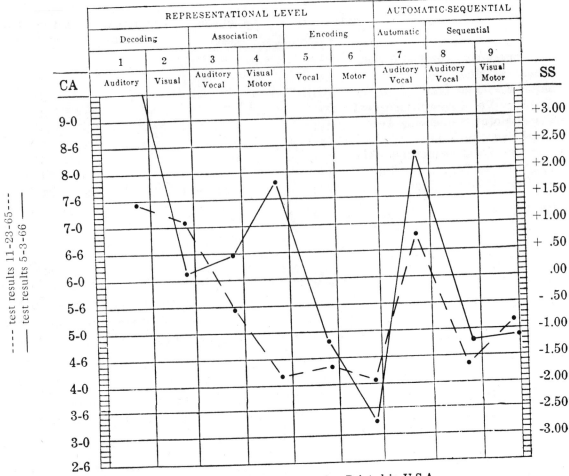

Aided by a grant from the United Cerebral Palsy Research and Educational Foundation and the Grotto Humanitarian Foundation.

The lowest area of linguistic functioning was motor encoding (the ability to express ones-self by way of gestures). Though this was the lowest area she was almost equally low in the areas of visual motor association (4.4—internal relating of visual stimuli), auditory vocal sequential (4.4—auditory memory), and vocal encoding (4.5—vocal expression of that which is seen and heard). We decided to train visual motor association on the assumption that motor expression would also improve. This was not the case. Three years 6 months progress was made in visual motor association (4.4—7.10) but she regressed one year in motor encoding. Motor encoding at the end of this test period was by far the lowest area of linguistic functioning. Training of this area in conjunction with academic assignments is indicated.

Test Summary	Raw Score	Language Age	Standard Score	Profile Test Numbers
Auditory-Vocal Automatic Test	* 14-19 * *	* 6-10 8-0 * *		7
Visual Decoding Test	19-20	A·N A·N	* * *	2
Motor Encoding Test	22-26	A·N A·N		6
Auditory-Vocal Association Test	22-24	8-3 A·N		3
Visual-Motor Sequencing Test	15-19	6-4 8-5		9
Vocal Encoding Test	16-16	6-4 6-4		5
Auditory-Vocal Sequencing Test	22-29	6-3 A·N		8
Visual-Motor Association Test	13-21	5-5 8-3		4
Auditory Decoding Test	27-34	7-11 A·N		1
ITPA Total	170-208	7-2 A·N		

* Score 11-23-65
** Score 5-3-66
*** Test Standardized to age 9

This boy was 11 years 1 month old at the beginning of the test period. He was 11 years 6 months of age when the test period ended. At the beginning of the period his language age was 7 years 2 months; at the end of the five months test period language age was above the norms of 9 years 5 months. This showed an overall gain in language functioning in excess of 2 years 3 months. Gains were made in all areas of language functioning except vocal encoding (vocal expression) which remained at the 6 year 4 month level. During this time an academic gain of 1 year 2 months was made by this boy which favorably correlates linguistic progress. Future plans for remediation include training of vocal expression. For this small sampling, it is interesting to note that reading progress appears to be almost consistently one month below linguistic progress.

CASE ILLUSTRATION #3

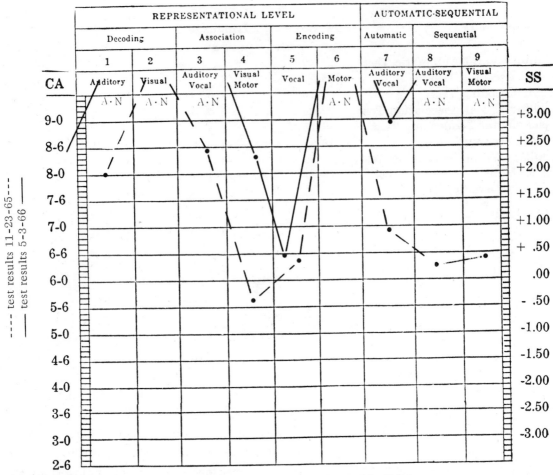

Aided by a grant from the United Cerebral Palsy Research and Educational Foundation and the Grotto Humanitarian Foundation.

These cases are presented to help clarify what we believe to be the relationship between linguistic functioning and academic performance. It is difficult, if not impossible, to isolate the two, but linguistic functioning or communication skills appear to be prerequisite to classroom achievement. It may be argued that linguistic functioning improved as the result of individualized, successful academic instructions, but the fact remains that such individual instructions encompassed, as a major part of its plan, the training of specific linguistic skills in conjunction with the presentation of didactic instructional materials. The question that remains unanswered is "Would the children have made the same academic progress had not we emphasized linguistic training?" This presentation should not be misconstrued to indicate that we believe linguistic training alone can and will produce increased academic productivity. We do believe that linguistic training is an important aspect of the child's development and should be included in his curriculum of instructions to emphasize, to enhance and to help make possible increased academic productivity.

INTELLECTUAL AND ACHIEVEMENT DEVIATIONS

Intellectual Deviations

We suspect that intellectual and academic potentials of these children are depressed by emotional handicaps and low linguistic functioning. However, as a rule we accept the children at their present level of intellectual functioning. We disregard, for the time, that which may be indicative of higher intellectual potentials. A distinction is therefore made between intellectual potential and level of intellectual functioning.

We do not expect that the children will progress academically at the same rate. We should not expect this in a "regular class" and cannot imagine it in the special classes. The children are allowed to progress at the rate their intellectual functioning and emotional stability will permit. The objective of each academic task is that success will be experienced in its completion. In light of linguistic functioning and emotional handicaps, the children are functioning intellectually as follows:

PROFILE OF INTELLECTUAL FUNCTIONING

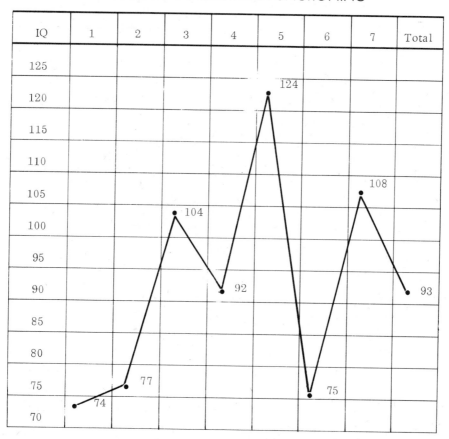

As a group they are functioning within the normal range of intelligence with a group I. Q. of 93. Individual ability ranges from dull normal to bright normal. The indications are that one child has potential for rapid academic progress (#5), others have potential for average progress (#3-4 & 7), and still others will make minimal progress and will require considerable assistance from the teacher for that progress which is made (#1-2 & 6). Some of the children are achieving at the level of their intellectual functioning and will require repeated success experiences to gain confidence and emotional security before we can realistically expect increased academic productivity.

Chronological Age and Mental Ability

Chronological age is characteristically a poor indicator of potential for achievement or academic performance. If there is a correlation between chronological age and potential for academic performance, it is not to be found in the classes for emotionally disturbed children in Elgin. There is no reason to believe that because a child has lived 7 or 8 years, he should be performing academically at the second or third grade level.

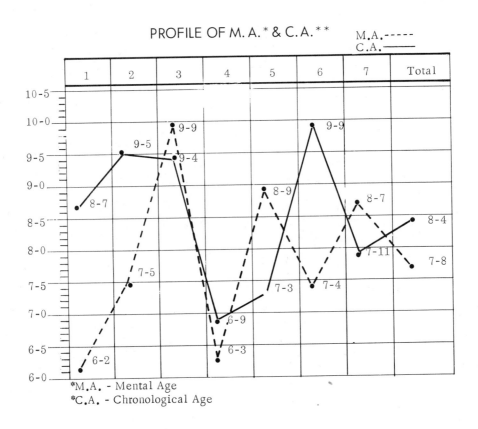

PROFILE OF M. A.* & C.A.**   M.A.-----
C.A.———

*M.A. - Mental Age
*C.A. - Chronological Age

(Continued)

(Continued from previous page)

No.	C.A.	G.E.*	M.A.	G.E.*
1	8-7	3-5	6-2	1-0
2	9-5	4-3	7-5	2-3
3	9-4	4-2	9-9	4-7
4	6-9	1-7	6-3	1-1
5	7-3	2-1	8-9	3-7
6	9-9	4-7	7-4	2-2
7	7-11	2-9	8-7	3-5
Average	8-4	3-2	7-8	2-6

*Grade Expectancy

This profile shows that some of the children have potential for academic performance above their chronological age, and others have potential below chronological age. Intellectual functioning ranges from 2 years 5 months below chronological age to 1 year 5 months above chronological age. There is no correlation between chronological age and intellectual functioning. If intelligence is a satisfactory indicator of potential for academic achievement, chronological age should be completly disregarded. A principle of education which seems to be most applicable is that we must: **accept the children at their level of achievement and allow them to progress at their own rate** in competition with themselves rather than with other members of the class.

Chronological Age and Unrealistic Expectations

Unrealistic expectations for achievement is often placed upon children because of their chronological age. Student #1 (Chart p. 244), because of chronological age, has been expected to achieve in the middle of the third grade level. When he entered the special class his level of intellectual functioning would not have permitted achievement at the third grade fifth month level, but at the first grade level. The same overexpectations have been placed on students #2-4 and 6. More than half the class have had unrealistic overdemands for achievement placed on them prior to admission to the special class. Other students have not been able to mobilize their potentials and produce at a level commensurate with their intellectual functioning. The postulated cause for this inability is emotional disturbance and all of its behavioral deviations discussed in Section I.

No.	Age	G.E.*	Reading	Spelling	Mathematics	Average Achievement
1	8-7	3.5	1.5	0	1.2	.9
2	9-5	4.3	2.2	1.9	2.2	2.1
3	9-4	4.2	3.3	2.4	3.5	3.1
4	6-9	1.7	0	0	0	0
5	7-3	2.1	1.8	1.8	1.5	1.3
6	9-9	4.7	1.0	1.0	1.0	1.0
7	7-11	2.9	1.4	1.5	1.8	1.3
	8-4	3.3	1.7	1.2	1.6	1.5

*Grade Equivalent for C.A.

Achievement Deviations

When admitted to the special class, the children had attended school an average of 3-1/2 years. During this time they had made an average of 1 year 5 months academic gain. They were making an average of 5 months academic progress per school year (10 months per school year), were becoming academically retarded at the rate of 5 months per school year. When admitted to the class they had accumulated an academic deficit of 1 year 8 months for chronological age. As a principle: **we should set expectations for academic performance according to potentials and level of achievement, rather than number of years lived**. Though we were concerned about the discrepancy between achievement and chronological age, special emphasis was made not to pressure on the basis of this information. The importance of the above mentioned principle is clearly illustrated when we compare achievement with potential for achievement and find:

COMPARISON OF ACHIEVEMENT AND CAPACITY

No.	M.A.	G.E.*	Reading	Spelling	Arithmetic	Average
1	6-2	1.0	1.5	0	1.2	.9
2	7-5	2.3	2.2	1.9	2.2	2.1
3	9-9	4.7	3.3	2.4	3.5	3.1
4	6-3	1.1	0	0	0	0
5	8-9	3.7	1.8	1-8	1.5	1-3
6	7-4	2.2	1.0	1.0	1.0	1.0
7	8-7	3.5	1.4	1.5	1.8	1.3
	7-8	2.6	1.7	1.2	1.6	1.5

* Grade Equivalent for M.A.

that Student #1 who was 2 years 8 months retarded for chronological age was over-achieving for his level of intellectual functioning. Student #2 was achieving at the level of his potentials. Other students were underachieving possibly because of the generalized condition of emotional disturbance. Success and confidence should be gained before Students #1 and 2 are likely to increase academic productivity. Individually, achievement ranged from kindergarten to third grade. We accept each child at his achievement level and select materials for the grade range. Potentials for the group were at the second grade six month level. They were achieving at the first grade fifth month level. As a group these children were achieving (at the beginning of the school year) 1 year 1 month below expected achievement for intellectual functioning. A realistic academic goal for the group was to close the distance between achievement and intellectual functioning. To achieve this goal it would be required that each child make the necessary academic progress each school year plus additional progress to decrease this deficit.

Major Educational Needs

It would appear that the major educational need is planned success experiences. The students have been conditioned through exposure to impossible tasks and persistent failure. If they are to be reconditioned, it would seem only logical that they must be exposed to repeated success experiences. The goal of the academic task must not be decided upon the basis of its academic value only, but upon the probability that the child will complete the task successfully. We believe that he must be forced to succeed — within the confines of potentials. We believe that success, success, and more success to reinforce success is needed if adequate reconditioning is to take place.

READING DISABILITIES AND THEIR REMEDIATION

Effort has been made to point out and illustrate the practical application of three principles of education.

1. Be aware of and reinforce the development of underdeveloped patterns of behavior.

2. Control deviate behavior to create an atmosphere conducive to success and positive learning experiences.

3. Accept the child at his level of achievement and allow progress academically at the rate potentials will permit.

The practical application of these principles of education are essential to the success of each child in the special classes for emotionally disturbed. The extent to which these principles are successfully applied determines to some great degree the success that will be attained in the total academic program for emotionally disturbed. Success in the application of these principles depends heavily upon the application of a fourth principle which has not yet been mentioned. This principle is: **Acquire knowledge and understanding of underdeveloped basic skills**.

We will use reading to illustrate this principle. However, the principle equally applies to all areas of academic endeavor. Two children may read at the same level, but the character and quality of their reading may differ vastly. When one is asked to read he is asked to perform processes which include, among others, the processes of: 1) word recognition, 2) word discrimination, 3) vocal production of words, 4) comprehension of that which is read. Deficiencies may exist in any one of these processes and the need for intensive training may be indicated in one area more than in another. It is therefore necessary to get an assessment of specific aspects of the reading process to determine areas of emphasis and instructions. Our analysis of reading consists of an assessment of oral reading, silent reading for comprehension, word recognition and word discrimination. We also make an analysis of specific errors made in the reading process and get an assessment of the child's ability to fuse sounds into words.

Analysis of Reading Profiles

The use of a profile to graphically illustrate oral reading, silent reading, word recognition, and word discrimination shows at a glance the strong and weak reading areas as related to chronological age and mental age.

READING PROFILE #1A

Oral reading	2.2
Silent reading	1.8
Word recog.	2.2
Word disc.	1.5
Average	1.9

Grade	C.A.	M.A.	Reading Tests			
			O	S	W.E.	W.D.
9	14-6					
8	13-6					
7	12-6					
6	11-6					
5	10-6					
4	9-6					
3	8-6					
2	7-6					
1	6-6					

This profile shows this boy to be 10 years 1 month of age, he is in a third grade class, according to his chronological age he should be in the fifth grade, he has capacity for performance at the fourth grade level but his reading performance is at the first grade ninth month level. The highest reading area is oral reading, the lowest is word discrimination. There is a deficit of three years three months between intellectual functioning and reading achievement. Our knowledge of behavioral deviations, linguistic functioning, intellectual output and newly acquired knowledge of reading behavior in the areas of oral reading, silent reading, word recognition and word discrimination provides a basis for developing an individualized program of reading remediation. Materials should be selected for this child at the first grade ninth month level. We should emphasize oral reading, his strongest reading area, to provide success experiences while training word discrimination, his weakest reading area, to improve composite reading.

Our basis for planning remediation is strengthened by knowledge of the kinds of mistakes made while reading. Two children may read at the same level, but may persistently and consistently make different kinds of reading errors. Identification of kinds of reading errors made provides a basis for objective remediation in the areas of reading deficit.

CLASSIFICATION OF READING ERRORS

1. **Faulty vowels**—mispronunciation in which the child alternates one or more vowel sounds.

Example:
A. **dig** read dug   B. **left** read lift
C. **not** read note   D. **core** read car

2. **Faulty consonants**—a mispronunciation in which the child alternates one or more consonant sounds.

Example:
A. **send** read sent   B. **tack** read tag
B. **sort** read short   D. **this** read his

3. **Reversals**—a mispronunciation in which the child reverses the **orientation of letters,** the **sequence of letters,** or the **sequence of words.**

Example:
A. Reversed orientation of letters
(b, d, p, g, u, n)
1. **dig** read big   2. **squirt** read spirt
3. **bone** read done

B. Reversed sequence of letters
1. **was** read saw
2. **on** read no
3. **left** read felt
4. **cord** read crod

C. Reversed sequence of words
1. Text: "Mother," he said
Read: "Mother," said he
2. Text: Once there was
Read: There once was

4. **Addition of sounds**—the child inserts one or more sounds

Example:
- A. **tack** read trace
- B. **pop** read pond
- C. **one** read once
- D. **till** read until

5. **Omission of sound** — the child omits one or more sounds of a word
   - A. **forming** read form
   - B. **core** read car
   - C. **blind** read bind
   - D. **report** read rost

6. **Substitution of words** — the child substitutes a word having no vowel or consonant sounds similar to the word
   - **Example:**
     - A. **lived** read was
     - B. **were** read had
     - C. **puss** read kitty
     - D. **the** read and

7. **Repetition of words** — the child repeats words or he repeats mispronunciation of words

   Example:
   Text: a boy had a dog
   Read: a boy a boy had a dog

   Text: once there lived a king
   Read: one one once there lived a king

8. **Addition of words** — the child inserts words

   Example:
   Text: Once there was
   Read: Once upon a time there was
   Text: saw his four feet
   Read: saw his four little feet

9. **Omission of words** — the child omits words from the text

   Example:
   Text: a little pig
   Read: a pig
   Text: Then the boy began to cry
   Read: The boy began crying

PROFILE #1B

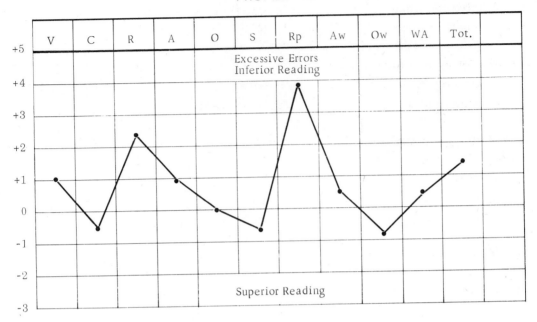

This profile of errors shows that in addition to being low in all reading areas and lowest in word discrimination, excessive repetitions and reversals are made in reading. We must therefore emphasize the correction of reversals and repetitions. Sound blending is adequate for first grade. We should therefore teach, through repeated assignments fusion of sounds into words.

READING PROFILE 2A

Oral Reading ----1-0
Silent Reading ---1-9
Word Recog. ----2-2
Word Disc. -----2-5
Average ------1-9

C.A. 9-6
M.A. 7-1

Grade	C.A.	M.A.	Reading Test				
			O	S	W.R.	W.D.	Total
9	14-6						
8	13-6						
7	12-6						
6	11-6						
5	10-6						
4	9-6						
3	8-6						
2	7-6	7-1					
1	6-6						

Sound Blending **1 grade**

This boy is 9 years 6 months of age. He has a mental age of 7 years 1 month. He is reading at first grade ninth month level; according to his chronological age we would expect performance at the fourth grade fourth month level. However, his intellectual output is like that of a child 7 years 1 month of age which indicates achievement for mental age at the second grade level; his academic productivity is at the first grade ninth month level. He is therefore producing academically at or near the level expected for intellectual functioning. The strongest reading area is word discrimination, the weakest area is oral reading.

This child will continue to need instructional materials at the second grade level. Oral reading should be emphasized by providing consistent opportunities to read orally and word recognition should be emphasized as the area in which reading success experiences may most easily be reinforced. His Profile of Errors shows:

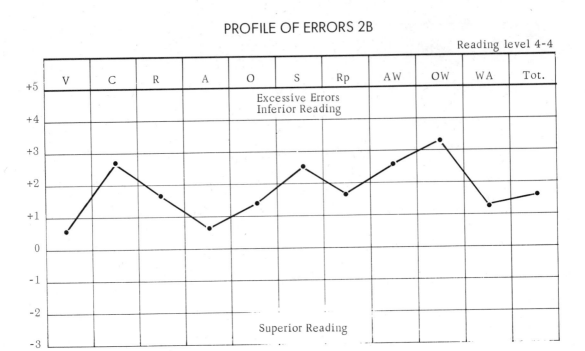

PROFILE OF ERRORS 2B

Reading level 4-4

omission of words and consonant errors are the reading mistakes most frequently made. These reading errors must be trained by way of repeated activities and a conscious awareness on the part of the child. Ability to fuse sounds is adequate for the second grade level and needs training to allow improved word attack skill which will enhance reading. There is need to experience repeated success and gain emotional stability that permits utilization of more intellectual potentials before we can expect improved academic performance.

Oral Reading------3-1
Silent Reading ----3-0
Word Recog.------3-4
Word Disc. ------2-9
Average   3-1

C.A. 10.4
M.A. 8-0

CASE ILLUSTRATION #3 — READING PROFILE 3A

Grade	C.A.	M.A.	Reading Test				Total
			O	S	W.R.	W.D.	
9	14-6						
8	13-6						
7	12-6						
6	11-6						
5	10.6						
4	9-6						
3	8-6						
2	7-6	8-0					
1	6-6						

Sound Blending 2 grade

This boy is 10 years 4 months of age. He has a mental age of 8 years. He is achieving at the third grade first month level. Based on chronological age he should be achieving at the fifth grade second month level. However, on the basis of intellectual functioning he should be achieving at the second grade tenth month level or the third grade. His reading achievement is at the third grade first month level. From all indications he is persistently producing at a level commensurate with ability.

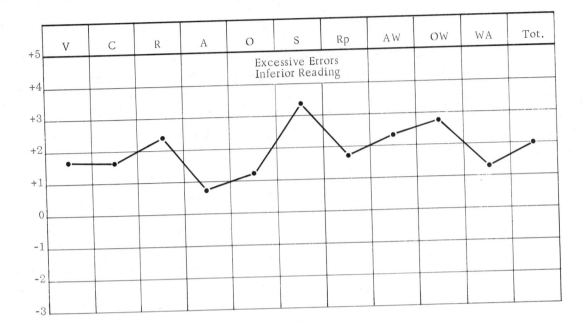

An analysis of reading areas shows that substitutions, omissions of words and reversals are most frequently made in reading. A plan for remediation should include reading instructions at the third grade level, emphasis on word discrimination as the reading area of deficit to be trained and oral reading as the area to reinforce success experiences. Sound blending is adequate for the fourth grade; indicating continued training. We cannot expect greater academic output until increased emotional stability and intellectual output is acquired. We hope that this can be acquired through a process of operate conditioning based upon knowledge of academic performance, intellectual functioning and planned repeated academic success experiences.

Remediation

Remediation of learning disabilities and development of skill areas consists of six levels in the program being discussed.

Outline for Remediation

I. Provide the child with knowledge of his disabilities
II. Teach him to discriminate his disabilities
III. Select materials to train disabilities
IV. Teach in small steps to assure success
V. Relate new learning to that which is known
VI. Proceed to a higher level of learning as rapidly as possible

Level 1—At Level 1 we endeavor to provide the child with knowledge of his disabilities. Usually for the first time in his life he is told of specific behavioral, linguistic and academic disabilities which seem to exist for him. This knowledge of these disabilities and the fact that we believe that he can help himself gives him a sense of direction and a feeling of security. Priority of disabilities to be worked on can be determined and with genuine interest on the part of the teacher the goal of the teacher becomes the goal of the child. Repeated activities to train specific behavioral and academic skills cease to be viewed as punitive. Academic assignments made that are far below grade expectancy for chronological age cease to be degrading. The child learns to see himself at a past, present, and future level of behavioral and academic functioning. Hopefulness gradually replaces hopelessness and defensiveness when disabilities are defined for a child in terms he can understand and remediation is objective.

Level 2—Knowledge of disabilities and acquisition of hope leading to motivation is but the first step in our remedial procedure. We must also teach the child to discriminate his disability from others so that he can help himself when he is not with his teacher. Knowledge and discrimination of individualized disabilities perpetuate motivation which may generalize to all aspects of the child's daily activities.

Level 3—Motivation will be perpetuated as long as it is reinforced by success experiences. It is therefore sometimes necessary to force a child to succeed within the confines of his present academic, emotional and intellectual capabilities. Each time he is forced to succeed the more he will want success and the greater would be his efforts to succeed. If allowed to experience frequent and prolonged academic failures in the special class, the existing attitude "I can't do it" will be reinforced, leading to intensified avoidance responses and defensive behavior. We thus achieve results opposite of that which we seek. At Level 3 we make a special effort to select and develop materials to train areas of disability and to provide successful academic experiences. The instructions may be as simple as teaching a child to raise his hands before he speaks or as complicated as teaching him to read. Much is to be said about teaching behavior. However, our focus for emphasis at this time is reading; we must therefore confine ourselves to this topic of discussion to avoid unessential confusion on the part of the reader. However, it should be emphasized that our outline for remediation is not limited to the area of reading but is helpful in other academic areas and in teaching standards of classroom conduct as well.

Level 4--Throughout this chapter the word "success" continues to reappear as a result of the writer's inability to find a substitute. For this writer there is no substitute for success: our special classes for emotionally disturbed children rely heavily upon reconditioning of attitudes about school and ability to succeed in school. Without such emphasis on success we believe the program is doomed to failure due to inadequate reconditioning attempts. We are equally aware of the fact that integrative responses to failure experiences must be learned, but believe that emotional stability must be gained to counterbalance the negative effect of failure for children who have experienced more than their share of failures. It is for this reason that we consider Level 4 to be a most important level of emphasis in our plan for remediation. At Level 4 we endeavor to **teach in small steps to insure success.**

Teaching Reading Sight Vocabulary in Small Steps

Teaching in small steps can best be illustrated by our procedure for teaching **sight vocabulary**. As the child reads from his textbook, words missed are recorded to be taught for sight recognition. The procedure for teaching such words is as follows:

I. **Present word sets for auditory memory** (child repeats set in sequential order after teacher; teacher says the complete set before child repeats words in sequential order). Example: camp, canary, basement, beach. The child repeats these four words in the order said by the teacher. The teacher says the word set in a variety of orders for exact repetition.

II. **Present word set for visual memory using a stimulus and response card** (see this, showing stimulus card, find one like it, turn stimulus card over, child points to word on his response card). Continue to completion of the set, allow much practice.

III. **Connect visual with auditory stimuli**—this word says _____ (showing stimulus card). Show me _____ (turning over stimulus card—child responds by pointing to correct word on response card). What does this word say? (showing stimulus card) child responds with correct auditory vocal response. Continue to completion of the set.

IV. Present words for visual discrimination. The auditory stimulus is supplied by the teacher. No stimulus card is used. The child responds by pointing to the correct word (show me _____. Show me _____ .) Continue to completion of set.

V. Present word set for auditory discrimination. Teacher supplies visual stimuli by pointing. The child gives the correct auditory vocal response without delay as the teacher points.

VI. The child reads the word set.

VII. Finger tracing of all words missed.

Level 5 — At Level 5 we make a conscious effort to relate new learning to that which is already known. Our outline for teaching phonetic skills emphasizes and illustrates the importance of this level of remediation. We are aware of the fact that a child should learn to recognize words at sight if he is to develop speed and accuracy in reading. However, it is equally important that he develop word attack skills that will permit him to recognize unfamiliar words based upon knowledge of sound symbols represented in the word. Our reading procedure is therefore one which equally emphasizes the teaching of phonetic skills and sight vocabulary.

Teaching Phonetic Skills

Teaching phonetic skills in the program under discussion consists of individual instructions in the reading of word drills which emphasize the recognition of increasingly difficult sounds and sound patterns. For this activity the Heggie, Kirk and Kirk Remedial Reading Drills is used. This period of instructions is structured as follows:

1. Individual instructions and reading of word drills.

2. Group sound dictations

   A. Teacher dictates sounds, children blend sounds dictated into words.

   B. Teacher dictates words, children say sounds of word.

   C. Children read sound patterns and words.
      Example: c-a-p c-ap cap
g-a-p g-ap gap
l-a-p l-ap lap
m-a-p m-ap map

D. Students write word at chalkboard from sounds dictated by teacher. Sounds, sound patterns and words are dictated as in C.

E. Student reads words written from sound dictation.

This procedure of teaching phonetic skills has all the advantages of having the qualities of a game. Sounds and sound patterns are rapidly learned during the training session, but are of little value if they are not retained and transferrable to the printed page of the textbook from which the child must read. We must therefore provide numerous opportunities to relate that which is newly learned in the training session to that which is already known and encourage the transference of this to all areas of instructions until it becomes an automatic process.

M. B. illustrates this point quite clearly. While reading from his textbook he pronounced a word which he was quite unfamiliar with at sight but was quite familiar with the sounds and the sound patterns which went to make up the word. He immediately stopped to make note of this remarkable discovery and commented, "Oh, those word drills", taking much pride in his ability to transfer knowledge gained from the training session to a realistic, typical classroom situation.

Level 6 — Though it is important to teach in small steps to assure success, it is equally important to proceed to a higher level of learning as rapidly as possible. Each child must achieve a feeling of accomplishment. Each child is believed to be achieving significantly below his true potentials if not below his level of intellectual functioning. He is required to make the necessary academic progress each year and generally needs to make additional progress if he is to close the distance between achievement and level of intellectual functioning. Within the confines of outlines presented in this section (remediation) we emphasize development of specific reading skills, of quickness of perception, strength of closure, sound blending and speed in changing sets.

RESULTS OF REMEDIATION

Academic achievement is the focus of emphasis and the medium through which we hope to recondition deviate behavior. The degree to which behavior is changed is clearly affected by the degree to which we are able to make children feel comfortable and adequate in academic tasks assigned them. Academic achievement is therefore a by-product — an instrument used in the process of rehabilitating behavior deviates in the special classes. Adaptivity, flexibility and creativity are the behavioral goals toward which we strive. Success in academic performance is directly related to the behavioral goals which we seek. Observations indicate that as academic performance improves, behavior becomes more flexible, less defensive and more spontaneously appropriate.

As academic performance improves the child is less threatened, more adaptive and creative in his behavioral responses. To help the children learn to adjust to school and its constellation of social situations is our goal. Education is our area of training and is therefore the tool used in effort to attain this goal.

We are aware of the fact that a child's academic output should be close to or commensurate with his level of intellectual functioning. However, we are more concerned about success in assignments made and know that if the child succeeds with assignments made at his level of achievement, the discrepancy between achievement and intellectual functioning will be dissipated. This is made possible by the fact that he gains confidence and ego strength when he experiences repeated success. Success in academic assignments and achievement progress is therefore often an indirect measure of gain in personality structure and emotional stability. This fact tends to be supported when children in the program are re-evaluated by the school psychologist. With this analogy in mind the following achievement evaluation for fourteen months of academic instruction is presented.

When admitted to the special class, after an average of 3-1/2 years in regular classes, the average academic retardation for chronological age was 1 year 8 months. This is significant only to the extent that it gives indications of the demands for achievement that had been placed upon the children. It is significant that they were achieving 1 year 1 month below level of intellectual functioning, had made an average of 1 year 5 months academic progress in the 3-1/2 years of school attendance and were becoming academically retarded at a rate of 5 months per school year. This information assists in determining the scope of the problem and provide guidelines for setting attainable academic goals for the class and for individuals of the class. Evaluation of achievement prior to admission to the special class also provides a basis for comparison of progress that is made in the special class.

The First 9 Months *

Academic progress during the first 9 months of special class placement was as follows:

One year 2 months academic gain was made during this 9 month period. This shows an academic gain of more than twice that made for the same period prior to admission to the special class. One year six months progress was made in reading, 6 months progress was made in spelling and progress of 1 year 3 months was made in arithmetic. Achievement progress ranged from a low of 2 months to a high of 2 years 3 months.

Achievement testing was done during this period to determine amount of progress

*This 9 month period excludes 3 month summer vacation

made in reading, spelling and arithmetic. The Wide Range achievement test was used for both pre- and post test results.

ACHIEVEMENT
(Reading, Spelling, Arithmetic)

No.	10-4-64	11-23-65	Academic Gain
1	.9	2.0	1.3
2	2.1	2.7	.6
3	3.1	3.3	.2
4	0	1.3	1.3
5	1.3	2.9	1.6
6	1.0	3.3	2.3
7	1.3	2.5	1.2
Average	1.5	2.7	+1.2

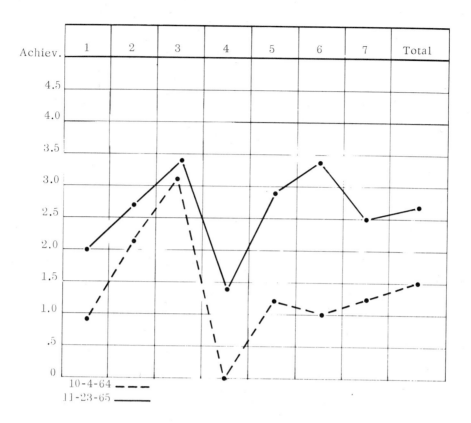

Achiev.	1	2	3	4	5	6	7	Total

10-4-64 _ _ _
11-23-65 _____

The Next 5 Months

At the beginning the next 5-month period diagnostic testing was done in the area of reading; the objective of which was to get an assessment of deficit areas in reading and to measure reading progress for the next 5 months. The Monroe test battery consisting of the following subtest:

    1. Gray's Oral
    2. Galt's Primary Reading Test (Silent reading for comprehension)
    3. Monroe Word Recognition
    4. Monroe Word Discrimination

was used to make this evaluation. These tests were administered 11-23-65 with the following results:

It was found that the weakest area in reading for this class was silent reading for comprehension. The strongest area was word discrimination. Oral reading for individuals of the class ranged from 0 to 3.4, silent reading for comprehension from 0 to 4.4, word recognition ranged from 0 to 4.9. Word discrimination ranged from 0 to 4.9 and composite reading ranged from 0 to 4.4. On the basis of this information instructional ma-

READING PROFILE

11-23-65 No.	Oral	Silent	Word Recognition	Word Discrimination	Average
1	1.0	1.9	2.2	2.5	1.9
2	3.1	3.0	3.4	2.9	3.1
3	3.6	4.4	4.9	4.9	4.4
4	0	0	0	0	0
5	1.8	3.2	3.6	4.5	3.2
6	3.4	2.9	4.2	4.2	3.6
7	3.1	2.4	4.5	4.2	3.6
Average	2.4	2.1	3.2	3.3	2.8

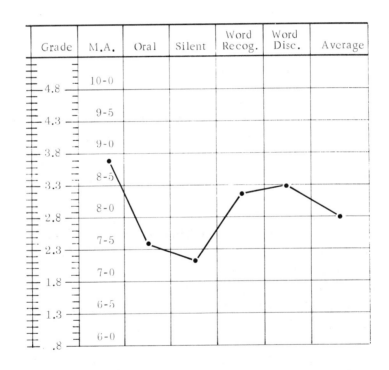

terials in the area of reading were selected ranging from kindergarten to fifth grade. Emphasis was placed on the lowest area, silent reading for comprehension.

An analysis of reading errors was also made. This analysis assists in determining the focus and emphasis of reading remediation for the class. Type errors made in reading was compared with mental age (8.9) of the class.

PROFILE OF READING ERRORS
For M. A. 8-9
Date — 11-23-65

(oral reading — silent reading
word recognition — word discrimination)

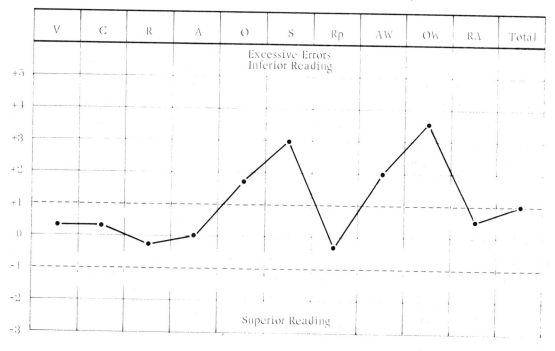

These results point out that the kinds of errors made most frequently by the class was substitutions and omission of words. The remedial program, based on results of analysis of reading, was (at this time) designed to emphasize silent reading for comprehension ranging from kindergarten to fifth grade and to correct substitutions and omissions of words in oral reading. The outline for remediation (p. 51) was followed.

SUMMARY OF READING RESULTS
(5 mo.)

	11-23-65	5-3-66	Months Progress
Oral reading	2-4	2-9	+ 5
Silent reading	2-1	3-0	+11
Word recognition	3-2	3-9	+ 7
Word discrimination	3-3	3-6	+ 3
Average Reading	2-8	3-4	+ 8

During the 5-month period that followed, an average reading gain of 8 months was made. Five months gain was made in oral reading (2.4 - 2.9), 11 months gain was made in silent reading for comprehension (2.1 - 3.0), 7 months in word recognition (3.2 - 3.9) and 3 months gain in word discrimination (3.3 - 3.6). Individual composite reading gain ranged from a low of 4 months to a high of 1 year 4 months. At this time Student #3 had been returned to "regular classes." Reading achievement was compared with intellectual functioning (M.A.).

The average M.A. at the time was 8.9. Average achievement was 2.7. Grade expectancy for M.A. at this time (G.N.=M.A. — 5.2) was 3.7. This shows an academic deficit of 1 year for M.A. Five months later the average M.A. was 9.2. Grade expectancy for this age was 4.0. Achievement at this time was 3.4. This shows a deficit in achievement for intellectual functioning of 8 months. Gradually the distance between achievement and intellectual functioning, which was initially 1 year 1 month, is being closed. The necessary academic progress plus additional progress is being made.

Changes in Reading Behavior

Both the quantity and the quality of reading changed during the period 11-23-65 to 5-3-66. At the beginning of this test period substitutions and omissions of words comprised the kinds of errors made most frequently in reading by the class. At the end of this period substitutions and omissions of words in reading were well within the normal range. Refusals and words aided in oral reading now represents a problem area. However, this problem area is not as intense as either of the former disabilities. A graphic comparison of reading errors for the period is as follows:

PROFILE OF READING ERRORS
For M. A. 8.9 & 9.2

(oral reading-silent reading
word recognition-word discrimination)

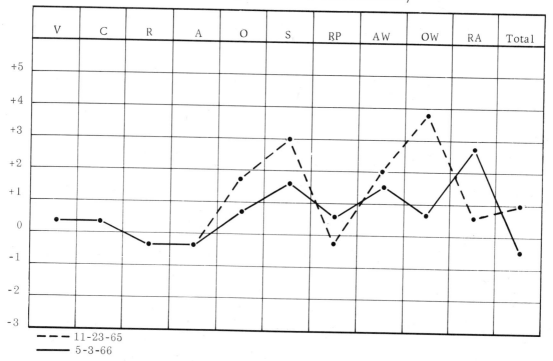

- - - - 11-23-65
———— 5-3-66

Vowel, consonant and reversal errors remained at the same level within the normal range. Omission of words, substitution of words and addition of words decreased in number of errors. Repetitions, refusals and words aided increased, and total errors made in reading decreased, remaining within the normal range. It should be noted that the basis used for comparing reading errors is not chronological age but level of intellectual functioning and grade norm indicated by this level.

Psycholinguistic Abilities

Assessment of psycholinguistic abilities revealed that the average communication skills of the class was at the 6 year 7 month level at the time of testing (11-23-65). There was a deficit of 2 years 10 months in communication skills when compared with chronological age. The average mental age of the class at this time was 8 years 9 months. Linguistic functioning revealed a deficit of 2 years 2 months in language functioning when compared with mental age (level of intellectual functioning). The children were achieving (2.8) 1 year 3 months above their level of communication skills (Language age 6.7 – G.E. 1.5) age.

Ability to **internally relate that which is seen** and **ability to remember that which is said** were the lowest areas of psycholinguistic functioning. The objective of our plan for remediation was to train these deficit communication skills. Success in training these abilities was as follows:

1. Ability to anticipate grammatical patterns increased 9 months (7.7 to 8.4).

2. Ability to understand that which is said remained at the seven year third month level.

3. Ability to express by way of gestures that which is seen and heard advanced 1 year 2 months (6.10 - 8.8).

4. Ability to internally relate that which is said gained 5 months (6.10 - 7.3).

5. Visual memory improved 5 months (6.4 - 6.9).

6. Vocal expression remained at the 6 year level.

7. Auditory memory advanced 8 months (5.11 - 6.7).

8. Ability to internally relate visual stimuli advanced 1 year 5 months (5.9 - 6.7).

9. Ability to understand that which is said improved more than 1 year 3 months (7.11 to above norms of 9.2).

The composite psycholinguistic gain for this 5-month period was 10 months (6.7 to 7.5). A composite of 8 months academic gain was made during the same period in reading.

Summary of Reading Results

During the 5-month period between 11-23-65 and 5-3-66 the class made an average of 8 months academic gain in reading. This progress ranged from a low of 3 months to a high of 11 months for individual students. Average reading at the beginning of this period was 2.7; average reading at the end of the period was 3.4. Progress in oral reading, silent reading, word recognition and word discrimination was as follows.

	11-23-65	5-3-66	Months Progress
Oral Reading	2.4	2.9	+5
Silent Reading	2.1	3.0	11 mo.
Word Recognition	3.2	3.9	+7
Word Discrimination	3.3	3.6	+3
Average Progress	2.7	3.4	+8

Comparison of achievement for 1 year 2 months (excluding summer vacation) shows that an average of 1 year 10 months progress was made. The necessary gain of 1 year 2 months was made, plus an additional 8 months. The deficit between achievement and intellectual functioning was closed by 5 months. Achievement deficit for intellectual functioning at the beginning of the class was 1 year 1 month; this deficit after 14 months was decreased to 8 months for intellectual functioning. The deficit was 1 year 8 months for chronological age; at the end of 14 months it had been reduced to 1 year 1 month for chronological age. The children are no longer regressing 5 months per school year but are making the necessary progress plus additional academic gain.

ACHIEVEMENT RESULTS
(Reading)

9 Mo. (Excludes summer vacation)		5 Mo.
10-4-64	11-23-65	5-3-66
1.5	1.9	2.3
2.2	3.1	3.5
3.3	4.4	*
0	0	.8
1.8	3.2	4.6
1.0	3.6	4.7
1.4	3.6	4.3
1.5	2.7	3.4
	(+1.2)	(+.8)

Returned to regular class

The purpose of this chapter has been to describe behavioral, intellectual, academic and linguistic disabilities of a class of emotionally disturbed children in Elgin's public school system. It has been the aim of this writer to point out a few of the controls and training procedures used to help these children compensate for their emotional handicap. Achievement results of 14 months' work with the children have been pointed to as support of our position and endeavors to assist emotionally disturbed children in returning to the main stream of school functioning. We do not classify our progress as a success, only time can make this classification. Success of children who have returned to the regular classes (5) will give us clearer indication of the success of this program and will no doubt result in revisions of the present program. Neither time nor space would permit the discussion of intake and return procedures or the role of the special class as related to the school in which it is located. The relationship between the special class and the school milieu is of such importance that it could easily consume a chapter. This relationship therefore merits a comment from the principals of the school in which the special class is located. The principal of Grant school at the time this class opened was Mrs. Leona Row, who makes the following observations:

"In the spring of 1964 it was evident that one room in the Grant school building would not be needed for a regular classroom. The speculation started: Could we use it for a remedial reading program (if a teacher would be provided), a special interest room (for art, drama, square dancing), etc. So many possibilities! A call from Child Study requested space for a pre-school deaf room or for a Socially Maladjusted room. Would we welcome a special class in the building? A new program?

A discussion with the staff indicated an openness to invite Child Study to establish one of the new programs in our building. It was understood that the pre-school deaf class would operate as a separate unit entirely. The Socially Maladjusted class would operate apart from the regular school program until a member was ready to participate, or begin to participate, again in the normal school program. Thus a selected class would act as a "half-way house" to gradually reorient the child into the regular activities and expectations of the normal classroom. We were told there would be no more than eight children allowed in the class so it sounded interesting but presented no threat to overloading any classroom, if a child did not work out in the regular classroom he would return to the Socially Maladjusted until he was ready. Surely there was a need for such a program! There seemed to be likely candidates in some of our classes.

In the fall the Socially Maladjusted class was instituted. The instructor was an experienced administrator as well as a master teacher. The class was gradually filled after proper staffing by the professional team (teachers — both referring and receiving), principal, nurse, social worker and psychologist.

The staff watched the progress of the new program with interest. To see the bare room with individual offices take on interest, corners with pictures, charts and books was deeply satisfying. Even more exciting was to see the aggressive child begin to assume responsibility for his own actions, or the timid and withdrawn child blossom out into a more outgoing and happy child! Progress seemed slow but sure.

At first there were comments — "only 8 children!", "anyone can manage a small number!", "sounds like an easy job." Later one could hear "He earns his pay!", "I'd rather have my 30!", etc.

A special class, such as this, doubles the load of the administrator in staffing time, evaluation with teachers, and working with parents, bus, and other problems. A great deal of time is demanded in transferring the children in and out of classes as they are ready to go — small details but necessary.

Even more important to the success of the new program was the cooperation with the other teachers in the building. When a child seemed ready to work normally he was placed for an hour of reading or arithmetic with a regular class daily. This added to the class load of the already full class, but the staff willingly agreed. With this type of mutual understanding and cooperation the program achieved success.

Principalship changed the following year but a basis for continuing a positive relationship with the school had been established. Mr. James Franck (Principal comments: "The relationship between special class and school not only enhances the growth of the emotionally disturbed children but has a direct effect upon the teaching staff as well. The presence of the children and particularly the teacher tends in general to cause the teachers of the general staff to look more favorably upon children who demonstrate emotional imbalance in their classroom. The teachers are far more likely to appreciate the difficulties facing children with such problems and reduces the chance of having teachers place such children in their class in the category of incorrigible.

Also, the long-term results of the teacher of the emotionally disturbed class helps teachers to recognize that rehabilitation actually can take place among children with problems of this nature.

Finally, the presence of the special teacher as a faculty member makes available to the staff new methods and approaches to the problems of teaching children with various emotional problems and even those which demonstrate quite normal behavior patterns. The special teacher can act as a resource person and can add significant contributions whenever teachers exchange ideas concerning student behavior and self control."

In conclusion then, the placement of the special classroom for the emotionally disturbed in the regular school setting is a logical arrangement. It is simply by its nature a co-operative enterprise.

ACKNOWLEDGMENT

I wish to thank Mr. J. T. Nelson (Director of Child Study Department—Elgin Public Schools), Mr. Richard Cutts and Mr. Morton Becker (School Psychologists—Elgin Public Schools) for their advice and council in preparing this chapter.

A very special thanks to Mrs. Lida Hunt (Special Teacher of Emotionally Disturbed Children—Elgin Public Schools) whose insight and experience in teaching emotionally disturbed children was freely given, and represent a major contribution to this chapter.

I also wish to thank Mrs. Leona Row and Mr. James Franck for their contributions to the chapter. Their position as principal, at different times, of the school in which this class is located is valuable for an understanding of the relationship of the special class to the total school program. The acceptance of the special class by the total school milieu determines to a great degree the success or failure of the special program.

References

1. Bender, L. PSYCHOPATHOLOGY OF CHILDREN WITH ORGANIC BRAIN DISORDERS. Springfield, Illinois: Charles C. Thomas, 1956.

2. Benton, A.L. RIGHT-LEFT DISCRIMINATION AND FINGER LOCALIZATION. N.Y.: Harper & Bros., 1959.

3. Durrell, D. DURRELL ANALYSIS OF READING DIFFICULTY, NEW EDITION. Chicago: World Book Co., 1955.

4. Gates, A.I. THE ROLE OF PERSONALITY MALADJUSTMENT IN READING DISABILITY. J. Genetic Psychol., 59: 77, 1941.

5. Graham, F.K., & Kendall, B.S. MEMORY-FOR-DESIGNS TEST: REVISED GENERAL MANUAL. Percept. Mot. Skills, 11: 147-188, 1960.

6. Gray, W.S. ON THEIR OWN IN READING. (Rev. Ed.) Chicago: Scott, Foresman, 1960.

7. Kephart, N.C. THE SLOW-LEARNER IN THE CLASSROOM. Columbus, Ohio: Charles E. Merrill, 1960.

8. Kirk, S.A. HEMISPHERIC CEREBRAL DOMINANCE AND HEMISPHERIC EQUIPOTENTIALITY. Comp. Psychol. Monogr., 11, No. 5, 1935.

9. Kass, C.E., and Bateman, B.D. THE EDUCABILITY OF PSYCHOLINGUISTIC FUNCTIONS IN RETARDED CHILDREN. Unpublished progress report, Project No. 1766. Illinois Psychiatric Training and Research Authority of the Illinois State Department of Mental Health, 1962.

10. Kass, C.E. SOME PSYCHOLOGICAL CORRELATES OF SEVERE READING DISABILITY (DYSLEXIA). Unpublished Doctoral Dissertation. University of Illinois — Urbana, Illinois, 1962.

11. McCarthy, J.J. THE ILLINOIS TEST OF PSYCHOLINGUISTIC ABILITIES — AN APPROACH TO DIFFERENTIAL DIAGNOSIS. Amer. J. Ment Def., 66, 399-412, 1961.

12. Kirk, S.A. ILLINOIS TEST OF PSYCHOLINGUISTIC ABILITIES: EXPERIMENTAL EDITION. Urbana, Ill.: Inst. Res. Except. Child., University of Illinois, 1961.

13. Montoe, M. CHILDREN WHO CANNOT READ. Chicago: University of Chicago Press, 1932.

14. Penfield, W., & Roberts, L. SPEECH AND BRAIN-MECHANISMS. Princeton, N.Y.: Princeton University Press, 1959.

15. Robinson, H.M. WHY PUPILS FAIL IN READING. Chicago: University Press, 1946.

16. Strauss, A.A., & Lehtinen, L.E. PSYCHOPATHOLOGY AND EDUCATION OF THE BRAIN-INJURED CHILD. N.Y.: Grune & Stratton, Vol. I, 1947.

17. Wepman, J.M. DYSLEXIA: ITS RELATIONSHIP TO LANGUAGE ACQUISITION AND CONCEPT FORMATION. Paper read at Dyslexia Conference, Johns Hopkins University, November, 1961.

UNTAPPED LEARNING ABILITY IN TRAINABLE MENTALLY RETARDED CHILDREN

David Rothenberg, Ph.D.,
Clinical Psychologist in Private Practice,
Miami Beach, Florida
and Consultant in Clinical Psychology,
Hope School, Miami, Florida

DAVID ROTHENBERG, Ph.D.

HISTORY

The question of the relationship between the concepts of learning and mental retardation dates back at least to 1799 when Itard (1932) attempted to educate the Wild Boy of Aveyron, and to Seguin's efforts with idiots in 1846. Since then the nature-nurture controversy has remained unsettled. The "naturalist," predominating before 1800, insisted that heredity was the primary cause of mental retardation, that treatment and education were precluded since "Once retarded—always retarded; nothing can be done." The use of "mentally retarded" as a distinct entity has been based primarily on the IQ score on an intelligence test, ranging from IQ 85 or below used by the American Psychiatric Association to IQ 75 or 70 and below as used by psychologists. Doll (1932) pointed out the inadequacies of the IQ based on a definition established more than thirty years ago; "It stops short at an arbitrary statistical gatepost and does not concern itself with the many ramifications of the conditions which, if adequately explored, would reveal the absurdity of its point of view."

That a lack of relationship may exist between an intelligence test score and the ability to learn may be seen in Gardner's study (1954) of severely retarded children. Divided into high and low groups, according to mental age (MA) as measured by the Cattell (1960) Infant Intelligence Scale, each subject (S) was presented with several learning situations. In the first situation the child had to learn to obtain a food reward from one of three boxes which was covered with a black cloth. In subsequent situations the size and position of the black cloth was varied. In the final situation Ss were able to generalize their learning and found food in the only box that was not covered with the black cloth. Gardner found that the performance of the low groups (MA 20-29 months) was not significantly different from the high group (MA 30-49 months) suggesting that the mental tests did not tap some uncovered abilities measured on this singular task. If a more encompassing measure had been used, a more meaningful comparison of abilities of these Ss might have been possible. Perhaps, in accord with Jastak's (1949) view of intellect as a capacity, potentiality, or power,

.....there is in every psychometric record an ability through which a person's latent intellectual power may be adequately approximated. It is the ability which yields the highest score.....we call this index of latent potential the Altitude Quotient.

It may be, however, that most existing measures of intellectual capacity are so highly multi-determined, item by item, even the factored tests, that they apparently do not measure a specific ability and seem unable to tap "latent" ability singly.

The Revised Stanford-Binet Intelligence Scales, the Wechsler Scales, the Seguin Formboard and related tests use items which require a multiplicity of modalities for response and are in this sense "global." Thus, vision, touch, and kinethesis are jointly involved in most test item requirements. Birch and Lefford (1963) reported investigation of intersensory function involving visual, kinesthetic, and haptic (manual exploration) modalities. They found these well developed in the normal school age children. The modalities were not evaluated separately, however. Furthermore, a prerequisite for evaluating the S was his ability to perform visual discrimination tasks perfectly on the Seguin Formboard. What may be said regarding nonperfect performance on this task? Is visual discrimination an all-or-none process? Perhaps even the Seguin Formboard tasks, like others purporting to measure some designated intellective skill, are so complex that for younger or retarded children the uncovered potential for learning is not being measured separately at all. The experimental tasks in the study required the same intermodal functions as the test to select the Ss.

Visual perception has received the most investigative attention of the various modalities, beginning with the historic study of Von Senden (1932) who reported that for Ss born blind and who later were able to see, certain stimulus classes had relative values for learning. Thus, he reported, if the color of an object was changed, the name of the object also had to be changed. Hebb (1949) also suggests that color perceptions may be nativistic or innate while form is learned.

Goldstein (1939), reporting on brain damaged individuals, gives evidence that they have difficulty in perceiving size and pattern (form). "This concrete dependence upon the size may be overcome by introducing the enlarged designs. The concrete dependence upon the 'design-pattern' may be overcome by presenting the designs 'broken up into squares.' "

As was noted by both Seguin and Itard, retarded children learned more readily when larger materials (letters of the alphabet, pencils, tools) were used. In terms of Hebb's (1949) model, grosser stimulus objects provide more stimulation at the sensory surface, producing more abundant excitation in the higher centers of the nervous system, and causing perceptual structures (cell assemblies) to develop more readily. The likelihood of excessive stimulation would suggest that the sensory input should not "over-load" the central nervous system.

The possibility that the usual sensory input is below the required optimal level is a frequently underscored rationale for using several sensory modalities or dimensions in a given perceptual task. Fernald (1943) demonstrated that slow learners are aided in learning words by tracing letters with the finger or stylus. By engaging more cortex and by including the motoric area of the brain, more opportunity for interfacilitation is provided, supposedly.

On the other hand, that the optimum stimulation may be exceeded is suggested in the study by Cruse (1961) and by Jones (1963). They dealt with the problem of visual distractibility in mentally retarded children utilizing an artificial simplification of the experimental situation, thereby limiting the total sensory input and distraction of attention. According to Hebb's model, attention is controlled through the delivery of facilitation from an active organizational structure (cell assembly) to another cell assembly not yet active. Thus, new learning may benefit from reduced distraction as a result of eliminating or minimizing irrevelant stimuli, or from training in attention (i.e., teaching S how to **exclude** irrevelant stimuli) as reported by Arnoult (1951, 1953, 1954).

Chansky and Taylor (1964) report that retarded children trained to perceive visually with greater precision and to organize these perceptions, increased in psychometric intelligence as much as two standard errors for the particular test used (WISC).

But what stimuli are irrelevant or otherwise detract from learning? Are additional information-bearing stimuli (e.g., Fernald's approach) necessarily beneficial to learning, or is too much information merely distracting to some learners? Are some classes of stimuli more adequate than others in their ability to elicit learning responses? Might not some learners benefit from restricting the problem to a single category of stimuli? Visual stimuli, for example, may be regarded in terms of shape, color, and size. Common test items (oddity type*) may present a problem even where the odd member of a set differs in all three categories. Are some learners being unknowingly overwhelmed with too much information so that some of it acts as interfering stimuli?

The above studies support the conclusion that the optimal stimulus type for learning required to solve oddity problems has not been established. Is color plus shape more facilitating for visual perceptual response than any one or a combination of two of these? Is there a significant difference in the effectiveness of particular stimulus classes

---

*The oddity type test item requires the Ss to select from a group of items the one that is in some way different from all the others.

for visual perception by retarded children? Is there an optimum number or combination of stimulus characteristics which may be utilized in the visual discrimination by retarded children?

The purpose of the investigation reported in this chapter was to determine if some previously uncovered learning ability might be demonstrated in trainable mentally retarded children.

HYPOTHESES

The hypotheses for this investigation centered upon the key notion that discrimination training with simplified cues would improve performance on complex items more than comparable training on other complex items. Also included were subsidiary predictions of relative efforts of the several types of training procedures utilized and an hypotheses regarding the role of Mental Age.

1. Moderately mentally retarded children will make more correct solutions of multiple stimulus class oddity items if they are first trained to discriminate items whose figures exhibit oddity in terms of a single stimulus class (Color, Form, Size).

2. Color, as a single stimulus characteristic will rank highest in the facilitation of visual discriminations.

3. Form, as a single stimulus characteristic will rank second in the facilitation of visual discriminations.

4. Size, as a stimulus characteristic will rank third in the facilitation of visual discrimination.

5. Test-taking practice will rank fourth in its facilitation of visual discrimination.

6. The level of initial ability as measured by the Revised Stanford-Binet will have a significant effect on the difference score between pretest and posttest.

PROCEDURE

Subjects

The Ss were sixty children (plus another twelve comprising an additional control group) whose scores on the 1937 Revised Stanford-Binet, Form L (Rev. S-B Scale), designated them as moderately retarded (IQ 25-50), MA 3 years 4 months to 4 years 6 months, chronological age (CA) 6 years 6 months to 16 years. Individuals described as displaying gross emotional or physical disabilities, as reported by the institution in which they were residing, were excluded. In this study, the research population was selected from Sunland Training Center at Ft. Myers, Florida (resident population, 960).

In order to determine the accuracy of using Pinneau's tables (1960) for calculating the Ss' current intelligence level from earlier tests, ten randomly selected Ss were readministered the Rev. S-B Scale, Form L. Table I indicates that the mean of the MAs obtained was not significantly different from that of the MAs projected from the tables for that test. Thus the projected MAs may be considered as an appropriate measure for matching Ss on that criterion. **(All tables at end of article.)**

Another group of twelve Ss, drawn from the same population, according to the same criteria, was used as an additional control group.

Materials:

The materials consisted of standard and especially made oddity items, as follows:

1. Certain items of the Columbia Mental Maturity Scale, 1959 Revision, which are detailed later. The full scale consists of one hundred items, each printed on a card 6"x 19". Each item consists of a series of from three to five drawings. The drawings depicted on the cards are, in general, "within the range of experience of most children, even for the handicapped whose environmental backgrounds may have been "limited" (Instruction manual).

In each item the task for the S is to select from the series of drawings the one which is different from, or unrelated to, the others in the series. The discrimination required is that of recognizing oddity, the picture which does not belong with the others, i.e., "the eduction of a principle for organizing the pictures so as to exclude just one." The bases for discrimination are differences in color, form, and size of geometric figures and/or familiar objects such as Cat — Automobile. The items are arranged in order of difficulty with an odd-even reliability of .89 (CA 4) to .92 (CA 10). The items selected were those rated at the MA level for the Ss to be used, and containing only geometric drawings for discrimination of the odd member of each set.

2. A series of **modified** C.M.M.S. geometric figure items, replicas of certain of the standard items, except that Color, Form or Size was the only stimulus property available to be discriminated as the "oddity" characteristic.

3. A series of **original** geometric figure items, in the C.M.M.S. style, using Color, or

Form, or Size, **only**, as the stimulus property to be discriminated as the "oddity" characteristic.

4. A series of **original** geometric items, in the C.M.M.S. style, the correct member odd in Color, Form and Size, simultaneously.

In the C.M.M.S. type items utilized in the present research, no basic changes in materials, procedures, or response style were made. Changes were restricted to those required to achieve certain discriminable stimulus property differences. The question arises of whether these changes invalidate the standard norms to the extent of removing the items from the mental-age range of the children used in the study.

Three major types of test adaptation for special populations have been reported: changing test materials; changing examiner's procedures; changing manner of examinee's responses. This practice has been investigated further, in terms of the a priori assumption that the adaptive use of a test does not necessarily invalidate the norms established on the standard mode of administering and responding to the test items. Maisel, Allen, and Tallarico (1962) concluded that, for their study with the Leiter International Scale, adaptive testing using standard norms was feasible. They caution especially, however, against modification in the size of the materials to be used, if standard norms are to be applied.

It was assumed, therefore, that since size of materials, procedures or responses were not changed the MA norms applicable to the standardized items would be valid for the original items, and that all were within the response range of the Ss tested.

Method

In summary, the total research population was first rated for intelligence level; random assignment then was made from Tables of Random Numbers (Edwards, 1959, p. 381) of Ss to one of five separate treatment groups. All Ss were then given a pretraining test, trained according to treatment group one week after, then given the posttraining test another week later to determine the effect on the treatment provided each group. Finally, forty-eight of the original sixty Ss (all who were still available) were retested a second time after a two month interval.

The sixth group, added as a further control group, was provided the same sequence of experimental procedures, beginning five weeks after the second posttest of the other five treatment groups.

Treatment groups $^TG_1$ (no training), $^TG_2$ (test-taking practice), and $^TG_6$ (training with color, form, and size cues simultaneously present) served as control groups.

Treatment groups $^TG_3$ (color training), $^TG_4$ (form training), and $^TG_5$ (size training) served as the experimental groups.

Tables 2 through 7 give data on each S by group. Table 8 shows the basic scheme of the experimental design. **(All tables at end of article.)**

Initial Test

The **pretraining test** was begun as follows: seated, facing the S across the table, the examiner said, "I am going to show you a card with pictures on it. You will see that one of the pictures does not belong there—does not go there. Point out the picture that does not belong with the others." The examiner then showed the S Card No. 3 of C.M.M.S. placing it before him on the table. The item numbers on each card were at the bottom of the card, and upside down, as it was presented to the S; the numbers were at the examiner's upper right. The S was expected to point to a drawing on the first card and, if he was correct, the examiner said "right" or "good" and proceeded to the next card. If the S erred on the first card, the examiner indicated the right answer and explained how it differed and why it was the correct answer, saying, "These two (pointing) are red squares and so they belong together. This is a blue circle, and so it does not belong with the other two." If necessary, the examiner used Card No. 4 and No. 10 as additional demonstration items, explaining in each instance how one of the drawings differed from the other on the card. No credit was given for any item that the examiner explained. All Ss were able to make a correct response after explanation of the first three items. All were considered, in accordance with the manual for this Scale, as thereby being measurable.

If an S made no response after 20-25 seconds, the examiner resorted to a question such as, "Which do you think it is?" to obtain either a correct response or definite indication of failure. The examiner continued to expose all the cards used in standard numerical order. All cards except the one to which the S was actually responding were kept face down or out of the S's sight to minimize distraction. If there was any examiner doubt that the S understood the requirements of this procedure, the examiner repeated the instructions before each item, saying, "Remember to point to the one that does not belong with the others." All correct responses elicited the word "good" or "right" from the examiner.

The examiner made certain that the S actually looked at all drawings on each card. Some Ss gave the correct response on one card and then on successive cards continued to point to the picture in the same position without considering the other pictures. When this seemed to be happening, the examiner repeated, "Look at all the pictures and then show me the one that does not belong."

Verbal responses were discouraged since the Ss may later have failed to designate a correct response merely because they could not name the drawing; or they may have indicated some other alternative merely because they could name it. Such a failure might have denoted a lack of familiarity with names rather than the deficiency of discrimination which the Scale is intended to measure. The pointing procedure was considered as the only scorable response and no oral responses, as an oral response, was credited. The S was required to indicate nonverbally what the correct response was; in no instance was it necessary to modify procedures in accord with any alternately available method of response.

The score on this procedure was number of correct responses made to the particular set of items used.

The pretraining and posttraining test included C.M.M.S. items as follows:

Standard C.M.M.S.	MA	Items
3	42	3
4	42	3
10	45	3
13	26	3
16	27	3
28	52	4

These items contain the multiple stimulus properties of Color, Form, and Size in combination, and all three demonstrate the "oddity" characteristic to be discriminated.

All Ss were administered, in addition, 18 "modified" C.M.M.S. drawings, each demonstrating oddity cue by only a single stimulus property. (6 Color: 6 Form; 6 Size). It was scored for each of the four subtests of 6 items each, as was the posttraining test. These items are reproduced as P-1 to P-21 in Figure I.

Posttraining Test

The posttraining test was the same as the pretraining test, including instructions to Ss.

Examiners

In order to eliminate the possibility of examiner bias in this research, two examiners were utilized. Both were experienced in the use of the Columbia Mental Maturity Scale with retarded children. The investigator provided the pretraining test of initial ability and the posttraining tests, while the Resident Staff Psychologist provided the training under the various experimental conditions as indicated. The examiner providing the

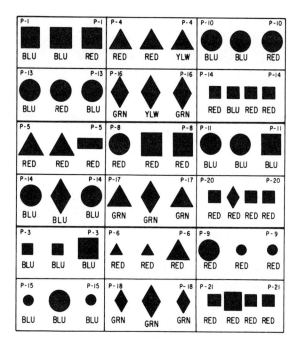

FIGURE 1

Testing Materials

pretraining and posttraining tests was not aware of the particular type of training given any specific S, in order to avoid bias in the acknowledgment of correct responses.

In order to minimize the effect of particular days of training and/or the order in which the Ss would be trained, the training order was systematically counterbalanced to the extent possible. In the initial tests of ability, Ss were provided the 6 Color; 6 Form; 6 Size cards in a systematically varied order, to balance for possible effects of such order. This order was repeated on posttraining tests.

Training Criterion

All training series were continued to a criterion of all correct in three separate sequences of eight items, or training was terminated after 96 trials, whichever came first.

The training items are reproduced as T-3 to T-23 in Figure 2 and T-5 to T-24 in Figure 3. Also shown in Figure 3 are items A-H, used for training with group $^TG_6$.

Training Group $^TG_6$

In reviewing this research after the procedures were completed in accordance with the

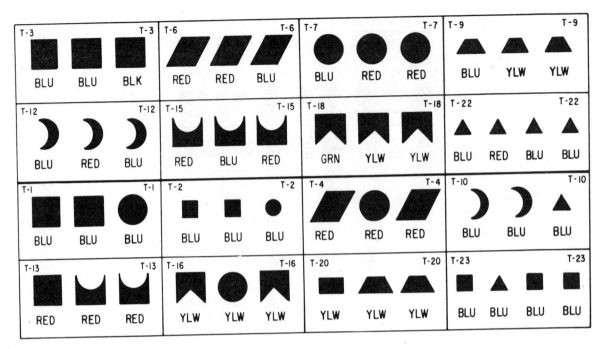

FIGURE 2

Training Materials

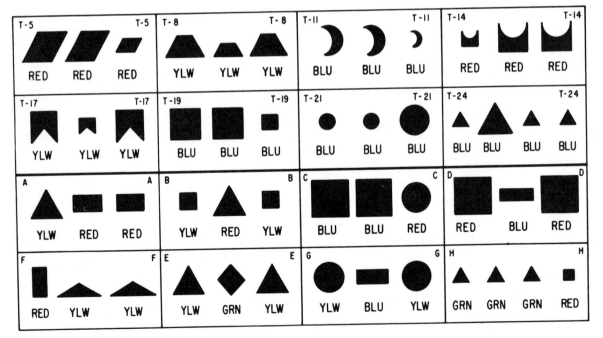

FIGURE 3

Training Materials

original design, it became apparent that another training group would be desirable as an additional control. This group was trained with a set of "C.M.M.S. type" items demonstrating oddity simultaneously via Color and Form and Size cues. The purpose was to answer the questions of whether the gains made on triply odd items by some training groups on the simplified single cue training items could have occurred as well with training on complex items.

This group, $^T G_6$, was selected from the same general population and according to the same criteria as the other training groups. The twelve Ss received the same pretraining test, training on item odd in CFS simultaneously, and posttraining test program as did the other Ss. The two examiners were the same, and performed the same functions.

There were, however, two variations from the procedure accorded the other groups. First, the examiner providing pre-posttraining tests was, of course, aware of the particular type of training these Ss received. Second, there was a succession of Ss with similar training, rather than the randomized order of the other variously trained Ss.

RESULTS

Analysis of Data

The pretest raw scores were first evaluated for normality of distribution.

Analyses of variance were then made of the scores for pretest—posttest by training groups and high-low intelligence levels, following the form in Edwards (1960, page 227).

A comparison of the means for the difference between pretest—posttest on all 24 criterion items and on the 6 C.M.M.S. subset items only was made in accordance with Scheffe (Edwards, 1960, page 154).

Also, a **t** test comparing the mean difference score on C.M.M.S. subset items for training group 6: 3 + 4 + 5 was computed.

The frequency distribution of the pretraining test total scores (the sum of all items correct) for all Ss was tested for goodness of fit and found not to differ significantly from a normal distribution, p. $\Rightarrow$ .16, df = 2, x^2 = 3.384 using Fisher's (1936) table.

The results of the analyses of variance of test scores for each S on pretraining and posttraining tests are shown in Tables 10 and 11. These results are described in relation to the several hypotheses stated earlier in this chapter.[*]

[*]See title HYPOTHESES

The total difference score means (i.e., using score difference pretest and posttest on all 24 criterion items) are shown in Table 13 and Table 14 and Figure 4.

The total raw score means are shown in Table 12 and Figure 5.

Scheffe's Test of Multiple Comparisons (1953) was utilized to determine the signficance of the differences among the total means of the difference scores for the treatment groups and for C.M.M.S. subset scores. This is shown in Table 15.

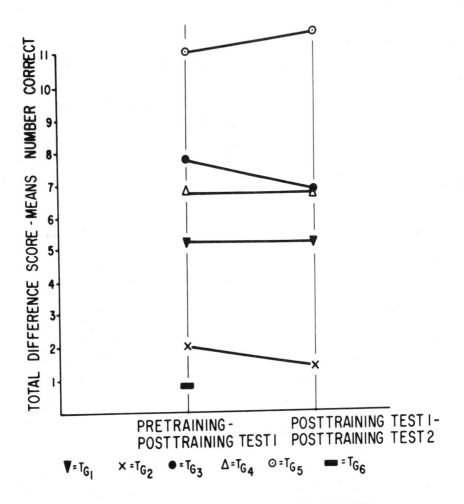

TOTAL DIFFERENCE SCORE MEANS PRETEST -
POSTTEST 1 -- POSTTEST 2   6 TRAINING GROUP

FIGURE 4

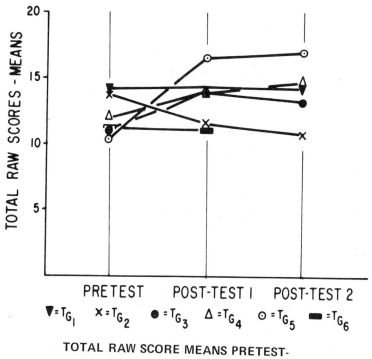

PRETEST   POST-TEST I   POST-TEST 2

$\blacktriangledown = T_{G_1}$ $\times = T_{G_2}$ $\bullet = T_{G_3}$ $\triangle = T_{G_4}$ $\odot = T_{G_5}$ $\blacksquare = T_{G_6}$

TOTAL RAW SCORE MEANS PRETEST-
POSTTEST 1 -- POSTTEST 2   6 TRAINING GROUP

FIGURE 5

The Stanford-Binet, Form L MAs projected to the same month for the initial 60 Ss, correlated by the product-moment method with the pretraining test total scores: $r = -.148$, $r = 1.114$, **p.** $= > .05$. Further, the additional S-B tests of 10 Ss described elsewhere (Table II) also failed to yield a significant difference suggesting that extrapolation of MA's was justified. The nonsignificant **r** for the S-B vs C.M.M.S. oddity item pretest are not measuring the same intellectual factors of these Ss.

Interpretation of Results

Visual training in single stimulus class was found to have a significant influence upon discrimination of multiple stimuli of Color and Form and Size. This appears in accordance with the hypothesis of Lashley and Wade (1946) that stimulus generalization may be established during testing by calling the Ss attention to a given stimulus characteristic.

This generalization may be considered as a positive capacity of the organism; and ability to generalize from absolute characteristics of stimuli or object (Razran, 1949). These results suggest however, that the "absolute characteristics" must first be apparent to the Ss before capacity for generalization can be assumed.

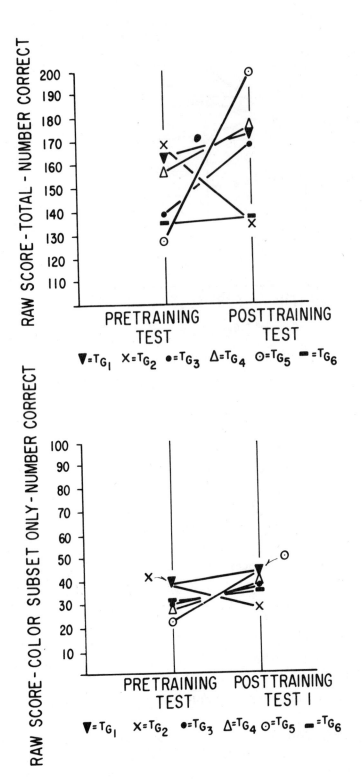

FIGURE 6

Total Raw Scores Pretraining Test -- Posttraining Test 1

6 Training Groups

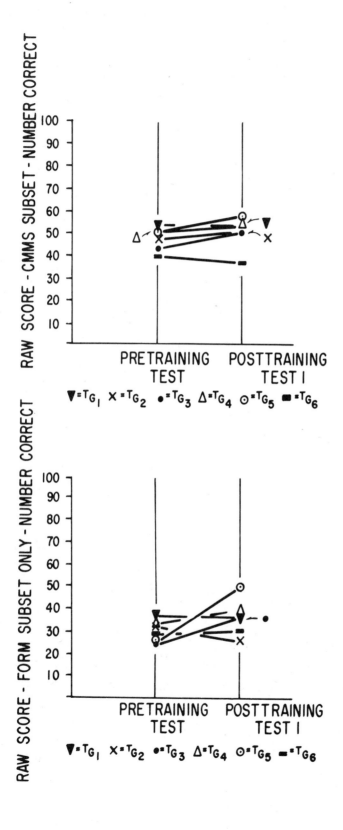

FIGURE 7

Total Raw Scores Pretraining Test -- Posttraining Test 1

6 Training Groups

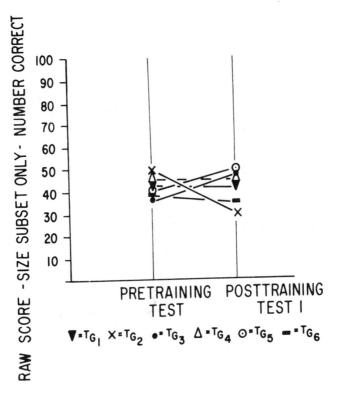

FIGURE 8

Total Raw Scores

Pretraining Test -- Posttraining Test 1

6 Training Groups

Facilitating effects of the stimulus characteristic were hypothetically ranked in the order: Color, Form, Size. These relative positions were not confirmed; however, Size characteristics were found to be a significantly greater influence on discrimination rather than either color or form.

This result may be interpreted in terms of a study by Grice and Saltz (1950). The authors assumed that the visual size dimension of the door was an intensity dimension and that "the total amount of reflected light would be a function of stimulus area." (p. 706). The gradient for generalization which they report is positively accelerated for larger stimuli.

The "test-taking practice not a facilitation factor" hypothesis in this study stated that training with irrelevant stimuli, as test-taking practice, would rank fourth, or lowest, in its facilitation of visual discrimination. This prediction was confirmed. As a matter of fact, this type of training did not facilitate discrimination at all. To the contrary, Ss trained in this manner did not do as well as those receiving no training, with a consistently poorer performance on Posttraining tests as compared to Pretraining tests, $p < .01$. The effects of the training of Ss to discriminate among line drawings were not generalized to geometric form discriminations. This would suggest that geometric forms provide "absolute characteristics" of a different stimulus class than line drawings. Thus, the form differences in the line drawings may have been obscured by the presence of properties involving the use of different intellective functions for discrimination. The significant loss could be interpreted as the result of the line drawing practice developing a "set" which interfered with performance with geometric figures.

Intellectual abilities and facilitation effects—the sixth hypothesis was not supported. The gross nature of the MA scores yielded by intelligence tests generally, and the Revised Stanford-Binet Scale specifically, may have masked the sensitivity to any differences in visual discrimination ability which may exist. Thus a specific "latent power" referred to by Jastak may have remained "hidden," if it does exist.

However, the lower intelligence level Ss did improve significantly, as compared to higher MA Ss, on color stimulus items, as a result of training provided. This suggests the level of learning offered in this type training was so "basic" that it benefited the more deficient Ss.

The discrimination activities demonstrated by the Ss in the present research may be considered as resulting in a transfer of training since the identical elements, certain stimulus characteristics, were transferred from one task to another. This is in accord with Goldstein's (1939, p. 268) concept of secondary rigidity, dependent upon the impairment of higher mental processes, i.e. intelligence or abstraction. Impaired individuals are not rigid.

DISCUSSION AND CONCLUSIONS

Simple Versus Complex Visual Discrimination

The purpose of the present investigation was to determine whether or not there exists in the impaired intellective abilities of mentally retarded children, as measured by visual discriminations tasks on the Revised Stanford-Binet Scale, certain abilities obscured by the multidimensioned nature of these measures. It was predicted that if these retarded individuals were trained to make discrimination of a single stimulus characteristic, such as Color, or Form or Size, there would be a significant effect upon their subsequent ability to discriminate these properties in multiple stimulus class items. This prediction was confirmed. However, training with single cue items resulted in significant improvement on similar single cue items. Training on multiple cue items did not result in significant gain on similar multiple cue items.

This is in accordance with concepts such as Hebb's (1949) suggestion that for optimum results total sensory input should be limited, and Zeaman's (1959) report of improved discrimination resulting from first focusing attention on the current stimulus dimension.

Thus, with the multiplicity of stimulus classes in visual discrimination tasks, the retarded child may find it beyond his ability to sort out or regroup these classes in order to develop a hypothesis which could be confirmed or dis-confirmed. These Ss were able to learn singular discriminations and, furthermore, were able to transfer this training to the subsequent multiple class discriminations of the traditional variety.

There may have been an influence of the "double complication" referred to by Piaget:

> The schemata subsume several objects whose mutual relationships it is a question of establishing....as a result, assimilation between the schemata ceases to work by simple fusion in order to give rise to diversified operations of inclusion or of hierarchical implication, of interference and even negation, that is to say, to multiple discriminations and regroupings (1952, p.232).

Thus, the inclusion of multiple cues for discrimination serves to distract or "overload" the capacities of the retardate rather than to facilitate, by requiring multiple discriminations and regroupings, thereby interfering with simple mutual relationships. If an intelligence test does not include items comparable to the single stimulus items used herein, certain learning abilities remaining in the retardate may be overlooked. Further, the investigation of these abilities is needed to determine whether individual retardates may be deficient in only certain abilities while retraining others.

In the past, measurement, in effect, has been concerned with the "acquired skills" (i.e., to solve complex test items) of retarded individuals based upon the presumption that they have had adequate opportunity for such acquisition. This presumption seems reasonably true for the non-retarded.

Have these atypical individuals had adequate time or opportunity for such acquisition, or simply been briefly exposed to typical occasions for acquisition which they lack the intellectual equipment to utilize?

There is present the issue of the time-repetition dimension which needs further investigation. Smith (1962) and Mueller and Smith (1964) report that training in language skills, as measured by the Illinois Test of Psycholinguistic Abilities, does not maintain the gain noted after a 13-14 month period. However, the Ss used by these authors were of a higher intellectual ability (Revised Stanford-Binet Scale I.Q. 50-80) and the training involved a different modality than the present research.

In addition, the deficit in learning ability of retardates may be "task specific" as interpreted by Baumeister (1963). The retarded Ss in his study, as compared to the normal

Ss, were as capable in retention of incidental material and superior in retention of intentionally learned material. These Ss were matched, however, by chronological age, in public schools and classified as normal or retarded on the basis of a paper and pencil intelligence test (Kuhlman-Anderson).

While it may not be meaningful to create a separate unit of measurement for these residual abilities for retardates, it is necessary to acknowledge that the current measures of intellectual potential may not provide valid comparisons of retardates and non-retardates. This point further emphasized by the nonsignificant correlation between the Stanford-Binet Intelligence Test levels and the single stimulus property series used in pretraining tests.

It is true that such measures as the revised Stanford-Binet Scale contain other types of items than the visual discrimination tasks. However, the other tasks contain additional requirements for the "eduction of a principle," as described in the CMMS manual, before an adequate response can be made. The two-dimensional, single sensory modality task of traditional test items may still be complex enough to confuse the retardate much more than the nonretardate who admittedly possesses additional and/or different (i.e., "higher") intellectual equipment. While these items may not be perceived by the retardate as singular, because of the multiplicity of stimulus characteristics which are intermingled, they required an analysis of such atomistic proportions as to be beyond his capacity for performance.

The durability of training retardates with single stimulus property items was indicated when 48 of the original group were retested after a two month interval and the significant improvement in test performance on complex items was retained.

Since this is a contradiction to the previously noted findings of Mueller and Smith (1964), further investigation may determine the long-range stability of the gains noted in the present research.

IMPLICATIONS

Practical application of these concepts to the field of education may be considered in the manner in which the teacher offers learning opportunities to retardates. After an adequate appraisal of abilities has been derived and specific areas of competence designated, trainable mentally retarded individuals may be most effectively taught through the use of materials and procedures which utilize single stimulus property items. Thus, a single color or a single size letter of the alphabet may enable visual discrimination by the stimulus of form only. Similarly, ruler markings which may be comparable in form and size can be more effectively discriminated if they are color coded. Visual discrimination between left and right, such as hands or shoes, for example, may be enhanced if different in color, since they are the same size and their relative forms are only reversals. The difference between nails and screws may become more apparent to trainable retardates if they are color coded, as would be true also for identification of specific door or drawers. Identification of personal belongings may be facilitated by one of the singular stimulus characteristics of Color, Form, or Size, rather than attention being directed to less constant stimulus properties such as texture, pattern or weight.

Most important, acknowledgement may be made that there may exist within each child learning ability that is yet to be tapped and that the challenge for such discovery is present.

TABLE 1

EXPECTED/OBTAINED STANFORD-BINET, FORM L MENTAL AGES

Subject	Date Previous Testing	M.A.	Expected M.A. 4/64 (Pinneau)	Obtained M.A. 4/64
1	7/61	3.50	4.33	4.25
4	9/60	3.58	4.25	4.33
13	2/61	4.25	4.25	4.25
16	3/59	3.58	3.58	3.67
29	10/55	3.08	3.92	3.83
30	7/60	3.50	4.00	3.83
39	11/61	4.33	4.33	4.42
43	1/61	4.08	4.50	4.42
45	8/60	3.17	3.67	3.33
50	12/61	3.50	4.17	4.08
			41.00	40.41

$M_D = .06$ $\sigma_D = .59$ $\sigma_{M_D} = .2$ $t = .03$ $p. > .05$

$r = .25$ $S_{E_R} = .35$ $p. = > .05$

TABLE 2

SUBJECTS: TREATMENT GROUP 1

Number	CA	MA*	Date Tested	Training and Testing Order and Time of Day**	CFS **** Orders
55	10-10	4-5	61-11	10-C	2
54	12-4	4-4	60-9	8-C	4
50	15-4	4-4	62-3	38-A	2
44	16-0	4-3	61-2	9-B	3
36	13-8	4-2	61-10	3-A	5
34	13-9	4-2(4-1)***	61-12(64-4)	50-D	2
28	14-5	4-1	60-11	15-D	3
21	10-1	3-11	61-1	14-D	2
18	9-6	3-10	61-6	20-A	2
14	13-11	3-8	61-11	26-B	2
8	12-11	3-6	60-9	35-D	5
5	12-0	3-5	60-3	42-B	6

* Projected from Pinneau's Tables.
** A--Early A.M.; B--Late A.M.; C--Early P.M.; D--Late P.M.
*** Obtained M.A. April 1964.
**** CFS ORDER indicates order of presentation of test items:
  1. color, form, size   2. color, size, form   3. form, color, size
  4. form, size, color   5. size, form, color   6. size, color, form

TABLE 3

SUBJECTS: TREATMENT GROUP II

Number	CA	MA*	Date Tested	Training and Testing Order and Time of Day	CFS**** Orders
59	16-0	4-6	60-8	54-A	6
51	16-0	4-4	61-3	34-D	4
47	13-5	4-4(4-5)***	61-11(64-4)	39-B	3
45	7-3	4-3	61-8	46-C	4
37	16-0	4-2	60-10	2-A	2
35	14-0	4-2	61-12	59-B	5
30	10-7	4-1	60-12	23-B	5
26	13-4	4-0(3-10)***	60-12(64-4)	30-D	6
19	12-5	3-10	60-8	5-B	5
24	16-0	3-7(3-8)***	59-3(64-4)	16-D	4
9	10-1	3-6	61-6	55-A	1
3	10-2	3-5	61-3	60-C	6

* Projected from Pinneau's Tables.
** A--Early A.M.; B--Late A.M.; C--Early P.M.; D--Late P.M.
*** Obtained M.A. April 1964.
**** CGS ORDER indicates order of presentation of test items:
   1. color, form size   2. color, size, form   3. form, color, size
   4. form, size, color   5. size, form, color   6. size, color, form

TABLE 4

SUBJECTS: TREATMENT GROUP III

Number	CA	MA*	Date Tested	Training and Testing Order and Time of Day**	CFS**** Orders
58	8-10	4-5	63-1	44-C	2
53	16-0	4-4(4-3)***	61-2(64-4)	37-A	1
49	16-0	4-4	62-6	40-B	4
43	14-8	4-3	61-9	47-C	5
38	12-8	4-3	61-12	51-D	3
32	14-5	4-1	61-12	52-A	4
23	16-0	3-11(3-10)***	60-10(64-4)	48-D	6
25	10-3	4-0	60-9	6-B	6
17	11-5	3-9	61-4	22-B	4
13	6-6	3-7	60-5	49-D	1
7	16-0	3-6	60-12	56-B	2
1	12-4	3-5	61-8	25-B	1

* Projected from Pinneau's Tables.
** A--Early A.M.; B--Late A.M.; C--Early P.M.; D--Late P.M.
*** Obtained M.A. April 1964.
**** CFS ORDER indicates order of presentation of test items:
   1. color, form, size   2. color, size, form   3. form, color, size
   4. form, size, color   5. size, form, color   6. size, color, form

TABLE 5

SUBJECTS: TREATMENT GROUP IV

Number	CA	MA*	Date Tested	Training and Testing Order and Time of Day**	CFS**** Orders
57	16-0	4-5	60-10	31-D	1
60	12-9	4-6(4-5)***	61-1(64-4)	43-C	1
48	11-6	4-4	62-7	24-B	6
42	16-0	4-3(4-3)***	61-2(64-4)	13-C	1
39	14-7	4-3	61-10	21-A	3
33	14-1	4-1	61-10	57-B	3
31	6-10	4-1	60-1	33-D	3
20	13-6	3-11	61-3	29-C	5
16	16-0	3-8	63-9	32-D	2
12	11-2	3-7	61-11	18-D	6
10	16-0	3-6	61-9	19-A	1
4	8-9	3-5	61-8	36-A	6

```
   * Projected from Pinneau's Tables.
  ** A--Early A.M.; B--Late A.M.; C--Early P.M.; D--Late P.M.
 *** Obtained M.A. April 1964
**** CFS ORDER indicates order of presentation of test items:
     1. color, form, size    2. color, size, form    3. form, color, size
     4. form, size, color    5. size, form, color    6. size, color, form
```

TABLE 6

SUBJECTS: TREATMENT GROUP V

Number	CA	MA*	Date Tested	Training and Testing Order and Time of Day**	CFS**** Orders
56	11-8	4-5	61-10	41-B	5
52	14-8	4-4	61-7	1-A	1
46	12-6	4-4	63-8	12-C	6
41	16-0	4-3	61-2	11-C	5
40	13-1	4-3(4-4)***	60-9(64-4)	45-A	3
29	14-5	4-1	61-10	53-A	5
27	16-0	4-0	60-12	17-D	5
22	13-4	3-11	63-9	7-B	1
15	11-6	3-8(3-4)***	60-8(64-4)	4-A	4
11	13-0	3-6	60-9	58-B	4
6	8-9	3-6	62-7	27-C	3
2	10-7	3-5	60-12	28-C	4

```
   * Projected from Pinneau's Tables.
  ** A--Early A.M.; B--Late A.M.; C--Early P.M.; D--Late P.M.
 *** Obtained M.A. April 1964.
**** CFS ORDER indicates order of presentation of test items:
     1. color, form, size    2. color, size, form    3. form, color, size
     4. form, size, color    5. size, form, color    6. size, color, form
```

TABLE 7

SUBJECTS: TREATMENT GROUP VI

Number	CA	MA*	Date Tested	Training and Testing Order and Time of Day	CFS*** Orders
61	14-9	4-0	60-9	63-A	3
62	10-1	4-1	62-8	61-A	1
63	11-9	4-2	64-4	64-A	4
64	7-1	4-3	61-1	71-C	5
65	10-0	4-4	61-4	69-C	3
66	14-4	3-6	61-11	68-B	2
67	14-7	3-6	63-7	62-A	2
68	13-10	3-5	61-11	67-B	1
69	13-3	3-7	60-9	70-C	4
70	16-0	3-11	55-10	65-B	5
71	16-0	4-2	60-10	72-C	6
72	16-0	4-4	61-3	66-B	6

   * Projected from Pinneau's Tables.
  ** A--Early A.M.; B--Late A.M.; C--Early P.M.; D--Late P.M.
 *** CFS ORDER indicates order of presentation of test items:
    1. color, form, size   2. color, size, form   3. form, color, size
    4. form, size, color   5. size, form, color   6. size, color, form

TABLE 8

SCHEDULE OF PROCEDURES

Treatment Group	Pretraining Test	Treatment	Posttraining Test	Retest 2 Month Interval
T_{G_1}	May 9, 10, 16, 17	No training	May 16, 17, 23, 24	July 11, 12
T_{G_2}	"	Test-taking practice	"	"
T_{G_3}	"	Color training	"	"
T_{G_4}	"	Form training	"	"
T_{G_5}	"	Size training	"	"
T_{G_6}	August 22, 23	Color, form, size training	August 29, 30	None

TABLE 9

TRAINING MATERIALS

Training Group	Item Type and Number	Item Content
T_{G_1}	No Training	
T_{G_2}	Standard C.M.M.S. #7, 8, 15*, 17 19*, 22, 23, 25*	Line Drawings: Familiar Objects
T_{G_3}	"Modified" C.M.M.S. #T3, 6, 7, 9, 12, 15, 18, 22*	Geometric Forms: Color offers the only oddity cue
T_{G_4}	Original "C.M.M.S. Style" #T1, 2, 4, 10, 13, 16, 20, 23*	Geometric Forms: Form offers the only oddity cue
T_{G_5}	Original "C.M.M.S. Style" #T5, 8, 11, 14, 17, 19, 21, 24*	Geometric Forms: Size offers the only oddity cue
T_{G_6}	Original "C.M.M.S. Style" #A, B, C, D, E, F, G, H*	Geometric Forms: Color/Form/ Size. All offer oddity cues

* These items contain four objects for forms, all other items contain three.

TABLE 10

ANALYSES OF VARIANCE—NUMBER CORRECT—PRETRAINING AND POSTTRAINING SCORES

Source of Variation	Sum of Squares	df	Mean Square	"F" Ratio	p.
1. *TOTAL SCORE - 24 ITEMS					
Between Training Groups	115.389	5	23.078	1.08	.05
M.A. Levels	106.777	1	106.777	5.02	.05
TRG. Gps x M.A.	81.639	5	16.328	.77	.05
Within Groups	1277.167	60	21.286		
Pre-Posttests	66.694	1	66.694	24.08	.01
Pre-Post x Trg. Gps.	249.899	5	45.980	16.61	.01
Pre-Post x M.A.	1.778	1	1.778	—	
Pre-Post x Trq. Gps. x M.A.	21.159	5	4.231	1.53	.05
Pre-Post x Within Gps.	166.114	60	2.769		
2. C.M.M.S. SUBSET ONLY - 6 ITEMS					
Between Training Groups	30.639	5	6.128	4.17	.01
M.A. Levels	2.250	1	2.250	1.53	.05
Trg. Gps. x M.A.	10.833	5	2.167	1.47	.05
Within Groups	88.167	60	1.469		
Pre-Posttests	2.250	1	2.250	2.59	.05
Pre-Post x Trg. Gps.	13.167	5	2.633	3.30	.025
Pre-Post x M.A.	1.777	1	1.777	2.14	.05
Pre-Post x Trg. Gps. x M.A.	6.640	5	1.328	1.60	.05
Pre-Post x Within Gps.	49.750	60	.829		
3. COLOR SUBSET ONLY - 6 ITEMS					
Between Training Groups	8.785	5	1.757	.84	.05
M.A. Levels	15.340	1	15.340	7.34	.01
Trg. Gps. x M.A.	27.451	5	5.490	2.63	.05
Within Groups	125.417	60	2.090		
Pre-Posttests	11.674	1	11.674	10.48	.01
Pre-Post x Trg. Gps.	23.284	5	4.657	4.17	.01
Pre-Post x M.A.	.839	1	.839	—	
Pre-Post x Trg. Gps. x M.A.	2.953	5	.591	—	
Pre-Post x Within Gps.	66.848	60	1.114		

* Total Score: 6 C.M.M.S. + 6 Color Only + 6 Form Only + 6 Size Only

TABLE 11

ANALYSES OF VARIANCE — NUMBER CORRECT — PRETRAINING AND POSTTRAINING SCORES

Source of Variation	Sum of Squares	df	Mean Square	"F" Ratio	p.
4. FORM SUBSET ONLY - 6 ITEMS					
Between Training Groups	10.472	5	2.094	.70	.05
M.A. Levels	1.000	1	1.000	.33	.05
Trg. Gps. x M.A.	7.584	5	1.517	.51	.05
Within Groups	179.834	60	2.997		
Pre-Post Tests	7.111	1	7.111	10.60	.01
Pre-Post x Trg. Gps.	19.806	5	3.961	5.90	.01
Pre-Post x M.A.	.446	1	.446	—	
Pre-Post x Trg. Gps. x M.A.	5.470	5	1.094	1.63	.05
Pre-Post x Within Gps.	40.278	60	.671		
5. SIZE SUBSET ONLY - 6 ITEMS					
Between Training Groups	8.000	5	1.600	.47	.05
M.A. Levels	14.694	1	14.694	4.31	.05
Trg. Gps. x M.A. Levels	8.556	5	1.711	.50	.05
Within Groups	204.500	60	3.408		
Pre-Posttests	.250	1	.250	—	
Pre-Post x Trg. Gps.	34.467	5	6.933	8.08	.01
Pre-Post x M.A.	2.250	1	2.250	2.62	.05
Pre-Post x Trg. Gps. x M.A.	5.333	5	1.067	1.24	.05
Pre-Post x Within Groups	51.500	60	.858		

TABLE 12

TOTAL RAW SCORES — MEANS
MAXIMUM POSSIBLE SCORE — 24

	T_{G_1}	T_{G_2}	T_{G_3}	T_{G_4}	T_{G_5}	T_{G_6}
Pretest	13.58	13.91	11.50	12.91	10.58	11.30
Posttest #1	14.08	11.91	14.42	14.66	16.33	12.04
Posttest #2	14.58	11.91	13.92	14.66	16.61	----

TABLE 13

DIFFERENCE SCORES PRETEST—POSTTEST

	T_{G_1}		T_{G_2}		T_{G_3}		T_{G_4}		T_{G_5}		T_{G_6}	
	(No Training)		(Practice)		(Color)		(Form)		(Size)		(Color, Form, Size)	
	M	SD	M	SD	M	SD	M	SD	M	SD	M	SD
TOTAL N = 24	.50	1.25	-2.00	1.47**	2.92	1.47**	1.75	1.01	5.75	3.02**	.74	2.88
CMMS Only N = 6	.08	1.03	.08	.87	.50	1.12	.33	1.04	.50	.96	.25	1.66
COLOR Only N = 6	.33	1.42	- .08	1.01	.75	1.16*	1.00	1.87	1.75	1.09**	.33	1.31
FORM Only N = 6	.00	.82	- .50	1.04	.83	1.23*	.50	.87	1.83	1.23**	.08	1.04
SIZE Only N = 6	.08	.97	-1.50	1.32**	.83	1.42*	- .08	1.48	1.66	.44**	.08	1.32

* = p .05
** = p .01

TABLE 14

DIFFERENCE SCORES POSTTEST #1 AND POSTTEST #2
(2-Month Delay)

	T_{G_1} (No Training)		T_{G_2} (Practice)		T_{G_3} (Color)		T_{G_4} (Form)		T_{G_5} (Size)		T_{G_6} (Color Form, Size)	
	M	SD	M	SD	M	SD	M	SD	M	SD	M	SD
Difference Scores Posttest #1 and Posttest #2 (2-Month Delay)												
TOTAL	.50	1.34	- .00	1.41	- .50	1.38	.00	1.60	.28	1.62		
CMMS Only	.00	.71	- .09	.67	- .09	.13	.00	.13	-.15	.83		
COLOR Only	-.13	.60	- .09	.76	.19	.85	.00	.60	-.15	.35		
FORM Only	.50	1.07	.36	.03	- .25	1.04	.18	.39	.29	.88		
SIZE Only	.13	.93	- .18	.57	- .25	.90	- .18	1.19	.29	.46		

TABLE 15

SCHEFFE TEST FOR MULTIPLE COMPARISON
SIX TREATMENT SUMS

Comparison	Total Difference Score p.	C.M.M.S. Subset Difference Score p.
1 vs 2	< .01	> .05
1 vs 3	< .01	< .05
1 vs 4	< .05	> .05
1 vs 5	< .01	> .05
1 vs 6	> .05	> .05
2 vs 3	< .01	> .05
2 vs 4	< .01	> .05
2 vs 5	< .01	> .05
2 vs 6	< .01	> .05
3 vs 4	> .05	> .05
3 vs 5	< .01	< .05
3 vs 6	< .01	> .05
4 vs 5	< .01	> .05
4 vs 6	< .01	> .05
5 vs 6	< .01	< .01

$$t \quad {}^{T}G_{6:} {}^{T}G_{3 + 4 + 5} = 2.10 \qquad p. \ < \ .05$$

References

1. Arnoult, M.D. FAMILIARITY OF RECOGNITION OF NONSENSE SHAPES. J. Exper. Psych., 4:265-276, 1951.

TRANSFER OF PREDIFFERENTIATION TRAINING IN SIMPLE AND MULTIPLE SHAPE DIS-CRIMINATIONS. J. Exper. Psych., 45:401-409, 1953.

STIMULUS PREDIFFERENTIATION: SOME GENERALIZATIONS AND HYPOTHESES. Psych. Bull., 4:339-349, 1954.

2. Baumeister, Alfred A. A COMPARISON OF NORMALS AND RETARDATES WITH RESPECT TO INCIDENTAL AND INTENTIONAL LEARNING. Amer. J. Ment. Defic., 68: 404-408, 1963.

3. Birch, H.G. and Lefford, A. INTERSENSORY DEVELOPMENT IN CHILDREN. Monogr. Society for Research on Children, March, 1963.

4. Cattell, P. MEASUREMENT OF INTELLIGENCE IN INFANTS. New York: Psychological Corporation, 1942, (Revised 1960).

6. Chansky, N.M. and Taylor, M. PERCEPTUAL TRAINING WITH YOUNG RETARDATES. Am. J. Ment. Defic., 68: 440-468, 1964.

6. Cruse, Daniel B. EFFECTS OF DISTRACTION UPON THE PERFORMANCE OF BRAIN-INJURED AND FAMILIAL RETARDED CHILDREN. Am. J. Ment. Defic., 66:86-92, 1961.

7. Doll, E. A., Phelps, W.M., and Melcher, R. MENTAL DEFICIENCY DUE TO BIRTH IN-JURIES. N.Y.: Macmillan, 1932.

8. Edwards, Allen L. EXPERIMENTAL DESIGN IN PSYCHOLOGICAL RESEARCH. N.Y.: Rinehart, 1959.

9. Ellis, N.R. LEARNING SETS IN MENTAL DEFECTIVES. J. Compar. & Physiol. Psychol., 51:79-81, 2/58.

10. Ellis, N.R. and Sloan, W. ODDITY LEARNING AS A FUNCTION OF MENTAL AGE. J. Compar. & Physiol. Psychol., 52:228-230, April 1959.

11. Fernald, G.M. REMEDIAL TECHNIQUES IN BASIC SCHOOL SUBJECTS. N.Y.: Mc-Graw-Hill, 1943.

12. Fisher, R.A. STATISTICAL METHODS FOR RESEARCH WORKERS. Edinburgh: Oliver and Boyd, 1936.

13. Gardner, L.P. RESPONSE OF IDIOTS AND IMBECILES IN A CONDITIONING EXPERIMENT. Am. J. Ment. Defic., 56: 59-85, 1945.

14. Goldstein, Kurt. THE ORGANISM. N.Y. American Book Company, 1939.

15. Grice, G.R. and Saltz, E. THE GENERALIZATION OF AN INSTRUMENTAL RESPONSE TO STIMULI VARYING IN THE SIZE DIMENSION. J. Exp. Psychol., 40:702-708, 1950.

16. Hebb, D.O. THE ORGANIZATION OF BEHAVIOR. N.Y.: Wiley, 1949.

17. Itard, J.M. THE WILD BOY OF AVEYRON. N.Y.: Appleton-Century-Crofts, 1932.

18. Jastak, J. A RIGOROUS CRITERION OF FEEBLEMINDEDNESS. J. Abn. & Soc. Psychol., 44:367-378, 1949.

19. Jones, R.W. Unpub. Doc. Diss., Coral Gables, Florida Univ. Miami, 1963.

20. Lashley, V.S. and Wade, M. THE PAVLOVIAN THEORY OF GENERALIZATION. Psychol. Rev., 53:72-87, 1946.

21. Maisel, R.N., Allen, R.M., and Tallarico, R.B. A COMPARISON OF THE ADAPTIVE AND STANDARD ADMINISTRATION OF THE LEITER INTERNATIONAL PERFORMANCE SCALE WITH NORMAL CHILDREN. Cerebral Palsy Rev., Sept.-Oct., 1962.

22. Mueller, M., and Smith, James O. THE STABILITY OF LANGUAGE AGE MODIFICATIONS OVER TIME. Amer. J. Ment. Defic., 68:537-539, 1964.

23. Piaget, Jean. THE ORIGINS OF INTELLIGENCE IN CHILDREN. N.Y.: International Universities Press, 1952.

24. Pinneau, S. IN STANFORD-BINET INTELLIGENCE SCALE. Boston: Houghton Mifflin, p. 339, 1960.

25. Razran, G. STIMULUS GENERALIZATION OF CONDITIONED RESPONSES. Psychol. Bull., 1949, 46:337-365, 1949.

26. Scheffe, H. A METHOD FOR JUDGING ALL CONTRASTS IN THE ANALYSIS OF VARIANCE. Biometrika, 40:87-104, 1953.

27. Smith, James Otto. GROUP LANGUAGE DEVELOPMENT FOR EDUCABLE MENTAL RETARDATES. Exceptional Child., 29:95-101, 1962.

28. Subes, J. Color Preferences of Children. ENFANCE, 2:117-142, 1959.

29. Von Sended, M. RAUM-UND GESTALT AUFFASOUNG BEI OPERIERTEN BLINDGE-BORESIEN VOR UND NECH DER OPERATION. Leipzig: Barth, 1932.

30. Zeaman, David. LEARNING IN RETARDATES. Train. Sch. Bull., 56:62-67, 8/59.

THE TEAM APPROACH IN THERAPEUTIC EDUCATION: SUCCESSES AND FAILURES

Harold Esterson, Ph.D.,
Mattie Cook, M. A.
Muriel Mendlowitz, M. A.
Charles Solomon, N. S. W.,
Manhattanville Community Centers, Inc.,
New York, New York

It has been apparent for some time now that we lack effective tools for helping the disadvantaged school child who is either disturbed, disruptive, or underachieving. The usual clinic referral is, in most cases, of little value, either because of poor motivation on the part of the family, or long waiting lists in clinics. In recent years, a variety of community-based approaches has been developed for therapeutic and preventative purposes. The program to be described is one of these attempts.

For nearly four years now, the Junior Guidance Classes Program (JGCP) of a local public school has been participating with Manhattanville Community Centers, Inc., an adjacent multi-functional social center, in the education and treatment of educationally retarded and emotionally disturbed children. During this time, approximately fifty-five children in five separate classes have been admitted to the program. Nearly all of the children were from disadvantaged homes and had been identified by their first grade teachers as being either disruptive, disturbed, or as not learning. The program which has been evolving is a team effort, jointly shared by the two agencies; it is clearly community-based, and its attempts are mainly designed to modify the various environments in which the children function and to provide needed services in their immediate environments. The educational personnel involved in the project are from the Junior Guidance Classes Program, while the clinical and social personnel are from Manhattanville Community Centers.

THE JUNIOR GUIDANCE CLASSES PROGRAM

The Junior Guidance Classes Program, initiated in 1960, now serves 1,850 children in 62 different schools, with 149 classes and 217 teachers. The program is administered by Louis Hay and Gloria Lee; the latter an educator and the former a clinical psychologist. According to them, the purposes of the program are as follows:

(1) Develop effective, economical procedures to identify emotionally and socially disturbed children in the earliest grades.

(2) Provide a resource for disruptive children who are damaging the normal functioning of regular classes, as well as of themselves.

(3) Prevent the development of serious maladjustment by helping troubled children before their problems become deep-rooted.

(4) Build a coordinated rehabilitative program under both educational and clinical supervision that will include teacher selection, teacher training, and a carefully planned curriculum, as well as other built in protections.

(5) Cooperatively develop school and community resources to mitigate the multiple detrimental controls in the child's malfunctioning.

According to Lee and Hay, the coordinators of the program, the basic orientations of the program are: "Weekly team meetings, the development of individual case histories, and a consideration of the class-group process by teachers and auxiliary professionals, counselors, psychiatrists, psychologists, social workers, and curriculum resource assistants." Currently, there are two different kinds of Junior Guidance classes: the closed register class with a pupil population of twelve to fifteen and an open register class with seven to ten pupils. Closed register Junior Guidance classes are limited to single grades, and a track is initiated with two classes, a second grade and third grade. Children are maintained in the program for at least one year, and after evaluation, for a second year. Children are drawn primarily from the host school. Open register Junior Guidance classes provide emergency therapeutic resources for the very disruptive boys within a two-year, two-grade span. The program we are discussing belongs to the closed register classes program.

MANHATTANVILLE COMMUNITY CENTERS, INC.

The cooperating, participating community agency which provides the clinical, social, and recreational services to the children and their families is Manhattanville Community Centers. This is a multi-functional agency, housing two day care centers, two group work oriented recreational programs, and a casework and mental health department. One of its centers is located in a low-cost housing project adjacent to the public school in a so-called deprived area in New York City. The proximity of the two institutions, their mutual concern for the community, and the availability of needed personnel made possible an exciting marriage which has generally been helpful to the pupils.

THE CHILDREN AND THEIR ENVIRONMENTS

For the most part, out children come from homes which suffer with all imaginable kinds of trouble and chaos; these problems range from economic deprivation to near incest. Many of the children do not have fathers living at home, and their mothers are nearly always overwhelmed and harrassed. The parents are either neglectful, threatening, or over-protective. As far as we can make out, there is little meaningful communication between the children and their parents. The children are sexually precocious, and their language, and sometimes their behavior, appears to be more like that of a disturbed adolescent than that of a seven or eight year old.

On the playgrounds, play can frequently appear to be friendly and enjoyable. Too often, however, it takes on jungle qualities, with children ganging up on one another. Only physical strength and power are respected. The underachieving and disturbed child perceives school as a place where he has little or no self-esteem. He is always in trouble. He develops counter-tactics of evasion, distraction, and attack. His anxiety about his ability to learn is quickly translated into aggressiveness or passive withdrawal.

Confronted with this picture, it was apparent that the once-a-week clinic visit, even if it did materialize, would be insufficient to reverse the children's perceptions, particularly if the world remained the same. Our approach, we thought, needed to be twofold: (1) to modify existing environments, and (2) to modify their perceptions of themselves and their worlds.

THE TEAM AND THEIR ENVIRONMENTS

Our team is made up of seven professionals, each having either a direct or nearly direct influence upon the children and/or their environments. They are: the teacher, guidance counselor, curriculum resource person, caseworker, group worker, therapist, and psychologist. With few exceptions, the above team members met once a week. On occasion, we had reports from other professionals; namely, physicians, nurses, and other specialists. The teachers, caseworkers, group workers, and therapists worked directly with the children or their families. The curriculum person and psychologist worked with the staff. The guidance counselor worked with the teachers, with the children's families, and sometimes with the children. She served with the chief caseworker as liaison between the two agencies.

As indicated earlier, our main purpose was to try to modify the several environments in which the children functioned. The obvious environments which needed modification, were: the inter-personal parent-child environment, the school and class environment, the leisure-time environment, the peer environment, and, finally, the child's inner environment. Each of our team members—or, by now, modifiers—was responsible for at least one environment. It was apparent from the start that we could easily manipulate and modify some levels of the environments, but that other levels and other environments were far less amenable. For example, under the JGCP, the class size was reduced to fifteen or less. The class size is undoubtedly a crucial variable in the educational scheme and in the education of disturbed and underachieving children. We could also enlist the children to participate in an after-school, group-work oriented, leisure-time program. Once, however, these programs were established, we were then faced with the more complicated issue of enlisting the collaboration of the children and their parents to participate in the programs in the manner we expected and for which the programs had been designed. It soon became apparent in the first 100 days that our population had no intention of standing still while we modified.

THE FIRST ONE-HUNDRED DAYS

The first days of the program were marked by considerable anxiety, hostility, and acting out on the part of most of the people involved in the program. The initial permissiveness of the teachers sparked the acting out children to great heights—such as swinging from the chandeliers. The school administrative personnel was critical of the Junior Guidance classes, since they did not look kindly upon the acting out. Some of the regular teachers felt that their colleagues in Junior Guidance had an easy time of it with such small classes, and they, too, were at times critical. The children themselves never had it so good, and the few and fragile inner restraints of the acting out children soon gave way. The tide of their acting out carried some of the more inhibited children with them. The hyperactive children, the horrified administrative personnel, and the occasional envious colleagues were joined by indignant parents who came marching on the program. Parents were angry on several counts. First, they insisted on seeing the Junior Guidance classes as being for dumb or crazy children. Secondly, they could not understand why their children did not have homework. (This had been the policy of the overall Junior Guidance Program.) Thirdly, they resented that the children were dismissed one hour earlier than the rest of the school. The reason for the earlier dismissal is that the teachers eat lunch with their children, and the last regular school hour is often used for various team meetings. All of these issues and feelings were brought to the team meetings. We were now face to face with two main issues: first, it was apparent that our modifying was being modified by the children and other interested people in the environment. While we were trying to modify in one direction, these others seemed determined to keep things the same. While we were somehow able to cope with the parents and school administrators, the matter of dealing with the children's anxiety was far more complicated. Each team member had to develop techniques to keep her situation from either slipping away or from deteriorating. Hence, our second problem was to develop ways and means of keeping our children from establishing relationships with us which were in keeping with their usual destructive life styles. This meant that all of the personnel who were giving direct service needed to develop clinical-like postures and skills to fend off their being integrated with the children in non-helpful, destructive ways. The development of these attitudes and skills became one of the main purposes of the team meetings.

TEAM MEETINGS

There are undoubtedly many successful and unsuccessful ways of teaching maladapted children. In our own experiences, we have been able to observe some teachers who managed excellent control over the children and who helped them to learn. Other teachers seemed unable to cope with the provocativeness of the children; these teachers became overwhelmed with their own anxiety and counter-hostility and preferred to leave the program. A specific definition and characterization of a so-called therapeutic teacher hinges on the methods and goals of therapeutic education. If management of the children is the main goal, as it has to be in some instances, then one kind of teacher and style is necessary. If, however, the goal is behavior modification, as well as learning and management, then it is obvious that the teacher needs more than her ordinary good skills. The clinical dialogue is specific, rooted in understanding of behavior and motivation and takes considerable skill and know-how. It appeared to us that while many of the teachers were presumably successful, only a very few seemed willing and able to take on the responsibility of teaching and treating. These teachers made maximum use of the team psychologist and team meetings.

The one characteristic of our most capable teachers was their ability to be in touch with their own feelings. This quality of in-touchness enabled them to report to the team meeting on the nature of their interactions with the children. This kind of reporting enabled the teacher, as well as the team, to understand the nature of the children's communications. At the first, the teacher who exposed her responses experienced anxiety; she was afraid of what the psychologist would think about her. When it was apparent that he was not going to be critical of her, she began to feel relief and support. She risked more of herself and, in time, admitted more of her irrational responses and the meaning she thought they had for her. She became adept at keeping her eye on herself and her feelings. Her timing of observations with the children became excellent, and she became skillful at selecting the time and place to offer interpretations. The experience was a profound one for her, and she reported that it had affected her personal life as well.

Generally, the atmosphere of the team meetings was open and free. At times, the team psychologist chose to challenge some of the institutional, public school behavior of the teachers. For example, the teachers tended to call each other by their second names at team meetings, a custom which apparently has not changed since the founding of the public school system. They became angry with him and said that they could not possibly use their first names in the presence of the children; the latter would undoubtedly take advantage of the situation and use it against the teachers. Actually, the psychologist was referring only to team meetings, but when they raised the issue of first names in school, he encouraged further discussion about their reluctance.

The general format of the meetings was for the teacher to present a problem she was having in her classroom. Other team members then added whatever knowledge and information they had about the children and their families.

CASEWORK, GROUP WORK, AND THERAPY

Unfortunately, all of these services were not always available to all of the children and their families. Some years, we were able to provide group work services for all of the children, and at other times we had to limit the number of children who would be served. The same is true of the casework service. In contrast to group work, however, which was accepted by nearly all of the families for their children, there was a good deal of resistance to casework. Many of the parents were quite suspicious of the social workers and refused service.

Only in very few instances were we able to involve the parents fully in a casework relationship. When we did offer services, they were mostly of a concrete nature, such as providing camp placements, beds, eyeglasses, and so forth. In one instance, we were able to modify a restrictive mother's attitudes; in another, a mother began to understand more fully the needs of her children.

Nevertheless, some of the parents began to feel more favorably disposed towards their children and towards the school as a result of the child's participation in one of the Junior Guidance classes. As the children began to do better in school and create fewer difficulties, the parents were no longer harassed by the school. Parents who were initially rejecting of the program came to feel more positively when it became apparent that they were not being called in daily by the teacher or assistant principal. So, while we have not been too successful in modifying the child's parental environment directly, it had been achieved sometimes indirectly.

Where no demands for participation were made on the parents, we could carry out most programs; namely, group work and therapy for the children. The children came to the center three times a week; twice to a friendship group, and once to an interest group. During the early days of the program, the group workers encountered considerable difficulty in maintaining any kind of program. The accepting and unstructured nature of the environment prompted some of the children to become quite anxious and aggressive. With time, the staff learned to introduce more structured programs, as well as to distribute children into several different groups rather than keeping them in their own groups. Unfortunately, again, we did not have as many staff members as we would have liked.

Two years ago, we began to provide individual therapy for some of the children. The therapists are doctoral students in clinical psychology and generally see the children once a week over a two-year period. It is quite stylish these days for our children to have what they call a "lady." In one of the classes, all of the girls have "ladies." We think they merely call them "ladies" because they can't quite identify the service they give. They don't see them in groups, so they are not group workers or teachers. They are like nothing they have ever seen before. These "ladies" pick up the children at school, spend about an hour with them, and return them. It is clearly a good thing in the lives of our children to have "ladies." We hope in the future to get "misters" as well as ladies.

EVALUATION

Our overall feeling about the program is that it is a good one. Very often, however, we are beset by doubts and anxieties. The problem is overwhelming, and the variables most complex. We can't be sure just how important the teacher is, the class size, the other services. We are convinced that the general approach is a correct one; namely, that help to these children needs to come through these special programs in the schools and from their own immediate communities. As it is, we have some definite impressions about the gains which the children make. First, the school attendance of the children is significantly better in Junior Guidance classes. Secondly, many of the children make significant gains in their I.Q. scores. Of eight children now completing two years in the program, four have made substantial gains, three remained the same, and one lost. Thirdly, the timid children became more assertive, and the aggressive children became more amenable to teacher and class controls.

We also know something about the kinds of children we can serve and how to select them. In the more permissive Junior Guidance classes, we do best with the more in-hibited and mildly acting out children.

One obvious limitation of the program is the lack of built-in research and follow-up. We are not certain how lasting the effects of the program are upon the children. We have contact with some of our graduates who seem to be doing well, but our knowledge, un-fortunately, is too general. There are a number of other unanswered questions. First, how important is the teacher and how important is the class size? Secondly, can specific teacher styles be defined? Thirdly, what kinds of programs need to be designed for the severely acting out children? Fourth, to what extent do the team meetings affect the teacher's understanding and handling of the children? These are only a few of the questions which have perplexed us and for which we will continue to look for answers.

THE DOMAN-DELACATO RATIONALE:
A CRITICAL ANALYSIS

Melvyn P. Robbins, Ph.D.,
Assistant Professor,
The Ontario Institute for Studies in Education,
Toronto, Canada,

Gene V. Glass, Ph.D.,
Assistant Professor,
Laboratory of Educational Research,
University of Colorado,
Boulder, Colorado

Early chemists attempted to create precious metals from base substances. They brought both enthusiasm and commitment to their task; but, lacking the tools of logic and science, they were unable to generate and test their ideas in a systematic manner. Consequently they failed in their endeavor. Today's scientists, focusing attention on logic and empirical tests, have succeeded in creating precious metals in the laboratory.

In many ways those of us concerned with educational therapy are like these early chemists. We lack neither commitment nor enthusiasm, but we fall short in the systematic generation and testing of ideas. Acceptance or rejection of ideas is more a function of publicity, tradition, and authority than of logic and empirical validation. Fortunately, we differ from the early chemists, for at our disposal are scientific resources of experimental design and standards for evidence.

If we wish to build a science, then we must insist upon ferreting out fact from fiction within our own fields of endeavor. Enthusiasm and commitment by themselves will not separate the useful from the useless.

In this paper we intend to apply standards of evidence to an existing theory in order to reach a rational conclusion as to its merits. Our focus is on the theory of neurological organization.

The paper is divided into four parts:

     I. The Theory of Neurological Organization.

     II. An Examination of Central Assumptions of the Theory.

     III. An Evaluation of Eleven Experiments on the Relationship between Neurological Organization and Reading.

     IV. Summary and Conclusions.

The first part, a background of the theory of neurological organization, is subdivided into five divisions: 1. History; 2. Central Concepts; 3. Treatment Rationale; 4. Treatment Applications; and 5. Popular and Professional Reaction.

The second part, an analysis of key assumptions underlying the rationale, is divided into three divisions: 1. Ontogeny Recapitulates Phylogeny; 2. Sequential Development, Brain Stages, and Localization of Function; 3. Sidedness (Laterality), Cerebral Dominance, and Human Superiority; and 4. Summary and Conclusions. Each of the first three divisions is further divided into the following subdivisions: A. Background; B. The Position of Theorists of Neurological Organization; and C. Refutation of the Position of Neurological Organization Theorists.

The third part, an appraisal of eleven experiments cited by Carl Delacato in support of his treatment rationale, is subdivided into eleven parts, one section being devoted to each experiment.

The fourth part, Summary, Conclusions, and Implications, completes the paper.

Part I. THE THEORY OF NEUROLOGICAL ORGANIZATION

The purpose of this part is to explore the history, central concepts, treatment rationale, treatment applications, and popular and professional reaction to the theory of neurological organization. This section provides only a brief introduction to the theory, the reader is advised to consult original source materials (Delacato, 1959; 1963; 1966b; Doman, G., undated; 1964; Doman, G. et al., 1963a; Doman, R. et al., 1960; Institutes for the Achievement of Human Potential, undated; 1964; LeWinn et al., 1966) or secondary resumes (Archdiocesan Reading Service, undated; Beck, 1964; Cecilia, 1966; Segal, 1966; Bird, 1967) for a more comprehensive introduction and elaboration of the rationale.

HISTORY

Approximately 27 years ago, an interdisciplinary team was formed under the direction of Temple Fay, a Philadelphia neurosurgeon, to consider the treatment of brain injured children. One result of the collaboration was the establishment of the Rehabilitation Center in 1959 and its successor organization, the Institutes for the Achievement of Human Potential, in 1962 at Philadelphia.

The essential tenets of the theory and practice of neurological organization were developed between 1955 and 1962 by two members of the team; Glen Doman, a physical therapist, and Carl Delacato, Ed. D., a school administrator. The first major presentation of the theory was made in 1959 by Delacato (1959), followed by an article in the JOURNAL OF THE AMERICAN MEDICAL ASSOCIATION (Doman, R. et al., 1960). A detailed history of the Institutes is available elsewhere (Institutes for the Achievement of Human Potential, undated).

CENTRAL CONCEPTS

The central concept of the theory is **neurological organization.** Although the concept **neurological organization** is not unique (see for example Minkowski et al., 1966) to the Philadelphia group, they defined the term in a particular way. In this paper **neurological organization** refers only to their specific definition.

Neurological organization posits that ontogeny, the process of individual development, recapitulates phylogeny, the process of species development; it assumes that the development of the individual proceeds in an orderly way, anatomically, in the central nervous system, progressing through the medulla and spinal cord, pons, mid-brain, and cortex, culminating in hemispheric dominance. According to the rationale, the individual's development with respect to mobility, vision, audition, and language parallels, and is functionally related to his anatomical progress. Advocates of the theory have further reasoned that differences in language facility, ranging from the inability to speak (aphasia) to success in reading, are a function of neurological organization. (Delacato, 1963)

The underlying rationale for the theory of neurological organization as advanced by associates of the Institutes for the Achievement of Human Potential, may be summarized in the seven following assumptions:

A. "The basic difference between the nervous system of man and that of slightly lower forms of mammals lies not in the number of cells, but in the differentiation and organization of those cells. Thus, we have for man the concept of Neurological Organization in addition to neurological development." (Delacato, 1966b, p5)

B. Man's ontogenetic development goes through four distinct phases: medulla and spinal cord, pons, midbrain, and cortex, and culminates in hemispheric dominance. According to the rationale, all phases of man's ontogenetic development recapitulates phylogenetic development of the species via fish, amphibian, reptile and primate. (Delacato, 1963)

C. Neurological Organization "... provides the organism with all the capabilities necessary to relate it successfully to its environment" (Le Winn et al., 1966, pp59-60), thus as a measure of ontogenetic progress it is an indicator of man's development, both motor (i.e., mobility, symbolic language, and manual competence) and sensory (i.e., vision, hearing, and tactility (Delacato, 1963).

D. Practitioners of the theory measure neurological organization along a continuum beginning with neurologically disorganized individuals who suffer from frank brain pathology, continuing through average or above average children with reading problems associated with poor neurological organization, and culminating in physically and intellectually superior individuals. (LeWinn et al., 1966)

E. Walking, writing, auditory understanding of language, tactile competence (LeWinn et al., 1966), as well as "Speech and reading are the final **human** result of neurological organization and hence are clinical indices of the nature and the quality of neurological organization of an individual." (Delacato, 1963, p7).

F. Advocates of the theory state that neurological organization can be evaluated by existing procedures developed at the Institutes for the Achievement of Human Potential. (LeWinn et al., 1966; Doman, R., et al., 1960; Delacato, 1959; 1963; 1966b)

G. The Institutes recommend simple, non-surgical exercises which can be imposed either actively or passively on the nervous system. They state that such exercises lead to improved sensory-motor function. (Doman, G., undated; Delacato, 1966b)

TREATMENT RATIONALE

The treatment program is formulated after an initial evaluation with either of the following two test protocols:

A. THE DOMAN-DELACATO DEVELOPMENTAL PROFILE (Doman, G. et al., 1963a; LeWinn et al., 1966) is used to evaluate the neurological age of brain injured children. Children are tested in six motor and sensory areas, each area comprised of seven levels.

A perfect score would yield 42 points (six areas times seven levels). The child's raw score is transposed to a neurological age equivalent through a conversion table.

B. The DELACATO TEST SUMMARY SHEET (Delacato, 1963, pp100-101) is utilized to evaluate older children who are not severely brain injured. The test consists of items measuring handedness, footedness, and eyedness in addition to subcortical skills. Unlike the DOMAN-DELACATO DEVELOPMENTAL PROFILE the DELA-CATO TEST SUMMARY SHEET does not yield a total score.

After a clinic visit the child returns home to carry out the program under parental supervision, returning in six to 12 weeks for a re-evaluation. Similar diagnostic procedures are employed when the program is administered on a group basis.

Treatment procedures consist of some on all of the following exercises: creeping, crawling, walking, reducing all muscular activities, sidedness exercises, establishing a sleeping posture, patterning, etc. (For a more complete list, other sources should be consulted.)

It is possible to be trained in those diagnostic procedures applicable to school age children within several hours (Delacato, 1963, p138). Intensive classes in treatment procedures are conducted at the Institutes. The classes range in length from one day to one year.

TREATMENT APPLICATIONS

Advocates of the theory have reported successful treatment applications for individuals with a variety of disorders: physical, developmental, learning and anatomical.

In 1959 (Delacato, 1959) treatment of the following amenable problems was reported: dyslexia, hyperactivity, asphasia, ataxic gait, reading reversals, stuttering, spelling deficiencies, low scholastic aptitude test scores (language scores lower than mathematical scores), motoric dysfunctions attributable to cerebral lesions or post-surgical recovery, low vocabulary scores, problems associated with premature birth — even when accompanied by blindness and stuttering, loss of adult speech (due to stroke and removal of the major part of the dominant cortical hemisphere in a 62-year-old-man), speech reversals, and difficulties attributable to mediocre parentage (Delacato, 1959).

In 1960 the group published a report indicating application of the treatment rationale to 76 children with mild to severe brain damage. The children had both unilateral and bilateral brain damage, including operated subdural hematomas, vascular malformations, non-specific hemiatrophy, and hemispherectomies. Sixty-one of the children had bilateral brain damage, most of which required surgical procedures. (Doman, R. et al., 1960)

A report in 1963 indicated that treatment application was extended to include delayed or poorly articulated speech, poor handwriting, behavior problems in school and at home, and strabismus (crosseyedness). (Delacato, 1963)

In 1966 an unusual case was reported. A child, who had been advised medically to have crooked feet surgically straightened, enrolled in the neurological organization program at school. After a short time in the program his feet straightened and no surgical intervention was necessary. (Delacato, 1966b, p153)

A suggestion has been made that in discussing this program "....we may be discussing a means for hurrying the evolutionary process." (Delacato, 1959, p80)

POPULAR AND PROFESSIONAL REACTION

Public acceptance of the treatment programs associated with the theory of neurological organization has been widespread. Thousands of children have been treated with the "neurological exercises" developed at the Institutes for the Achievement of Human Potential. "There are presently schools and clinics in every state which are either experimenting with or using neurological organization in the diagnosis and treatment of reading problems." (Delacato, 1966b p. 180). The Philadelphia center reports a 10-year waiting list. (Krippner, 1966, p 16.)

The widespread popular acceptance has probably resulted in some measure from extensive publicity. Accounts of individual cases and treatments have been published in many magazines and newspapers:

(1) "Miracle in Pennsylvania" in GOOD HOUSEKEEPING (Ernst, 1962).

(2) "A Boy Who Would Not Die" in LOOK (Brossard, 1962).

(3) "Hope for Brain-Injured Children" in READER'S DIGEST (Maisil, 1964).

(4) "Unlocking the Secrets of the Brain" in the CHICAGO TRIBUNE (Beck, 1964).

(5) "When Kids Can't Learn" in THE SATURDAY EVENING POST (Bird, 1967).

(See also Delay, 1963; Segal, 1966; Time, 1963; Bird, 1967; an unfavorable report was published by NEWSWEEK—Clark, 1964).

Associates of the Institutes have contributed to public acceptance of their theory by writing magazine articles. Some of the titles suggest a direct appeal to the mass market.

(1) "You Can Teach Your Baby to Read" in LADIES HOME JOURNAL (Doman, G. et al., 1963b).

(2) "Train Your Baby to be a Genius" in MC CALLS (Doman, G. and Delacato, 1965).

Despite positive factors such as (1) the popularization of the theory through the mass media; (2) the large number of children treated with the "neurological exercises"; (3) the reported 10-year waiting list for entrance into the Philadelphia center; (4) the reported results; and despite claims of scientific validity such as the following:

> *The concepts and procedures of the Institutes, although relatively new, are based on sound and established neuroanatomic, neurophysiologic and neurodynamic principles as well as extensive experience.* (Institutes for the Achievement of Human Potential 1964 p10).

The reaction of professional writers and organizations has been less than enthusiastic.

Reviewers of the theory in general and two of Delacato's (1959, 1963) books in particular have characterized his work and the rationale as follows:

> *(1) faddist* (Money, 1962, p28)

> *(2) a dangerous book* (Cole, 1964, p354)

> *(3) The Madison Avenue treatment of Delacato's claims (in the mass media) have, however, been little different from statements which appear within the book itself and in fact are often outdone by the unsupported evidence presented in the book.* (Wepman, 1964, p352)

> *(4) ....Delacato's data on which his theories are based are fallacious, his rationale poor and his conclusions untenable.* (Oettinger, 1964, p125)

> *(5) Neurologists will be unlikely to find this book scientifically in-*

formative. It is of some passing interest if viewed as an excursion into the realm of science fiction. (Brown, 1964, p600)

(See also Glass and Robbins, 1967; Hudspeth, 1964; Perkins, 1964; and Spache, 1965).

One of the authors (Robbins) has reported the results of two experimental studies which tested the relationship between neurological organization and reading. The data failed to support either the basic assumptions or the practicality of the theory. (Robbins, 1965a; 1965b; 1966a; 1966b; 1966c; 1967).

In an exchange of letters (Delacato, 1966a; Robbins, 1966d) one of the authors (Robbins) suggested that Mr. Delacato participate in a major research project to test the theory.

> *Our joint efforts would allow advocates of the theory to have confidence in the correct interpretation and application of the theory through Mr. Delacato's participation. Assistance from authorities in research design and statistical analysis could be sought to assure detractors of the theory of the adequacy of the study.* (Robbins, 1966 d, p201)

This suggestion had the support of prominent leaders in reading and special education. To this date, Mr. Delacato has not responded.

Statements to the public that the treatment efficacy is largely unsubstantiated have been issued by many major professional organizations including the Pennsylvania Society for Crippled Children and Adults (Clark 1964), the Pennsylvania Association for Retarded Children (Clark, 1964) and the American Academy of Pediatrics (Executive Board, 1965).

Part II. AN EXAMINATION OF CENTRAL ASSUMPTIONS OF THE THEORY

The theory of neurological organization is based on a series of assumptions which are said to rest upon data and logical justifications from numerous scientific disciplines (Delacato, 1966b); however, many of their theoretical formulations are contradicted by established knowledge. The following related tenets of the theory will be discussed here: 1. Ontogeny Recapitulates Phylogeny; 2. Sequential Development, Brain Stages, and Localization of Function; and 3. Sidedness (Laterality), Cerebral Dominance and Human Superiority. Each of the preceding divisions is further divided into subdivisions: A. Background, B. The Position of Theorists of Neurological Organization, and C. Refutation of the Position of Neurological Organization Theorists. Because the presentation of both the position of neurological organization theorists and our refutation are technical and terse, we have included a background section for each division of Part II. These sections contain such topics as definitions of key terms, origins of theories, critical issues, and other information essential to understanding the argument.

ONTOGENY RECAPITULATES PHYLOGENY

Background

Ontogeny is the developmental history of the individual, beginning with the ovum; phylogeny is the developmental history of the species, beginning with the origins of life. If one accepts the general concept of evolution, it is reasonable to expect structural and developmental similarities among species.

In 1828 von Baer reached several conclusions regarding embryonic development. In 1866 Haeckel modified von Baer's conclusions in a form known as the Biogenetic Law which postulated that ontogeny recapitulates phylogeny (Kraus, 1964, pp157-158). Haeckel's position extended only to the embryonic stage of human development, and is currently discredited (Kraus, 1964, pp157-158; Moody, 1962, p50).

The Position of Theorists of Neurological Organization

Theorists of neurological organization have extended Haeckel's law beyond the embryonic stage, to include childhood. They posit five distinct brain stages and suggest certain point-to-point correlations in neurological structure, function, and integration between man and his ancestors. (Delacato, 1959; 1963; 1966b; Doman, G. et al., 1963a) (This is elaborated further in Section 2.— Sequential Development, Brain Stages, and Localization of Function.)

Refutation of the Position of Neurological Organization Theorists

The position of neurological organization theorists is untenable for at least three reasons: (1) Haeckel's Biogenetic Law upon which it is based is discredited; (2) it extends Haeckel's Law beyond fetal development; and (3) neurological recapitulation is anatomically untenable.

DeBeer (1958) in reviewing evidence relative to the recapitulation theory concluded that the affinity between species was not strong enough to support the biogenetic hypothesis. He reported marked deviation between the ontogeny and phylogeny of man, for as ontogeny progresses within a species the individual members of that species grow more dissimilar from their ancestors over time. The theory is discredited in terms of fetal development; furthermore, there seems to be no merit in the extension of Haeckel's Law into childhood.

The assumption that lower brain stages of man structurally recapitulate the development of lower animals is anatomically untenable. Although certain areas of the human brain grossly correspond with brain areas of animals below the level of man, there are gross structural and functional differences (see for example, Gardner, 1963, pp235-237) which mediate against accepting the position of neurological organization theorists on this point.

The doubtful validity of the recapitulation theory in general, and as modified and advocated by neurological organization theorists in particular, has been pointed out by others:

> ...Delacato makes as his basic theoretic concept the recapitulation theory, that the ontogenetic organization and development of man recapitulates phylogenetic development. Not only does evidence from comparative neurology fail to support this theory in any detailed way, but it has long been discarded in the educational and psychological fields from evidences on the development of behavior. (Perkins, 1964, p120)

> This neuroanatomical development supposedly follows the structural changes found in ascending the phylogenetic scale. However, this comparison is based only upon gross structural similarities. In addition, there appears to be no one-to-one functional-structural correspondence as one follows the phylogenetic scale. (Hudspeth, 1964, p127)

SEQUENTIAL DEVELOPMENT, BRAIN STAGES AND LOCALIZATION OF FUNCTION

Background

If the defunct biogenetic law of Haeckel is applied to the development of man's central nervous system and his corresponding behavior from conception to maturity, then a series of deductions follows: first, there is an ordered pattern or sequence in the development of man's nervous system and functional behavior; second, this pattern of development recapitulates species development; third, particular behaviors in man and animals are associated with their developmental brain stages; fourth, a specific brain stage is identified with a particular point in either human or species development; and fifth, animal and human behavior of any particular brain stage are similar, subject to anatomical limitations.

Specific brain stages can also be attributed to particular archetectonic areas of the nervous system. This concept, known as localization of function, holds that particular areas of the brain assume maximum importance for specific functions.

The Position of Theorists of Neurological Organization

Theorists of neurological organization suggest that human development is divided into five separate levels, each level dependent upon the development of a previous level and associated with a specific part of the brain. Correspondingly, each level is also associated with a particular stage of animal development. The five brain stages with their associated developmental levels, animal and human, are as follows: (Delacato, 1963; Doman, G. et al., 1863a)

> **Medulla.** — Phylogenetically, this stage corresponds to the behavior of the fish. The gross trunkal movement, birth cry and reflex activities of the newborn are ontogenetic manifestations of the medulla stage.

> **Pons.** — In phylogenetic terms the pons stage corresponds to the behavior of the amphibian, with ontogenetic manifestations of this stage consisting of crawling, meaningful crying, and gross visual, tactile, and auditory perceptions of the one-to-four-month old child.

> **Midbrain.** — The midbrain stage corresponds phylogenetically to the behavior of the reptile. Creeping, creating meaningful sounds, greater awareness and interpretation of visual, tactile, and auditory stimuli and the prehensile grasp of the four-to-13-month old child are the ontogenetic manifestations of this stage.

> **Early Cortex.** — The early cortex stage corresponds phylogenetically to the behavior of the primate. Ontogenetic manifestations of this stage consist of crude walking, cortical opposition, ability to speak and understand a limited vocabulary, depth perception through visual and tactile means of the eight-month to six-year old child. Each of these functions approaches maturation during this stage.

> **Cerebral Dominance.** — There is no phylogenetically equivalent species for this level. The development of lateral dominance and as-

sociated functions of the eye, ear, leg and hand, full maturation of speech and hearing, and elementary reading skills of the three-to eight-year old child are the ontogenetic manifestations of the cerebral dominant stage. It is at this point that man achieves his ultimate phylogenetic and ontogenetic development.

Theorists of neurological organization state that "If a lower level is incomplete, all succeeding higher levels are affected both in relation to their height in the central nervous system and in relation to the chronology of their development." (Delacato, 1959, p19) Neurological organization theorists advocate specific developmental stages which must occur in a prearranged order for normal human development. "The basic premise of the neuro-psychological approach as outlined by the author is that if man does not follow this schema he exhibits a problem of mobility or communication." (Delacato, 1963, p7)

Briefly, the neurological organization position may be summarized as follows: (1) There is a relationship between ontological and phylogenetic neural development, (2) There is a sequence of development which is followed in normal, adequate humans, and (3) There are particular areas of the brain which have responsibility for particular functions.

Refutation of the Position of Neurological Organization Theorists

(1) Ontogenetic and Phylogenetic Stages

One test of the recapitulation theory would be a comparison of specific human and animal development attributed to a particular brain stage. Gross differences between human and animal behavior would contradict the position of neurological organization theorists. Peiper's (1963) work indicates the presence of this contradiction:

> The infant does not pass even a temporary stage of being a pure quadruped nor does he become temporarily quadrumanous. (p240)

Other contradictions are suggested by Peiper's findings. The human infant possesses demonstratable swimming movements not found in anthropoids (p218). On the other hand Peiper (1963, p241) "....was never able to find genuine climbing movements in the infant," a behavior common to species below man.

(2) Sequential Development

The concept of sequential development as postulated by theorists of neurological organization is contradicted by existing knowledge: (a) The assumption that earlier stages can predict the quality of later development is not supported and in some instances there is evidence to the contrary; (b) The exact order of developmental levels, if one does exist, has not been established; and (c) Individuals have been known to omit specific developmental stages without apparent ill effects on their maturation.

If a specific developmental sequence does in fact occur, it should be easy to establish a correlation between early and later developmental levels. However, Perkins (1964) has indicated that material of Shirley (1933) as well as Dearborn and Rothney (1941) clearly cause one to question the assumption that early motor performance predicts later intellectual development. Analyzing the data from the Harvard Growth Studies, they found a near zero correlation between motor development and later intellectual development.

Robbins (1965b) found that many children who did well on Delacato's test of laterality had difficulties with purportedly earlier developmental levels such as creeping, in contradiction to the theory.

Neurological organization theorists believe

> ....that there are critical periods for the appearance of motor and perceptual activities, like crawling, walking, etc., and that these must occur to full development in a certain order. Certainly, there is current interest in evidence on critical periods from ethology, but there are many contradictions in material from this field and very little evidence on human behavior. ....Evidence from child development certainly indicates that many children omit a phase like crawling, without showing later handicaps. (Perkins, 1964, p120)

Hudspeth (1964, p127) indicates that

> ....studies of human development have shown that specific developmental stages are not followed in the same order by all individuals. In fact, some individuals omit a few stages. All of these reversals and omissions do not appear to produce any more reading difficulty than is found in the population at-large. Thus, it would seem that the required developmental sequence proposed by Delacato has little empirical support.

(3) Localization of Brain Function

Several authors have attacked the assumption of localization of brain function made by neurological organization theorists. "The postulation of a point-to-point correlation between structure and function has been found to be untenable in other scientific attempts." (Wepman, 1964, p352) Hudspeth (1964, pp127-128) wrote:

> In assigning developmental roles to the various areas of the central nervous system Delacato has postulated what is termed localization of function. Modern studies of functional neuroanatomy have shown that the brain is not so simply constructed....over thirty years ago Lashley discovered that no single area of the brain was responsible for the learning of a specific habit.

Hudspeth also indicated that areas such as the pons and midbrain are involved in all behaviors requiring attention or shifts in attention. "No specific intellectual process is localized in any cortical area such that a loss of function invariably follows removal of that region." (Shure and Halstead, 1958, p28)

In postulating five specific brain levels of development the neurological organization theorists have negated the importance of other areas of the brain such as the reticular formation. This area, phylogenetically preceding man, is important to higher cognitive processes. (Bower, 1966)

SIDEDNESS (LATERALITY), CEREBRAL DOMINANCE AND HUMAN SUPERIORITY

One of the most controversial aspects of the neurological organization theory is the emphasis on cortical hemispheric dominance in diagnosis and the suggestion that certain exercises can develop laterality and cerebral dominance. Because of the complexity surrounding the concepts of **laterality** and **cerebral dominance**, the following background section is extensive.

Background

This section contains (1) definitions of several concepts and (2) the relationship between handedness and speech dominance.

(1) Definitions

The definitions which follow are consistent with current medical and educational thought. It is important to note that neurological organization theorists use some terms differently; these differences are pointed out in Section B.

> **Cerebrum.** — The cerebrum is the upper, main part of the brain consisting of two hemispheres. The exterior portion of the two hemi-

spheres is called the **cortex.** Although severing of the corpus callosum (transverse fibers which connect the cerebral hemispheres) in both man and animals has demonstrated that the two hemispheres are capable of functioning as independent brains (Sperry, 1964; Mishler, 1964); in normal individuals the hemispheres are inter-related in an unknown manner. (Penfield and Roberts, 1959)

Cerebral dominance. —The concept of cerebral dominance posits that one of the two hemispheres is the controlling agent for either one particular function or a series of functions, e.g., speaking, walking, writing, eating. Neurologically, a hemisphere is considered dominant for a particular function or series of functions if disease, damage or experimental intervention produce dysfunction. The concept does not imply that one hemisphere is dominant for all receptive or expressive behavior, nor does it suggest that the dominant hemisphere acts independently of other parts of the brain for any given function.

Decussation. —Many of the nerve fibers within the body are connected to the contralateral (opposite side) hemisphere. The crossover of these fibers is termed decussation. Not all the fibers decussate; some are connected to the ipsilateral (same side) hemisphere. For example, about 75 per cent of the corticospinal motor fibers which connect the hands with the hemispheres decussate (Gardner, 1963, p143). Because of this decussation, in normal individuals motor performance of the right hand is controlled by the contralateral (left) hemisphere. The left hand and right hemisphere are similarly related. Disease and surgical removal of a hemisphere have demonstrated that each hemisphere is capable of controlling skilled manual behaviors.

Sidedness or laterality. —The concept of sidedness posits that for certain skilled behavior, both receptive and motor, one hand, eye, leg, and ear is favored over the other. A person is lateralized if the skilled performance of all four of these elements occurs with consistency on the same side of the body. Individuals who do not possess consistent sidedness are called mixed or non-lateralized. Laterality is determined through various tasks, such as writing, kicking, sighting, tactual discrimination, etc. (Harris, 1958; Delacato, 1959; Luria, 1966). Laterality, a measure of external body function, is contrasted with dominance, a measure of cortical control. The

relationship between dominance and laterality has not been resolved.

(2) The Relationship Between Handedness and Speech Dominance

Several factors have contributed to the hypothesis that speech and language are controlled by the cerebral hemisphere contralateral to handedness. Although considered
fallacious by current clinical and experimental data, the hypothesis persists (Bakes, 1966,
p450) because "....there are....independent....tendencies....for humans (1) to be right-
handed and (2) to develop speech organization or dominance in the left hemisphere of
the brain."(Osgood and Miron, 1963, p51)

Penfield and Roberts (1959, pp89-90) attribute the origin of the hypothesis to Bouillaud
and Broca. When they advanced the theory in 1865, they did not have access to an
adequate number of left-handed cases. The theory was based primarily on data from
right-handed individuals with brain lesions (injuries) of the left hemisphere.

The relationship of sidedness, as measured by functional tests, to symbolic language at-
tainments has been emphasized by some (Delacato, 1959, 1963, 1966b; Harris, 1956,
1957, 1958; Orton, 1937; Orton and Travis, 1929; Travis, 1931) and minimized by others
(Gates, 1947; Money, 1962; Perkins, 1964; Hudspeth, 1964). The relationship between
laterality and reading disability has been empirically confirmed (Harris, 1957) and
rejected (Johnstone, 1942; Belmont and Birch, 1965). (Also see part (3) of section (C),
"Sidedness and Reading," below.)

No satisfactory test for measuring laterality which meets criteria of objectivity, reliability,
validity and adequate standardization norms has yet been developed (Buros, 1953,
1959, 1965).

Because of the absence of strong evidence to support the relationship between sidedness
and language, the connection is currently considered tenuous. Summary statements of
the literature indicate that the evidence is equivocal and depends upon the bias of the
investigator (Johnson, 1957; Smith and Carrigan, 1959).

The Position of Theorists of Neurological Organization

Complete presentation and interpretation of the assumptions made by theorists of neurological organization regarding dominance are difficult due to inconsistencies in definition
and terminology. Their position may be summarized as follows:

The culmination of adequate neural development is cerebral dominance, the climax of
phylogenetic and ontogenetic development. According to this rationale (note the dif-

ference in the definition given by the neurological organization theorists and that stated in the previous section), the concept **dominance** suggests that one hemisphere controls most of man's skilled activities, both receptive and motoric; however, control of tonality is suggested to fall in the subdominant hemisphere. Therefore, when the right hemisphere is dominant, it controls speech; tonality is controlled by the left hemisphere, and the individual is left-eyed, -footed, and -handed. (Delacato, 1963, pp64-65)

According to the rationale, cerebral dominance and neurological organization can be determined and measured by a series of tests within the **Delacato Test Summary Sheet** (Delacato, 1966b, pp18-23) and the **Doman-Delacato Developmental Profile** (LeWinn, et al., 1965, p64).

Theorists of neurological organization maintain that animals, because they do not possess dominance, cannot perform the following human functions: stand fully upright, create musical sounds, use a symbolic language system, see stereoscopically, and exhibit single sidedness. (Delacato, 1963, p46) Since the crux of the theory depends upon these theorists' definition of dominance, refutation of any aspect of their interpretation would tend to undermine the entire theory.

Refutation of the Position of Neurological Organization Theorists

The assumptions of neurological organization theorists regarding sidedness (laterality), cerebral dominance and human superiority are challenged in this section, which is divided into seven parts: (1) Contradictions in Logic; (2) Inconsistencies in Laterality: Sensory and Motor; (3) Laterality and Linguistic Functions: An Unsubstantiated Relationship; (4) Laterality and Speech Dominance: A Pseudo-Relationship; (5) Eye Dominance: A Contradiction to the Theory; (6) Human Superiority, Sidedness and Dominance: Contradicted Assumptions; and (7) Dominance: An Elusive Concept.

(1) Contradictions in Logic

Tonality. —Delacato (1963) states that infants possess the ability to make vowel and tonal (musical) sounds. Two inherent contradictions arise from this statement: first, if tonality is a function of the subdominant hemisphere which is not developed at birth, then the infant should be unable to emit these sounds; second, if, as purported by the theory, the infant is at the medulla stage, he should not possess skills more advanced than this phylogenetic level, represented by the fish.

Thumb sucking. —According to one theorist (Delacato, 1959, p74), parents should permit thumb sucking only of the sub-dominant hand. If cortical function begins at the age of one year (Delacato, 1963), the parents would be unable to distinguish the dominant from the sub-dominant hand before this age. Gesell and Ames (1947) reported that inconsistent use of a hand before consistent handedness is established persists until the age of eight years.

Speech and Reading Development. — The theory suggests that cerebral dominance takes place during the fifth to eighth year (Delacato, 1963, p63), with speech and reading the final result of neurological organization (Delacato, 1963, p7). This contention leaves unexplained the relatively complete speech ability of the three-year-old or the emphasis placed on early training in reading (Doman, G., 1964).

(2) Inconsistencies in Laterality: Sensory and Motor

The theory suggests that laterality is the normal condition in well-functioning individuals, with both receptive and expressive functions (except for tonality) primarily associated with one side of the body. However, current research reveals that constant sidedness is not a normal situation. Sensitivity and eye dominance are independent of handedness. "....the various functions, e.g. language, handedness, eyedness, establish themselves independently...." (Goodglass and Quadfasel, 1954, p525). Consequently, the sidedness hypothesis of the neurological organization theorists is refuted.

Consistent Sidedness. — Cole (1964, pp352-353) seriously disputes Delacato's (1963) position that the normal pattern in man is single sidedness:

> *Current literature on the subject does not substantiate this statement, nor do clinical studies now in progress at the Language Clinic of the Massachusetts General Hospital. So-called crossed or mixed patterns of laterality occur with great frequency in the normal population.*

The review of Hecaen and Ajuriaguerra (1964) reaches the same conclusion.

Sensitivity. — The theory of neurological organization postulates that both receptive and expressive acts should be associated with one consistent side of the body. However, this assumption cannot be supported by recent work on somatosensory representation.

Semmes and others (1960) have shown that right-handed subjects were more sensitive to pressure stimulation on the left rather than the right hand. They reported that additional studies confirmed this result for normal subjects, the brain injured and individuals with peripheral sensory injuries regardless of handedness. The authors cited an unpublished study involving 60 left-handed and 60 right-handed subjects which found that

> *....the left hand tended to show greater sensitivity to pressure in both groups. The left forearm and the left sole were also more sensitive than the right in a majority of subjects in both groups.* (Semmes et al., 1960, p10)

Additional follow-up studies led Weinstein (1964, p166) to conclude: "The majority of normal right-handed individuals were more sensitive on their left forearms and soles, as were the majority of normal left-handed individuals." He further rejects the notion that hand dominance, sensory dominance and speech dominance are related.

> *....the fact that various dissociations of handedness from sensory dominance (whether auditory or tactual), and sensory from speech dominance suggests that these functions are anatomically independent, despite frequent coincident relationships.* (Weinstein, 1964, pp166-167)

(3) Laterality and Linguistic Functions: An Unsubstantiated Relationship

Neurological organization theorists posit relationships among laterality, tonality, stuttering and reading. In actuality, these relationships are unsupported, and in some cases contradicted, by the literature.

Dominance and Tonality. — The theorists maintain that tonality is a function of the subdominant hemisphere, but cite no research evidence beyond their own opinions (see Delacato, 1963, p45, footnote 20). A search of 100 different references from the field of neurology failed to reveal one source supporting this position.

Dominance and Stuttering. — Delacato (1963, pp17-18) acknowledges Orton as a pioneer in relating dominance to language functions but neglects to mention that despite attempts by Orton (1937), Orton and Travis (1929) and Travis (1931), the theoretical relationship between dominance and language was not substantiated.

Travis was unable to relate dominance to stuttering despite "....a rather exhaustive series of experiments in stuttering, in which he tried to demonstrate that inference with established cerebral dominance, or lack of dominance, was a cause of stuttering." (Bakes, 1966, pp450-451). "....by the 1940's this theory and procedure was abandoned by Travis and his followers, since the evidence clearly showed that these methods did not work." (Perkins, 1964, p120)

Sidedness and Reading. — The relationship between mixed cerebral dominance and reading performance is equivocal and depends upon the bias of the investigator. Reviews of the literature have failed to substantiate a consistent relationship. (Johnson, 1957; Smith and Carrigan, 1959)

Fernald (1943, p150), as a result of remediating children with reading disorders, concluded:

> *The right-handed cases and the cases of matched eye-hand dominance resemble the cases in which the dominance is not matched, are as serious in their deficiency, learn by the same methods, and are as successful in the final outcome....the subject with unmatched eye and hand dominance learns to read and is able to read in an entirely normal manner with eye and hand dominance still opposite.*

In two studies Robbins (1965a; 1965b) failed to find a relationship between sidedness and reading. The first study used the **Harris Tests of Lateral Dominance** (Harris, 1958) with normal second graders, the second employed Delacato's laterality tests (Delacato, 1963) to retarded readers from grades two through eight. Considerable amounts of evidence have been presented recently which show no statistical correlation between "mixed-dominance vs. uni-laterality" and reading performance. (See Balow, 1963; Balow and Balow, 1964; Belmont and Birch, 1965; Capobianco, 1966, 1967; Coleman and Deutsch, 1964; Flescher, 1963; Hillerich, 1964; and Silver and Hagin, 1960. See Harris, 1957, and Zangwill, 1962, for dissenting opinions.) Moreover, apparent correlations between degree of neurological organization and reading performance which Delacato presented to support his theory have been shown to have arisen from a failure to partial out the effects of chronological age (Glass and Robbins, 1967).

If neurological organization and consistent sidedness were essential to reading and other linguistic skills, as maintained by neurological organization theorists, then one would not expect to find normal and superior readers with laterality problems; however, the latter do exist in contradiction to the theory. "A very large number of individuals who have never had the slightest reading disability, many with distinctly superior reading skill, have unmatched eye and hand dominance." (Fernald, 1943, p161) "It is extremely difficult to understand why some ill-lateralized children have reading problems and others, almost certainly the great majority do not." (Zangwill, 1962, p112)

(4) Laterality and Speech Dominance: A Pseudo-Relationship

Those who advocate the theory of neurological organization state that there is a positive relationship between speech dominance and handedness. They contend that the speech functions of a right-sided individual are controlled by the left hemisphere and that the speech of a left-sided individual is controlled by the right hemisphere. Even if the notion were maintained that consistent sidedness for eye, hand, leg and ear is normal (and desirable), the suggested relationship to speech dominance is contradicted by a growing body of evidence. As indicated by the evidence below, speech of normal individuals is generally controlled by the left hemisphere regardless of sidedness.

> *There is not a causal dependency relation between handedness and laterality of speech representation. Rather, there are strong and independent tendencies (environmental or hereditary) for humans (1) to be right-handed and (2) to develop speech organization or dominance in the left hemisphere of the brain.* **(Osgood and Miron, 1963, p51)**

The false historical association between hemispheric control for both handedness and speech has probably been caused by the intersection of these two independent tendencies.

Evidence from Aphasia. — Penfield and Roberts (1959, pp90-91) cited 136 cases of aphasia without involvement of the right hemisphere. Fifty-three cases were right-handed, 65 cases were left- or predominantly left-handed, and in 18 cases handedness was not known. The researchers concluded that the purported relationship between handedness and speech dominance is false, and that speech is normally controlled by the left hemisphere. They attributed most cases of right hemispheric control of speech to a childhood lesion in the left hemisphere.

Evidence from Experimental Aphasia. — Intracarotid injection of Sodium Amytal induces a temporary loss of function in the ipsilateral hemisphere. This procedure has provided an experimental means of inducing aphasia through injection into the suspected speech-dominant hemisphere. Results of this procedure tend to confirm other evidence that speech in the case of left-sided individuals is not confined to the right hemisphere, in contradiction to the theory of neurological organization. (Wada and Rasmussen, 1960)

Evidence from Post-Neurosurgical Aphasia. — Patients who underwent neurosurgery for a variety of reasons were classified by handedness. Penfield and Roberts (1959, p102) reported "....no difference in frequency of aphasia after operation on the left hemisphere between left- and right-handed." Similar results were reported for operations on the right hemisphere. The researchers (p102) concluded: "Brain function and handedness may be unrelated except by disease."

Evidence from Electro-cortical Interference. — Electric current has been applied to the exposed cortex in order to map various areas of the brain. Based on data gathered from 114 patients Penfield and Roberts (1959, p137) concluded:

> *From the standpoint of cerebral dominance; the data from electrical interference support the conclusion....that the left hemisphere is usually dominant for speech regardless of the handedness of the individual, with the exclusion of those who have cerebral injuries early in life.*

Evidence from Brain Injuries.—Zangwill (1960) reviewed 492 cases of unilateral brain injury at the Oxford Head Injuries Bureau. There was a tendency for both right and left-handed individuals to have speech difficulties associated with the left hemisphere. This "....raises the possibility that even in those who are fully left-handed the dominant hemisphere may be the left." (p5)

Additional case material and a review of the literature led Zangwill (1960, p26) to conclude:

> *....the relation between handedness and cerebral dominance is somewhat less clear-cut than was at one time supposed. In left-handed individuals, the dominant hemisphere — insofar as this can be inferred from the clinical manifestations of brain damage — is more often the left than the right....*

(5) Eye Dominance: A Contradiction of the Theory

Although both hemispheres are involved in visual functions, dominance is a property of the right temporal lobe:

> *We have known for a number of years from the investigations of Dr. Brenda Milner, and more recently from the work of Dr. Lansdell, that visual perception in man is impaired by a right temporal lobectomy. In fact, the impairment can be detected in patients with right temporal epilepsy even before a removal is made; the surgery simply exacerbates the impairment. But curiously, this deficit in response to complex visual material is not found in patients with left temporal epilepsy, not even after the left temporal lobe has been removed. Clearly, the right temporal lobe in man is dominant for visual functions.* (Mishkin, 1962, p105)

The location of visual dominance in the right hemisphere contradicts the theory on two points: first, the theory suggests that both visual and speech dominance reside in the same hemisphere—an impossibility since speech dominance is normally located in the right hemisphere and visual dominance in the left; and second, since visual dominance is in the right hemisphere regardless of sidedness, the assumption of the theory that this dominance is contralateral to sidedness is contradicted by all normal individuals who happen to be lateralized on the right side.

(6) Human Superiority, Sidedness and Dominance: Contradicted Assumptions

Theorists of neurological organization maintain that because man alone possesses cerebral dominance, he exclusively is able to perform the following tasks: (Delacato, 1963, p46)

(a) stand fully upright
(b) create musical sounds
(c) use a symbolic language system
(d) see stereoscopically
(e) exhibit single sidedness

Alternate explanations or contrary evidence for man's uniqueness can be offered for each of these characteristics.

The ability to stand upright. — Upright posture in man is difficult to attribute to one factor since it "....entails a whole series of anatomical changes as compared to the structure of primates which do not have this posture." (Moody, 1962, p229) The anatomical changes include shifts in the relationship between skull and spinal cord, addition of the lumbar curve in the vertebral column, changes in the pelvic girdle, etc. These changes seem to offer a satisfactory explanation without reference to cerebral dominance.

The ability to create musical sounds. — As suggested by Spache (1965, p409) lower species, particularly birds, display tonality by creating musical sounds, in contradiction to the theory.

The ability to create symbolic language. — According to Dr. Lilly there is no evidence for dominance in the dolphin, yet he is capable of language-like communication definitely symbolic in nature. (Jung, 1962, p269)

The ability to see stereoscopically. — Numerous animals, including birds, dolphins and monkeys possess depth perception despite any indications of dominance. Lilly (1962, p113) reported stereopsis in the dolphin, and Hudspeth (1964, p128) found it in the monkey.

The ability to exhibit single sidedness. — Sidedness is considered a trait found only in **homo sapiens**, yet animals not possessing dominance have been found to possess sidedness or laterality, "....including the lowly rat." (Hudspeth, 1964, p128)

(7) Dominance: An Elusive Concept

The concept of dominance which evolved from studies in neuro-pathology may not be viable for normal individuals. Attempts to measure dominance in normal subjects have proven unsuccessful due to the seeming instability and inaccessibility of the phenomenon. Hecaen and Ajuriaguerra (1964, p148) reported the "....absence of anatomical and electrophysiological data in favor of cerebral dominance...." and suggested that many recoveries in human functioning after unilateral lesions mitigate against a rigid concept of dominance.

Child (1964, p257) stated,

> *Judging from behavior, the relations of dominance and subordination within the cortex are not definite and fixed, but shift from moment to moment, according to the impulses coming in and the physiological state of the various cells.*

An analysis of the intellectual processes of 72 post-neuro-surgery cases led Shure and Halstead (1958, p28) to conclude, "Abstraction ability is not significantly more impaired by lesions in one hemisphere than in the other."

Luria (1966, p89) also noted that "....the degree of dominance of the hemispheres varies not only from subject to subject, but also from function to function."

The concept of consistent dominance is used as a cornerstone for both the theory and practice of neurological organization. Advocates of this rationale have not been able to demonstrate its validity — neither has anyone else.

Conclusion

The central assumptions of the theory of neurological organization have been presented here. The examination has provided a background of related information, a statement of the position of theorists of neurological organization, and refutation of the theorists' position, on the following interrelated topics: ontogeny recapitulates phylogeny; sequential development, brain stages, and localization of function; and sidedness, cerebral dominance and human superiority.

Theorists of neurological organization have failed to provide the evidence upon which the fundamental tenets of their theory are based. Our examination of these assumptions indicates that the tenets are either unsupported or overwhelmingly contradicted when tested by theoretical, experimental, or logical evidence from the relevant scientific literature. As a scientific hypothesis the theory of neurological organization seems to be without merit.

Part III. AN EVALUATION OF ELEVEN EXPERIMENTS ON THE RELATIONSHIP BETWEEN NEUROLOGICAL ORGANIZATION AND READING

Each of the studies considered in this review comes from one of the three following sources: C.H. Delacato, THE TREATMENT AND PREVENTION OF READING PROBLEMS (1959); C.H. Delacato, THE DIAGNOSIS AND TREATMENT OF SPEECH AND READING PROBLEMS (1963); C.H. Delacato, NEUROLOGICAL ORGANIZATION AND READING (1966) Although Delacato performed only two of these studies himself, they are all cited by him as evidence in support of his system of therapy to remediate poor readers and improve the performance of good readers through improving neurological organization.

Sources of the empirical studies which will be discussed in the remainder of this paper appear below:

1. The 1959 Delacato Study pp98-100 in Delacato (1959).
2. The Piper Study pp152-166 in Delacato (1959).
3. The 1963 Delacato Study pp170-173 in Delacato (1959).
4. The Sister M. Edwin Study pp50-53 in Delacato (1966).
5. The Masterman Study (Chp. 12)*
6. The McGrath Study (Chp. 13).
7. The Noonan Study (Chp. 17).
8. The Kabot Study (Chp. 14).
9. The Glaeser Study (Chp. 16).
10. The Sister M. Alcuin Study (Chp. 18).
11. The Miracle Study (Chp. 19).

The experimental studies of the Doman-Delacato theory of neurological organization and its relationship to reading are exemplary for their faults. They were naively designed and clumsily analyzed. They suffer from a multitude of sources of invalidity. They appear to have been executed and reported in an atmosphere of relative insensitivity to basic considerations of empirical, experimental research.

Campbell and Stanley (1963) have identified influences which threaten the validity of findings from experiments. These influences may operate in any given instance to produce a "gain" from a pretest to post-test or an advantage for an experimental group over a control group. When an experiment has been executed in such a manner that one or more of these invalidating influences has gone uncontrolled and unnoticed, the experimenter may mistake their presence for an "effective treatment" or a "treatment which makes a difference." Among the sources of experimental invalidity identified by

*The chapter number in parentheses is the chapter which the study constitutes in Delacato (1966).

Campbell and Stanley are the **following:***

History — events affecting the experimental units (persons or classrooms, for example) between a first and second observation of the units. For example, suppose an evaluator was measuring the effect of a science curriculum on "interest in astronomy" and he was able to show a large pretest—posttest gain over the period of a semester. A dramatic space launching of men to the moon occurring between the pretest and posttest might cast some doubt on the validity of the evaluator's assertion that the curriculum stimulated interest in astronomy. The "space launching" is a source of possible internal invalidity which we might classify under **History.**

Maturation — biological, physiological, or psychological "processes within the respondents varying systematically with the passage of time" but not as the result of specific events (including the experimental treatment) external to the respondents, e.g., growing older, more tired, better coordinated, etc. Suppose an experimenter claimed that a series of prescribed play activities were effective in promoting **bladder** control in infants; as evidence he showed that two per cent of the 15-months-old infants starting his experiment had control, and 75 per cent of these infants achieved control nine months later. His claim is questionable since the normal infant develops bladder control during this period naturally.

Testing — the effects of taking a test on the outcomes of subsequent administration of the same or a highly related test. Taking some cognitive-ability tests may increase your score by several points on a second administration of the same test or a parallel form of it.

Instrumentation — changes in the instruments (tests, judges, various measuring devices) with which persons participating in an experiment are observed may produce changes in the scores over time which are mistaken as treatment effects. For example, judges observing and rating some performance may be more lenient from time 1 to time 2. Or Form A is given as a pretest in an experiment, and Form B is used as posttest.

Statistical regression — the inevitable tendency of persons whose scores are extreme (high above or far below the mean) on Measurement A to be less extreme (less high above or less far below the mean) on Measurement B. This phenomenon of "regression toward the mean" will be observed whenever Measurements A and B are **not** perfectly correlated, which for all practical purposes is always. Francis Galton recognized almost

*The definitions of the sources of experimental invalidity in this list are based on D.T. Campbell and J.C. Stanley's EXPERIMENTAL AND QUASI-EXPERIMENTAL DESIGNS FOR RESEARCH ON TEACHING, Chapter 5 in Gage, N.L. (Ed.) Handbook of Research on Teaching (Chicago: Rand-McNally), 1963. All material which is a direct quotation from this source is enclosed in quotation marks.

one hundred years ago that the sons of very tall fathers had a shorter average height than their fathers and that the sons of very short fathers had a taller average height than their fathers.

Selection — all of those factors which conspire to make the experimental and the control groups unequal at the outset of an experiment in ways which **cannot** be properly taken into account in the analysis of the data. For example, **selection** might invalidate a comparison of curricula A and B if older, more experienced teachers were selected to teach the more difficult curriculum. It appears that in almost all instances the only feasible way to guard against selection bias is by employing the **random assignment** of persons or classrooms to treatments and then using statistical analyses of the final data which are based on the randomization procedure.

Experimental Mortality — the differential loss or "dropping out" of persons from two or more groups being compared in an experiment. If attrition is greater under curriculum A than curriculum B, a comparison of A and B at the end of one school year might be biased in that the students completing A would be brighter — on the average — than those completing B. This is true simply because the slower students were fatalities under curriculum A.

It is important to note that these sources of invalidity can interact in a single experiment to produce a combined invalidating influence. For example, **selection** and **experimental mortality** interact in an experiment comparing curricula A and B when more experienced teachers are selected for curriculum A and greater demands they place on the students cause a greater number of students to drop out of curriculum A than curriculum B.

In the evaluation of each study reported in Delacato's three books, an attempt will be made to avoid caviling at and carping about the myriad statistical **faux pas**. Nor will the game of conjuring up improbable alternative explanations of gains and differences be played. Whenever an attempt is made to explain the obtained results in terms of factors other than the effectiveness of Delacato's therapy, the explanation offered is considered **probable** by the authors and not simply in the realm of possibilities. In many instances, possible explanations of gains shown by a treated group or of a difference favoring the experimental group over the control group are rejected and not mentioned because they seemed to be mere possibilities. To facilitate the reader's independent evaluation of the studies to be reviewed here, a summary of the points to be raised in connection with each study is presented in Table 1. For each of the eleven experiments to be reviewed, an indication is made of those sources of internal invalidity which exist as alternative explanations of treatment effects which were attributed to the effectiveness of the Doman-Delacato therapy.

A detailed critical analysis of empirical studies of the Doman-Delacato therapy has appeared elsewhere (see Glass and Robbins, 1967). In the remainder of this review the criticisms raised elsewhere will be mentioned briefly and, in most instances, supplemented by new evidence and argument. Thus, this review supplements and extends the previous critique cited above.

THE 1959 DELACATO STUDY

The sole empirical study, other than case studies, reported in THE TREATMENT AND PREVENTION OF READING PROBLEMS (1959 pp98-100) was performed on 30 pupils who evidenced moderate reading problems. To qualify for this study, a pupil had to be in the lower third of his class and had to perform at least one and one-half years "below his expectancy level" on a reading achievement test. Doman-Delacato therapy was administered for eight weeks, after which a posttest was administered.

No detailed analysis of the data from this experiment was presented. It was merely reported that the maximum, median, and minimum "gain" on an unnamed test of reading performance were 2.3 years, 0.9 years, and 0.4 years in grade-placement units, respectively. At least three sources of gain **other than** effectiveness of the therapy can be identified. First, the time elapsing from pretest to posttest was 0.2 years. An "average" group would be expected to gain 0.2 years from normal reading instruction. One might hazard the guess that the maximum, median, and minimum "gains" from all factors other than "normal growth" between the pretest and posttest were 2.1 years, 0.7 years, and 0.2 years, respectively. (This assumption about normative growth will be viewed critically later.) A second influence which undoubtedly produced some pretest to posttest increase—but an influence which is difficult to evaluate without a special empirical study—is the practice effect on the posttest resulting from having taken the same test eight weeks previously. The third influence which could easily have been mistaken for "gains" due to therapy in this "experiment" was probably the strongest. The regression effect would be expected to produce gains from pretest to posttest which are much greater than those to be expected from both the facilitating effect of repeated testing and the effect of normal growth during the experimental period. Pupils chosen because of their low scores on a pretest will show "gain" on a posttest regardless of the length of time or the nature of the events which intervene between the pretest and the posttest.

THE PIPER STUDY

The study was performed by Gayle L. Piper of Mingus Union High School, Jerome, Arizona. Fourteen pupils experiencing reading difficulties were tested in February of 1962 with Form 1 of the GATES BASIC READING TEST. Delacato therapy was administered for six weeks at which time Form 2 of the Gates test was given. After six weeks

TABLE I

Probable Sources of Invalidity for the Eleven Experiments Being Reviewed

Source of Invalidity	1 '59 Delacato	2 Piper	3 '63 Delacato	4 Sister Edwin	5 Masterman	6 McGrath	7 Noonan	8 Kabot	9 Glaeser	10 Alcuin	11 Miracle
A. History				X	X				X		
B. Maturation	X	X	X			X	X				
C. Testing	X	X	X			X					
D. Instrumentation								X			
E. Regression	X	X	X		X	X	X				
F. Selection				X					X	X	X
G. Experimental Mortality		X			X			X	X		
H. Inappropriate or Inadequate Statistical Analysis	X	X	X	X							

further therapy, Form 3 of the Gates test was administered on May 1, 1962. Therapy was suspended during the summer; on September 6, 1962, Form 4 of the Gates test was given.

Effectiveness of the therapy was measured by gain scores. Any difference between a test score on a child and one obtained earlier on the same child was considered evidence of gain; no attempt was made to correct this "gain" for an increase to be expected from the normal passage of time in school.

The following data were recorded for the experimental subjects:

Mean Grade-placement Scores on the Gates Basic Reading Test

	FEBRUARY 1, 1962	MARCH 15, 1962	MAY 1, 1962	SEPTEMBER 6, 1962
MEAN =	5.07 yrs.	5.55 yrs.	5.43 yrs.	6.38 yrs.

At least four plausible explanations of why posttest scores exceed pretest scores can be identified:

1. Since the subjects were chosen for therapy because of poor reading and academic performance, their scores on subsequent administrations of the reading test should increase because of the inevitable phenomenon of regression toward the mean.

2. One might expect that increases in achievement test scores would result from familiarity with the format of the test—and other factors referred to as the "practice effect of testing"—when four alternate forms of the same test are administered in a seven-months period.

3. "Posttest—Pretest" measures of gain can be expected to be positive because of the normal growth in reading performance of any pupil receiving instruction in reading.

4. In calculating the means for the four testing occasions, Piper failed to account for the fact that the mean for Sept. 6, 1962, was based on 13 **S**'s, one subject having dropped out of the experiment between May and Sept. If the pupil who dropped out between May and Sept. had been present on the final testing and contributed a score of 3.6 (his three previous scores in order were 3.5, 3.8, and 3.6), the mean for Sept., 1962, would have dropped to 6.18 years.

Piper offered no statistical analyses of the data. Such analyses were performed by the authors and will be summarized here. It must be kept in mind that the following tests of statistical hypotheses are merely **descriptive** of the variation in the data and do not

352

constitute tests of the scientific hypothesis that Delacato therapy is effective. The data from Piper's study are suspect at the outset in a way that no statistical test can correct. The mean gain from pretest to posttest following six weeks of therapy is 0.48 grade-placement units; the variance of the gain scores is 0.33. This difference between pre-test and posttest means is significant at the .01 level when a *t*-test was applied to the 14 gain scores. If the gain scores are corrected for elapsed time, i.e., if six weeks = 0.15 grade-placement units are subtracted from each gain score,[*] the mean gain is 0.33 grade-placement units. The *t*-statistic for testing the significance of this gain is 0.33/0.33/14 which is approximately 2.15; this value of *t* barely misses statistical significance at the .025 level with a one-tailed test. With confidence, it can be concluded that a non-random gain in scores occurred, although it remains moot whether the gain can be attributed to regression, the practice effect of testing, or the inappropriateness of a "correction for maturation" of 0.15 grade-placement units.

The mean gain over the twelve-weeks period from the beginning to the end of therapy was 0.36 in grade-placement units, the variance of the gain scores is 0.28. The mean gain less elapsed time (twelve weeks) equals $0.36 - 0.25 = 0.11$. The *t*-statistic for testing the significance of the difference between .11 and zero is less than unity. One cannot conclude with any confidence that there is a significant difference between the means of the grade-placement scores in February and in May over and above the expected gain due to elapsed time.

The mean gain from the pretest in February to the final posttest in September was 1.19 grade-placement units. This gain is statistically significant even when elapsed time is subtracted from the gain scores. (It must be pointed out, however, that the elapsed-time score does not include two months of the summer recess. Thus, if some or all of the subjects received instruction in reading during the summer, the elapsed-time score used to correct the gain scores in the analysis would have been too small. Piper does not report whether the subjects were instructed in reading during the summer recess). The significance test, it must be remembered, reflects only on the reliability of the gain; it does not reflect on the cause of the gain. The gain from February to May is smaller than the gain from February to September even when corrected for elapsed time. This is to be expected from data whose movement is governed by the regression effect. Since Form 1 in February correlates higher with Form 3 in May than it does with Form 4 in September, the regression toward the mean will be greater when measured from February to September than from February to May.

---

[*]*This technique, used repeatedly by Delacato in NEUROLOGICAL ORGANIZATION AND READING (1966), will be viewed critically in the review of the McGrath study.*

THE 1963 DELACATO STUDY

The 25 members of the Junior class of a private school for boys were the subjects in this experiment. As part of the College Entrance Examination Board's testing program, all of the 25 subjects took the SCHOLASTIC APTITUDE TEST. Their scores on the Verbal subtest of the SAT were recorded. At this point, Delacato formed an experimental and a control group. There is only about one legitimate way in which to do this: **randomly** assign some number of subjects to the group which will receive neurological training and place the remaining subjects in the control group. There are numerous ways to form the two groups so that unknown amounts of bias result: (a) try to "match" subjects in predesignated control and experimental groups, (b) ask for volunteers for the experimental group, (c) let the boys who play football be the control group, etc. Of all the incorrect ways of forming the groups, Delacato chose, perhaps unwittingly, the poorest and the one which was most biased in his favor. The nine lowest scoring subjects on the pretest with the SAT-Verbal were designated the "experimental group", and the 16 highest scoring subjects, the "control group." As can be seen by anyone who understands the rudiments of statistical regression, the "design" is certain to show "gains" for the experimental group and much smaller "gains" or even losses for the control group irrespective of the effectiveness of the treatment given to experimental subjects.

Neurological training was administered to the nine experimental subjects for one-half hour each day for six weeks. At some unspecified time following the end of the six-weeks experimental period, the **Scholastic Aptitude Test** was administered a second time. The following results were obtained:

	PRETEST MEAN	POSTTEST MEAN	MEAN "GAIN"
CONTROL GROUP (n≈16)	547.4	5 54.2	6.8
EXPERIMENTAL GROUP (n≈9)	397.7	463.5	65.8

It should come as a surprise to no one that the mean "gain" for the experimental group was considerably larger than the mean "gain" for the control group (65.8 points versus 6.8 points). How might one account for the large "gain" of the experimental group? How can one explain the fact that the control group actually gained from pretest to posttest instead of regressing downward?

The answer to the second question is simple. The regression effect does **not** imply that a group chosen because of their high scores at Time 1 will have a smaller mean at Time 2. This will only be necessarily true if the mean and variance of the total group from which the "high group" was selected do not change from Time 1 to Time 2. If both sets of scores (Time 1 and Time 2) are standardized to the same mean and variance, the "high group" at Time 1 will yield a lower mean at Time 2. In Delacato's study the mean of the total group of 25 scores increased 28 points from the pretest to the posttest, probably as a result of maturation on the subjects and the practice effect of having taken the SAT-Verbal test once before. Frankel (1960) found a practice effect of 19 points on the SAT-Verbal. In a well-designed study of the effect of previous administrations of the SAT-Verbal, Pearson (1948) showed a practice effect of 20 points over a two-month period after the maturation effect was removed from the results. It is not unreasonable to assume that the practice effect of pretesting was of the order of 20 points in Delacato's study). Both maturation and the practice effect of pretesting operated to increase the scores of both the control and experimental groups. The regression effect joined these two influences to produce a large "gain" for the experimental group; in the control group, it militated against these influences which were strong enough, nonetheless, to produce a pretest to posttest gain where it might not have been expected.

Delacato made an attempt to provide somewhat better control for this experiment than his first control group of 16 students by going into the records of the Junior class of the previous year to measure the gain made by the nine lowest scorers on the SAT-Verbal test from a first to a second testing. With this "control group" the interval between the pretest and posttest was seven months. Since Delacato did not report the time interval between the pretest and the posttest for his experimental group, the appropriateness of the improvised control group is questioned. This consideration aside, the results Delacato obtained on these nine students are nothing short of amazing. Not only did they not regress upwards—they were the nine lowest scorers on the SAT-Verbal for the previous Junior class—not only did they fail to show a normal gain in verbal skills due to growth during the year, not only did they show no gain due to the practice effect of taking the test, but they actually showed an average loss of 19 points from the pretest to the posttest. This result is known to be so atypical that this improvised "control group" is without question inappropriate.

The Educational Testing Service, the agency which constructs, administers, and scores the Scholastic Aptitude Test, gathered the following data over a seven-months span from May to December, 1965.* For those pupils tested in May and the following December, a gain from 474.93 to 494.15 was observed. The correlation between the two sets of scores was .88. An average score of 547.4—the mean for Delacato's "control group"—would be expected to regress naturally under standard conditions to a score of 556.8, which is less than 3 points from the posttest mean for Delacato's "control group." An

*(Dr. Gary L. Marco, personal communication, 24 January, 1967).

average score of 397.7—the mean for Delacato's "experimental group"—would be expected to regress naturally to a score of 427.4. The greater regression of the mean for Delacato's "experimental group" might be attributable to the fact that his 9 experimental subjects were the most extreme in the group in which they were pretested; they were not merely a group lying one standard deviation below the mean of the general population.

THE SISTER M. EDWIN STUDY

A total of 108 kindergarten children began the experiment; 84 children "were able to participate in the total program to the end of the study," producing a "mortality rate" of 22 per cent. The experimental period was six weeks. Subjects were pretested on June 24 with the HARRISON-STROUD READING READINESS TEST. Of the 84 children who persisted in the experiment, 43 were in the experimental group and 41 were in the control group.

The experimental group was placed on a daily 80-minute regimen of neurological training. The control group participated in coloring, games, lunch, and a rest period, but was given no neurological training. Oddly enough, the experimental group listened to stories, folk songs, and nursery rhymes for 25 minutes each day. The only possibility for the control group to receive a comparable activity was provided by the teacher asking the mothers or some older members of the families of the control children to read or tell a story to the child for at least 10 minutes each day. Even if the families of the control subjects followed this suggestion faithfully—which is difficult to imagine—each experimental child would still have been exposed to approximately five or six more hours of such activities than each control child. **It is difficult to conceive why the researchers allowed this "historical" influence of exposure to the reading and reciting of material to differ so greatly from the experimental to control group.**

Little data and almost no statistical analysis of the objective results of this study were given. It was reported that in the experimental group the "per cent of increase in score at the time of the second test averaged 82.4 per cent." The comparable per cent—and it is unclear what this per cent means or how it was calculated—was 37.2 for the control group. Does this statement mean that 82.4 per cent of the experimental subjects made a higher score on the posttest than on the pretest? Or would the author of the report have considered a gain from a score of 100 to one of 182.4 a "gain of 82.4 per cent?" The author's intended meaning was not clear.

The following data have been summarized from the research report and statistical significance tests have been performed:

VARIABLE AND ITS MEASUREMENT	Experimental Group		Control Group		Z-TEST OF DIFFERENCES BETWEEN INDEPENDENT %'s
	Frequency	Percent	Frequency	Percent	
GAIN IN CONTROLLED ATTENTION SPAN	34	79.1	20	48.7	z - 2.7
GAIN IN UNCONTROLLED ATTENTION SPAN	30	69.7	24	58.5	z - is less than 1.0
GAIN FROM READING READINESS CATEGORY TYPE 5 TO TYPE 4	7	16.2	3	7.3	z - 1.2

The above table shows that there was a significantly larger proportion of subjects making gains on a test of controlled attention span in the experimental group than in the control group. The differences between the two groups on the other two variables were not statistically significant.

The statement in the research report that the experimental group had better than a 200 per cent advantage over the control group in moving from category Type 5—the level at which pupils are considered not ready for first-grade training—to Category Type 4 is grossly misleading. Such a statement is not altogether unlike claiming that coin A is more than twice as apt to turn up "heads" than coin B, because in these 10 tosses of both coins, A yielded 7 heads and B yielded only 3.

THE MASTERMAN STUDY

A group of 422 children between 7 and 13 years of age at two separate summer remedial reading centers was involved in a six-weeks experiment comparing pupils receiving neurological training with a control group. The 422 subjects were assigned to experimental and control groups in some unspecified manner. Nineteen teachers, each teaching two classes, participated in the experiment. **Arbitrarily, each teacher's first-period class was designated "experimental" and the second-period class "control."** We see, then, that if there is any advantage to studying in the first-period as opposed to the second-period class of a teacher, this advantage would favor the experimental group in Masterman's study. Hence, "history" is a possible source of variation which might invalidate the results of this study.

Subjects in the 19 experimental classes were required to report to class 15 minutes early and stay 15 minutes after class for neurological training. Of the 422 subjects who started the study, only 282 persevered or were retained through the six-weeks course, the posttest and the final matching of control and experimental subjects. Thus, the mortality rate was 33.2 per cent. From the 282 subjects who completed the study, 141 pairs containing one experimental and one control subject each were formed so that pair-mates matched on sex, age and grade placement.

The data (Delacato, 1966, p113) show the experimental and control groups perfectly matched on pretest scores on the GRAY ORAL READING PARAGRAPHS TEST, each with a mean of 3.80 years. On the posttest with the Gray Test, the 141 experimental subjects scored 4.36 years, and the 141 control subjects scored 4.22 years. A statistical hypothesis test (correlated t-test) of the difference between the control and experimental group means gave a t-value of 2.46, significant at the .01 level with a one-tailed test.

Of the 422 subjects who began the experiment, 282 persevered to the end. It is not clear from Masterman's report whether the matching of subjects into matched pairs took place before or after the experiment. We shall assume that the determination of pairs matched with regard to sex, age, and pretest score on the Gray Test took place before the experiment. Might the fact that 33 per cent of the matched pairs dropped out of the study indicate a possible bias in the comparison of the control and experimental groups?

It seems likely that when a subject actually left the experiment, i.e., withdrew from summer school, his matched pair-mate was not forced to leave the experiment. The pair-mate's score would simply be disregarded in any analyses, though he would be allowed to stay in school. Now if a greater number of withdrawals from the experiment are initiated in the experimental group, the result would be a tendency for the 19 experimental classes to be smaller than the control classes. These smaller experimental classes with the attendant greater opportunities for individual attention from the teacher would benefit more from normal instruction than would the control classes. *

The high mortality rate coupled with matching techniques operates to produce another source of bias. If the rigorous experimental regimen drives S's away from the experimental group, this is equivalent to cutting out the poorly motivated S's. Since there is an imperfect correlation of motivational and intellectual variables across matched pairs, eliminating the poorest S's from the experimental group also eliminated their matched pair-mates who are systematically higher on these same variables. In a very real sense, this is an example of the regression phenomenon. Hence, if poorly motivated S's were drop-outs from the experimental group, throwing out the matched-pair-mates from the

*We are endebted to Gustave Lieske for pointing out this source of bias to us.

control group has the effect of reducing the net motivational assets of the control group below those of the experimental group. This effect creates a bias which favors the experimental group. (There is evidence in the Glaeser study—chapter 16 in Delacato (1966)—that **S**'s left an 8 a.m. experimental group for reasons of low motivation at a greater rate than **S**'s left a 10 a.m. control group). For a more lengthy discussion of the above point, see Glass and Robbins (1967).

THE MC GRATH STUDY

Ninety-two pupils, ranging in age from approximately 12 to 16 years, were tested at the beginning of the summer on Form Am of the METROPOLITAN READING TEST. All 92 students were reading below their grade level. Having been chosen for their poor performance on the reading test at the outset of the experiment, one would expect them to regress upwards toward the means of the groups from which they were selected on subsequent testings. For six weeks, neurological training was administered in the form of cross-pattern creeping and walking, homolateral patterning, and attempts to establish hemispheric dominance by blocking vision with the subdominant eye. At the end of the six-weeks experimental period, an alternate form, Form Bm of the METROPOLITAN READING TEST, was administered.

Father McGrath presented no statistical analysis of the data. Analysis was provided in a footnote by Delacato on page 117. The average gain from pretest to posttest for the 92 subjects was 0.63 grade-placement units. The elapsed time (six weeks) equaled 0.14 grade-placement units. A correlated **t**-test was run on the pretest to posttest gains for testing the hypothesis that the difference between the pretest and posttest population means was 0.14. The value of the **t**-statistic was 5.10.

In actuality, an irrelevant hypothesis was tested. One can identify at least two influences other than the simple passage of instructional time (six weeks or 0.14 years) which would cause a pretest to posttest "gain." As mentioned earlier, the regression effect was undoubtedly operative in this experiment. Indeed it may account for the major portion of the observed "gain" in scores over the six-weeks period. McGrath made no attempt to control this influence either by forming a control group or by estimating the expected increase from pretest to posttest due to regression. The second influence which was probably operative to a lesser extent than the regression effect was the practice effect on the posttest of having taken an alternate form of the test only six weeks previously. (That any sizable portion of the pretest to posttest gain could be attributed to non-equivalence of Forms Am and Bm of the METROPOLITAN READING TEST is considered only a remote possibility and not a major criticism.) Thus, given the experimental design and knowledge of how the experiment was carried out, one would expect a greater increase in scores from pretest to posttest than that attributable to the passage of time alone, viz., 0.14 years.

The necessity of a control group in this situation to control for "normal growth rate" is emphasized by consideration of a study reported in Chapter 18 in Delacato (1966). A group of 40 **control pupils**, ranging in age from 6 to 14 years and with reading performance below grade level, showed a gain on the STANFORD READING ACHIEVEMENT TEST of 0.40 years in a **six-weeks** summer remedial reading program. These pupils did not receive neurological training. In Chapter 12 of Delacato (1966), a group of 141 **control subjects** was given the GRAY ORAL READING PARAGRAPHS TEST immediately before and after a six-weeks summer session. The average gain for the group in grade-placement units was 0.42 years. In Chapter 14 of Delacato (1966), Kabot's **control group** of 96 subjects showed a mean gain of 0.60 years in an eight-weeks study. While these studies do not indicate that a "natural" gain of about 0.40 years should have been expected for the six weeks period in McGrath's study, they do highlight the dangers of **assuming** without evidence that a non-existent control group should show an increase in reading achievement of 0.14 years in the six-weeks summer session. The attempt made in several of the studies being reviewed to use test norms as a "control" for growth in reading performance has additional deficiencies. "Normative growth" is obtained in a cross-sectional study as opposed to a longitudinal study. For example, what constitutes typical reading performance for third and fourth grade pupils is determined by administering a test to third and fourth grade pupils at a single point in time. The facts that this "point in time" is usually in the remote past and that "growth" from the third to fourth grades was not determined by following a single group of pupils for two years are both important considerations. It is gratuitous to assume that a non-randomly chosen group of third-graders and a different group of fourth-graders at a single moment in the past will show a difference equal to the growth of a single group of third-graders followed into the fourth grade. There exists another danger in the use of test norms as a "control group." Typically, a standardized test grade-placement norms are determined by administering the test at the beginning and end of the year and interpolating between these two points to determine monthly grade-placement scores. The interpolation is linear, hence the assumption that growth proceeds in equal steps from the beginning to end of the year. However, recent evidence gathered from repeated testing during the year shows that the rate of growth in academic subjects in the elementary school is not at all linear during the school year (Beggs and Hieronymous, 1967). In fact, the period from January to April shows the greatest growth during the school year, far greater than any other three-months period. Moreover, a substantial loss in achievement for language and arithmetic is observed over the summer months. This normative loss over the summer would make a summer school class which did nothing but hold its own appear to gain in reading achievement. Note that the norm groups typically will not have the advantage of summer school. These data expose as gratuitous the assumption that a class ought to show an increase of 0.20 grade-placement units during any eight-week period of the year.

THE NOONAN STUDY

Nine retarded readers in the sixth and seventh grades were placed in an experimental group to test the effects of Delacato therapy. Each subject was tested in September on Form Am of the IOWA SILENT READING TEST. Two subjects entered the experimental group in the second semester. Form Bm of the IOWA SILENT READING TEST was administered in June. During the entire year, 45 minutes of neurological training was given each day.

Noonan reported only the mean differences in grade placement scores from September to June for the eleven subjects: (1) Reading rate: gain of 3.3 years; significant at .01 level. (2) Comprehension: gain of 3.1 years; significant at .01 level. (3) Directed Reading: gain of 3.2 years; significant at .01 level. (4) Word Meaning: gain of 1.4 years, non-significant at .01 level. (6) Sentence Meaning: gain of 1.2 years; nonsignificant.

The same influences which invalidated the McGrath study are present in this experiment: scores would increase from September to June because of the phenomenon of regression toward the mean; scores might increase somewhat because of a practice effect on the test, using the test norms to control for expected growth or maturation is fraught with numerous deficiencies.

A correlated *t*-test was used to assess the significance of the difference from zero of the mean "gain" score. A "gain" score equaled (Posttest grade placement) — (Pretest grade placement) — (Elapsed time). The "Elapsed time" was taken to be 0.88 years, i.e., 1.0 years for the eleventh subject. (Although subjects #10 and #11 participated in the therapy only 6 months and 2 months, respectively, there is some indication in Noonan's report that they were pretested in September which would imply that the "elapsed time" should have been 1.0 years for all eleven subjects.) The assumption that the experimental subjects would be expected to show a normative true growth (apart from the regression effect) of 1.0 years during the school year was questioned in connection with the McGrath study. As Noonan pointed out parenthetically, seven of the eleven experimental subjects participated in a remedial reading class the previous year and made gains of from 1.0 to 1.5 years in reading achievement. This fact casts doubt on the assumption that the experimental group of eleven subjects should show a normal rate of growth of 1.0 years during the experimental period and as a consequence makes the "elapsed time" correction of 0.88 years somewhat dubious.

THE KABOT STUDY

A control versus experimental group design was employed with both pretesting and posttesting. Kabot reported that the STANFORD READING ACHIEVEMENT TEST was used as a pretest and the CALIFORNIA READING TEST as a posttest.

Ninety-six experimental and ninety-six control subjects were matched with respect to reading achievement on the STANFORD READING TEST. Matching was also performed on KUHLMANN-ANDERSON IQ, "reading retardation, and laterality." For eight weeks, the ninety-six experimental subjects received remedial reading instruction and exercises "advocated by Dr. Delacato for building body balance and laterality," and the control group received only remedial reading instruction. Kabot gave no indication whether the control and experimental groups had the same or different teachers, met at the same or different times during the day, etc. Posttest observations were made and gains were calculated using scores on the STANFORD READING TEST as the pretest and the CALIFORNIA READING TEST as the posttest. A logical question to ask is "Were the groups initially matched with respect to the CALIFORNIA READING TEST?" By no means can it be confidently answered "yes." If one inspects the two tests in question, one finds that they are substantially different in content. The reading section of the STANFORD TEST comprises 50 items in which sentences in context must be completed by choosing the appropriate word from among four options. Only 20 of the 85 items of the CALIF-ORNIA READING TEST are of this sort. The remaining 65 items of the Californa Test involve recognizing synonyms and antonyms (40 items), identifying spoken words (15 items) and following directions (10 items). No evidence was given in the research report that the two groups were comparable on the CALIFORNIA READING TEST at the be-ginning of the experiment.

The following data were reported by Kabot:

	MEAN IQ	STANFORD TEST	CALIFORNIA TEST	MEAN IMPROVEMENT
EXPERIMENTAL GROUP	96	2.3	3.1	.8
CONTROL GROUP	96	2.3	2.9	.6

A correlated t-test, employing the differences between matched-pairs gain scores, was run to test the hypothesis that the population mean of such scores was zero. There were thirteen matched pairs of subjects at the beginning of the study; two of these pairs were dropped from the study when one member of the pair transferred out of school during the eight weeks of therapy. The t-statistic for the correlated t-test run on the 11 pairs taking the CALIFORNIA READING TEST immediately after therapy equaled 1.54, which is nonsignificant at the .05 level with a one-tailed test.

Delacato reported that retests (**of an unspecified type**) were given one year after therapy. He reported that a difference in gain of 0.54 years (t=2.84, significant at the .01 level) favoring the experimental group over the control group was obtained. **Without explanation, however, the sample size shrunk from 11 to 7 matched pairs.** Again the high mortality of subjects raises the concern for comparability of the control and experimental groups on variables related to any possible differential mortality factors which have not been "matched out" but which might be acting on the two groups. It must also be noted that the 96 matched pairs mentioned at the beginning of Kabot's report are never mentioned again.

THE GLAESER STUDY

In the summer of 1964, sixty-six students volunteered for two reading clinic classes which met for two hours daily for seven weeks. The class of 30 students which met from 8 a.m. to 10 a.m. each morning was arbitrarily designated the experimental group. The second-period class of 36 students which met daily from 10 a.m. until 12 noon was designated the control group. Obviously, the effect of "time of day" is confounded with the effect of the experimental treatment producing a source of invalidity classifiable as "history." In discussing the assignment of students to control or experimental groups, the authors claimed only that the students enrolled in either the first or second class of the day "in the usual chance manner." Undoubtedly, there is very little that is random about a student's decision to sign up for the 8 a.m. class instead of the 10 a.m. class.

Both the experimental and control groups received reading instruction for seven weeks. For the experimental group, one hour of each two-hour class period was spent in a wide variety of exercises designed to improve neurological organization. At the end of the seven-weeks experimental period, the experimental and control groups were compared in terms of pretest to posttest "gains" in seven subtests of the STANFORD ACHIEVEMENT TEST (Form L). The analyses of the data in Tables I and II on page 140 of Delacato (1966) showed significantly greater gains for **15** experimental subjects than for **24** control subjects on two of the seven subtests: Paragraph Meaning and Word Meaning. No significant differences in average gain for the experimental and control groups were found on the Spelling, Language, Arithmetic Reasoning, Arithmetic Computation, and Study Skills subtests.

It is impossible to account for the dropping of several subjects from the experimental group prior to analysis of the data, to justify the switching of subjects between the experimental and control, or to measure the influence on the results of the selective mortality of subjects during the experimental period.

At the outset of the experiment, the control group contained 36 subjects and the experimental group contained 30 subjects. Posttest data from which "gains" were calculated and on which the two groups were compared was reported for only about 14 experimental subjects and 24 control subjects.

Accounts were given of the loss of only eight pupils from the experimental group and eight from the control group. Given the initial figures of 36 on the control group and 30 in the experimental group, one would expect that final analyses of the data from the experiment would be based on 28 control subjects and 22 experimental subjects. However, unaccountably, only about 14 of the experimental subjects and 24 of the control subjects were represented in the data analysis. No explanation of why the data for approximately 8 experimental subjects and 4 control subjects do not appear was offered.

THE SISTER M. ALCUIN STUDY

This experiment was different from the preceding experiments in that three comparison groups were involved: Experimental Group—40 students receiving reading instruction and neurological training; Control Group I—40 students receiving only reading instruction; Control Group II—40 students receiving reading instruction and some unspecified type of psychological treatment. Prior to the opening of the six weeks summer session, the 120 pupils, ranging in age from 6 to 14 years, were tested with the STANFORD READING ACHIEVEMENT TEST, the LARGE-THORNDIKE INTELLIGENCE TEST, the KEYSTONE VISUAL SURVEY TEST, and Delacato's tests of laterality and neurological organization.

The manner in which subjects were assigned to the experimental or control group I or II was not described by the author of the report. It was simply stated that a pupil's score on the "STANFORD READING ACHIEVEMENT TEST along with teacher judgment" determined whether he was placed in the experimental or one of the control groups.

The average gains on the STANFORD READING ACHIEVEMENT TEST over the six-weeks experimental period were as follows: Experimental Group, 0.75 years; Control Group I, 0.40 years; Control Group II, 0.44 years. Application of the Scheffe method of multiple comparisons by the authors showed that the mean gain of the experimental group was significantly different (at the .01 level) from the mean gains of the two control groups. There was no significant difference between the control group means.

The report of this experiment is quite brief and many questions are left unanswered. How did the three groups compare initially on several variables (e.g. reading achievement, motivation) which might be related to the gains they might be expected to make? It was shown above that the Experimental Group was significantly younger than either Control Group. Is this important? How much control was exercised over the instruction in reading during the experiment? Even though students from each group being compared were present in each of six different classrooms, within each class Control Group I was taught by a different teacher (p152). In what respects and to what extent did the teachers of the Experimental Group and Control Group II differ from the teachers of Control Group I?

THE MIRACLE STUDY

Forty students ranging in age from 8 years 7 months to 11 years 4 months and reading at least one year below grade level (on the IOWA TEST OF BASIC SKILLS) were used as subjects. The range of grade-placement reading scores of these fourth and fifth grade pupils was 1.9 years to 4.1 years. Prior to the start of the eight-weeks experimental period, the neurological organization of each pupil was evaluated. Six tests of handedness, four tests of footedness, and five tests of ocular dominance were administered.

Four groups of ten subjects each were compared in the experiment. Group A received reading instruction ("whole" or "sight methods" plus structured and phonetic analysis of words) for thirty minutes daily plus thirty minutes of cross-pattern creeping and cross-pattern walking. The thirty minutes of creeping and walking each day constituted the entire program of neurological training. Group B received only neurological training in the form of **thirty minutes of** cross-pattern creeping and walking daily; Group B did **not** receive any reading instruction. Group C received the same remedial reading program as Group A; Group C was not given neurological training. Group D received **neither reading instruction nor neurological training.** The following diagram depicts the 2 x 2 factorial design employed:

	REMEDIAL READING	NO READING INSTRUCTION
NEUROLOGICAL TRAINING	GROUP A	GROUP B
NO NEUROLOGICAL TRAINING	GROUP C	GROUP D

Miracle reported that the group of 40 subjects was divided into four groups of ten students each **at random.** If so, this experiment represents the only experiment under review here in which random assignment of subjects to groups took place. Hence, Miracle's study would represent the single experiment in which one could be confident that the groups being compared were initially equivalent (randomly) on all variables. Unfortunately, either Miracle obtained an unlucky random split of the 40 subjects or else some non-chance factor influenced the assignment of subjects to the four groups. This can be seen from an analysis of the pretest data which Miracle presented. Before the experiment, the mean number of items correct for the four groups on the Reading Ability subtest of the IOWA TEST OF BASIC SKILLS were as follows: Group A = 12.10, Group B = 14.30, Group C = 10.70, Group D = 10.30. Miracle did not report variances for each group; however, he did report the results of "Fisher t-tests" for the pretest data in Table

VI. Knowing the means, sample sizes, and value of the t-statistic for any comparison of two groups, it is possible to approximate the average within sample variance. The approximation to the average within sample variance turned out to be 14.19. The value of the mean square between the four groups on the pretest of reading ability could be calculated exactly; it equaled 32.63. The F-ratio for testing the hypothesis that the four samples of ten scores each were assigned to the four groups at random equaled 32.63/14.19 = 2.30. This F-ratio exceeds the 90th percentile in the F-distribution with 3 and 36 degrees of freedom. Consequently, the differences between the means of the four groups obtained on the pretest were so great that they would occur less than 10 per cent of the time, **when assignment of subjects to groups is strictly at random.** Either the assignment of subjects to groups was not strictly random, as Miracle reported it was, or we must believe that an event occurred when the odds against it occurring were nine-to-one. It should also be noted that the assignment of subjects to groups favored the two experimental groups, Groups A and B. The brighter subjects tended to fall into these two groups.

One cannot learn from the research report whether the four groups had the same or different teachers, whether the groups met at the same or different times of the day, whether the subjects were treated individually or as intact groups. Failure to report such information is a serious omission.*

Miracle reported the following pretest and posttest means on the Reading Ability subtest of the IOWA TEST OF BASIC SKILLS for each group:

	GROUP A	GROUP B	GROUP C	GROUP D
n	10	10	10	10
PRETEST MEAN	12.10	14.30	10.70	10.30
POSTTEST MEAN	18.00	21.10	13.40	12.40

Miracle presented t-tests of the differences between the above posttest means. Of course, this multiple t-testing of the data is not legitimate and tends to show a spuriously large number of significant differences. Tukey multiple comparisons of the posttest means performed by the authors revealed that Groups A and B did not differ significantly from each other but differed significantly from Groups C and D; Groups C and D did not differ significantly.

Questions remain concerning the initial comparability of the four groups (they were significantly different on the **pretest** of reading abilities at the .10 level) and the comparability of the experimental conditions for each group (the four groups may have been treated as intact groups, in which case the experiment did not yield a valid estimate of

*Nor did such information appear in Miracle's dissertation, which was also examined in the course of writing this review.

error). Apart from these considerations, the data from the experiment were quite surprising. The remedial reading program which was carried out for eight weeks appears to have been ineffectual. Group B made a greater gain (numerically, though the difference is not statistically significant) from pretest to posttest than did Group A, even though Group B received no reading instruction. The average gains shown by Groups C and D, 2.70 points and 2.10 points, were not significantly different, even though Group C was given eight weeks of remedial reading and Group D was given nothing! Miracle concluded that cross-pattern creeping and walking **alone** are more effective in improving reading performance than is remedial reading instruction. Miracle reported that the "students who showed greatest progress in this study (Groups A and B) were probably more interested in participation than were the students in Group C." This may have been only one of several systematic differences between the four groups.

CONCLUSION

Not being thoroughly acquainted with Delacato's position, the reader might have assumed falsely that therapy to bring about neurological organization should show effects only on persons suffering serious neurologically dysorganization initially. It would follow from this assumption that any study in which Delacato therapy was given to normal pupils would constitute neither a valid test of his theory nor an appropriate evaluation of Delacato's therapy. However, with remarkable sanguinity, Delacato has argued that this therapy should be effective for both the neurologically dysorganized (including the brain injured, genetically deficient, and environmentally deprived) and the pupil whose neurological organization is normal.

"The author further feels that a child with good reading can be helped to have even better language facility and better language aptitudes through the system of setting up a neurological organization which operates as a unity. **No doubt as man has evolved he has set up certain environmental blocks to his complete utilization of his neurological structure.** Hence if we can, through preventative activity or through educative activity, teach people neurological unity, we shall have done them a great service and shall perhaps make our good students even better, our good language people (sic) even better, our good spellers even better, our fluent speakers and listeners even better. Indeed, we may be discussing a means for hurrying the evolutionary process." (Delacato, 1959, p80)

"....the author feels that the approach used above and the results thereof certainly indicate that the rationale contained herein is quite applicable to the normal classroom activity for children who present slight deviations in reading as well as for children who present gross reading retardation." (Delacato, 1959, p100)

It seems advisable that at least two distinct groups of subjects be identified in any experiment on the effect of neurological organization on reading performance: "normal" pupils who do not give evidence of marked neurological dysorganization, and pupils who possess marked neurological dysorganization. It is important to distinguish these two subgroups because the effects of the Delacato therapy may not be the same for each group. Delacato has maintained that his therapy is effective on both groups (see THE TREATMENT AND PREVENTION OF READING PROBLEMS, p80). It may be, however, that only the markedly neurologically dysorganized can benefit from attempts to establish hemispheric dominance and other conditions which constitute adequate organization. More adequate designs than those which have been employed thus far in investigating the effects of Delacato's therapy would involve stratifying the sample of subjects into at least the two groups mentioned at the beginning of this paragraph and looking for the possible differential effectiveness of the therapy. This has not been done in any of the studies reviewed in this paper. The subjects who participated in almost all of the experiments reviewed in this paper could not be characterized as seriously neurologically dysorganized.

A special statement dated December 1, 1965, from the Executive Board of the American Academy of Pediatrics holds true today: "....there is as yet no firm evidence substantiating the claims made for the Doman-Delacato methods and programs. What is needed are well controlled studies by recognized experts." A generous assessment of the research Delacato cites as evidence for the effectiveness of his therapy might be as follows: all of the empirical research reported thus far has failed to produce cogent evidence that Delacato's therapy has any effect whatsoever on the reading performance of apparently **normal subjects** evidencing mild or serious reading problems. The possibility exists that Delacato's therapy is effective on subjects suffering serious neurological dysfunction, though this hypothesis has not been subjected to adequate empirical tests. If it were to be reliably and validly established that the highly neurologically impaired child could be rehabilitated as Delacato maintains, it would represent a truly valuable contribution to the technique of remediation of certain special learning difficulties. Of course, we would have to relinquish hope that a "means for hurrying the evolutionary process" had been found, or that Delacato's neurological exercises can make good readers even better; but then we should all be accustomed to having our Utopian dreams dispelled by the intransigent facts of life by now.

SUMMARY

Our purpose in preparing this paper was to apply standards of evidence to the assumptions which underlie the theory of neurological organization and to experimental data cited in support of the purported relationship between reading and neurological organization. The analysis is an attempt to reach a rational conclusion concerning the merits of the theory.

The paper is divided into four parts: The first part, The Theory of Neurological Organization, provided background material; the second part, An Examination of Central Assumptions of the Theory, evaluated the essential tenets of the theory in terms of internal logic and existing scientific knowledge; the third part, An Evaluation of Eleven Experiments on the Relationship Between Neurological Organization and Reading, assessed the scientific merit of a series of experiments cited in support of the theory; the fourth part, Summary, Conclusions, and Implications completes the paper.

CONCLUSIONS

1. The fundamental tenets of the theory are overwhelmingly refuted by internal inconsistencies, a lack of supporting evidence, and direct contradiction by established knowledge.

2. Studies which purportedly support the relationship between neurological organization and reading lack sophistication and proper controls consistent with current scientific procedures.

3. There is no empirical evidence to substantiate the value of either the theory or practice of neurological organization.

IMPLICATIONS

The scientific and professional community have standards which remain unaffected by the publicity surrounding a theory. If the theory of neurological organization is to be taken seriously by this scholarly community then its advocates are under an obligation to provide reasonable support for the tenets of the theory and a series of experimental investigations, consistent with current scientific standards, which test the efficacy of the rationale.

The costs of production of this paper were partially met by U.S. Office of Education Grant #OEG-4-061860-0812 to the Laboratory of Educational Research of the University of Colorado.

The authors wish to acknowledge the invaluable assistance of Jean Russell Miller, Herman L. Saettler, Florence Goldberg and Richelle Lisse.

References

1. Archdiocesan Reading Service. A HANDBOOK OF INFORMATION ON THE CARL H. DELACATO NEUROLOGICAL APPROACH TO READING INSTRUCTION. 126 North Des Plaines Street, Chicago, Illinois, undated.

2. Balow, I.H. LATERAL DOMINANCE CHARACTERISTICS AND READING ACHIEVEMENT IN THE FIRST GRADE. Journal of Psychology, 55:323-328, 1963.

3. Balow, I.H. and Balow, B. LATERAL DOMINANCE AND READING ACHIEVEMENT IN THE SECOND GRADE. American Educational Research Journal, 1:139-143, 1964.

4. Bakes, F. SPEECH, LANGUAGE AND HEARING. In F. Falkner (Ed.), Human Development. Philadelphia: W. B. Saunders, Chapter 14, 433-458, 1966.

5. Beck, Joan UNLOCKING THE SECRETS OF THE BRAIN. Chicago: Chicago Tribune, 1964.

6. Beggs, Donald L. and Hieronymous, Albert N. UNIFORMITY OF GROWTH IN THE BASIC SKILLS THROUGHOUT THE SCHOOL YEAR AND DURING THE SUMMER. American Educational Research Association Paper Abstracts, 62-63, Feb. 1967.

7. Belmont, Lilian and Birch H. LATERAL DOMINANCE, LATERAL AWARENESS AND READING DISABILITY. Child Development, 36 (1):57-71, 1965.

8. Bird, J. WHEN CHILDREN CAN'T LEARN. Saturday Evening Post, 240(15):27-31 and 72-74, 1967.

9. Bower, G. NEUROPHYSIOLOGY OF LEARNING. In E. Hilgard and Bower (Eds.), Theories of Learning. (3rd Ed.) New York: Appleton-Century-Crofts, Chapter 13, 426-479, 1966.

10. Brossard, C. A BOY WHO WOULD NOT DIE. Look, 26(16): 60-66, 1962.

11. Brown, J. Book review: DIAGNOSIS AND TREATMENT OF SPEECH AND READING PROBLEMS by Carl H. Delacato. Neurology, 14(6): 599-600, 1964.

12. Buros, O. (Ed.). THE FOURTH MENTAL MEASUREMENTS YEARBOOK. Highland Park, New Jersey: Gryphon Press, 1953.

13. Buros, O. (Ed.). THE FIFTH MENTAL MEASUREMENTS YEARBOOK. Highland Park, New Jersey: Gryphon Press, 1959.

14. Buros, O. (Ed.). THE SIXTH MENTAL MEASUREMENTS YEARBOOK. Highland Park, New Jersey: Gryphon Press, 1965.

15. Campbell, D.T. and Stanley, J.C. EXPERIMENTAL AND QUASI-EXPERIMENTAL DESIGNS IN RESEARCH ON TEACHING, Chapter 5 in Gage, N.L. (Ed.) Handbook of Research on Teaching, Chicago: Rand McNally, Chapter 5: 781-785, 1966.

16. Capobianco, R.J. OCULAR-MANUAL LATERALITY AND READING IN ADOLESCENT MENTAL RETARDATES. American Journal of Mental Deficiency, 70: 781-785, 1966.

17. Capobianco, R.J. OCULAR-MANUAL LATERALITY AND READING ACHIEVEMENT IN CHILDREN WITH SPECIAL LEARNING DIFFICULTIES. American Educational Research Journal, 4: 133-138, 1967.

18. Cecilia, Sr. Joseph. THE DOMAN-DELACATO APPROACH TO THE TEACHING OF READING. Montana Education, 42(9): 17-22, 1966.

19. Child, C. PHYSIOLOGICAL FOUNDATIONS OF BEHAVIOR. New York: Hafner, 1964.

20. Clark, M. PATTERNS OF RECOVERY. Newsweek, 63(18): 84-85, 1964.

21. Cole, E. Book review, THE DIAGNOSIS AND TREATMENT OF SPEECH AND READING PROBLEMS by Carl H. Delacato. Harvard Educational Review, 34(2): 351-354, 1964.

22. Coleman, R.I. and Deutsch, C.P. LATERAL DOMINANCE AND RIGHT-LEFT DISCRIMINATION: A COMPARISON OF NORMAL AND RETARDED READERS. Perceptual Motor Skills, 19: 43-50, Aug. 1964.

23. Dearborn, W. and Rothney, J. PREDICTING THE CHILD'S DEVELOPMENT. Cambridge, Mass.: Sci-art Publishers, 1941.

24. de Beer, G. EMBRYOS AND ANCESTORS. (3rd Ed.). Oxford: Clarendon Press, 1958.

25. Delacato, C. THE TREATMENT AND PREVENTION OF READING PROBLEMS. Springfield, Illinois: Charles C. Thomas, 1959.

26. Delacato, C. THE DIAGNOSIS AND TREATMENT OF SPEECH AND READING PROBLEMS. Springfield, Illinois: Charles C. Thomas, 1963.

27. Delacato, C. LETTERS TO THE EDITOR: DELACATO REVISITED, Exceptional Children, 33(3): 199-200, 1966a.

28. Delacato, C. NEUROLOGICAL ORGANIZATION AND READING. Springfield, Illinois: Charles C. Thomas, 1966b.

29. Delay, J. RETURN TO BABYHOOD: MAVERICK METHODS GIVE HELP TO BRAIN-INJURED CHILDREN. Life, 55(8): 31-38, 1963.

30. Doman, G. TREATMENT PROCEDURES UTILIZING PRINCIPLES OF NEUROLOGICAL ORGANIZATION. Philadelphia: The Institutes for the Achievement of Human Potential, undated.

31. Doman, G. HOW TO TEACH YOUR BABY TO READ. New York: Random House, 1964.

32. Doman, G. and Delacato, C. TRAIN YOUR BABY TO BE A GENIUS. McCalls, 92(6): 65ff, 1965.

33. Doman, G. Delacato, C. and Doman, R. THE DOMAN-DELACATO DEVELOPMENTAL PROFILE. Philadelphia: The Institutes for the Achievement of Human Potential, 1963a.

34. Doman, G., Stevens, G., and Orem, R. YOU CAN TEACH YOUR BABY TO READ. Ladies Home Journal, 80(4): 62 ff, 1963b.

35. Doman, R., Spitz, E., Zucman, Elizabeth, Delacato, C. and Doman G. CHILDREN WITH SEVERE BRAIN INJURIES. Journal of the American Medical Association, 174(3): 257-262, 1960.

36. Ernst, P. MIRACLE IN PENNSYLVANIA. Good Housekeeping, 55(32): 32-36, 1962.

37. Executive Board-American Academy of Pediatrics. DOMAN-DELACATO TREATMENT OF NEUROLOGICALLY HANDICAPPED CHILDREN. Newsletter of the American Academy of Pediatrics, 16(11): 1, 1965.

38. Fernald, Grace. REMEDIAL TECHNIQUES IN BASIC SCHOOL SUBJECTS. New York: McGraw Hill, 1943.

39. Flescher, I. OCULAR-MANUAL LATERALITY AND PERCEPTUAL ROTATION OF LITERAL SYMBOLS. Genetic Psychology Monographs, 66: 3-48, 1962.

40. Frankel, E. EFFECTS OF GROWTH, PRACTICE AND COACHING ON SCHOLASTIC APTITUDE TEST SCORES. Personnel and Guidance Journal, 38: 713-719, 1960.

41. Gardner, E. FUNDAMENTALS OF NEUROLOGY. (4th Ed.). Philadelphia: W. B. Saunders, 1963.

42. Gates, A. THE IMPROVEMENT OF READING. (3rd Ed.). New York: MacMillan, 1947.

43. Gesell, A. and Ames, Louise. THE DEVELOPMENT OF HANDEDNESS. Journal of Genetic Psychology, 70(2): 155-175, 1947.

44. Glass, G., and Robbins, M. A CRITIQUE OF EXPERIMENTS ON THE ROLE OF NEU-ROLOGICAL ORGANIZATION IN READING PERFORMANCE. Reading Research Quarterly, Vol. 3, 1967, pp. 5-51.

45. Goodglass, H. and Quadfasel, F. LANGUAGE LATERALITY IN LEFT-HANDED APHA-SICS. Brain, 77(4): 521-548, 1954.

46. Harris, A. HOW TO INCREASE READING ABILITY. (3rd Ed.). New York: Longmans, Green, 1956.

47. Harris, A. LATERAL DOMINANCE, DIRECTIONAL CONFUSION, AND READING DISABILITY. Journal of Psychology, 44(2): 283-294, 1957.

48. Harris, A. HARRIS TESTS OF LATERAL DOMINANCE: MANUAL OF DIRECTIONS FOR ADMINISTRATION AND INTERPRETATION. (3rd Ed.). New York: Psychological Corporation, 1958.

49. Hecaen, H. and Ajuriaguerra, J. LEFT HANDEDNESS: MANUAL SUPERIORITY AND CEREBRAL DOMINANCE. New York: Grune and Stratton, 1964.

50. Hillerich, R.L. EYE-HAND DOMINANCE AND READING ACHIEVEMENT. American Educational Research Journal, 1: 121-126, 1964.

51. Hudspeth, W. DELACATO IN REVIEW: THE NEUROBEHAVIORAL IMPLAUSIBILITY OF THE DELACATO THEORY. In M. Douglass (Ed.), Claremont Reading Conference: 28th. Yearbook. Claremont, California: Claremont Graduate School and Curriculum Laboratory, 126-131, 1964.

52. The Institutes for the Achievement of Human Potential. HISTORY. Philadelphia: 8801 Stenton Ave., undated.

53. The Institutes for the Achievement of Human Potential. A SUMMARY OF THE CONCEPTS, PROCEDURES, AND ORGANIZATION. Philadelphia: 8801 Stenton Ave., 1964.

54. Johnson, Marjorie. FACTORS RELATING TO DISABILITY IN READING. Journal of Experimental Education, 26(1): 1-21, 1957.

55. Johnston, P. THE RELATION OF CERTAIN ANOMALIES OF VISION AND LATERAL DOMINANCE TO READING DISABILITY. Monographs of the Society for Research in Child Development, 7(2), Washington, D.C.: Society for Research in Child Development, 1942.

56. Jung, R. SUMMARY OF THE CONFERENCE. In V. Mountcastle (Ed.), Interhemispheric Relations and Cerebral Dominance. Baltimore: Johns Hopkins Press, Chapter 11, 264-277, 1962.

57. Kraus, B. THE BASIS OF HUMAN EVOLUTION. New York: Harper and Row, 1964.

58. Krippner, S. EVALUATING PRE-READINESS APPROACHES TO READING. Education, 87(1): 12-20, 1966.

59. LeWinn, E., Doman, G., Delacato, C. Doman, R., Spitz, E. and Thomas, E. NEURO-LOGICAL ORGANIZATION: THE BASIS FOR LEARNING. In J. Hellmuth (Ed.), Learning Disorders Volume 2, Seattle: Special Child Publication, 47-93, 1966.

60. Lilly, J. CEREBRAL DOMINANCE DISCUSSION. In V. Mountcastle (Ed.), Interhemispheric Relations and Cerebral Dominance. Baltimore: Johns Hopkins Press, Chapter 6C, 112-114, 1962.

61. Luria, A. HIGHER CORTICAL FUNCTIONS IN MAN. New York: Basic Books, 1966.

62. Maisil, A. HOPE FOR BRAIN-INJURED CHILDREN. Readers Digest, 85(510): 135-140, 1964.

63. Minkowski, A., Larroche, J., Vignaud, Jacqueline, Dreyfus-Brisac, C., and Dargassies, S. DEVELOPMENT OF THE NERVOUS SYSTEM IN EARLY LIFE. In F. Falkner (Ed.), Human Development, Philadelphia: W.B. Saunders, Chapter 11, 254-325, 1966.

64. Mishkin, M. A POSSIBLE LINK BETWEEN INTERHEMISPHERIC INTEGRATION IN MONKEYS AND CEREBRAL DOMINANCE IN MAN. In V. Mountcastle (Ed.), Interhemispheric Relations and Cerebral Dominance, Baltimore: Johns Hopkins Press, Chapter 6A, 101-107, 1962.

65. Mishler, Katherine. WHY TWO BRAINS? Smith, Kline and French Psychiatric Reporter, 13: -6, 1964.

66. Money, J. (Ed.) READING DISABILITY: PROGRESS AND RESEARCH NEEDS IN DYS-LEXIA. Baltimore: Johns Hopkins Press, 1962.

67. Moody, P. INTRODUCTION TO EVOLUTION. (2nd Ed.). New York: Harper and Row, 1962.

68. Oettinger, L. DELACATO IN REVIEW: THE THEORY FROM THE STANDPOINT OF PEDIATRICS. In M. Douglas (Ed.), Claremont Reading Conference: 28th Yearbook. Claremont, California: Claremont Graduate School and Curriculum Laboratory, 123-126, 1964.

69. Orton, S. READING, WRITING, AND SPEECH PROBLEMS IN CHILDREN. New York: Norton, 1937.

70. Orton, S. and Travis, L. STUDIES IN STUTTERING: IV. ARCHIVES OF NEUROLOGY AND PSYCHIATRY, 21: 61-68, Jan. 1929.

71. Osgood, C. and Miron, M. APPROACHES TO THE STUDY OF APHASIA: A REPORT OF AN INTERDISCIPLINARY CONFERENCE ON APHASIA. Urbana: University of Illinois Press, 1963.

72. Pearson, R. EFFECTS OF GROWTH AND RETESTING ON SAT-VERBAL SCORES. The College Board Review, No. 5, 57: 68-71, Fall 1948.

73. Peiper, A. CEREBRAL FUNCTION IN INFANCY AND CHILDHOOD. New York: Consultants Bureau, 1963.

74. Penfield, W. and Roberts L. SPEECH AND BRAIN-MECHANISMS. Princeton: University Press, 1959.

75. Perkins, F. DELACATO IN REVIEW: PROBLEMS ARISING FROM ASSERTATIONS OR ASSUMPTIONS OF DELACATO. In M. Douglass (Ed.), Claremont Reading Conference: 28th Yearbook. Claremont, California: Claremont Graduate School and Curriculum Laboratory, 119-123, 1964.

76. Robbins, M. THE DELACATO INTERPRETATION OF NEUROLOGICAL ORGANIZATION: AN EMPIRICAL STUDY. Unpublished doctoral dissertation, University of Chicago, 1965a.

77. Robbins, M. INFLUENCE OF SPECIAL PROGRAMS ON THE DEVELOPMENT OF MENTAL AGE AND READING. Report of Project No. S-349. Washington, D.C.: Cooperative Research Branch, Office of Education, U.S. Department of Health, Education and Welfare, 1965b.

78. Robbins, M. A STUDY OF THE VALIDITY OF DELACATO'S THEORY OF NEUROLOGICAL ORGANIZATION. Exceptional Children, 32(8): 517-523, 1966a.

79. Robbins, M. CREEPING, LATERALITY AND READING. Academic Therapy Quarterly, 1(4): 200-206, 1966b.

80. Robbins, M. THE DELACATO INTERPRETATION OF NEUROLOGICAL ORGANIZATION, Reading Research Quarterly, 1(3): 57-78, 1966c.

81. Robbins, M. LETTERS TO THE EDITOR: DELACATO REVISITED—A REPLY. Exceptional Children, 33(3): 200-201, 1966d.

82. Robbins, M. TEST OF THE DOMAN-DELACATO RATIONALE WITH RETARDED READERS, 1967, (in preparation).

83. Segal, Marilyn RUN AWAY LITTLE GIRL. Readers Digest, 89(535): 259-300, 1966.

84. Semmes, Josephine, Weinstein, S., Ghent, L., and Teuber, H. SOMATOSENSORY CHANGES AFTER PENETRATING BRAIN WOUNDS IN MAN. Cambridge: Harvard University Press, 1960.

85. Shirley, M. THE FIRST TWO YEARS: A STUDY OF TWENTY-FIVE BABIES, VOLUME II: INTELLECTUAL DEVELOPMENT. Institute of Child Welfare Monograph Series, No. 7. Minneapolis, Minnesota: University of Minnesota Press, 1933.

86. Shure, G. and Harlstead, W. CEREBRAL LOCALIZATION OF INTELLECTUAL PROCESS. Psychological Monographs: General and Applied, 72(12). American Psychological Association, 1958.

87. Silver, A. and Hagin, R. SPECIFIC READING DISABILITY: A DELINEATION OF THE SYNDROME AND RELATIONSHIP TO CEREBRAL DOMINANCE. Comprehensive Psychiatry, 1: 126-134, 1960.

88. Smith, D. and Carrigan, Patricia. THE NATURE OF READING DISABILITY, New York: Harcourt, Brace, 1959.

89. Spache, G. ANOTHER APPROACH TO LANGUAGE PROBLEMS. The Reading Teacher, 17(5): 409-410, 1965 (A review of Delacato, 1959).

90. Sperry, R. THE GREAT CEREBRAL COMMISSURE. Scientific American, 210(18): 46-48, 1963.

91. TIME. CAN MAN LEARN TO USE THE OTHER HALF OF HIS BRAIN? Time, 81(2): 46-48, 1963.

92. Travis, L. SPEECH PATHOLOGY. New York: Appleton-Century, 1931.

93. Wada, J. and Rasmussen, T. INTRACAROTID INJECTION OF SODIUM AMYTAL FOR THE LATERALIZATION OF CEREBRAL SPEECH DOMINANCE: EXPERIMENTAL AND CLINICAL OBSERVATIONS. Journal of Neurosurgery, 17(2): 266-282, 1960.

94. Weinstein, S. DEFICITS CONCOMITANT WITH APHASIA OR LESIONS OF EITHER CEREBRAL HEMISPHERE. Cortex, 1(2): 154-169, 1964.

95. Wepman, J. ON CLAIM AND EVIDENCE. Contemporary Psychology, 9(9): 351-352, 1964. (A review of Delacato, 1963).

96. Zangwill, O. CEREBRAL DOMINANCE AND ITS RELATION TO PSYCHOLOGICAL FUNCTION. Edinburgh: Oliver and Boyd, 1960.

97. Zangwill, O. DYSLEXIA IN RELATION TO CEREBRAL DOMINANCE. In J. Money (Ed.), Reading Disability: Progress and Research Needs in Dyslexia. Baltimore: Johns Hopkins Press, Chapter 7, 103-113, 1962.

TESTS INCARNATE:
THE GAP BETWEEN TEACHING AND TESTING

Frank Garfunkel, Ph.D., Director,
Headstart Evaluation and Research Center,
School of Education,
Boston University,
Boston, Massachusetts

Introduction

Educational and psychological tests were developed as tools for obtaining information about individuals and groups, which were used to assess and facilitate the educational process. After teaching a unit of history or science, a teacher would devise a variety of questions that students would be required to answer. Questions were closely tied to curriculum. Scores obtained by students were, at the same time, a sampling of accomplishment and, indirectly, an indication of future achievement. Requirements of mass education have led to large scale standardization, which has fractionated the relationship between teaching and testing. The national character of test development has led to the construction of tests that are maximally useful in diverse geographical, social, political and economic circumstances. Furthermore, the "market" calls for instruments that can be used with as many grade levels, subjects and sexes as is possible. Although this has led to reliability and widespread use, it has also resulted in either a growing irrelevancy of tests for teaching, or the domination of curriculum by tests and testing.

The Status Quo

Any test score can be conceived as being a point n-dimensional space. Rigorous definition depends on articulation of dimensions and careful accounting of sets and subsets which include particular points. Conditions of definition and description are necessary for relevance, but they are not sufficient. This depends on the existence of an empirically determined system of variance and invariance which provides geometric trivia with a well ordered and logically consistent isomorphism which gives substance to the mapping process of abstracting behaviors by providing a necessary superordinate structure. It does not necessarily follow that the language (mathematics) and the thought (structure of relationships) have always to be in communion with each other, but only that paucity of language (and agents) should not debilitate the development of useful structural entities even if, albeit, it will always present a severe limitation. Myopic concern with selected trees and often weeds precludes attending to forests and perhaps jungles. Resulting intellectual intercourse produces defective offspring with a dominant genealogy. But the defect becomes the norm and the dominance provides edification which permeates journals and textbooks and justifies budgets and procedures. The resulting rather decrepit Maypole dance has ritualistic attractiveness, even if the children are not quite laughing and everyone knows some of the words.

The best that can be said for this mockery is that the phony war is being fought with phony weapons so that maybe no one is getting hurt. A lot of children (and adults) are inefficiently learning a behavior called test-taking, which occasionally makes a difference, but usually does not. Scores can be processed in record times, which would appear to be a not too important corollary to Parkinson's Law. Test development has been engulfed by the massive mediocrity which is inherent in mass education. The irony is that the demands of staffing and operating a purportedly democratic school system have imposed an authoritarian structure on test development. Witness the ludicrous debate between the "scholars" and the "testers." (Hoffman, 19) Also the requirement that the Bureau of the Budget approve instruments to be used in research sponsored by the Federal Government. These reflect an attitude about testing that is as futile as it is sterile. We know how to control abuses of testing, but it costs time and money. If there is a single commandment that directs test development and usage, it would appear to be that we should collect the most amount of data with the least expenditure of effort.

Test usage is characterized by the implicit assumption that the only important source of variance is subjects. Examiner, situation, test format, sex and social class are assumed to be more or less invariant. There is a fair amount of discussion about these other sources of variance, but it has had little or no effect on procedures. For a while, there was some discussion of culture-free tests, and several tests appeared on the market, but the assumption of invariance was implicit even in these tests and in their development. No strategies were developed to deal directly with social class variance while, at the same time, either controlling for or dealing directly with subject variability. There are, of course, many reasons why social class has not been attended to in test development or standardization, just as there are reasons why education of lower class children has been largely ignored. What is not so clear is that defects of tests which have been developed and standardized with middle class children not only apply to their use with lower class children, but with any children. The arbitrary restriction of the test space does not, in general, lead to only restricted validity. On the contrary, it confuses the issue because it inflates the contributions of both systematic and error variance while ignoring extraneous variance.

This does not mean that social class by child interaction will be uniform from child to child, from age to age, or from sex to sex, but that such effects have been described and, therefore, must be considered. It is not enough to take note of the ignoring of important sources of variance and then to deal with factors that seem relevant. More important is why they were ignored. The fact that the Stanford-Binet either assumes or imposes invariance over examiner, situation, previous experience of child, social class, sex, and time, is a reflection of a view of testing which deals rather summarily with much of the variance of the test space. Apparently, for the sake of comparability and economy, researchers are willing to indulge themselves in a fail-safe fantasy which justifies any violation of sampling or testing by appealing to tradition and expediency. One could easily take the contrary position that results are acceptable only if all sources of variance are systematically controlled. However, this would hardly be compatible with current funding practices or with usual procedures for collecting data from samples of children. the facade of reliability and consequent implied invariance covers a wide variation of precision. One is reminded of the statistic that three per cent of the population is mentally retarded. This really means that, whatever the criteria, there are always three per cent that are lower than the ninety seven per cent above them. But the critical spuriousness of the statistic is that the three per cent are not distributed equally in different social classes, sexes, or age levels. Similarly, reliability presumes invariance which is closely tied to sampling variability. A given standard error varies in an ascertainable way — ascertainable if we take the time and effort to find out.

Test development can and, unfortunately, probably will continue to be dominated by traditional Euclidean paraphernalia. We can play mathematical and discursive games using multivariate and multilingual test spaces, but the powerful and pervasive machinery for developing and using tests as screening devices will probably maintain the orthodoxy, even though some sampling dimensions will have to be extended. This was exemplified a few years ago when several thousand Negro elementary school children in five southern states were given the Stanford-Binet in order to set up norms. (Kennedy, **et al.**, 1961). It is difficult for us to see the justification for this activity, particularly in light of the fact that a good deal of time was spent with several thousand Negro school children and the only data reported were score distributions and central tendencies. Such blind adherence to an artificially restricted test space would appear to be completely unjustified. The blanket assumption of invariance does violence to even a most cursory skepticism.

There have been efforts in recent years to map out a more elaborate test space than is represented by either conventional intelligence or achievement testing. Stimulation for this has come from factor analysts (Kelley, Thurstone, Guilford, Dingman, Meyers, Cattell), clinicians (Wepman, Sievers) and developmental psychologists (Bruner). But even this has arbitrarily excluded significant dimensions and, as McNemar (1964) has summarized, we are still left with a dominant verbal factor and a quantitative coattail. In viewing the phenomena of mental testing one would infer that intelligence has been conceptualized as being largely independent of social and economic environmental and social interactions. The antiseptical process of standardization has produced a library of instruments that have purchased precision at the price of obliterating sensitivity, and predictability at the price of observing educability.

There is a remarkable naivete in discussions of tests and testing regarding how arbitrary item selections can be and, if not arbitrary, how several monumental psychometric principles can outweigh pedagogic and clinical considerations. Examples abound of tests used in ways which contradict or are inconsistent with their standardization: Inferring sex differences from tests that have either controlled for sex (eliminated discriminatory items) or ignored it in their development; inferring change due to special interventions from tests that have maximized developmental (age) variation making educational decisions from the results of tests that have been developed independently of any kinds of educational interventions. The rules of this Orwellian test game call for maximal reliability to be obtained uniformly over diverse samples of subjects. This demand for uniformity (invariance) over extraordinary ranges of sample, child and situational variation is completely at odds with most applications, with the possible exception of prediction studies. It amounts to the elimination of possibilities of measuring instability (change) or within subject variability. Prediction necessitates this, but diagnosis calls for careful attention to dimensions which are ordinarily suppressed. Furthermore, the items and instruments that are precipitated from prediction studies depend on stability, while, at the same time, generating this same stability. The most successful individuals in academics provide the base for selecting test items which are, in turn, used as a basis for selection. On the other hand, interventions are developed in order to foster instability in the system. Tests are needed to identify the non-predictables and to measure, or rather infer, change. an approximation might be made by simply changing the criteria and utilizing a conventional predictive model. I would contend that this would be a waste of time as it would end up in a trap of restricted dimensionality. The strategy for measuring change must address itself to questions of timing and technique, which amounts to exhaustive studies of innumerable dimensions. Where there is a question of cost, we had better risk inefficiency, because the margin is so narrow that it will be difficult to describe even if we attend to all possible relevant sources of variance.

Strategies for Tests Development

It has been the contention of this paper that existing tests are largely inappropriate for measuring changes that are due to special interventions which are directed towards children in general or, in particular, children from lower socio-economic backgrounds whose probability for success in school is minimal. The problem of testing change in sub-normal children of any background is a special case of testing change in children from any background. Just because tests are inadequate for particular groups of children who show various kinds of disabled behavior does not necessarily mean that tests are sensitive for any children. Rather, it means that the inadequacies of tests are more obvious when they are used in situations where changes are more imperative and where the status quo is less desirable.

The problems of testing lower class children and, in particular pre-school lower class children, bring into relief the deficiencies of tests and the way they are used to describe the total tests space, which includes characteristics of children, culture, situations, special abilities and interventions. The fact that examiner variation is important when pre-school children are being tested, and particularly when they live in lower social class homes, does not countermand the fact that examiner variation is generally ignored in any testing situation. The platitude that examiners must have good rapport with children in no way helps the researcher to ascertain which children have had good rapport and which have not.

To carry this example further, it is necessary to realize that the examiner is a teacher and the teacher is an examiner. The assumption that examiner variation is either trivial or irrelevant is untenable unless we assume that this is also true for teachers. Furthermore, it is necessary to question whether it is desirable to promote a testing system that, by implication, denies teacher variability.

If we are to develop tests in such a way as to minimize examiner variation, then some serious questions have to be raised about what we are excluding from the tests and what the significance is of that which remains. Sources of variance that have meaning for the educational situation are hardly those that should be eliminated in order to give the appearances of test reliability and force some sort of pseudo simplification on data collection processes.

This is brought out even more forcefully by considering the effect on test variance of knowing whether a particular child is an experimental or a control subject. It is readily admitted in the literature that this is a consideration, and it is suggested that "blinds" should be maintained in order to minimize possible biasing effects. Again, the recourse is to hide an important source of variance rather than to deal with it by thoroughly exploring the effect of various kinds of knowledge on the examiner and of finding out which children are more noticeably affected by this kind of bias, and which are not.

Testing situations involving either individual groups of children or interpersonal situations do not uniformly enhance or impair a child or an examiner. It is certainly true that systematic design procedure can cancel out interpersonal effects by systematically randomizing examiners with children as well as by systematically randomizing a number of other variables of the testing situation. However, we must ask ourselves whether such suppression, even if unbiased, is desirable in light of information that is being lost, which might be extremely relevant for assessing the possibility and probability that a child will change and that this might be brought about by a particular kind of teacher.

What too often happens is that responses to protocols are systematically recorded and scored and produce quantifiable data, while other kinds of responses to situations are discussed and written up in anecdotal form or are rated in rather crude ways. For all practical purposes, this is a "no contest" situation where the quantifiable results dominate any interpretations that are made and contribute disproportionately to decisions that are made about children. This has not been empirically justified, but is, rather, a procedure that is traditionally done. One cannot deny that it has served a purpose of providing "hard" data which can be generated in diverse situations. However, one can seriously question whether this strategy is uniformly valid for all children in all situations. It might very well be that data other than that which are produced by the currently quantifiable component of a test situation are of crucial significance. It is likely that these "hard" data would be considerably more meaningful if they were obtained in a context that allowed for rigorous control of interventional and motivational components.

We can see from many cross-sectional and longitudinal studies that children learn, and that this learning is reflected in responses to a variety of standardized tests (Bloom, 1964). It is not quite so clear as to what the roles of teachers are in this learning process, and there is some reason to believe that their roles are, at best, quite indirect. In terms of direct measures of achievement, teachers do not seem to make any difference. It may be because we do not measure the right things, or because our measurements are not accurate enough, or, what is even more likely, that material is always presented at an age of maximal readiness when the developmental curve is so steep that one could hardly hope to extract any teacher variance from it. This is perhaps less so with intellectually and emotionally disabled children, whether or not they come from lower social classes. But it seems clear that we cannot directly relate teacher behavior to variations in learning behaviors of children, when such behaviors are defined as referring to cognitive functions.

On the other hand, it would seem to be quite clear that teachers do have effects on children and that these effects, in turn, most probably affect a child's ability to learn. We might variously call this effect attitude, value, motivation, expectation or self concept. All of these are extremely difficult to measure and are confounded with other more potent sources of variance.

The strongest sources of variance are social class and developmental level. It is easy to succumb to these sources and to build tests so that they are the only variation that comes to the surface. However, a contrary view is that sources of variance in tests should be related to teaching situations and to possible effects of educational interventions. We already know a good deal about what can and cannot be measured by paper and pencil tests and rating scales irrespective of other sources of variance besides that which is explicitly gotten at in the test. We have to revise our strategy from that of considering the test to be the major unit for data collection about educationally relevant cognitive and non-cognitive abilities, and switch to alternative strategies which consider the test situation to be the major unit. This is based upon the assumption that the first order of business in studying the effects of educational interventions is to delve more immediately into the direct effects on children of different kinds of tutorial and group activities.

In quasi-laboratory situations where particular children are exposed to specific educational techniques and content, one can look directly to measurements of that content as criteria of the effects of interventions. Attitudinal and interactional changes would then be secondary criteria, which could only be justifiably looked at if the changes in the primary criteria could be demonstrated.

However, with pre-school children few programs aim at such specific behavioral changes that they are amenable to direct observation of cognitive behaviors. Although we know that children of any intellectual level can be specifically affected by experimental techniques, it is not at all certain that these are particularly meaningful to the child's learning-how-to-learn and his ability to transfer knowledge into different areas of behavior. For the most part, in studies of mentally retarded children, such transference has not been found, and children who have learned many subtle discriminations are not more able to learn after they have been through a training program than before. The argument that no matter what the means, the ends of learning certain specific discriminations or specific tasks will enable a child to go on to other areas of learning is a moot one and has been seriously questioned in many areas of educational research.

Action Goals

Programs that aim at specific remedial procedures can justifiably depend on specific testing operations to evaluate their success. On the other hand, programs which are more global with regard to very specific abilities or skill areas, such as most Headstart programs and most pre-school interventions, should look more directly at the **action goals** of programs in order to determine what criteria for what success should be used. The success or failure of a program, and, therefore, the strategies for observing behavior, should depend explicitly on educational procedures that are used and their immediate goals. These goals may or may not be defined in the curriculum or by the teacher, but they should certainly be implicit in classroom procedures as they evolve throughout the year. This is true disregarding what the stated goals of a program are, and also disregarding whether the program identifies with a particular school of thought. The translation of generalized goals to **action goals** is often quite tedious and unrealistic because of the liberties that are necessarily taken by teachers. We have seen this operate in a highly controlled one-to-one situation where teachers were instructed very specifically on how to teach young children how to work with electric typewriters. Many sessions were spent training teachers both before the program started, as well as at periodic intervals throughout the program, and there were two-way observational facilities so that the intervention could be carefully monitored. In spite of this, teacher variation certainly becomes a crucial issue in determining whether stated goals of an educational program are relevant to evaluation. The greater the teacher variation, the more it is necessary to look to interactional and longitudinal goals as the basis for accurately describing changes that have taken place both in children and teachers, and the educational system in which they exist.

What is being called for here is the systematic abstraction of goals that cut across teacher variation and that are anchored in classroom procedures rather than goals and philosophies that teachers and administrators give lip service to. Whether the articulated system and the actual system are compatible or congruent is another question which also must be attended to, but which is dependent upon the establishment of the workability of the natural situation as it evolves over time and the implicit goals (**action goals**) accomplished.

The first step in this procedure is to establish **action goals** for a variety of classes, so that degrees of fulfillment can be measured in situations with comparable goals. This can probably be best done by carefully observing classes over an extended period of time and categorizing them according to the curricular directions that exist. The success of the class would, in this first analysis, be evaluated in terms of which classes with similar **action goals** are more successfully achieving them. The measurement of goals would involve long term observation by multiple observers of clusters of contrasting classes. These goals would then be operationally defined in terms of specific children and group behaviors that they would affect, and then independent measures would be taken of these behaviors, in order to ascertain the extent to which diverse classes are accomplishing similar and different things.

The second phase of such a program would be to compare **action goals** with articulated goals of teachers. The latter would be obtained by developing seminars with selected groups of teachers who would have opportunities, over an extended period of time, to discuss their goals and to communicate them to other teachers and researchers in such a way as to develop an orderly presentation. This might then give the researcher an alternative set of goals to work with in the development of criteria, and it would move him still closer to his ultimate goal of obtaining measurements over many children in many classes of generalized changes in intellectual and social functioning.

The thing that is most disturbing about the evaluations of many educational programs is that they leave out the core of the educational process and, at best, randomize internal effects. If it worked, one could possibly be happy with such an arrangement, even though it can have little effect on teacher behavior. But the fact of the matter is that, in general, it does not work, and we really do not know why. The tentative solution is to search more deeply into the workings of the "little black box" so that we can more immediately get on with the work of studying the differential effects of educational programs on different children.

Attention should be directed towards the effects of changing classroom environments on individual children. Any description of teaching must be modified by a specific object-child. The authoritarian class ceases to be relevant—rather we can describe the more or less controlled environment of particular children as they experience (and effect) situations. This would call for large scale revamping of traditional normative procedures in favor of positive strategies that describe correlates of intra-individual variation. To accomplish such strategies would require research models which focus on differentiation rather than prediction and change rather than reliability. It would necessarily mean that the teacher's functional unit of observation and application would become the researcher's guideline for methodological development.

Part of this chapter was presented as a paper at Headstart Research Conference, Temple University, Philadelphia, Pennsylvania, February 15, 1967.

References

1. Bloom, B. S.   STABILITY AND CHANGE IN HUMAN CHARACTERISTICS, New York. Wiley, 1964

2. Hoffman, B. THE TYRANNY OF TESTING, New York: Crowel-Collier, 1964

3. Kennedy, W. A., Van DeReit, V. and White, S. C. The Standardization of the 1960 revision of the Stanford-Binet Intelligence Scale on Negro elementary-school children in the Southeastern United States. Washington: Cooperative Research Program, Office of Education, 1961.

4. McNemar, Q. "Lost: Our Intelligence—Why?" AMERICAN PSYCHOLOGIST, 1964, 19, pp. 871-82.

TEACHER-CHILD RELATIONSHIPS IN PSYCHOEDUCATIONAL PROGRAMMING FOR EMOTIONALLY DISTURBED CHILDREN

Peter Knoblock, Ph.D.,
Associate Professor of Special Education,
Division of Special Education and Rehabilitation,
School of Education, Syracuse University,
Syracuse, New York

Ralph A. Garcea, M. S. S.,
Guidance Services Associate, Syracuse Public Schools,
Syracuse, New York

PETER KNOBLOCK, Ph.D.   RALPH A. GARCEA, M. S. S.

Increasing awareness, mandatory state and federal legislation, and humanistic concerns are all combining to foster the development of public school programming for emotionally disturbed children. In the majority of instances the educational design takes on some form of grouping referred to as the special class.

It is to this programming approach of the special class that this paper addresses itself. Many school systems invest considerable energy and funds in the selection and hiring of trained teachers of disturbed children, grouping of children, and utilization of other school personnel and resources. This paper will attempt to look behind some of the major operations within such classes to see what the implications are for relationships between teachers and children and teachers and other staff members.

In recent years the concept of relationship has seemingly won almost universal acceptance as an integral factor in the helping process. Most schools of psychology, psychiatry and social work remark that an initial task in the helping process is the establishing of a relationship between the helping person and the person or group who is to be helped.

Yet the meaning of this concept appears quite different as it is viewed in different settings. The Social Worker working as a Probation Officer uses himself quite differently than the clinician in private practice. The use of authority and lack of choice on the part of the client, in marked contrast to the feelings of suffering and seeking out of help demonstrated by the private patient, is ample illustration of the difference. Despite such wide differences, both practitioners claim that a worker-client relationship is central in their treatment process.

People concerned with the special problems of educating problem children have also embraced this concept of the essentialness of the relationship between the teacher and the pupil. What is this all important "thing" we call relationship? Is it a condition of happiness or good will? Is it a sharing of conflict? Has the older term, rapport, just been replaced with a more modern, yet identical, term? To most of us this concept probably means all of these things and perhaps more.

Our problem is its meaning to teachers of difficult children. The uniqueness of the special education setting, its group nature, its authoritarian factors, its comparison to "regular school," its concern for academia on the one hand and healing on the other have all contributed to the confusion often felt by the teacher of the emotionally disturbed child. It is our attempt to reexamine this concept as it may exist for the special teacher.

Perhaps the initial focus of such a clarification should be on the goals or purposes of the relationship. Why do we bother to develop relationships in the first place? Are teachers' goals different from, or similar to, pupils' goals? Does it make any difference if these goals are similar or dissimilar?

For some the formation of relationships is a goal in and of itself. The idea of the healing potential which can result from the effective communication between human beings is quite understandable. The lack of significant, positive bonds between emotionally disturbed children and others is generally presumed to be a major cause of disturbance. Most theoreticians in the behavioral sciences have pointed to negative and destructive feelings that exist between emotionally disturbed children and their parents. Further, case studies usually demonstrate that these same kinds of negative feelings are often felt by these same children when in contact with other adults. It is therefore assumed that the many negative relationships which the child experiences becomes a dominant factor in his view of how others perceive him. This in turn negatively alters his behavior and his performance. The special teacher therefore sees the importance of the positive relationship between himself and his emotionally disturbed pupil as a significant break in pupil cycle of negative feelings and relationships with other people.

Another goal often described by the special teacher is the development of a relationship in depth. This process is seen as similar to the previous example but "something more." The something more may refer to the difficulty of developing meaningful ties with disturbed children. To some teachers it may be a defensive tactic used to favorably compare themselves to regular classroom teachers. To still others, it may be the purposeful use of self in a very sophisticated manner including the manipulation of transference phenomena. In general this concept is quite confused yet widely accepted.

Frequently the teacher's goal incorporates the idea of helping the child to control his behavior. This is most frequently the case regarding the acting-out, anti-social pupil. The rationale in this instance is certainly understandable. The acting-out behavior is usually a prominent factor in the pupil's referral to the services of the special teacher; the "reason" he needs help. In addition, his acting-out performance as a member of the special group jeopardizes his chances of help, even in the special setting. Most special education programs are organized on the basis of some group participation by the pupils. The acting out pupil's continual difficulty with his peers and with the authority of the teacher's role is a constant threat to his potential for success.

The special teacher therefore faces the immediate task of successfully dealing with this behavior as a premise for keeping the pupil in his group. In other words, no other benefits of the program can come to the pupil unless some modification can be made regarding his aggressive behavior. For some pupils this goal is so difficult to accomplish that it can become the primary and seemingly almost exclusive purpose for the relationship.

The special teacher has often been concerned and frustrated over his pupils' lack of academic achievement. This poor performance cannot usually be justified on the basis of an I.Q. It is often attributed to emotional factors which have caused the child to reject the reality of the outside world and that often includes school work. Many teachers believe that successful performance in this area will lead to a reality based competitive status. This then will be the child's way back to the normal world. In addition to this rationale, the teacher's knowledge and use of sophisticated educational techniques makes this goal a natural and desirable one.

Many teachers see the relationship as a means of helping a particular child with a particular problem. For example, a lonesome child who has great difficulty making friends might be helped to overcome this problem in the classroom. The teacher will design activities which will enhance this child's self esteem and his relationship with other pupils in the class. In this case, the teacher hopes the social success experienced by the child will carry over to new situations.

Some teachers have a primary, although perhaps unconscious, goal of achieveing personal success through the achievement of the group. Although all helping professions are prone to this malady, perhaps the special teacher is even more vulnerable. Unlike offices in a mental health clinic, school rooms in the same building often use competitive methods. Even if the special classes tend to deemphasize this phase of the school program, they are usually in physical proximity to regular groups of children. In addition to many other positive as well as negative effects, it does stimulate the competitiveness mentioned above. It takes a mature, goal directed teacher to escape from risking his class inappropriately so that he can show others in the building that he is a good teacher.

The goals outlined above, and undoubtedly many others not touched on, propel many teachers toward purposeful interactions with disturbed chilcren. But what of other teacher-child interactions which remain at arm's length?

The absence of meaningful encounters between adults and children leads to less satisfying ways of filling the relationship vacuum. A dramatic example of this is Claude Brown's (1965) description of his institutionalization in a training school for delinquent boys.

"We all came out of Warwick better criminals. Other guys were better for the things that I could teach them, and I was better for the things that they could teach me...." (p. 146)

The question must be asked—why is there such a shying away from an emphasis on the dynamics of teacher-child relationships? Teachers traditionally verbalize considerable differential diagnosis anxiety. They either claim that they have too many "problem" children for whom they are unable to plan effectively, or that they have the children, but cannot spot them in a clear and meaningful manner. Regardless of the reason, the message is clear. Large groups of classroom teachers have tended to pull back from a positive use of their relationships with disturbed children. **In our experience, one of the major distinguishing characteristics of psychoeducationally oriented teachers, whether they are regular or special class teachers, is the belief that they are in a position to effect changes in the attitudes and behaviors of children via this relationship.**

For a number of reasons, not the least of which has been the potential threat of being introspective regarding one's philosophic view of children, we have tended to rely heavily on mechanistic teacher and curriculum approaches. A careful search of the existing literature on teacher-child relationship reveals a remarkable dearth of attention. Short of the many textbooks on mental health approaches in the classroom, few professional workers identified with the education of disturbed children specifically focus on conditions which enhance teacher-child relationships. Educational researchers have observed that one reason for the present confusion regarding the issue of teacher effectiveness and competence is the avoidance of studying the impact of teacher behavior on children.

For the psychoeducator, this is the crucial consideration; namely, how does a teacher go about effectively using himself as a vehicle of change? Needless to say, whatever form the relationship takes would be vitally related to the other characteristic concerns of these therapeutic educators. For example, it is now well recognized that the teacher's approach to group behavior profoundly influences his impact on individual as well as group relationship. The kinds of interpersonal relationships individual teachers establish with other members of the school who are also involved with emotionally disturbed children such as guidance counselors and school psychologists—regardless of whether these other workers are viewed as a team or not—would certainly have an impact on how the teacher's feelings would spill over into contact with children. One complexity leads to another. One could and should maintain that the possibility of this kind of chain-reaction occurring would in turn be dependent upon the ego status of the adult. It would also be dependent upon a great variety of other factors such as what some workers refer to as the presence of "conflict-free areas" of ego functioning on the part of the teacher. Certainly, if we were to base our belief in the potential potency of the quality of the interaction between teacher and child on experimental or hard data, we would have little to fall back upon. At this juncture we are willing to put this forth as a testable hypothesis.

To be sure, the majority of teachers believe in developing relationships with children in their classrooms. It would be interesting and undoubtedly revealing to gather the perceptions teachers have of just what is meant by a "relationship." The present authors are of the opinion that many teachers have been gripped by an "all or none" quality. A kind of mystique has been created which has negatively served our purposes. The implication is that a "real" relationship is something only a very few people, teachers included, have been able to effect. To talk in such global terms about such an amorphous concept has prevented us from asking more relevant questions. Do all disturbed children need the same dosage of relationship? Or is it conceivable that a different relationship approach is needed in accordance with the particular needs of a child at certain times in the school year or at certain times in his development. What seems important to remember is the perception of a relationship as a dynamic concept which by necessity must flex itself to the very special situations and stages in which children find themselves.

One implication of the above discussion is that many educators have been guilty of either completely avoiding the dynamics of teacher-child interactions or have tended to encompass uncritically the necessity of developing a relationship with disturbed children. Both orientations, if adhered to, may have a common outcome—namely, to gloss over the interpersonal complexities in such interactions. Accounting for this would seem to be a prevalent approach to looking at the teacher-child interaction solely as an outcome variable, something to be achieved or a goal a teacher can seek to reach. We take the view that present knowledge also demands that we look at such interaction patterns in process terms. That is to say, relationships as we typically think of them are in reality found to occur in many sizes and shapes and may progress or remain static depending on a whole host of variables, some of which impinge on the environment of the special pupil and are outside the control of the teacher. It is this relationship process that we will devote attention to in this article.

One other "given" in the teacher-child interaction should be mentioned and then hopefully tucked away only to reappear within a sounder theory. All too often we take up the plight of a disturbed child and proceed to make a unilateral decision as to his need for a "relationship." We then proceed to apply whatever it is that is necessary to accomplish that goal. Those professional workers, for example, who have long been involved in working with acting-out children no longer make such a grand assumption. Through painful experiences they have come to recognize that the expectations for learning and relating that youngsters have may differ markedly from those of adults.

Some children, especially when they are first placed in a special education program, experience overwhelming anger. For them the only goal is to "get out." They see themselves as serving time in this special place. For such children the placement in a special program may very well represent but another episode in the lifelong pattern of adult and parent imposition. They didn't want to come to the program in the first place and they just can't wait to get out. For such children the goal of getting out is with no strings attached. That is, they would like to be released without any change in behavior or personality, and without any pain or effort on their part. For such children, the use of relationship may very well be to manipulate the teacher into allowing him to be removed from the program.

A secondary goal for such children, when getting out becomes impossible, is to manipulate the teacher. He may attempt to fight, steal, or engage in any other anti-social activity which suits his needs for the moment and then to use his relationship with the teacher to escape any punishment or consequences which would normally follow such actions. Such goals are seen as variations of the original theme, getting out of the program, and are all aimed at instant impulse graitification.

For some children, the relationship with the teacher becomes primarily a method of protection from the outside world. Such children, overwhelmed by their own feelings of inadequacy, and in turn overwhelmed by their environment, find the teacher a constant source of comfort, one who may fight his battles and favorably represent him to the outside world. Because of the extensive period of time that the teacher and pupil have contact with each other, for such children the program with the teacher can represent a new home, one which he never wishes to leave. For such a child, the goal is to stay and to continue to be protected.

For some children, the relationship with the teacher represents the opportunity for positive identification with an adequate adult. The opportunities for such prolonged and intimate contact with a positive adult like the teacher are extremely rare for most disturbed children. In this case it means several hours each day, five days a week, month after month, throughout the school year. Not only does the child have the opportunity to see the teacher in more formal situations but he can view him in informal situations too; eating food together, playing games together, making mistakes together, being embarrassed together. This is truly a unique opportunity in our society and for some children it becomes the most important factor in the entire program. For some children, the relationship with the teacher becomes primarily a method by which the child makes a contact with the outside world. For these children the failures in peer relationships have been outstanding and consistent. In the classroom setting the teacher directs the child in appropriate behavior toward his peers, and in fact, has some control over the other children's responses. Such an opportunity can give this type of child the courage to try again, experiencing limited success at first, and this in turn may encourage more attempts at successful social interaction in the future.

Still another major goal for relationship with the teacher for some children is the need on the part of the child to learn. Certainly encompassed in the role of the teacher is the concept of a knowledgeable person who has the potential to impart his knowledge to others. For some children the frustration of not being able to learn, despite the higher expectations of others, has resulted in a frustrating and bewildering life. Pressures at home to achieve become almost unbearable and yet learning does not take place. For such a child, the relationship with the teacher who represents knowledge and the ability to teach can become an all-encompassing interest.

A PSYCHOEDUCATIONAL FRAMEWORK

Clinical and teaching experience with emotionally disturbed children seems to highlight the essential ingredient of any framework: namely, that it encompass both relationship conditions fostered by the teacher and environmental conditions created to enhance the interactional pattern.

One of the major stumbling blocks to articulating the characteristics of effective teachers in terms of their relatability has been the apparent diversity of their role. Redl and Wattenberg (1959) make a convincing case for the many hats teachers find themselves wearing. It may be reasonable to view certain relationship qualities as generic and applicable to many groups involved in interpersonal relationships, including teachers.

For our purposes, we are intrigued with the possibilities discussed by Truax and Carkhuff (1967) in identifying three relationship qualities which they maintain account for what has come to be known as necessary and sufficient conditions for enhancing relationships and fostering improvement.

Based on their own research and organization and integration of existing data and theory, they have advanced the following characteristics as important for the helping person.

The effective helping person:

(1) "is integrated, non-defensive and authentic or **genuine** in his therapeutic encounters.

(2) can provide a non-threatening, safe, trusting or secure atmosphere by his acceptance, unconditional positive regard, love, or **nonpossessive warmth** for the client.

(3) is able to "be with", grasp the meaning of, or **accurately and emphatically** understand the client on a moment-by-moment basis." (p. 1).

While their book deals primarily with the functioning of counselors and therapists, it is our impression that much of what they have to say is equally applicable to teachers and others who find it imperative to enhance the quality of their communications with disturbed children. Truax and Carkhuff present some provocative ideas including the feasibility of specific training procedures to increase the level of communicating the above three conditions. Also central to their approach are the premises that therapeutic conditions have generalizable benefits regardless of the type of individual you are confronting and that it is the helping person, not the target individual, who determines the level of the relationship condition as specified above.

RELATIONSHIP AND PSYCHOEDUCATIONAL PROGRAM CONDITIONS

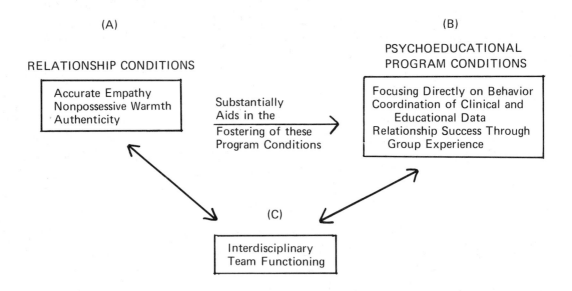

Clinical and educational experience with disturbed children has convinced us that both sides of the framework chart must be called into action. That is, those teachers epitomizing satisfactory relationship conditions as specified above appear to call forth those psychoeducational behavior and environmental conditions which compliment the relationship stance of the teacher. Our premise is that in order for a total psychoeducational environment to exist and have its impact on teaching and learning behaviors of teachers and children the relationship conditions (A) must be present in high enough degrees to create psychoeducational behaviors and environmental conditions (B).

A central position is given to the utilization of a variety of other program personnel (C).

400

The notion is that by the time most children are placed in a special class program they are in need of multiple interventions by professional workers. It is further hypothesized that the adult's handling of himself with his program colleagues is in many ways as important as the level of relationship conditions established with the children in the program. Experience has also shown us that psychoeducational program conditions are dependent upon the removal of certain situational restraints, many of which involve other special class program personnel.

Focusing Directly on Behavior

The placement of children into a special class carries with it certain crisis dimensions. Despite the fact that many of these children have long presented schools and teachers with placement and handling problems, what frequently propels them into a special class is "something" they have done. Not infrequently, they have lost control of their feelings and in some instance this breakdown of ego functioning is translated into physical acting-out.

Rarely do we know the kinds of feeling such children bring to a special class setting. The developmental nature of the problem may very likely take a back seat to what is happening in the present. After all, if he has repeatedly lost his control the mere placement in a special program offers no guarantee of preventing such a reoccurrence. The task of the teacher and program personnel is to assist the child in sorting out the kinds of concerns and anxieties he may have while in his new group. And it is here that the teacher has the advantage of sharing with the child the many bits of behavior and affect he displays. They are in it together, both sharing and experiencing the other. While the teacher may know of the past horrors in a child's life, it is difficult, if not impossible to, experience such events and constellations from the past. But she can feel the child's anger at being told by another teacher in the cafeteria that he should "watch his table manners." Not only can she empathize with him, even possibly conjuring up images of lots of children hustling for food around a sparsely set dinner table, but more importantly, she can project herself into the equation. It seems increasingly more difficult to armchair the development of empathy. Accurately perceiving the dilemmas faced by children must surely be a participant process. To be there, both physically and psychologically, offers unique possibilities to teachers for conveying to disturbed children their understandings of what is happening and even greater opportunities for effecting the outcome of the behavioral incident.

The potential for change would appear to reside in the interactional effects of the teacher constantly being in a position to not only help the child deal with his feelings about himself as a learner, group member, and larger school community member, but to continually communicate to him the impact of his behavior on others — including the teacher. The feelings of helplessness and despair communicated by so many disturbed children serve as paralyzing forces in their motivational systems. To be constantly fed as much interpersonal reality by a teacher who repeatedly presents herself as one inextricably involved holds great promise.

To focus on the present reality enables the teacher to maximize his use of self in translating relationship conditions into practice. The following are brief examples of such conditions:

Authenticity: *The question of whether a particular teacher is real has absorbed much space in the popular press as well as in the conversations and stereotyped impressions of the public — the great majority of whom were former students in contact with teachers. How many of us look back with a sense of satisfaction at those teachers whom we considered firm but fair. A kind of personal challenge was met when we found we could succeed with such a teacher. Most considered this a studied teacher strategy, but in more cases than not we were and are excited by the realness of the person. What we were experiencing were teachers with expectations about what learners could achieve and who were not running in a popularity contest. They seemed to be comfortable with allowing a relationship and rapport to nurture and grow, as it often did.*

Accurate Empathy: *Rollie, a ten year old boy, characterized by his special class teacher of last year as extremely anxious and somewhat depressed, began this current school year in a regular classroom. Entering his new classroom and confronting the teacher, he exclaimed, "Oh, no! Not you! I don't want to stay in this class, I want Miss Jones!" His teacher then very calmly stated, "You know, I always get a little nervous the first day of school. Is that how you feel now?" His teacher had obviously made good use of her own reactions to accurately "read" Rollie's dilemma. Faced with a new teacher and group, he was in immediate need of hurdle help. Rather than resorting to convincing techniques, she communicated her awareness of his concern and did so in a nonjudgmental and face-saving manner.*

Nonpossessive Warmth: *A teacher in a residential treatment center for emotionally disturbed children was confronted with a 14 year old boy with marked conceptual deficits. His years of aggravated defeats at the hands of adults did little to allow him to do battle with formal learning tasks. A level of hostility never really determined by those of us who worked with him kept him apart from us and vice versa.*

He did not strike us as brittle but rather immovable. This youngster was truly an example of a child who hates (Redl and Wineman, 1951). After considerable effort and frustration on the part of the teacher, she related her feelings by stating that the depth of this boy's learning problem was repulsive to her. In this instance, acceptance by the teacher was dependent upon high priority needs of the teacher. For this youngster the job of grappling with his own difficulties, while at the same time meeting unrealistic expectation levels of his teachers, tended to immobilize his school functioning. No movement seemed the safest to him and his passive orientation remained very much in evidence.

Coordination of Clinical and Educational Data

The expectation here is that we are encouraging the development of diagnostic or clinical teaching. Confusion regarding the proper role for teachers of disturbed children appears to be a reflection of the teaching versus therapy argument. The contention being advanced in this section is that clinical and educational data as it applies to daily and long range programming can not be separated or compartmentalized. The development of realistic curriculum and behavioral goals for disturbed children is predicated on the bringing together of seemingly diverse bits of information.

As a point of departure, one is even hard pressed to clearly delimit educational from clinical data. First grade teachers will take an enormous number of behavioral and antecedent variables into consideration when planning a school program. Would consideration of a child's motor development reflect concern of a clinical or educational nature? Operating on the assumption that by operationally defining our terms we could make this distinction, the real question is whether such a distinction is useful. When we consider the interrelationship of visual-motor maturation and success with curriculum tasks such as adequate perception of pictures, words, and writing, the separating out of clinical from educational appears to be, in part, an artificial distinction.

If, instead, we think in more global terms of coordinating such seemingly diverse but related information, then perhaps the following data collection approaches, while not inclusive, will convey the diagnostic possibilities for teachers.

1. Only collect such information which appears to be directly related to present behavioral or curriculum plan or problem. Earlier events of childhood, while offering some tantalizing hypotheses in terms of cause and effect relationships, are often at an inferential level which yields little direct programming or relationship interventions for the teacher.

2. Recognizing that many relationship stances of disturbed children may either have their origin in peer contacts or are acted out in classroom groups, teachers of disturbed children are finding sociometric analyses of their special class group to be extremely helpful. Several designs are possible, including pre-middle-post testing, and collecting sociograms of one group in varying settings such as in the special class and in physical education where the special group may be merged with other groups as well.

3. In our opinion, the past emphasis on supplying teachers with information pertaining to the educational status of children created a degree of diagnostic apathy which is just now becoming dissipated, largely due to the efforts of those encouraging an approach to the learning disabilities of exceptional children. Much of the diagnostic excitement for teachers has long disappeared and in its place is the cumulative folder and results of standardized reading and achievement tests. Intelligence test results have not fared much better with the "boiling down" process in such an advanced state that many teachers are handed only the score along with a cursory analysis of the results. The common failing in all of this has been the extreme difficulty in translating such information into educationally relevant terms. What is meant here by educationally relevant is information which directly contributes to changing some specified learning or adjustment problem.

4. The present trend toward the fractionating of learning and behavioral qualities has created some major planning problems for teachers. Not the least of these has been the difficulties encountered in putting all of the findings back into some coherent diagnostic picture of the child. For the above reason, several broad-gauged diagnostic approaches are being experimented with by teachers and clinicians. One would be the utilization of instruments based on some underlying theory or framework such as the Illinois Test of Psycholinguistic Abilities (ITPA). Developed as an outgrowth of Osgood's communication model this instrument offers teachers a diagnostic procedure with reasonably direct intervention and remediation possibilities (Kirk and Bateman, 1962). A second example would be in the utilization of an instrument such as the Conceptual Styles Test (Kagan, Moss, Sigel, 1963). In the investigating of a child's approach to learning tasks, the information obtained by the teacher would seem to yield greater usable data than the more piecemeal orientation of specifying various aspects of a child's functioning pattern. In this test, a determination can be made, based on the child's response to stimulus pictures and his rationale for his responses, as to his approach to learning situations in terms of cognitive dispositions such as inferential and analytic. Behaviors such as reflective are believed to be associated with high analytic scores and impulsivity with low scores. Thus, we see not only a way of looking at the learning stances of children but certain implications for behavior predicated on such cognitive styles.

5. Direct observation of children's behavior appears to be a lost art. And perhaps the

implicit involvement required of the observer is what has deterred some school workers from engaging in such activities. The other side of this is that there are now several observation procedures which bear directly on major, at least from our standpoint, interpersonal attitudes of teachers and children. Amidon and Hough (1967) have organized much of the significant research and theory dealing with Interaction Analysis. This particular observation technique focuses directly on degrees of teacher directness and indirectness through a relatively simple ten category system. Of interest here is that many professional workers are modifying the original category system as developed by Flanders to meet highly idiosyncratic purposes such as observations in special classes for disturbed children in which teacher talk patterns seem to differ so markedly from regular classroom teacher behavior. Certainly a number of other observational schemes would be just as appropriate. One major criterion in the selection of such a technique within a psychoeducational framework would be its promise for contributing to teacher practices which in turn contribute to change. The ongoing collection of observational data just so we know what is going on, while important, no longer seems sufficient.

It does not seem adequate to merely exhort special class teachers to adopt a clinical-diagnostic role. A degree of dynamic orientation must be present which allows and entices one to speculate and integrate such information. A great many factors appear to impede the development of such a role. Perhaps the most prominent has to do with the issue of role definition. Most frequently a special class program is established with as little fanfare as possible. It is gently oozed into the ongoing school program to as great an extent as possible. The not so hidden message is that if we can "look like the others" in the school, then we will stand a better chance of assimilation. There is certainly an element of truth in this notion of job-alike similarity and congruence. If special class teachers can be seen as teachers performing tasks familiar to other staff members, then perhaps initial suspicion and distrust can be minimized. The long range consequences of playing down one's special role, however, may outweigh immediate acceptance, which, in practice, is never quite that immediate. To feel forced to go underground in presenting yourself and your special class program creates a sense of tension which invariably bubbles to the surface at crucial points in the school year. Certain tasks of the teacher and other program personnel require direct exposure and confrontation with other school staff.

Most schools have rigidly locked teachers into what has vaguely been referred to as the teaching function. As indicated earlier, a passive diagnostic role has been fostered and encouraged by the environment, but not without acquiesence by special class teachers. Basic to many teachers' negative or over-reaction to engaging in organized diagnostic behaviors may be a large component of passiveness. One implication behind the collecting of information is that something will need to be done with the data. Perhaps the insular nature of many special class programs has forced many teachers into the attitude of "we know what the problem is, but doing something about it is the problem." The bind is often a paralyzing one. To function diagnostically is to isolate oneself from many of the other staff members; and to engage successfully in those activities too often leaves a teacher with a feeling of uncompletion. Raised to a level of awareness and sophistication regarding a disturbed child's status along a number of dimensions the school environment may either not be supportive of such data gathering activities or the school and community environments may not offer outlets for the translation of such information into sound programming.

There would appear to be a prevalent belief that formal testing and even informal diagnostic procedures such as observation of individual and group behavior interfere with the relationship. Such thinking may reflect attitudes toward the use of diagnostic instruments and thinking as mechanistic and unreal. There is frequently a sharp cleavage between diagnostic activity and relationship behavior. In practice, however, the distinction is not very clear. A relationship may need and involve clear diagnostic information and thinking. In the eyes of the child the teacher's individualized-diagnostic approach may be perceived as involvement and need not necessarily convey negative implications for the relationship.

To diagnose, in the broad sense of the term, is to make demands on the child. Many teachers are comfortable making academic demands, but when confronted with disturbed children a pulling back by teachers is often apparent. It may be a matter of feeling that the child has already been through enough in terms of evaluation procedures, or again, there may be a feeling that first a degree of rapport is needed in an effort to help the child adjust to the special class. The dilemma becomes one of asking ourselves the question of how far can we go in our plans with the child and group before developing accurate perceptions of what it is that is in need of change.

Relationship Success Through Group Experience

The school room is the setting for the special education program. Even if the program is part of a treatment center, the teacher's area is designated as the school. For most teachers and children this label has very definite implications regarding the group structure under which learning takes place. These implications are drawn from the regular school grouping of children.

Such regular school groupings may be based on a range of factors such as level of academic achievement or alphabetic sorting according to the child's surname. Once grouped, the children sit in the same room together and carry on parallel activities. There is relatively little interaction among the children that is goal directed. The emphasis is on group instruction, for convenience, which hopefully results in individual learning for each child in the group. In short, there is little conscious attention directed at the potential of the group as an entity within itself. The dynamics of the group tend not to be maximized as a helping tool. The interactions tend to be singular between the teacher and the individual student.

Many, if not most, students have need for successful group experience. Further, their previously unsuccessful experiences with adults makes it difficult for them to operate in the singular interactional experience with teachers. Generally, these two factors may explain the failure of many children in school and may be the basis for their referral to the special program.

The contention is that the special needs of many emotionally disturbed children warrants a different concept of the classroom group, one in which interactions between all group members are viewed as meaningful; and in which the dynamics of the group are purposely used by the teachers as a tool to help the children academically, socially, and psychologically.

In order to do this the teacher must view the group as an exclusive entity, not as merely a collection of individuals. Although the quality and character of the group is greatly determined by the individuals involved, no study of the individuals will suffice in rendering an understanding of the group as a whole. The number of individuals when brought together becomes something more than their sum total; this is the group character and this necessitates special study.

Of primary importance is the fact that the children do not comprise a natural group. They are instead grouped through one process or another by the school or institution. This means that friendships must be started, roles must be defined and goals must be developed. All of the characteristics of the natural group are lacking and must be injected before a meaningful group process can be developed.

Another complication which further hinders the development of adequate group processes is the expectation of the children. As the previous description of school room groups indicated, there is little or no expectation on the part of the child that he is expected to interact meaningfully with his classmates. The teacher therefore is faced with the problem of a formed group of children whose expectations in the classroom do not include meaningful interactions with their classmates.

Another important ingredient is the role of the teacher. Many factors result in the teacher being thrust in a role of exclusive leadership. First, is the fact that the teacher is adult, the pupils children. The authoritarian implications of the traditional role of teacher is another factor. Added to this is the inability of the group to quickly select its indigenous leadership because of the artificial nature of its formation.

The group also tends to lack a common goal. The teacher's perception of where the group should be going may be very different from that of the children. The children themselves probably differ markedly in their perception of where they are going.

The above concepts are mentioned, if only briefly, to illustrate the complexity of using the group constructively. Only when these issues have been dealt with by both teacher and children can the group come alive. Many teachers, by dint of natural ability and intuition, have made constructive use of the group but the special education teacher cannot depend on such coincidences. The pathology of the children in addition to the many factors which can prevent the formation of a working group makes it imperative for him to systematically study and direct the group before it can be a helpful and healthful influence on the lives of the children involved.

Interdisciplinary Team Functioning

The successful coordination and integration of clinical and educational data depends greatly upon the quality and extent of the interrelationships between special class teachers and other program personnel. The concepts behind team functioning remain highly elusive. Once we go beyond agreeing to the anticipated value of collaborative efforts the implementation of such activities remains elusive.

For illustrative purposes it may be instructive to explore the interpersonal behaviors of special class program personnel when involved in the activity of assisting a child's family as part of the total special class program effort.

Some unique problems are faced by the special class teacher once the program undertakes extended contact with the child's family. Not the least of such problems is the possibility of arousing a host of angry feelings they may have about parents of disturbed children. Many teachers can manage to keep such feelings reasonably under control as long as some distance can be maintained between what the teacher is doing with the child and the child's interaction with the parent. Once contact with parents becomes part of the special program design, such distance is no longer possible.

Certainly, one could speculate as to the dynamics behind teachers' reactions, feelings and concerns regarding parents of children in their classes. After all, it is the teacher who may be left with the residue of feeling left over from the child's encounters at home. For every step made by the child, there is the lingering concern that the ego skills being acquired may be adequate for school adjustment but they may not hold up under conditions at home.

Harboring such negative or potentially negative feelings about families of disturbed children may at some point get in the way of attitudes about professional colleagues who may be spending the time with parents in counseling situations. The very message that teachers of disturbed children find so distressing — "I don't know how you can manage to work with them" — is the very message that many of them send out to the social workers and psychologists who spend the time with parents. It is almost as if the personnel of a program are being asked to take sides — much as we often do against regular classroom teachers in the same building.

For the teacher, the introduction of an approach to parent counseling within the context of a special program seemingly enlarges the child's problem and ultimately the teacher's management problems. In many ways it is easier for all of us to zero in on a problem when the variables with which we have to cope are kept within some reasonable boundary. The teacher operating with data obtained within the classroom interactions may feel that having to now react and appraise the family dynamics as they impinge on the child's classroom functioning presents a rather awesome task. One wonders how powerless many teachers come to feel when faced with some of the harsh realities of family life as perceived and experienced by many disturbed children.

Basic kinds of questions immediately present themselves. What diagnostic weight should be given to here and now observations and behaviors of the child interacting with the teacher and group in comparison to more inferential but now somewhat closer data regarding home conditions? What are the educational and management treatment implications arising from the parent contacts? Do we now change our classroom approach because of what we are learning from our program colleagues who are seeing the parents? To say we can remain aloof from this data seems unlikely, but it is difficult to determine just how it influences our behavior.

Some observers of special class programs also detect a certain rivalry among personnel once contact with parents is part of the program design. Who then holds the position of central importance with the child? Is it the teacher who in reality has the most contact with the child, or is it the social worker or psychologist who is seeing the parents and might actually be in a position to change home procedures and routines of direct concern to the child? We think the resolution of these kinds of questions matter very much. It is just a short step to the raising of questions such as the handling of confidential information and does the school still represent the interests of the child along with those of the parent, or does a decision have to be made?

SUMMARY

Psychoeducational programming is based on effective and purposeful relationships. Central, is the educationally therapeutic relationship which must exist between teacher and pupil. Equally important is the concept of interdisciplinary team functioning and of the relationship factors that exist between team members.

This article is not intended as a primer on psychoeducational programming for emotionally disturbed children. It does, however, attempt to show the dependence of this method on adequate interpersonal relationships. Further, it describes some of the complexities of understanding and therefore effectively utilizing such relationships.

References

1. Amidon, E. J. & Hough, J. B. INTERACTION ANALYSIS: THEORY, RESEARCH AND APPLICATION. Reading, Mass.: Addison-Wesley, 1967.

2. Brown, C. MANCHILD IN THE PROMISED LAND. New York: Macmillan, 1965.

3. Kagan, J., Moss, H.A. & Sigel, I.E. Psychological significance of styles of conceptualization. SOCIETY FOR RESEARCH IN CHILD DEVELOPMENT MONOGRAPH, Serial #86, 28: 73-112, 1963.

4. Kirk, S.A. & Bateman, Barbara. Diagnosis and remediation of learning disabilities. EXCEPTIONAL CHILDREN, 29: 73-78, 1962.

5. Redl, F. & Wattenberg, W.W. MENTAL HYGIENE IN TEACHING. 2nd edition, New York: Harcourt, Brace and Co., 1959.

6. Redl, F. & Wineman, D. CHILDREN WHO HATE. Glencoe, Ill.: Free Press, 1951.

7. Truax, C.B. & Carkhuff, R.R. TOWARD EFFECTIVE COUNSELING AND PSYCHO-THERAPY: TRAINING AND PRACTICE. Chicago, Ill: Aldine, 1967.

TREATMENT METHODS AND THEIR EVALUATION IN EDUCATIONAL THERAPY

Marianne Frostig, Ph.D.,
Phyllis Maslow, M. A.
Marianne Frostig Center of Education Therapy,
Los Angeles, California

MARIANNE FROSTIG, Ph.D.

During the last decade an ever increasing number of children have been grouped into special classes labeled "children with learning difficulties," "educable retarded," "neurologically handicapped," "perceptually handicapped," "emotionally handicapped," "brain damaged," or some other term reflecting either a prime symptom or suspected cause. Certain teaching procedures have usually been recommended for each group but though at times considerable improvement resulted the amount of academic success and the degree of improvement in behavior and learning ability have varied greatly, and the proportion of children reintegrated into regular classes has often been low.

There are a number of reasons for this comparative lack of success. A fundamental one is that the assumption has often been made that children gathered under a single label will all have the same pattern of learning difficulties and will respond equally well to a standard pattern of educational approaches. It may be that the group labels tend to confuse the issue by designating either a single characteristic symptom of disturbance such as "perceptually handicapped," or "emotionally disturbed." In fact, the children show a variety of symptoms, and even the individual children often exhibit multiple symptomatology. Nor can one always suggest a single cause of the disturbance, such as "brain damage" or "perceptual handicap," when in fact the causes may be multiple too. None of these labels is of great significance for the educator, whose actual task is to educate children who for various reasons show a variety of difficulties in learning, ranging from inability to pay sustained attention to poor handwriting.

An alternative solution to strict classifying is to disregard labels and to provide specific training programs based upon a detailed analysis of each child's current psychological and educational abilities. At the Marianne Frostig Center of Educational Therapy, the children's abilities are assessed in six major developmental areas — sensory-motor development, language, perception, higher cognitive functions, and emotional and social adjustment.* Four tests serve the basis for planning the appropriate remedial programs — the Marianne Frostig Developmental Test of Visual Perception.**, the Wepman Test of Auditory Discrimination,*** the WISC**** and the Illinois Test of Psycholinguistic Abilities.***** These basic tests are supplemented by a detailed survey of sensory-motor functions, projective testing, interviews with parents and child, careful observation, and the additional use of other formal tests as required in particular instances. [1]

Both the Frostig Test of Visual Perception and the Illinois Test of Psycholinguistic Abilities were designed to serve as the basis for remedial programs. Training programs based upon them have been developed at the Frostig Center in sensory-motor functions, visual perception* and language.** In addition a physical education program has been prepared on the basis of results of various factor analytic studies of movement.*** The total remedial program is individualized as far as possible to take into account each child's needs and deficits as diagnosed during the comprehensive evaluation.**** [2]

DIFFICULTIES OF CHILDREN WITH LEARNING DEFICITS

There are four broad areas of difficulty with which the educational therapist must deal. One is the amelioration of specific developmental lags and inadequacies. This involves selecting training exercises for each child from the remedial programs on the basis of

[1]

*Frostig, Marianne, "The Education of Children with Learning Disabilities" in PROGRESS IN LEARNING DISORDERS edited by Helmer R. Myklebust for Grune & Stratton, Inc., New York, N.Y. (1966).

**Frostig, M., Lefever, D.W. and Whittlesey, J.R.B., THE MARIANNE FROSTIG DEVELOPMENTAL TEST OF VISUAL PERCEPTION, Palo Alto, California: Consulting Psychologists Press, 1964.

***Wepman, Joseph M., WEPMAN TEST OF AUDITORY DISCRIMINATION, Chicago: Language Research Associates, 1958.

****WECHSLER INTELLIGENCE SCALE FOR CHILDREN, New York: The Psychological Corporation, 1949.

*****Kirk, S.A. and McCarthy, James P., ILLINOIS TEST FOR PSYCHOLINGUISTIC ABILITIES, Urbana, Illinois: University of Illinois Press, 1961.

[2]

*A manuscript summarizing the reports received from users of the Frostig Perceptual Program is in preparation.

**Other language programs based on the ITPA have been developed by Lloyd Dunn, Douglas Wiseman and Dr. N.S.W. Hart. Barbara Bateman has summarized literature on the ITPA.

***Guilford and 78 others, summarized by Nicks and Fleishman. Other suggestions came from Kephart and Mosston.

****Although all of these programs are in use at the Frostig Center, they are not all at an equal stage of development. The sensory-motor and visual perceptual programs are the most advanced, and have been published. A language program is now being used experimentally in selected school districts as well as at the Center.

the initial testing and observation. Specific training is thus provided for specific disabilities in each developmental area.

The second aim of the remedial teacher is to help academic progress by teaching subject matter, by methods which take the child's developmental difficulties into account. The analysis of the child's strengths and weaknesses, which results from the initial evaluation, indicates how this can be done. For example, if a child is shown to have severe disabilities in visual perception which make reading difficult for him, he can be taught new content orally or by means of a tape recorder, while at the same time receiving carefully programmed training in visual perception. As his ability to read improves, the supplementary methods are gradually reduced until he is able to master the material by reading books appropriate for his age level.

The third remedial task is to aid emotional and social development. In severe cases, psychotherapy or counseling might be required for the child or parents or both, but it is the task of the teacher to manage the classroom, the playyard activities and the interactions of the children in a therapeutic way. Of prime importance is the teacher's relationship with the child. She must guide him, help him to succeed, set limits, accept his feelings whether positive or negative, and assure him of her continual attention, concern and interest. She should maintain steady verbal interaction, afford children who need to do so the opportunity to ventilate, and clarify their feelings for them when they are confused. Behavior which harms or disturbs others cannot be tolerated, but the teacher who recognizes that unacceptable behavior is usually a sign of tension, will adjust her reactions and her demands, and remain friendly even when she has to be firm. The teacher must also be aware of the importance of peer group relationships for the child's total development, and should lose no opportunity to promote social cohesiveness in the group.* A therapeutic classroom atmosphere is one in which the teacher helps the children, the children support and help each other, everybody shares in the daily tasks, and every child feels accepted and respected whatever his contribution.

The fourth main task is to ameliorate the global and more pervasive disturbances which cannot be pinned down to a specific developmental deficit. Disorganization, impulsivity, hyperactivity, inability to follow a sequence of stimuli, inability to focus attention at will, and so on, are familar manifestations of global disturbances. These defects can be conceptualized as defects in ego development, which affect all behavior—in psychoanalytic terminology, all ego functions—motility, perception, language, thought, social behavior and emotional reaction. **Three main approaches are used in the classroom to**

Not only the daily experience of teachers but also the beautiful animal studies of Harlow, assure us of the beneficial effects of good peer relationships.

417

ameliorate global symptoms—focusing attention, providing structure, and **promoting ego growth by reducing anxiety.**

1. **Focusing attention can be achieved through:**

    (a) Stimulus reduction—the use of bare walls, masked windows, cubicles, a restricted program and the presentation of simple stimulus patterns. We use this approach sparingly.

    (b) Stimulus accentuation—the use of color, boundaries, or movement, to accentuate a stimulus and set it apart from others. For example, writing a word to be learned in a color which differentiates it from other words; using pointers; "framing" pertinent stimuli with lines or materials. Stimulus accentuation should be used all through the school day.

2. **Providing structure in:**

    (a) Behavior, by maintaining basic rules of classroom conduct consistently.

    (b) Tasks involving sequences of action, whether buttoning a jacket or solving a problem in multiplication, by analyzing them carefully and teaching them in successive small steps.

    (c) Time, by referring to events in both the immediate and more distant past, and naming the period of time that has elapsed. Reference to future actions gives the children the confidence and security to be derived from predictability. They should know what schedule is planned for the day, and they should be well prepared for changes of activity. For example, the teacher might say, "In a few minutes we shall go out to the play yard. When I clap my hands you are to close your books, stand up quietly and walk to the door, where you must wait in line."

3. **Promoting ego growth through reduction of anxiety:**

    (a) Good teacher/child relationship, with frequent reassuring contacts.

    (b) Promoting reassuring contacts among the children.

    (c) Providing tasks precisely geared to the child's abilities, so that he regularly advances and experiences of failure are kept to a minimum.

    (d) Teaching by careful step-by-step progression.

(e) Giving each child an immediate reaction to his work or behavior (feedback).

(f) Providing rewards which are appropriate to the child's level of maturity and known needs. These may range from candy to praise, from a paper star to the provision of ideas and ideals.

(g) Showing the child graphically what he has accomplished (by collecting his work and keeping records of his progress).

EVALUATION OF THE RESULTS OF THE TOTAL PROGRAM

The treatment of learning difficulties is thus a complex task. The symptoms are commonly multiple, the causes commonly multiple, and the treatment procedures therefore, to be fully effective, must usually be multiple. What, then, about the task of assessing the success of treatment programs, when so many variables are involved? How can we evaluate the degree to which changes in a child's test scores reflect changes in his emotional and social adjustment due to classroom procedures or extra-school factors, as opposed to the impact of specific teaching techniques and program? And how do we take into account the differences between teachers in assessing the effects of a program? Teachers differ in their approaches to children in many ways that cannot easily be assessed.

Despite these difficulties, and although many methodological problems have not been clearly delineated, let alone solved, we have embarked upon a preliminary program to explore the efficiency of the integrated remedial programs used at the Frostig Center. The evaluation is currently tentative, being concerned only with the changes occurring in the WISC scores of 61 children after periods of training at the Center ranging from seven to twenty-three months. The children in our sample met the following criteria:

(1) Initial full scale WISC score was 78 or over.

(2) Initial tests of Frostig, Wepman and WISC were given within six months of beginning training. (In all but three cases all testing was completed prior to beginning training).

(3) Chronological age of child at time of initial testing was above 6 years but below 10 years of age. This limit was chosen because approximate scale scores for the Frostig Test cannot be used above age 10, and the WISC cannot usually be administered before 6 years of age.

(4) The children had no known uncorrected sensory defect.

The children were either enrolled in the day school in classes of 5-12 children, each conducted by a teacher and assistant teacher, or they continued in regular or special public school classes but attended the Center for additional tutoring. (Many children who fail to progress in regular school are able to do so when they receive specialized tutoring which includes the training of defective developmental abilities). The decision whether to use full-time attendance or a tutoring program was made on the basis of the test performance, the need for structure, and the child's age, social maturity, and available public school facilities. In general, children in the tutoring group may be assumed to have had less severe academic and/or behavior problems than those in classes, but this may not be true when comparing individual children. The children in the sample were not differentiated according to etiology or severity of academic difficulty.

The mean chronological age at time of initial testing was 93 months (7 years, 9 months), and the mean full scale WISC I.Q. was 94.7, with a range of 78 to 121. The sample, we believe, may be described as representing children expected by public school personnel and by their parents to benefit from regular public school curricula, but who in fact had only been able to work in public school under great stress and had progressed minimally, if at all. The children had to be helped to make progress both in their academic work and in the underlying abilities which make learning possible. One measure for studying changes in underlying abilities was the readministration of the WISC and a careful analysis of the changes in scores.

The following tables summarize the average changes in WISC subtest scale scores, and in verbal performance and full-scale I.Q. scores.

IMPLICATIONS OF FINDINGS

It can be assumed that the changes in the **overall I.Q. scores** are the result of the total remedial program for each child—the measures taken to remedy specific developmental lags and inadequacies, the teaching of academic subjects by methods which take developmental difficulties into account, the attention paid to emotional and social development, and finally the measures taken to ameliorate the pervasive global disturbances through classroom management. The changes in the mean I.Q. scores, it seems, indicate the general effectiveness of the total approach, here termed "educational therapy." With regard to changes in individual I.Q. scores, it is the policy of the Center, whenever an I.Q. drops more than five points, to initiate a multidisciplinary case review. In our experience, if a particular child's I.Q. does not advance or at least remain stable, there is a strong possibility of an untreated or deteriorating neurological condition being present (undiagnosed petit mal, for example), or of a deleterious total life-situation. (See Appendix).

AVERAGE DIFFERENCES 1ST AND 2ND WISC

	According to Age Level*				According to Training		
	Under 6-1/2 yrs **N -9	6-1/2-7-1/2 N -19	7-1/2-8-1/2 N 14	8-1/2-9-1/2 N 18	Classroom N - 31	Tutoring N -24	Spec.Class & Tutoring N - 6
INF	- .33	- .68	+ 1.64	.00	+ 1.32	+ .16	+ 1.00
COMP	+ 1.88	+ 1.10	+ 1.57	- .44	+ .77	+ .75	+ .83
ARITH	+ 3.22	+ .26	+ .57	.00	+ 1.32	+ .54	+ 1.33
SIM	+ 2.11	+ 2.26	+ .78	+ 1.16	+ 2.06	+ .91	+ 1.16
VOC	.00	+ 1.47	+ .71	+ 1.05	+ 1.26	+ .34	+ 1.16
DS	+ 1.44	+ 1.05	- 1.14	- .66	+ .13	- .20	+ .66
PC	+ .55	- .21	- .92	- .50	- 1.00	+ .12	+ 1.16
PA	+ 1.77	+ 1.47	+ .84	+ .58	+ 1.30	+ .65	+ 1.50
BD	+ 1.33	+ .68	- .14	+ 1.33	+ 1.00	+ .08	+ 2.16
OA	+ .77	+ 1.89	+ 1.28	+ 1.58	+ 1.30	+ 1.45	+ 3.00
CODE	+ .33	+ .94	+ 2.42	+ 1.11	+ 1.70	+ .91	+ .66
VIQ	+ 9.11	+ 6.16	+ 4.36	+ 3.55	+ 6.87	+ 2.50	+ 7.33
PIQ	+ 7.00	+ 6.63	+ 4.07	+ 6.44	+ 6.16	+ 4.37	+11.00
FSIQ	+ 9.22	+ 6.31	+ 4.78	+ 5.16	+ 6.80	+ 3.75	+ 9.83
Average Number of Months							
Between 1st & 2nd WISC	16	16	16	14	15	16	16
In Training	13	14	15	12	14	13	15

* One child was excluded because he was over 9-1/2 years old.

Average Age (at first WISC)   93.00 months   Standard deviation: 14.03
Average FSIQ (at first WISC) 94.70 months   Standard deviation: 9.57

**N refers to number of children.

AVERAGE DIFFERENCES 1ST AND 2ND WISC

	According to Initial Difficulties*				General Average N - 61	SE of Measurement of WISC Tests at 7-1/2 yrs
	Frostig and Wepman N = 22	Frostig only N = 22	Wepman only N = 5	Neither N - 10		
INF	+ .77	+ 1.27	- 1.20	+ 1.10	+ .83	1.75
COMP	+ .68	+ 1.27	- 3.80	+ 2.00	+ .77	1.92
ARITH	+ 1.14	+ 1.45	- 1.20	+ .60	+ 1.03	1.82
SIM	+ 1.72	+ 1.22	+ 2.50	+ 1.90	+ 1.52	1.75
VOC	+ .95	+ .52	- 2.00	+ 2.90	+ .94	1.44
DS	+ .63	- .31	- 1.20	+ .11	+ .05	1.90
PC	+ 1.36	- 1.22	- 3.00	- .40	- .34	1.92
PA	+ 1.45	+ 2.09	- .40	- 1.22	+ 1.03	1.59
BD	+ .95	+ .45	+ .40	+ 1.40	+ .75	1.20
OA	+ 1.50	+ 2.04	_ .20	+ .77	+ 1.46	1.82
CODE	+ 1.31	+ 1.27	+ .20	+ 1.00	+ 1.28	1.90
VIQ	+ 5.36	+ 6.27	- 5.60	+ 9.10	+ 5.22	5.19
PIQ	+ 8.86	+ 6.68	- 3.40	+ 4.00	+ 5.93	5.61
FSIQ	+ 7.72	+ 7.13	- 5.00	+ 5.90	+ 5.90	4.25

Average Number of Months						
Between 1st & 2nd WISC	15	16	14	15		
In Training	13	14	13	13		

* Two children were excluded because of invalid results in their Wepman Tests.

AVERAGE DIFFERENCES 1ST AND 2ND WISC

	According to Gains and Losses in Full Scale IQ Points						
	No Change or change ± 5 IQ points N-18	Gains from 6 thru 11 IQ points N-22	Losses from 6 thru 11 IQ points N-5	Gains from 12 thru 17 IQ points N-6	Losses from 12 thru 17 IQ points N-2	Gains from 18 thru 23 IQ points N-5	Gains from 24 thru 35 IQ points N-3
INF	+ .38	+ 1.45	- 2.00	+ 3.16	.00	+ .20	+ .66
COMP	- .11	+ .86	- .80	+ 4.00	- 3.50	+ 1.80	+ 2.66
ARITH	+ .47	+ 1.68	- 2.60	+ .66	- 2.00	+ 2.60	+ 5.66
SIM	+ .11	+ 1.22	+ .20	+ 2.00	- 2.00	+ 8.20	+ 4.66
VOC	- .11	+ 1.40	- 1.60	+ 1.66	+ 1.00	+ 1.20	+ 6.50
DS	- 1.50	- .19	+ 2.40	- .33	- 2.00	- 3.60	+ 3.33
PC	- 1.44	- .04	- 1.00	+ 1.33	- 7.50	+ 1.60	+ 2.66
PA	- .05	+ .90	- 1.20	+ 3.40	- 1.50	+ 4.00	+ 5.00
BD	+ .16	+ 1.27	.00	+ 1.00	- 2.50	+ 1.20	+ 4.00
OA	+ .61	+ 2.45	- .20	- .40	- 2.50	- 2.20	+ 6.66
CODE	+ .52	+ 1.59	- 2.40	+ 3.16	+ 2.00	+ 3.60	+ 1.33
VIQ	- 1.05	+ 6.95	- 8.00	+12.16	- 9.00	+17.60	+27.33
PIQ	- 1.22	+ 8.86	- 7.60	+15.16	-17.00	+17.60	+27.33
FSIQ	- 1.27	+ 8.04	- 8.60	+13.33	-14.00	+20.00	+29.33
Average Number of Months							
Between 1st & 2nd WISC	16	14	16	15	19	19	15
In Training	14	13	12	15	17	16	12

We have assumed the average significant change in **specific sub-test scores** for this sample to reflect, at least in part, the efficacy of the basic ability programs — the developmental programs administered according to test results in the developmental areas of sensory-motor functioning, language, perception and higher cognitive functions. It was assumed that subtest changes which were consistently strongly positive or consistently negative reflected particular strengths or weaknesses in our basic ability (developmental) training programs, and statistical group changes in subtest scores have been used empirically as a basis for revising programs.

As the tables show, we divided our sample in four ways: by age level; by organization of training (tutoring versus day school); by initial perceptual difficulties as revealed by the Frostig and Wepman tests; and by 6-point steps of gains and losses.

If we look at the table of findings with these tentative foci, several comments seem to be in order.

(1) Although the gains and losses in subtest scores for this sample are all within the standard error of measurement, it is interesting to note that all changes are positive, except in the subtest for picture completion.

(2) Younger children show the greatest gain. This finding is congruent with years of clinical observation, with results reported consistently by other workers, and with the experience of certain Head Start programs. The earlier that developmental training is instituted, the better the results.

(3) Tutoring children gained less than children in the Center's day school — the classroom program allowed for more training, integration, and practice in the basic psychological abilities. Also the stress upon marginally adjusted children of attendance in regular public school classes is considerable. On the other hand, the children who attended **special** classes in public school showed more improvement than any other group. The tutoring sessions with these children did not include so much help with academics, homework or preparation as was required by the children who came for tutoring but were in **regular** public school classes. Their sessions could be concentrated instead upon intensive ability training, with daily practice at home whenever possible.

(4) The picture completion subtest and the digit span subtest show a generally consistent pattern of negative changes in scale score. Picture completion is influenced by visual memory (imagery) and associative processes — the child has to compare mentally a present stimulus pattern with his memory of previous experiences in order to be aware of what is missing. The digit span subtest taps attention to auditory stimuli and immediate auditory memory for sequences.

These facts indicate that we must explore whether there is an under-emphasis on certain memory and associative functions in our training program. Training in memory for visual sequences is included in both the program for the development of visual perception and our language program, but it may well be that more attention should be given to aiding visualization, associative processes, and auditory memory, and that more effective exercises should be developed in these areas.

Another line of evidence supporting the need to emphasize exercises designed to aid in visualization and memory is that 74.4% of a different but comparable sample of 78 children referred to the Center, showed initial difficulties on the visual-motor sequencing subtest of the ITPA.* Unfortunately, systematic testing with ITPA had been initiated too recently for retest results to be available for all of the children who were retested with the WISC. Also the language program had not been developed when training was started for 12, or 19.7% of the children in our current sample. If the language program, which does have many suggestions for helping memory functions, had been consistently used for all children, the retest results with the WISC might have been different.

(5) Additional evidence indicating a probable weakness in our basic ability programs is given by the changes in test scores of the five children in our sample who had no difficulty in visual perception on initial testing, but who did have auditory perceptual problems as measured by the Wepman. Their comparative lack of progress suggests that a stronger program of training in auditory perception and auditory memory is needed.

SUMMARY

In summary then, this paper has been concerned with the progress of a group of children with learning difficulties. On the basis of comprehensive testing and observation, developmental programs were planned to ameliorate deficits in sensory-motor, perceptual, language and cognitive functions, in emotional and social adjustment. All-pervasive global symptoms were also taken into account and a therapeutic classroom environment was planned. A beginning has been made in assessing the value of this approach by retesting children with the WISC. The general trend so far is sufficiently encouraging to justify continuing with current methods and curricula. The variables are many, however, and much work has yet to be done in pinpointing specific strengths and weaknesses in the program, and assessing the causes of changes in the children's performance.

Over-all changes in behavior, I.Q. or academic progress probably reflect the changes brought about by the total environmental influences, and are due to a multiplicity of

*Analysis of this sample assisted by IBM programs at Western Data Processing Center.

factors. But it seems likely that the efficacy of developmental ability training programs can be inferred from the differential changes in specific sub-test scores.

It seems likely that changes in academic success alone, or in global I.Q. alone or in adjustment alone, cannot be used to prove the efficacy of a total educational program. It is necessary to measure the efficacy of all phases and aspects of the educational program—overall changes brought about by classroom management and a therapeutic environment, specific changes brought about by developmental programs (such as that for visual perception), and also the changes in academic achievement.

Revision of a paper presented at Symposium: EXPERIMENTAL APPROACHES IN EDUCATIONAL THERAPY. Chairman: Cynthia Deutsch, Ph. D. American Psychological Association, New York, September 2, 1966.

APPENDIX

One most significant factor in any child's performance is yet to be mentioned, and that is the child's life-situation outside the school. Sometimes psychiatric help is available for families in turmoil, sometimes teachers are able to help parents to understand their children and modify their behavior according to the child's needs. But often family situations have a deleterious effect upon a child, even when the maximum help is available. Conversely, an improvement in a child's life-situation is likely to bring about an improvement in his performance. This also has to be taken into consideration.

The only way of taking this variable into account seems to be to compare longitudinal studies of school performance with the material from carefully compiled case histories. The results of two such assessments are appended, the performances of Ariro and Martr. Their test performances varied widely, while those of the rest of their class seemed fairly consistent. An explanation is suggested when a comparison is made of the dates of crises within the family, with the dates of testing.

COMPARISON OF WISC TEST AND RETEST RESULTS
WITH RELATIONSHIP TO PARENTS AT THE TIME OF TESTING

ARIRO (girl)	Birthdate 7/29/55
Jan. 1964	Referred
July 1964	I.Q. scores: Verb. 86 Perf. 85 Full 84
Apr. 1965	Child described as "infantile, clinging, discouraged, teasing. Her father regards her as hopeless. She is teased by older siblings. She is the center of a battle between the parents."
June 1965	I.Q. scores: Verb. 94 Perf. 83 Full 88
	Despite the conflict between the parents and her father's hostility towards her, she was able to benefit from educational therapy, and her scores improved slightly.
June 1965	Child terminated at end of school year, at father's insistence.
Nov. 1965	Re-enrollment requested. Ariro had, of course, failed in public school. She was accepted provided mother received counseling. The father was also seen intermittently.
March— June 1966	Rift between parents widens. Child feels that much of the fault is hers.
Apr. 1966	Teacher's report includes these remarks: "Sometimes makes errors which she corrects herself when her attention is brought to them. . .I feel that there is an emotional problem which is slowing up learning."
June 1966	Divorce proceedings instituted.
July 1966	I.Q. scores: Verb. 82 Perf. 76 Full 77
	Test examiner remarked: "Ariro indicated a great deal of anxiety beneath a smiling exterior. She gave up on questions if she thought her answer might be wrong. . .Her thinking often seems to be disjounted. . .I feel that negative feelings about herself and her performance increased her anxiety and brought about scores which do not reflect her real capabilities."
	(Total loss in I.Q. scores: 7 points)

MARTR (boy) Birthdate 2/18/57

Aug. 1964	I.Q. scores: Verb. 87 Perf. 85 Full 86

Jan. 1965   Referred for tutoring and therapy. In special class in public school. He is diagnosed as neurologically handicapped, with an overlay of emotional disturbance. Traumatic events in his life included an injury to his hand when he caught it in a lawn-mower at age 4; the death through illness of his older sister when he was five; the subsequent illness of his mother.

The mother described herself as "overly fastidious, compulsively clean, unrelaxed." She overprotects the boy, and he is full of anxiety. The father is essentially passive.

Apr. 1965   "Martr will have nothing to do with talk of death. His puppet play suggests he feels responsibility for his sister's death, and possibly a fear that he may be punished by dying also." Martr's mother sees him as less satisfactory than his dead sister. She has to protect him from her own impulses. This is a time of crisis for the mother, who has to face and talk about her daughter's death for the first time."

May 1965   "Martr's mother is concerned because he has so many tics and twitches. She should understand that this is an expression of tension and cannot be nagged out of existence." "The death of Martr's sister is a shadow in this house which affects the relationships between all family members. The mother is now involved in plans to visit the cemetery on the anniversary of her daughter's death."

June 1965   "The boy is beginning to show some direct evidence of feeling. Anger is displaced from his mother to his therapist."

July 1965   "There is a greater outpouring of anger on the part of the mother. She even threatens the boy with banishment to his own apartment.

Sept. 1965   "The mother has made progress and been much more consistent with Martr. She accepts his limitations in schooling, gives him more freedom in the neighborhood. They are both more open to each other. The father takes a more active role."

Nov. 1965   I.Q. scores: Verb. 94   Perf. 89   Full 91

Apr. 1966   "Martr's mother is doing her best to make the boy less dependent. This is very difficult for her. However, the parents are now able to plan for a week's vacation without him."

June 1966   "Martr has become more venturesome in forming relationships in the neighborhood, but is still anxious. He accepts more responsibilities in the home."

Aug. 1966   I.Q. scores: Verb. 97   Perf. 94   Full 96

(Total gain in I.Q. scores: 10 points)

References

1. Bateman, Barbara, THE ILLINOIS TEST OF PSYCHOLINGUISTIC ABILITIES IN CURRENT RESEARCH. Urbana, University of Illinois: Institute for Research on Exceptional Children, April, 1964.

2. Dunn, Lloyd and Smith, James O., PEABODY LANGUAGE DEVELOPMENT KIT. Minneapolis: American Guidance Service, Inc., 1965.

3. Frostig, Marianne, THE EDUCATION OF CHILDREN WITH LEARNING DISABILITIES in Progress in Learning Disorders, Helmer R. Myklebust. New York: Grune & Stratton, Inc., 1966.

4. Frostig, M., Lefever, D.W. and Whittlesey, J.R.B., THE MARIANNE FROSTIG DEVELOPMENTAL TEST OF VISUAL PERCEPTION, Palo Alto, California: Consulting Psychologists Press, 1964.

5. Guilford, J.P. A SYSTEM OF PSYCHOMOTOR ABILITIES, Amer. J. Psychology, 71: 164-174, 1958.

6. Harlow, H.F. and Harlow, M.K., THE EFFECT OF REARING CONDITIONS ON BEHAVIOR, Bull. Menniger Clinics, 26:213-224, 1962.

7. Hart, N.S.W., EXPERIMENTAL LANGUAGE DEVELOPMENT PROGRAMME, based on OSGOOD'S LANGUAGE THEORY AND ITPA PROFILES, mimeographed, available from the author: Dept. of Education, University of Queensland, Brisbane, Australia.

8. Kephart, N.C., THE SLOW LEARNER IN THE CLASSROOM. Columbus, Ohio: Charles E. Merrill Books, Inc., 1960.

9. Kirk, S.A. and McCarthy, James P., ILLINOIS TEST FOR PSYCHOLINGUISTIC ABILITIES. Urbana, Illinois: University of Illinois Press, 1961.

10. Mosston, Muska, DEVELOPMENTAL MOVEMENT, Columbus, Ohio: Charles E. Merrill Books, Inc., 1965.

11. Nicks, Delmer C. and Fleishman, Edwin A., WHAT DO PHYSICAL TESTS MEASURE— A REVIEW OF FACTOR ANALYTIC STUDIES. Technical Report 1 prepared for the Office of Naval Research by the Departments of Industrial Administration and Psychology, New Haven, Yale University Press, 1960.

12. WECHSLER INTELLIGENCE SCALE FOR CHILDREN, New York: The Psychological Corporation, 1949.

13. Wepman, Joseph M., WEPMAN TEST OF AUDITORY DISCRIMINATION. Chicago: Language Research Associates, 1958.

14. Wiseman, Douglass E., THE EFFECTS OF AN INDIVIDUAL REMEDIAL PROGRAM ON MENTALLY RETARDED CHILDREN WITH PSYCHOLINGUISTIC DISABILITIES. Unpublished doctoral dissertation, University of Illinois, 1965.

AN ENGINEERED CLASSROOM DESIGN
FOR EMOTIONALLY DISTURBED CHILDREN

Frank M. Hewett, Ph.D.
Assistant Professor of Education and Medical Psychology
and Head, Neuropsychiatric Institute School, University of California,
Los Angeles, California

FRANK M. HEWETT, Ph.D.

Once a society dedicates itself to the goal of providing educational opportunities for all individuals and possesses the resources for fulfilling such a goal, growing concern may be expected when certain individuals fail to respond and learn by traditional methods. During the past two decades as special education in this country has struggled toward maturity, one group which has aroused concern, particularly in the public schools, is the emotionally disturbed. Children acquire the label of "emotionally disturbed" when their deviate behavior in a learning situation cannot be explained on the basis of physical, sensory, neurological, intellectual or disadvantaged factors. It is a nebulous label with many meanings and it covers a multitude of problem behaviors including inattention, withdrawal, acting out, immaturity, and interpersonal conflicts.

This chapter reports on an approach still in the experimental stage which attempts to extend sound educational practice so that many children labeled "emotionally disturbed" can be included rather than excluded from public school and learn more efficiently in the classroom. (5) The approach was suggested by the work of Bijou and others with institutionalized retardates. (2) It was modified for use with emotionally disturbed children in the Neuropsychiatric Institute School in the Neuropsychiatric Institute (NPI), a California State Department of Mental Hygiene facility located in the University of California, Los Angeles (UCLA) Center for the Health Sciences. The NPI School provides an education program for inpatient children and adolescents hospitalized on the Children's Service of the NPI. These individuals are severely emotionally disturbed and require 24-hour care and supervision.

Despite success in the NPI School setting with the goals and methods to be described, the author was well aware that a far greater number of problem learners who were not so severely disturbed and who did not require hospitalization existed in the community and were dependent on the public schools for their education. This number has been estimated by Bower (3) to be as great as 10% of the entire school population. In an effort to assess whether or not the NPI School procedures were applicable to the public school the author attempted to enlist the support and cooperation of several school districts. Unfortunately, suggestions for innovation in education are often met with reactions of extreme caution and even mistrust and it was initially somewhat difficult to locate school districts willing to investigate a unique approach.

The Tulare County schools in California, however, provided the first opportunity for exploration (4) during a five week summer session. During the next school year the Santa Monica Unified Schools initiated several classes in cooperation with the author. The following summer the University of Hawaii cooperated by setting up a demonstration class for five weeks with children from the Palolo School District in Honolulu.*

After these initial successes in public school settings, a large-scale opportunity for investigating the engineered classroom was provided by the Santa Monica Unified School District in California. Dr. Alfred Artuso, Superintendent of the District, and Mr. Frank Taylor, Director of Special Services, expressed an interest in incorporating the engineered classroom design in the district-wide program for the educationally handicapped. The State of California encompasses children with emotional problems within this classification along with children manifesting minimal neurological impairment and learning disabilities. The Santa Monica Schools had previously utilized several other approaches with educationally handicapped children but none had proven wholly satisfactory. As a result, a unique university and public school liaison was established between the author and the Santa Monica Unified School District, based on research concerns for the development of more effective educational approaches with the emotionally disturbed and the demands placed on the public schools for more adequate service. A U.S. Office of Education Demonstration grant (OE Project 62893) was awarded to the author and the Santa Monica schools to assess the effectiveness of the engineered classroom design and Mr. Thomas J. Taglianetti appointed as coordinator for the project. In the later sections of this chapter many of the procedures and materials described were largely developed in this project and represent contributions made by the Santa Monica staff.

With this introduction to the development of the engineered classroom design we will discuss the nature of the educational problems presented by emotionally disturbed children, the goals and methods inherent in the design and then the specific operations and program of the engineered classroom itself.

Rabinow (7) has aptly called attention to the fact that emotionally disturbed children are often 1) not ready to be in school, 2) however, ready to learn something, and has further pointed out that the dilemma facing the educator is 3) getting such children ready to be in school while they are actually attending school.

*The author is indebted to Mr. Lou Rienzi and Mrs. Blanche Warson of the Tulare County Schools and Dr. George Fargo and Miss Sylvian You of the University of Hawaii for their contributions to the development of the engineered classroom design.

The author has interpreted "not ready to be in school" in a broad context and considers a disturbed child who maintains appropriate behavior in the classroom but who is an inefficient learner "not ready". Being ready to learn implies the capacity to attend to learning tasks and the teacher, to retain information, to respond to a school learning situation, to follow directions, to conform to classroom limits, to readily explore the environment and function appropriately in relation to teachers and peers. The child who does not possess these capacities is in trouble in school.

The uselessness of the label "emotionally disturbed" for the teacher has been alluded to earlier. The entire practice of diagnostic labeling has perplexed and appalled many special educators including the author. Descriptions of children's behavior are inevitable in the process of attempting to understand and help them but when such descriptions are restricted to "second-hand" nomenclature borrowed from the psychiatrist, neurologist, pediatrician or clinical psychologist, they have little, if any, value in the classroom. In an attempt to link diagnosis and description with educational operations a developmental hierarchy of educational tasks has been conceived which delineates seven stages of learning and the tasks which must be accomplished at each level if efficient learning is to occur. This hierarchy is illustrated in Figure 1.

According to the hierarchy the child must learn to pay attention, respond in learning, order his behavior, explore his environment, and function appropriately as a member of a group if he is to master intellectual skills and achieve intrinsic motivation for learning. These levels overlap and the use of the hierarchical framework is primarily for expository purposes. The levels described are related to stages of development basic to the writings of Piaget, Freud, Erikson and Havighurst. By means of the hierarchy the emotionally disturbed child may be described in terms of his deficits in learning readiness. Level-by-level the following tasks are of central importance:

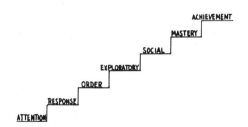

FIGURE 1
A Hierarchy of Educational Tasks

Level-by-level the following tasks are of central importance:

LEVEL	TASKS
Attention	Attending to assignments.
	Preferring reality instead of fantasy.
	Attending to behavior which supports learning rather than ritualistic, compulsive behavior.
	Having appropriate interests and beliefs.
	Attending to the teacher.
	Retaining information.
Response	Responding to assignments
	Not evidencing constriction in learning performance.
	Responding to a wide range of learning interests.
	Approaching teacher and peers.
	Responding in a classroom setting.
Order	Following directions.
	Displaying controlled behavior in learning.
	Functioning within classroom limits.
	Completing assignments.
Exploratory	Acquiring complete and accurate knowledge of the environment.
	Independent interest in exploring the environment.
	Being competent in sensory-motor exploration of the environment.
Social	Obtaining the approval of others.
	Not being overly dependent on the attention and praise of others.
Mastery	Utilizing intellectual capacity in self-care.
	Acquisition of intellectual and academic skills.
Achievement	Pursuing learning on the basis of intrinsic motivation.

Description of the child's behavior according to the hierarchy enables the teacher to replace "second-hand" diagnostic information with terms relevant for classroom instruction. For purposes of illustration the following parallels exist between certain traditional clinical diagnostic terms and the first four levels of the hierarchy.

Attention problems — autism, psychosis, schizophrenia.

Response problems — school phobia, neurotic traits, schizoid personality.

Order problems — primary behavior problems, conduct disturbance.

Exploratory problems — perceptual-motor dysfunction.

Of course, the problems manifested by schizophrenic children are not restricted to the attention level but often the primary task which must be accomplished by the teacher before learning can begin is to help such children learn to pay attention. Similar examples might be given with relation to problems of school phobia, conduct disturbance and perceptual-motor dysfunction.

The hierarchy of educational tasks assists the teacher in locating the "somethings", particularly the initial "something", the child needs to learn. The tasks on the lowest levels which the child has not accomplished have priority over those on higher levels. Children who are competent on the mastery and achievement levels but who lack adequate response, exploratory and social skills should be oriented toward the lower levels even at the expense of academic assignments.

The major contribution of the hierarchy is to alert the teacher to deficits which interfere with the child's learning in school and to focus on emotionally disturbed children's difficulties within a "first-hand" educational rather than "second-hand" psychiatric context.

Two examples from the research literature will illustrate problems commonly displayed by emotionally disturbed children in school. Although these examples do not involve school-age children they will demonstrate why emotionally disturbed children are "not ready" to learn, the fact that they are "ready to learn something", and finally how to "get them ready to be in school while they are actually there."

The first example concerns Peter, a three-year-old participant in a famous experiment done by Jones during the 1920's. (6) Peter was a normal, healthy boy with one exception. He had an aversion toward rabbits and white, furry objects in general. When a rabbit was brought near Peter he exhibited extreme distress. In fact, at such times Peter was not ready to pay attention, respond, order his behavior, explore his environment, function appropriately with others, much less master intellectual tasks. Under such stress Peter's readiness for learning was reduced practically to zero.

Emotionally disturbed children often develop an aversion to the school setting which, like the rabbit for Peter, reduces their readiness to learn to a near zero level. School, however, is not a discrete stimulus but a collection of physical, emotional, intellectual and social cues, many of which converge on the child simultaneously.

Johnny must arrive in the classroom before 9:00 in order not to be tardy, hang his coat up on a hook with his name on it, place his lunch directly overhead, walk in an orderly manner to his desk, sit quietly, ignore the teasing and poking of Billy, his neighbor, across the aisle, and pay attention to the teacher as she starts a spelling lesson, for he may be called on to recite without warning.

While normal children manage to take such stresses and expectations in their stride, the emotionally disturbed child may not be ready to deal with them and when the teacher arbitrarily imposes demands without any consideration of his lack of readiness to be in school in the first place, she is, in effect, demonstrating the same lack of understanding that might have been shown by an individual who directly confronted Peter with a rabbit and impatiently glared at him as he became upset and was unable to adjust to the situation. The case of Peter illustrates that regardless of our knowledge of the "somethings" children need to learn and are ready to learn, unless we give careful consideration to the manner in which we impose our demands on them we may fail before we start.

How can a child like Peter be helped to overcome his fear of rabbits and how can emotionally disturbed children be aided in getting ready for school while they are actually in school? Despite the apparent dissimilarity of problems, the measures taken to help Peter have direct relevance in the classroom. Peter was seated in a room at a table. On the table were many of his favorite foods, including ice cream and a selection of toys which appealed to him. He was immediately drawn to the food and toys, sat quietly and apparently was quite happy eating and playing. In fact, Peter was so content that he hardly noticed when a door, some distance away, was opened and someone stood there holding a rabbit. The rabbit was in the general vicinity of Peter but so rewarding and positive were the activities in which he was engaged that these positive stimuli dominated whatever negative stimuli might have been associated with the rabbit. The rabbit, however, was not brought in and given to Peter at this time. No doubt, had this occurred, Peter would have become upset, ice cream or no ice cream. But a starting point was established in a program to help Peter overcome his aversive reactions to rabbits and he was being helped to get ready to tolerate rabbits while one was actually in his presence.

On subsequent days the rabbit was moved closer and closer but never at a rate which upset Peter. In fact, if Peter had displayed discomfort despite the rewarding objects on the table, the rabbit would no doubt have been withdrawn a distance until he relaxed.

This approach taken with Peter illustrates the significance of three basic factors in learning. First a **suitable task** must be provided all learners. Second, a **meaningful reward** must be present, and third, **structure** must be imposed by the teacher in the presentation of the task which determines the conditions under which the reward is made available.

In another study done by Allyon and Haughton (1) institutionalized psychotic adult patients with severe eating problems were aided in a somewhat similar manner. In most mental hospitals patients who refuse to eat present serious difficulties. A great deal of staff time and effort must go into coaxing and supporting them during mealtime. In some cases spoon-feeding is required to get them to eat. The investigators in this study decided that patients who refused to eat but who had no physical problems which precluded them feeding themselves could be helped to improve their level of functioning. A group of patients with serious eating problems were placed together on a ward. With the cooperation and participation of the medical staff a program was instituted that required all patients to enter the ward dining room in order to be fed. There were to be no exceptions. The initial **task** was to go to the dining room, the **reward** was the obvious receipt of food and the **structure** imposed was that no food would be made available outside the dining room itself. Despite initial reluctance most patients responded. The steps in the program designed to help these patients paralleled the levels of the hierarchy (although this was not the purpose of the study) and demonstrated how gradual introduction of increasingly complex demands can bring about dramatic changes in behavior.

Step I involved the patients being told when it was time to eat and then being allowed an hour to get to the dining room. They were expected to **attend** to the nurse's announcement and the clock and **respond** by going to the dining room. Step II required entrance into the dining room during shorter and shorter periods of time following the nurse's announcement—a half hour, then 15 minutes, and finally five minute intervals were imposed. At this step the task and reward remained the same but the structure was altered and a greater degree of **order** introduced. Step III required that each patient stop by the nurse's office and pick up a penny to deposit in a can at the door to the dining room in order to gain admittance. This step involved an **exploratory** behavior of picking up a coin and placing it in a designated place. Step IV was at the **social** level. Each patient had to get the assistance of a fellow patient in order to obtain a penny. A device was placed in the ward with two buttons on it some seven feet apart. Pennies were available only when the two buttons were pushed simultaneously. The patients quickly adapted to this increased demand and the degree of interaction among them increased considerably as a result.

Had the investigators imposed Step IV initially it probably would have been difficult to achieve success with these patients. It was the selection of a suitable starting point, the systematic provision of a meaningful reward and gradual increase in the structure imposed that insured the success.

The engineered classroom design attempts to incorporate the principles of learning illustrated in these two studies. It considers emotionally disturbed children essentially victims of incomplete or faulty learning, ready, however, to learn something and attempts to get them ready for school while they are actually in school by adherence to the goals of the hierarchy of educational tasks.

In this regard it is important to point out that the goals in the classroom are more critical than the methodology utilized to achieve them. The two studies briefly described are illustrations of the application of behavior modification or conditioning techniques to individuals with behavior problems. The case of Peter was an example of the deconditioning of respondant or involuntary behavior while the work of Allyon and Haughton represented the use of operant conditioning to promote acquisition of behaviors under voluntary control. Other examples of these approaches may be found in a text by Ullmann and Krasner. (8)

Behavior modification methodology is extremely useful in education because it focuses the teacher's attention on small increments of learning and stresses the importance of rewards and systematic structuring in the learning process. It does not, however, delineate appropriate educational goals and, as a result, may be rejected by educators. Over the past three decades an interesting contrast has existed with respect to emphasis on goals and methodology in the education of the emotionally disturbed child. The field was initially strongly influenced by the psychoanalytic approach which stressed resolution of the child's psychic conflicts before imposition of rigid demands for learning. While this approach contributed many educational goals (e.g. development of trust between the child and teacher, initial acceptance of maladaptive behavior) it was limited in terms of the practical methodology it made available to the teacher for achieving these goals. On the other hand the interest in recent years in the behavioristic approach has provided teachers with a practical methodology but few well-defined educational goals.

The hierarchy of educational tasks provides the educational goals for the engineered classroom and the behavior modification approach, the methodology for achieving these goals. The design of the classroom will now be presented in several sections devoted to class size and composition, provision for teacher and an aide, physical arrangement of the classroom, the check mark system, daily schedule, curriculum and classroom operation, and interventions.

CLASS SIZE AND COMPOSITION

Deciding how many emotionally disturbed children can be grouped together in a classroom depends on the degree of disturbance of the children, the number of teachers available, as well as the teaching resources at hand. Some children require individual tutoring while others may work efficiently in groups ranging from two to twenty. The engineered classroom design is based on nine students with a teacher and teacher aide. This number has been arrived at after several years of trial and error exploration and makes possible the organization of the class into subgroups of three students each for various activities. There is no magic in the number nine and engineered classrooms of 10 and 11 students have been successful. However, as class size increases beyond this number, problems of classroom management arise which conflict with the approach central to the design.

In the group of 9 students the author prefers to include 3 children with essentially attention and response problems, three with problems at the order level and three with exploratory and mastery problems. In most groupings of emotionally disturbed children it is hard to find students without problems at the social level and hence these are usually common to all nine children. Again, classes have successfully been set up with different compositions but the author doubts the wisdom of combining 9 extreme response problems in one class group.

To date, the major development of the engineered classroom has been with children from 8 to 12 years of age. Although adaptations have been made with both younger and older levels, the program discussed in this chapter refers, in the main, to the upper-elementary age level.

TEACHERS AND AIDE

The announcement that a teacher and an aide are required in an engineered classroom often elicits a groan from teachers and supervisors who see this as an extravagance beyond the means of most school districts. However, it has been found that an aide is highly desirable and that volunteer parents and high school and college students can be trained to work effectively as aides. One of the goals of the engineered classroom is to make assistance for any student not more than a short time away, and one teacher working alone is not as easily able to meet such a demand. As will soon be apparent, the engineered classroom design is highly structured and creates an unique role for the teacher. The term "engineered" refers to a constant manipulation of the three essential ingredients in learning mentioned earlier—the learning task, provision of meaningful rewards for learning and maintenance of a degree of structure—to insure success for each student. Such a role is demanding for the teacher, particularly at first, and it is probably well to admit at the onset that not all teachers are comfortable having to function in a program that holds them accountable to such an organized system of instruction. While the operations of the classroom appear contrived and mechanistic to some, the majority of teachers who have utilized the engineered approach find that there is more than enough room for expressions of their "teaching artistry". This matter will be discussed again at the close of the chapter.

PHYSICAL ARRANGEMENT OF THE CLASSROOM

The engineered classroom should be set up in a large room which provides at least 100 sq. ft. per student. Rooms with floor plans of 1200 to 1500 sq. ft. have been found to be ideal. Each student is provided with a double desk 2 x 4 ft. and the desks should be separated so that there is several feet between each student. The double desk permits a large working surface for the child and promotes separation from students so that each child has a well defined, independent working area. A large desk also facilitates individual instruction by the teacher by allowing the teacher to sit alongside the child at his desk in a business-like manner.

The room is divided into three major working centers correlated with the levels on the hierarchy. The student desk area is the focal point of the **mastery and achievement center,** and assignments are given here in reading, written language and arithmetic. Also as a part of this center are two study booths or offices which are used by students for academic work. These offices are carpeted, contain upholstered easy chairs and are presented to the students as attractive working areas to help them work free from visual distraction. They are not presented as isolation booths.

The second major center is the **exploratory-social center**, usually set up in the vicinity of the classroom sink. Here, science, art, and communication activities will be undertaken, each at a different table. Science is viewed as an extremely useful exploratory activity because of the opportunity it affords for multisensory exploration and reality testing. Art activities are less structured and allow the child a greater degree of self expression. The communication area provides games which two or more children may engage in and is designed to foster social interaction and development of cooperative behavior. A listening post is included in this area where one or more children may engage in listening to music and story records.

The **attention-response-order center** is the other major defined area in the classroom. It includes two tables and a storage cabinet set up in one corner of the room. The purpose of this center is to engage the child in direction following activities which focus his attention, elicit active participation, and take him through a sequence of steps leading to a conclusion.

There are four bulletin board areas in the room. One is designed as a Student Work Board and is used to display assignments done by the students each week; another is an Assignment Board and features a large wheel used in assigning students to various activities; a third and fourth board are used in connection with the check mark system which is discussed next.

THE CHECK MARK SYSTEM

As has been stressed several times up to this point, an effective learning situation must provide some form of meaningful learner reward. In regular classrooms with normal children this is not a difficult matter, for school is essentially very rewarding. Teacher attention, satisfaction from task accomplishment, sensory-motor rewards of looking, listening, touching and moving, teacher praise, peer group status, and skill acquisition are all available for the child whose performance in the class is such that he obtains them. For the emotionally disturbed child many of these rewards are non-existent, at least if he is placed in a regular classroom. In an effort to guarantee that some meaningful reward is available for even the most resistant learner, the engineered classroom uses a system of token rewards—check marks—which have an exchange value for tangible items such as candy, toys, and trinkets.

The check mark system is an extension of the more traditional reward system relied on by all teachers in classrooms every day and does not preclude the child's developing motivation for other types of rewards mentioned above. In the author's work over a several year period with autistic and other severely disturbed children, he has never found a single child who did not eventually begin to respond for the promise of social attention, task accomplishment, sensory rewards, and even grades. The check mark system functions as an initial procedure which helps get children started learning in a classroom situation which may have an essentially non-rewarding connotation for them as a result of previous experience. The use of check marks along with the small class size, the help of two teachers, and the unique physical arrangement of the room, establishes a totally different educational environment which is intriguing and satisfying. In this respect it serves much the same function as favorite toys which were given Peter. These helped create a totally positive situation before the negative rabbit was introduced.

Each morning as the child enters the classroom he picks up a Work Record Card at the door. This is a 4" x 6" card which is ruled with 200 squares and is kept in a holder on the wall with the child's name on it. As the child goes through the day he receives check marks on the card reflecting his classroom functioning and task accomplishments. Usually, a possible 10 check marks are given following each 15 minute work period. Two checks are given if the child started his work, three if he followed through on the assignment and a possible five bonus checks are administered for "being a student". In an engineered classroom "being a student" refers to different criteria for each student. Teachers use the bonus check marks to reward those aspects of the student's behavior which are most critical to his learning problem and most basic to his deficits on the hierarchy. An extremely inattentive student might be given the five bonus checks for a disordered child for attempting to follow directions; a child not given to ready exploration of his environment if he becomes more involved; a child with social difficulties for displaying appropriate group behavior, cooperating, or waiting his turn; and finally, the child whose primary problems centered around academic deficits would receive his five bonus check marks for doing assignments given him correctly. As the child falls short of the minimal expectation the teacher has for him the number of bonus checks is reduced.

In the giving of the check marks the teacher functions in a non-personal manner much as a shop foreman does when paying workers on an assembly line what they have actually earned during a work period. The attempt is to use the check mark system as a non-conflictual meeting ground for the emotionally disturbed child and the teacher—at least initially devoid of an interpersonal emphasis. The teacher communicates to the child: "This is what you have earned" not "I'm giving you this because I like you" or "Because you did what I asked". Although the interpersonal element obviously cannot be eliminated it is limited at first, particularly with children with serious social problems. As the child gains in his competency at the attention, response, order, exploratory and social levels the emphasis might change and the teacher may acknowledge "I'm pleased because you did that just the way I wanted you to". One of the most important advantages of the check mark system is that it guarantees teacher contact with each child at least three times an hour.

The child totals up his check marks each day and these are graphed on a Work Report kept on his desk. This is illustrated in Figure 2 and allows the child to compare his individual progress day by day. While some children may become preoccupied with the total number of checks being given to their classmates and become competitive regarding comparisons it has been found that a reminder such as "In this room every student earns check marks for doing what he needs to do. Since everyone is working at their own level checks are given for different reasons" causes such behavior to rapidly diminish. All children obtain approximately an equal number each day.

In addition to giving check marks following 15 minute work periods, the teacher may also use the "surprise bonus". When a given child is displaying some behavior close to one of the teacher's goals for him he may be surprised and given five or ten extra check marks on the spot. At other times when the class is having difficulty settling down the teacher may announce "Each student who is ready to work and who has followed my directions will receive five extra check marks". These are then immediately given out to those students who fulfilled the teacher's expectations. No additional comment is made about the students who were "not ready" and who did not receive surprise bonus check marks.

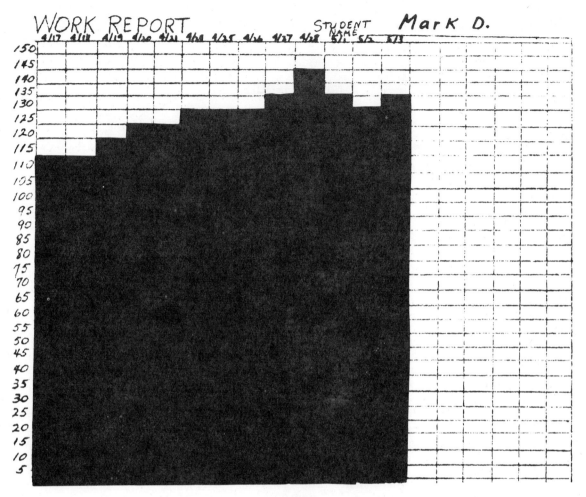

FIGURE 2

Work Report

Completed check mark cards may be exchanged weekly for tangible items and an Exchange Board displays one, two, and three card items. The cost of each item usually averages 5¢ for one card, 10¢ for two cards and 15¢ for three cards. The monetary value of the exchange items has been found to be very insignificant and it appears that the most important factor is that they are earned in the classroom. Children with enough money in their pockets to buy the equivalent of the teacher's entire supply of exchange items at the local 5 & 10¢ store display delight with a five cent item earned with the check marks.

It should be mentioned that the first day of the class when none of the children have ever been in the room before, the teacher places a candy unit on top of each check mark given during the first two hours of the class. Following this, the children are ex-

447

pected to save their check marks and turn completed cards in after longer and longer periods of delay.

DAILY SCHEDULE

The class operates on a 240-minute daily schedule, in line with the State of California minimum for special classes for educationally handicapped children. It runs from 8:30 a.m. to 12:30 p.m. The schedule, including provision for check marks is as follows:

TIME	ACTIVITY	POSSIBLE CHECK MARKS & CRITERIA
8:30 a.m.	Flag salute and Opening exercises	3: Coming on time. 2: Picking up card and going to seat - ready to work
8:35 a.m.	Order	10: Doing order worksheet 2: Starting 3: Following through 5: Bonus for "being a student".
8:40 a.m..	Reading (Skill reading, individual reading, work study).	10: check marks each 15 minutes. (Same criteria as above)
9:40 a.m.	Recess (Outside room)	10: check marks following recess. 2: Leaving the room 5: Behavior during recess 3: Returning and being ready to work.
9:50 a.m.	Arithmetic (skill arithmetic, individual arithmetic, and activity arithmatic)	10: check marks each 15 minutes (same criteria as for reading)
10:50 a.m.	Recess (Nutrition - Inside room)	10: check marks for this period 5: Behavior during recess 5: Being ready to return to work.
11:00 a.m.	Physical Education	10: check marks 2: Leaving the room 5: Behavior during the period 3: Returning and being ready to work.
11:20 a.m.	Exploratory (Science, art, and communication).	10: check marks following each 15 minutes (same criteria as for Arithmetic and Reading)
12:20 p.m.	Check Out	Total number of check marks received for the day are graphed on the child's Work Report on his desk.

CURRICULUM AND CLASSROOM OPERATIONS

The initial **order period** is designed to settle the students down and involve them in a short direction-following task stressing control and completion. Commercially available perceptual motor training worksheets are used along with simple tracing, design copying, and visual discrimination tasks designed by the Santa Monica staff.

The **reading program** takes place three times weekly, and as can be seen from the schedule, is divided into three 15 minute periods. The assignment wheel shown in Figure 3 assigns three children to each of the three activities in rotation. The center wheel is turned every 15 minutes. **Individual reading** is done at the teacher aide's desk with each child. The child brings his work reader (a basal or remedial text close to his actual functioning level) to the desk and reads aloud for a three minute period. The three minutes are timed by a small hour-glass which the child turns over when he is ready to start reading. As the child correctly completes each line of reading material the teacher aide deposits a candy award (M & M) in a paper cup beside him. The aide also keeps a record of each word the child miscalls and these are printed on a 3 x 5 file card for later study. At the end of the 3 minute period the child is asked several comprehension questions and then takes the cup of candy and new reading words back to his desk. Candy is used in this activity rather than check marks because of the high motivation exhibited by students for practicing their reading before going to the teacher aide's desk and their good concentration during oral reading. The presence of the candy does not seem to distract the child and careful attention is given by the teacher to the level of the child's work reader so that he will both achieve success and learn new words. Inevitably the question is raised about dental and health problems in relation to the giving of candy during the activity. Where such problems exist raisins, sunflower seeds, or peanuts have proven equally effective.

FIGURE 3

Assignment Wheel for Reading Period

After each child in a given group has had individual reading the center wheel is turned, the teacher has all students put down their work and both teacher and aide circulate giving children their check marks. This takes approximately three to five minutes and the children are expected to wait quietly for their check marks. The bonus check marks given for "being a student" will reflect such "waiting" behavior.

Next, the groups move to either **word study** or **skill reading. Word study** is done at the child's desk. The teacher circulates (while the aide continues individual reading with another group of three students) and goes over accumulated reading words with each child. The cards are flashed before him and he is held for recognition. As the child correctly reads a word the teacher puts a plus on it and after three successive correct readings the card is filed away alphabetically in a small file box on the child's desk and no longer reviewed. Spelling words acquired during story writing to be discussed later are also reviewed at this time.

Following word study the center wheel is turned and check marks are given all students. It is important to point out that during the check mark giving period not only is the previous assignment corrected and acknowledged with check marks but the next 15 minute assignment is introduced. It has been found that this type of individual transition period is very useful in maintaining the work-oriented atmosphere in the class. The teacher does not rely on verbal directions from the front of the class or repeatedly calling out "Boys and girls! Boys and girls! That means you too, Henry! Give me your attention! I am waiting for two people in row three." etc.

Skill reading involves an independent vocabulary and comprehension building activity and commercial materials, including programmed units, are used. The Santa Monica staff has developed several types of word games, decoding exercises, and other activities for use with poor readers who cannot work for any extensive periods of time in reading. The interventions used to assist a child who cannot do a reading assignment or any other assignment for a period of time will be discussed in a later section.

Twice a week **story writing** is done by the entire class rather than in small groups. The teacher usually makes a short motivation presentation in some area of interest to the class (e.g. knighthood, deep sea life) and the students are expected to write about the topic. This is a difficult activitiy to get children with severe reading and spelling problems to engage in and alternate activities are available for those unable to write. The Santa Monica staff has prepared simple sentence completion and picture labeling materials for these children.

Following either reading or story writing, the class is dismissed for recess. This is taken outside the room and as each child leaves he puts his Work Record Card away in its holder. Upon returning the card is picked up and the children receive a possible ten check marks for the recess period.

The **arithmetic** period occupies the next hour. Students work for 15 minute intervals on two or three types of number work. The entire class works on the same type of assignment although it is individualized for each child. Arithmetic fundamentals including basic addition and subtraction, facts and concepts, the multiplication tables and process, and division are assigned as appropriate. Following this, arithmetic skills are put to work in problem solving. Students are given specially prepared worksheets or use standard texts. For the student who is able to pursue longer work periods this activity may take up two 15-minute intervals, although the child will be asked to stop his work in order to receive check marks half-way through. The Santa Monica staff has developed multi-level arithmetic drill sheets which can be quickly altered to fit a particular child's level in addition, subtraction, multiplication, or division and these may be used with slower students during both the drill and skill periods. For the child who cannot handle a 15-minute work period in arithmetic, work sheets involving measurement, counting, form discrimination, and coloring are utilized for one or more intervals. It is important to stress that during arithmetic, however, all students receive check marks following each 15-minute interval.

The 10-minute nutrition period is held in the room and the children have a snack. They are allowed to move about the room and various free-time activities are available. Ten check marks are given following this period and the children leave the room for physical education. Work Record Cards are taken outside to the playground and checks given when students reach the play area, finish their play, and return to the room.

Following the physical education period a 10 to 15 minute group listening activity may be used to help students effect a transition from the active play on the playground to the more restricted behavior in the classroom. During this time the teacher reads a portion of a continuing story aloud.

The final period of the day is devoted to **exploratory** activities. For this period the wheel shown in Figure 4 is utilized. The same groupings used during the reading period are employed. Each 15 minutes three children go to the science area, three to the art area, and three to the communication area. The teacher remains in the science area and introduces a specific science task to each group as they rotate to the area. The aide circulates between the art and communication areas. Following each 15 minute interval all children return to their desks, receive their check marks and are reassigned by means of the wheel. The Santa Monica staff has devised a series of science tasks in such areas as magnetism, air, sound, light, chemistry, and has prepared cards for each task similar to the one illustrated in Figure 5. Each task is selected for its intriguing interest value

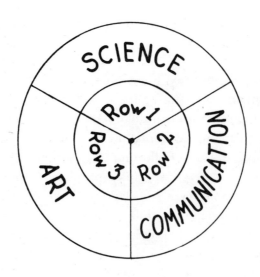

FIGURE 4

Assignment Wheel
for Exploratory Period

TASK Nº 1 \ MAGNETS

FIGURE 5
Science Task Card

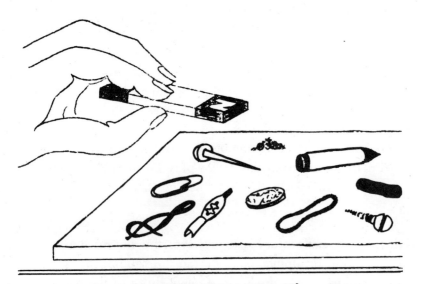

DIRECTIONS

1. Hold a magnet near each item placed on display table.
2. List the items that a magnet attracts
3. List the items that it won't attract.

rather than because it falls within any particular grade level curriculum. It may be re-called that the exploratory level falls below the mastery level and hence science ex-periments are chosen for their multisensory rather than intellectual value. Nevertheless, simple, accurate descriptions of all science experiments are given by the teacher to each group. Following the introduction of each day's science task, the card is filed at the center and is available for students during the interventions to be described in the next section.

Art activities are varied and have been organized by the Santa Monica staff to include projects, such as the one illustrated in Figure 6. An attempt is made to keep these tasks simple so that they can be completed within a 15 minute work period. However, the children may continue them one day to the next. The art task cards are also filed at the art area for later reference and replication.

TASK N°. 3 SCRIBBLE DESIGN

Material: crayons, glue,
9"x 12" white construction paper,
dark construction paper,
scissors, brush, watercolor.

DIRECTIONS

1. Using a yellow crayon, make a scribble design on a 9"x12" sheet of white construction paper.
2. Color each section a different color, out-line each section with black crayon.
3. Apply a watercolor wash over design.
4. Cut out and mount on dark paper.

FIGURE 6
Art Task Card

Communication tasks similar to the one shown in Figure 7 are introduced during the exploratory period and are also kept filed at the communication area for later usage. Since games entered into by two or more children inevitably involve a winner, those based more on chance rather than skill have proven most successful.

After the final 15-minute exploratory interval the children return to their seats and the final check marks are given. Following this the child's total number of checks received during the day are counted by the teacher and entered on his Work Report. The children then return their cards to the Work Record holder and leave the room. Check mark exchanges are held once a week, usually on Friday, at the end of the day.

FIGURE 7

Communication Task Card

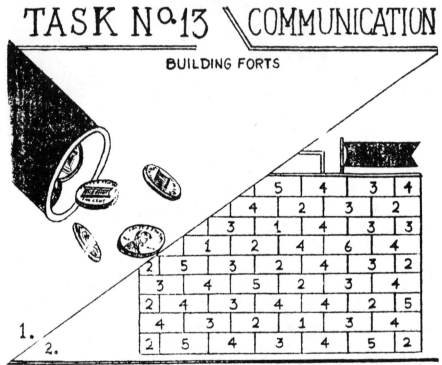

TASK N⍛13 \ COMMUNICATION

BUILDING FORTS

DIRECTIONS

1. Each player is given a fort to "build" (a blank sheet).

2. Each player shakes a cup filled with six pennies, and rolls the pennies on the table.

3. The player colors in the bricks of his fort, depending on how the pennies turn up. (Each head equals one point.)

INTERVENTIONS

Whenever it becomes apparent that a given task cannot be successfully accomplished by the child the teacher must be prepared to re-assign him so that he does not fail. Just as the rabbit occasionally had to be moved back from Peter when it was brought too close during de-conditioning, the teacher must be prepared to reduce school expectations to insure that the emotionally disturbed child is successful at any given moment.

In the engineered classroom this is taken care of by means of a series of interventions which involve descending the hierarchy of educational tasks until a level is found where the child can succeed and earn check marks. As long as the student can function with an assignment at any of the levels of the hierarchy he earns his full complement of check marks. There is no penalty attached to re-assignment at lower level tasks.

The interventions will be discussed one by one. In actual practice the teacher may try them one at a time or, most likely, select the one that appears to be most appropriate for a given child at a given moment. An intervention is necessary when a child exhibits resistance, withdrawal, anxiety, or frustration. The ideal time for initiation of an intervention is in anticipation of the actual problem, or very shortly after the first sign of inability or unwillingness to do an assigned task. The first seven interventions are considered "student interventions" because they involved the child's continuing to earn check marks at all times. Interventions eight and nine are "non-student interventions" because they do not enable the child to continue earning check marks.

1. Send Student to Study Booth. (Mastery level)

The first intervention involves sending the child to work on an assigned mastery task in one of the study booths or "offices". It has been pointed out that these booths are presented to the children in a positive manner and as a result they are desirable working areas. In being sent to the booth the child picks up a "pass" (cut-out wooden key painted yellow) from the teacher's desk and hangs it on the wall inside the booth. This signifies his assignment to the study booth for a period of time. It has been observed that merely allowing the child to change position and move around in the room appears to interrupt a period of boredom or upset effectively.

2. Modify Assignment. (Mastery level)

The next logical intervention in terms of the hierarchy and the engineered classroom philosophy is to change the mastery task given the child, either making it easier, different, or perhaps more difficult in an effort to get him involved. Sending the student to the study booth with a modified assignment may also be used at this time.

3. Re-structure Verbally. (Social level)

When the mastery interventions described above are not successful or appear inappropriate an intervention at the social level is next in line for consideration. This intervention involves verbal restructuring on the part of the teacher, using social approval or disapproval as leverage. The child is reminded of the teacher's expectation for him in relation to the assigned task and his behavior. It has been previously mentioned that interactions between teacher and child in the engineered classroom are largely task-oriented because of the poor relationships with adults previously experienced by many emotionally disturbed children. Nevertheless, with some students a reminder by the teacher regarding what is expected may be all that is necessary to help them improve their behavior. This intervention is perhaps most often used by teachers in regular classroom with children who display problem behavior and often reinforces the child's negative concept of school and teachers. Therefore it should be only used after careful consideration and it is often deleted in the intervention process.

4. Send to Exploratory Center. (Exploratory Level)

The next intervention re-assigns the child to another task center in the room. Upon direction the child picks up a blue pass key from the teacher's desk and goes to the exploratory center where he hangs it on the wall, signifying re-assignment to this area. The teacher selects one of the previously demonstrated science, art, or in some cases, communication tasks and assigns it to the child, making sure all the materials are available and that he understands what to do. Assignments at the exploratory center are always teacher-selected.

5. Send to Order Center. (Order Level)

Since the exploratory center involves a high degree of stimulation it may not be as appropriate for some disturbed children at a given time as the Order Center. After picking up a red pass key at the teacher's desk, the child hangs it on the wall by the order center and is given a simple direction-following task such as making a puzzle, copying a pegboard design, stringing beads, deciphering a secret code with the aid of a key, or constructing a model of plastic or metal components.

6. Take Student Outside and Agree on a Task. (Response Level)

In an effort to maintain contact with the student and keep him earning check marks an intervention at the response level may be undertaken outside the room. Both student and teacher go out of the classroom and agree on some task the child will undertake, such as turning somersaults on the lawn, swinging on a swing for 15 minutes, punching a punching bag, or even resting in the nurse's office for a period of time. If the student successfully completes the task he is given his full complement of check marks and returned to the room. Following a response intervention the teacher attempts to select some assignment in the classroom to insure the student's success.

7. Provide Individual Tutoring and Increase Check Marks. (Attention Level)

The intervention corresponding to the lowest level on the hierarchy involves the teacher devoting full time to individual instruction with the student. Such individual tutoring is not always possible for extended periods of time because of the needs of the other students, but it is the next logical step to take in order to help the child. It may also include doubling the number of check marks given the child during a 15 minute period or in some cases going back to placing a candy unit on top of each check mark.

8. Time Out. (Non-student)

Interventions eight and nine are non-student interventions and require that the child give up his Work Record Card and the opportunity to earn check marks for a time. During the time-out intervention the child is told that he cannot earn check marks for a five, ten, or fifteen minute period, during which he must sit in isolation, usually in the principal's office. Following this time-out period the child is immediately returned to the class with no questions asked. As long as he sat quietly during the time-out period he is able to return to the classroom and begin earning checkmarks again. In returning the child to class the teacher will select an intervention level which seems to hold promise of successfully re-integrating him back into class. There is no extracting of promise that the child "be a good boy" or statement to the effect that "you can return when you feel you can control yourself". The student's return is based solely on the clock and there is no verbal pressuring on the part of the teacher or principal. In regard to this and the final intervention, the importance of total school support, including the office clerks and the principal cannot be minimized. Fortunately, in the Santa Monica project, there has been consistent cooperation evident from the Superintendent's office to each level in the individual schools.

9. Exclusion (Non-student)

When the child is unable to tolerate a given time-out period or has to be placed in a time-out intervention three times in one day, he is immediately excluded from school and if at all possible, sent home. There is no "lecture" given by anyone in the school. He is merely told he cannot remain in school because it appears he cannot "function as a student". He will be permitted to return the next day "with no hard feelings". If a given student has to be sent home three times in one semester he must earn his way back into class and can only attend one hour the first day; two the next, and so on.

As can be seen from the nature of the interventions, an attempt is made to move the "noxious rabbit" of school demands as far out of the picture as may be necessary in order to maintain the child in a successful learning situation. When it is apparent that no amount of task manipulation will successfully engage the student in learning, the final consequence of exclusion is the only resource left. It should be stressed again that time-out or exclusion carries no "bad boy" connotation with it, but represents a "fact of life" which the student must be made aware of when he is unable to meet the school and the teacher even a small part of "half-way".

Many aspects of the engineered classroom design have been utilized by teachers of emotionally disturbed children for years. The use of an aide, small class groupings, activity centers and an individualized instructional approach is not new to education; nor is the notion that children who are not ready to learn must be helped to get ready in school a novel one. In the past, teachers of children with learning problems have been aware that a different task orientation was required with their students but the importance of providing meaningful rewards for learning and maintaining systematic structure often has been overlooked. While "success experience in school" has become the major goal for all exceptional children, including the emotionally disturbed, suitable methodologies to aid in the attainment of such a goal have been slow to develop. The model utilized by Jones with Peter and the rabbit demonstrated such a methodology, as did the systematic shaping of behavior accomplished by Allyon and Haughton with institutionalized psychotic patients.

The engineered classroom design attempts to take the goal of "success experience" and implement it through behavior modification methodology. Few educators would argue with such a goal, but often there is a considerable reaction to the means utilized in the engineered classroom design for achieving it. Concerns typically center around reliance on extrinsic rewards, questions about eventual reintegration into the regular classroom, and the "technician" status of the teacher in the engineered classroom.

The use of tangible rewards in school has been viewed by some as an unwholesome compromise with educational values and as outright bribery. This reaction is probably related to the term "reward" rather than the principle of acknowledging certain appropriate behaviors in school through systematic positive consequences. Providing the grade of "A" for outstanding effort constitutes an acceptable means of acknowledging a student's performance in the classroom but rewarding him with check marks which have a tangible exchange value may not be seen in the same light. Actually, there is little difference between the two approaches except that the grade represents a more sophisticated and highly socialized acknowledgment as compared with check marks which are more concrete and primitive in nature. The principle of acknowledgment of accomplishment, however, is identical.

Emotionally disturbed children are often less sophisticated and socialized learners than children who function effectively in regular classrooms and the provision for tangible rewards is viewed as a logical and temporary extension of the traditional system of acknowledgment relied on by all educators. The term "temporary" is used advisedly, for in the author's experience the check marks and later tangible exchange items lose their potency fairly quickly and once the child is involved in a successful learning experience he naturally moves toward the seeking of more traditional educational rewards such as task accomplishment, sensory motor experience, social status, praise and grades.

In this regard reintegration of children back into regular classrooms from the engineered classroom has proven surprisingly uncomplicated. The fears of those who would predict that children given tangible rewards in school for learning would have to be followed around for the rest of their lives and immediately rewarded with candy for each task they accomplish are completely unfounded. As the child learns to pay attention, respond, follow directions, explore his environment, obtain status as an accepted member of a peer group in the classroom and master the basic academic skills he becomes a ready candidate for reintegration. The engineered classroom is presented to the student from the very beginning as a special program to help him "catch up" as quickly as possible. Often children express continued interest in going back to their regular classroom and once their achievement level is close to their expected grade level they are reintegrated for limited periods each day. The true value of the engineered classroom seems to be that in this totally unique classroom environment where success is guaranteed and small units of accomplishment are continuously acknowledged on an immediate and concrete basis the child gains confidence and ability, and rather than regressing he begins to progress, in some cases for the first time in several years.

The role assigned to the teacher in the engineered classroom is also unique. This role is based on the assumption that a task-oriented relationship between teacher and child is more conducive to remediating learning deficits rather than one with an interpersonal emphasis. The teacher is directed to use non-verbal means of relating to students whenever possible. Excessive verbiage is seen as a hindrance when working with emotionally disturbed children because of the vagueness of word symbols and negative associations with adults who "lecture" and "criticize".

The giving of checkmarks every 15 minutes and correcting each child's work during this period admittedly places an extra burden on the teacher, as does the systematic reassignment of students who experience difficulty during the day. While the engineered concept probably runs counter to some teacher's personality and teaching style to such a degree that it would be unwise to expect them to implement it, the author has found that most teachers of emotionally disturbed children respond positively to it, once they establish the routine.

It seems that provision of rewards for teachers in teaching is often minimized or over-looked. With emotionally disturbed children these rewards may be few and far between because of the unpredictability and variability of the children themselves. The engineered classroom design increases the probability of the teacher receiving rewards because, through a constant assessment of what each child needs and can do success-fully, a clearer picture of teaching goals is provided, and more frequent indications of the child's progress made available.

It is not the intent of the engineered classroom design to reduce the teacher to the level of a mere "technician". While the emphasis on structure and routine and non-verbal direction alters the traditional teacher's role, there is still a great deal of room for pro-fessional teaching competence and creativity. It is also not the intent of the program to impose such a role on the teacher indefinitely. The engineered classroom is largely a plan for building emotionally disturbed children's competency at the attention-response, order and exploratory levels, and hence "launch" them into learning. In future years variations of the engineered classroom may be developed which focus on social mastery, and achievement levels to a greater degree.

This chapter has reported on a classroom design still in the experimental stage, which attempts to help emotionally disturbed children get ready for school while they are actually in school. It views emotional disturbance in an educational context as a lack of readiness for learning and postulates a hierarchy of educational tasks which provides the program goals. Behavior modification techniques are utilized in providing meaning-ful rewards and establishing suitable structure in the classroom. While the use of tangi-ble rewards and the degree of structure and routine in the program is in direct contrast to some of the more traditional approaches with emotionally disturbed children, the design has been found practical and effective in the public schools with children who have long histories of maladaptive behavior in the classroom, including serious learning deficits.

A portion of the work presented herein was performed pursuant to a grant from the U.S. Office of Education, Department of Health, Education and Welfare.

References

1. Allyon, T., & Haughton, E., CONTROL OF THE BEHAVIOR OF SCHIZOPHRENIC PATIENTS BY FOOD, Journal of Experimental Analysis of Behavior, 5:343-354, 1962.

2. Bijou, S., Birnbrauer, J., Wolf, M., and Kidder, J., PROGRAMMED INSTRUCTION IN THE CLASSROOM. In L. Ullman & L. Krasner (Eds.) Case Studies in Behavior Modification, New York: Holt, Rinehart and Winston, 1965.

3. Bower, E.M., THE EDUCATION OF EMOTIONALLY HANDICAPPED CHILDREN, Sacramento, California, California State Department of Education, 1961.

4. Hewett, F., THE TULARE EXPERIMENTAL CLASS FOR EDUCATIONALLY HANDICAPPED CHILDREN, California Education, 3:6-8, 1966.

5. Hewett, F., EDUCATIONAL ENGINEERING WITH EMOTIONALLY DISTURBED CHILDREN, Exceptional Children, 33:459-471, 1967.

6. Jones, M.C., A LABORATORY STUDY OF FEAR: THE CASE OF PETER, Pedagogical Seminary, 31:308-316, 1924.

7. Rabinow, R., THE ROLE OF THE SCHOOL IN RESIDENTIAL TREATMENT FOR CHILDREN, American Journal of Orthopsychiatry, 25:685-691, 1955.

8. Ullman, L. & Krasner, L., CASE STUDIES IN BEHAVIOR MODIFICATION, New York: Holt, Rinehart & Winston, 1961.

THE STATUS OF RECENT AND CURRENT BEHAVIORAL RESEARCH WITH IMPLICATIONS FOR NEW EDUCATIONAL PROGRAMS FOR THE RETARDED

Max G. Frankel, Ph.D.,
Associate Professor and Director,
Education of the Exceptional, School of Education,
The Catholic University of America,
Washington, D. C.

MAX G. FRANKEL, Ph. D.

Realization of the goals of prevention and remediation of mental retardation requires extensive research and service programs in the behavioral, biological, and social sciences.

With the development of educational programs for the culturally disadvantaged and the retarded , the need for closer articulation between the two areas is becoming more and more evident.

The purpose of this paper is to review the current tides of behavioral research which have implications for the education and training of the mentally retarded individual. This being a huge task, accordingly, this article will limit itself primarily to supported research and to that which has direct bearing on education. Among the many areas to which the research lends itself, we have selected those in which actual research is currently being undertaken. It is also our object to briefly discuss the more recent findings and program suggestions for the culturally deprived where this is appropriate to the discussion of the major topic.

The substantive areas of behavioral research which holds a challenge to the behavioral and social scientists interested in mental retardation are: language development and communication; the multiply-handicapped; motivation; cultural deprivation; learning; free-operant conditioning; and motor functions.

SOCIAL BEHAVIOR

Current research is attempting to deal with the problem that available measures of social adaptation are inadequate in evaluating the development of social adaptation.

An apparent step in this direction is current research utilizing an urban population in which an effort is being made to gain information concerning attitudes toward child rearing practices and these compared with analysis of records of services in the community for the mentally retarded. Other studies focus on vocational rehabilitation from the standpoint of seeking to discover the psycho-social factors accounting for occupational success or failure or are investigating the problem of improvement of the social perceptions, social inferences and the behaviors of the mentally retarded adolescent in social situations. Study in the social sphere aims to find out to what extent educable mentally retarded children can be helped to participate in group activities for normal children. Other research is concerned with the major attitudes of parents toward their children and the relationship this may have to social growth of the child, and with study of relationships between parental attitudes and social adjustment of pre-school retarded children which is contributing to an understanding of the attitudes of parents toward retarded children. Study of self-attitudes and emotional adjustment in the mentally retarded is increasing understanding of the dynamics of their behavior, both for the institutionalized and the non-institutionalized. Meanwhile study is in progress to examine the reactions of a large number of parents to information that their child is suspected of mental retardation.

PERSONALITY

Current research seems to be designed along the lines of ascertaining the basis of the discrepancy between performance and potential and the role played by anxiety, early social experiences and early learning experiences in the development of this discrepancy. These investigations seem to be geared along the lines of naturalistic studies of the everyday behavior of the retarded which might reveal information about the most appropriate aspects to study and which could yield concepts which are particularly applicable to this study of the personality.

A growing body of research literature is available on the effects of psychotherapy with the mentally retarded. Much of this has been conducted by clinical psychologists and some by psychiatrists. Considerable controversy exists in the field as to the extent and degree of personality disorders found among the mentally retarded. In spite of the fact that very few of the studies can be classed as experimental since no adequate control groups are used, nevertheless, these investigations have value in contributing to general knowledge.

Relationships between serious emotional factors and mental retardation are being looked at in several current researches. These range from inter-disciplinary programs aimed toward remediation, to studies of work preferences of retarded psychiatric patients and to the study of the exposure of mental deficiency following treatment of children with psychosis. They include the study of the manifestations of the etiology of anti-social behavior at its very beginning in the early childhood years, where retarded children are included in the population, and also include seeking a reliable means of describing the "problem" behavior of adolescence and are contributing toward a concise understanding of adaptive behavior based on a "behavioral diagnostic system."

The retarded delinquent has also been given some attention in the rehabilitation setting where the principle of reinforcement is applied to modify and eliminate undesirable anti-social behavior.

Research is in process to study the effects of a retarded child in the family upon the personalities of fathers.

CULTURAL DEPRIVATION

The recent interest in the educational problems of the deprived has included an awareness of their kinship with the educational problems of the mentally retarded.

From the recent research findings a general conclusion may be drawn that the culturally deprived develop different linguistic patterns than those of the predominant middle class culture. These studies also bear out the conclusion that the infants from the high income class families are sharply contrasted to the infants from low income families by the faster speech sounds they develop.

Present research in intellectual development in lower class urban children is directed to establish correlations between the disadvantaged and/or significant underachievement and specific characteristics of a child and his family background.

Some studies made in the field of speech development suggest that the children of low income groups master only the "public language." In contrast, the middle class child can use, in addition to the public language, a formal language which he develops at home through conversation with parents. It is this factor which is believed to strongly handicap the lower class child's success.

In addition, personality differences are also reported in a number of studies dealing with social and economic deprivation. Also, feelings of inadequacy and insecurity are reported to increase with their growth. There is indisputable evidence of a much higher incidence of severe behavior disorders among the deprived than is found in the middle classes. It is not surprising that the motivational frame of the retarded is apparently different from those of normal individuals. They suffer a definite disadvantage because they lack the setting of a culturally-sound home, responsible and prudent parents, and early experiences of success and encouragement.

Low income groups also have been found to possess a verbal skill which is consumed in general intelligence and fails to find expression through some specific area of ability.

A growing body of research literature is available which suggests the kind of curriculum necessary if the culturally deprived are to achieve their full academic potential. Still, there is in evidence a growing need for extensive investigation to identify the psychological and cultural factors which influence the development and adequacy of functioning in various spheres of behavior.

MOTIVATION

Motivation and cognitive factors and the role they play in the performance of the mentally retarded is the subject of current research. Studies on motivation being closely linked with those of learning and personality development, it is, indeed, difficult to discuss motivation separately.

Because of a continuous chain of inadequate performance in evaluative situations, the retarded individual is skeptical of himself and, so, performs in school with high anxiety. Recent studies show that the retarded are not charged with high achievement motivation and are content with lower levels of accomplishment in comparison with normal individuals.

A current piece of research on motivation is specially directed to determine the influences of external motivators — such as praise, censure, and aspiration — upon the performance of retardates on a manipulation task.

In a study related to but not specifically dealing with retardates, new findings lend to support the generalization that cerebral-palsied children are adequately or highly motivated when a group of children are individually compared. Further work needs to be done on the relationship of motivation to other personality characteristics, and on the determination of motivation or lack of it in cerebral-palsied children, on self-attitude and attitude toward others and the parents' attitude toward the child, from whence the child's own attitudes are presumably learned.

ADJUSTMENT

Concern is presently with factors affecting vocational rehabilitation training success such as socio-economic status and parent participation while similar factors are being related to the retardate's success in school. Another study is interested in the extent to which the persons identified as retarded during childhood years are still identified as retarded after reaching adulthood.

The occupational needs of the young adult retardate are being looked at through investigation of the value of various behavioral indices in predicting work performance along with an attempt to suggest possible patterns of services that could be developed in the rehabilitation setting.

Attention is being given to the counseling needs of these youngsters which involve research to evaluate client-counselor communication in counseling.

Also under investigation is the adolescent's expressed level of understanding of selected occupations and the degree of realism with which he regards the jobs that he thinks he can obtain when leaving school.

INTERDISCIPLINARY APPROACHES TO DIAGNOSIS

There is evidence now of studies and demonstration projects which emphasize a comprehensive approach to diagnostic assessment and evaluation of children and adults with mental retardation both on a resident and out-patient basis. Included are such features as a university branch-wide interdisciplinary plan which includes training personnel in all concerned professions at several levels of experience.

ACADEMIC

The relationship between training experience and selective personality characteristics of teachers and the school progress of retarded children is now under scrutiny. Teacher effectiveness is defined in terms of the progress of the children and when this factor is related to effectiveness this has a potential for revealing some important basic factors in such areas as teacher selection, structuring teacher training programs and developing improved teacher certification codes.

Academically oriented research leading toward the development of materials and methods is the aim of current study comparing several selected approaches to the teaching of reading which hopefully point to innovations in educational programs.

In evidence is research designed to test the efficacy of a specific curriculum and method for teaching mentally retarded children as compared with standard types of programs.

Based on the notion that dependency is a basis for effective socialization it is noted that a partial failure in learning dependency contributes to learning problems of the retardate, according to current research. Following these assumptions the purpose of the research is to determine whether dependency relationship can be used to increase the effectiveness of audio-visual teaching techniques with the young retardate.

Along the same line are researches in evidence to investigate number concept development in retarded children including the concept of numerical equivalence.

LANGUAGE DEVELOPMENT AND COMMUNICATION

Until recently, most of the research on the linguistic problems of the mentally retarded has been of a descriptive nature and little was achieved to determine whether speech and language could be modified. It is fortunate that currently interest in this area has been oriented toward practical application.

Perhaps the most encouraging feature of research on speech and language had been the development of assessment devices, for these tests are stimulating research. The most recent devices are represented by the theory-based tests which concentrate on assessing linguistic abilities per se: the Differential Language Facility Test, the Illinois Test of Psycholinguistic Abilities, and the Peabody Language Scale. The research on these tests accounts for the phenomenal growth of the recent research literature on the subject.

It is likely that the same factors which lead to mental retardation also contribute to linguistic problems. With this in view, current supported research is concentrating on the study of the incidence and nature of the interaction produced by the co-existence of intellective and linguistic defects, and the damage this interaction causes to both functions.

There are two known major causes of intellectual and linguistic defects: environmental and genetic. Certain researchers tend to equate environment with "culture." The old concept that the large proportion of retarded mental development was due to hereditary factors largely unamenable to treatment is giving way to the realization that environmental sources, more amenable to control, contribute substantially to the problem. Current research is concerned with approaches to communication behavior among this specified population and with investigating learning and language processes in this group.

Social interaction is also being considered in relation to communication behavior. Efforts are continuing to assess the speech and language abilities of lower social class mothers and their children using the traditional pattern of language. It has been established that there exists a clear link between the linguistic retardation in these mothers and corresponding deficits in their children.

The bulk of research on receptive linguistic ability has been on hearing problems. But, the relationship of sensory processes to each other in language learning and usage is largely unexplored. There have been numerous attempts at improving the linguistic abilities. In general, encouraging results have been obtained with the educable retarded, though the trainable child remains a problem.

Recent research suggests that there is much room for research on the more affective aspects of linguistic behavior including not only reinforcement but motivational and purely affective factors as well. Several theories have emerged with regard to the linguistic behavior of retarded children. The role of theory, however, is one of chief value to this area because the research within the past decade on the linguistic problems of the retarded has sprung from one of these theories.

THE MULTIPLY-HANDICAPPED

Mentally deficient children frequently have multiple handicaps. Present investigations do throw some light, though not adequately, on the relation between the retarded child and multiple handicaps. Much thought is currently being given to the education of multi-handicapped children, but to date less research and less understanding is available regarding this group of exceptional children than for any of the other clinical groups.

An investigation of techniques of testing sub-normal children and adults to determine the sensitivity of hearing is part of investigation to uncover the most suitable training program for retarded blind and deaf children.

Recent related research suggests a serious need exists for services to multi-handicapped children with visual impairment. Handicaps in addition to blindness present unique problems for which radical solutions exist through the modification of methods of instruction. As the schools attempt to provide for as many exceptions as possible, the number that will be identified as having secondary deviations or multiple handicaps will automatically increase.

The hopelessness and confusion which have characterized the situation of multi-handicapped children, has of late deservedly caught the attention of the research experts. The residential schools, too, have a function to perform with multiply-handicapped children where mental retardation is a primary concern. Recent survey material shows that most residential schools have not accepted this as a major responsibility but should be urged to do so.

NEUROLOGICAL CONSIDERATIONS

Since 1950, the literature has become increasingly marked by clinically oriented articles reporting studies of disabilities relating to the general concept of minimal brain dysfunction in children.

It is now possible to diagnose various neurological and sensory disorders at a very early age. If proper treatment is started at once, some forms of mental retardation can be prevented.

Study continues of the concomitants of cerebral lesion in children. Motor performance characteristics are being studied in association with such behavioral characteristics as distractability and hyperactivity. Comparison of groups of children with well defined cerebral lesion with "minimal brain damage" and those without known cerebral lesion are being carried out relative to the effects of known abilities relating to various known cerebral lesion variables.

MOTOR FUNCTIONS

In order to test whether a motor handicap would result in cognitive integrative ability, certain tests have recently been devised. The results have indicated that there is a significant decrease in integrative ability in children with a motor handicap, with a tendency for increased severity of handicap to result in a corresponding decrease in integrative ability. There is no evidence, however, that a motor handicap produces a kind of deviate thinking in the child, or necessarily forces him to extremes of deviate thinking.

Certain recent studies have shown that imbecile level mental retardates do respond differentially to different kinds of incentives. Investigations have also been conducted to determine motor performance of retardates as a function of competition with same and opposite sex opponents.

Retardates, particularly those who are nonambulatory, may need special training in order to develop motor skills. According to an ongoing study, exercise in large-scale "total" motion makes even severely handicapped children more independent over a period of weeks. Training of the purely manual skills should come only after such motion education.

To gain data not attainable by the present tests, visual motor functions have more recently come under scrutiny in the form of the development of measures for use during the developmental process.

COGNITIVE PROCESSES

In evidence are studies dealing with cognitive functioning and specific handicaps in verbal facility. These are related to non-verbal conceptual and symbolic learning and transfer tasks. Other efforts are in the direction of applying the conceptual framework of developmental psychology to thought processes. Current direction of investigation is following up on findings that the differences between retarded and average children on a variety of measures are lessened when the developmental levels are equal and when the tasks are appropriate to the group. Certain productive thinking traits of both groups are also being examined and compared as well as are the frequency and classification of productive thinking experiences.

The relationship between intelligence and acquisition of conservation is being explored as to the effects of training and to allow for the study of the process of intellectual growth of retarded children.

PERCEPTION

Current research activities are directed toward exploring abilities starting with basic sensory and motor tasks, continuing through perceptual functions, to reasoning, memory and integrative functions. One objective is to then compare the development of abilities in retarded children with that of normal children.

Other research is addressed to the investigation of the role of perceptual experience as a cognitive process and is wide enough in scope to encompass multiple aspects of both normal and variant behavior. Studies with infants allow for control of stimulus values in order to identify relationships between selective behavior and specified perceptual feedbacks. Sensory and intra-organismic as well as ontogenetic studies are among the areas being investigated as being a part of this relationship.

Perceptual characteristics continue to be correlated with different etiologies and diagnostic categories as a means of identification.

Continuing studies focusing upon context and upon organismic factors involved in the processes of time sense are leading to investigation of intersensory differences, conditions of stimulation, response requirements, scaling processes, anchoring of defects and some personality variables.

Specific research is in evidence relative to training of retardates in the area of focal attention to determine any possible effect it may have upon the emergence and development of higher level functions.

LEARNING

A measure of learning potential is being studied as a supplementary indicator of ability to function more adequately than is suggested by a failing school record in educable mental retardates. Initial response and response subsequent to a tutorial session with non-verbal reasoning tasks employed have been demonstrated to involve consistently differing levels of performance on a variety of non-verbal psychometric, cognitive, and learning tasks.

Most of the available research suggests that a prompting procedure may be more efficacious with college students in simple verbal learning, but the limited research with retarded subjects does not, in general, corroborate these findings.

A number of studies concern themselves with learning problems. The nature of learning pattern and determinants of learning in the mentally retarded have led to investigation of the effectiveness of various reinforcers. Some of this research is on the learning of multiple comparable problems as contrasted with the learning of a single problem.

Some of these efforts are concerned with the problem of establishing developmental and comparative differences between normal and retarded children in the learning process. Still other studies are applied to the role and functions of reinforcement and the nature of clustering in free recall and a possible relationship between personality and learning in the retardate.

Research is in evidence which may serve to make the free-operant conditioning method a more powerful analytic and training technique. Efforts are being made to apply reinforcement techniques to the analysis of discrimination performance, control and training, as well as stimulus control.

STIMULUS VARIABLES

There is now in evidence research dealing with how the retardate integrates multiple and independent stimulus cues as well as the salutary and obstructive effects of presentation of materials where two modalities are emphasized. In the first instance, implications have to do with reading while in the second they have to do with discriminative decision or forming precepts. Other studies are concerned with growth of the ability to integrate modalities and the relationship it may have with measure of field dependence in mental retardates. Auditory stimuli is currently being studied to develop a clinical tool designed to specifically determine auditory thresholds in normal and retarded children, among others.

BEHAVIOR

The application of behavioral principles, behavioral style and level of functioning and the relationship of adaptive behavior to EGG phenomena is occupying the attention of research scientists. In all these studies predictive significance is being sought as to a retarded child's behavioral style and such factors in adaptive behavior as personal self-care, social behavior, and educational achievement.

The influence of verbal reinforcement and its counterparts is being assessed as to its effect on the performance of mentally retarded children.

PROGRAMMED LEARNING

Studies to investigate the development of discriminations of progressive difficulty implying operant discrimination of patterns and group use of programmed materials are being pursued. Efforts are being made to relate basic self-instructional techniques in the tool academic subjects with student and teacher training in the application of the materials and procedures developed. Efforts are now in evidence to adapt principles of learning and techniques of programmed instruction to the teaching of reading to the retarded.

Verbal learning is being further investigated by way of variables as they may be applied to the area of programmed instruction.

More general research in this area sets upon the assumption that the debility in many retardates is specific to certain abilities, and that areas of normal aptitudes might exist. One aim of this effort then is to build a repertory of basic skills and another is to examine learning processes in general. A particular piece of research is employing classical eyelid conditioning techniques.

Matching random and systematic events is being investigated as a possible process for observing differentials in age, intelligence and ethnic group in retarded and average subjects.

Applying behavioral principles in the technique of behavior modification or behavior shaping is currently occupying the attention of researchers interested in its implications for utilization in the classroom for exceptional children. Such techniques have also been recently applied to toilet training severely retarded children, self-care behavior and to studies of rates of responding where operant conditioning procedures have been applied.

FREE-OPERANT CONDITIONING

With regard to the education and treatment of retardates a number of recent and current researches dealing with free-operant conditioning indicate promise, particularly, for analyzing the behavior of severely retarded children.

The apparent value of the introduction of "programmed instruction" or "teaching machine" programs, which are based on this approach, has led to continuing research along several lines. For example, current research is investigating the utilization of operant behavior analysis to determine the role of perceptual experience among retarded children which is generated by their own behavior with respect to their cognitive development. It is being used to study social and symbolic behavior, its effectiveness for training in self-help with severely retarded adults, and the roles and functions of reinforcement in learning and learning deficits of the mentally retarded.

Reinforcement theory has recently been applied to such variables as those controlling the productivity of retardates in work situations and in a laboratory free-operant situation to demonstrate temporal relationships between reward and punishment as an important determinant of conflict performance.

Previous findings and current trends in this area of endeavor appear to demonstrate the efficacy of the free-operant method for therapeutic and prosthetic purposes in producing apparently "normal" uniformity in a group of retarded children. A review of current and proposed research reveals that still little, if any, has been oriented toward development of devices which automatically measure "behavior deficit." It also portends the need for research to make the free-operant method a more powerful analytic and training technique.

SUMMARY

In summary, an attempt has been made to review the status of current research in psychology and education which impinges upon the development of educational programs for the mentally retarded.

References:

1. Gardner, William I. BEHAVIORAL AND SOCIAL RESEARCH: REPORT OF THE TASK FORCE, PRESIDENT'S PANEL ON MENTAL RETARDATION. The President's Panel on Mental Retardation, U.S. Department of Health, Education and Welfare, Washington, D.C. 20021, 1964.

2. MENTAL RETARDATION ACTIVITIES. The Secretary's Committee on Mental Retardation, U.S. Department of Health, Education and Welfare, Washington, D.C. 20021, 1965.

3. MENTAL RETARDATION: ACTIVITIES OF THE U.S. DEPARTMENT OF HEALTH, EDUCATION AND WELFARE. The Secretary's Committee on Mental Retardation, U.S. Department of Health, Education and Welfare, Washington, D.C. 20201, 1963.

4. Seidenfeld, Morton A. MENTAL RETARDATION: A FURTHER ASSESSMENT OF THE PROBLEM. Rehabilitation Service Series N. 63-62, Vocational Rehabilitation Administration, Washington, D.C. 20025, 1962.

5. Clements, Sam D. MINIMAL BRAIN DYSFUNCTION IN CHILDREN: TERMINOLOGY AND IDENTIFICATION, PHASE ONE OF A THREE-PHASE PROJECT. U.S. Department of Health, Education and Welfare. Public Health Service Publication No. 1415. Washington, D.C., 1966.

6. NOTICES OF RESEARCH PROJECTS: SCIENCE INFORMATION EXCHANGE. Smithsonian Institution, Washington, D.C., 20036.

7. RESEARCH RELATING TO CHILDREN: CLEARINGHOUSE FOR RESEARCH IN CHILD LIFE. U.S. Department of Health, Education and Welfare. Public Health Service Publication. Welfare Administration, Children's Bureau. Bulletin No. 18, Washington, D.C., 1964.

8. SPECIAL EDUCATION: STRATEGIES FOR EDUCATIONAL PROGRESS, SELECTED CONVENTION PAPERS. 44th Annual Convention of the Council for Exceptional Children. Toronto, Canada, April 17-24, 1966.

AN EVALUATION OF THE EDUCATIONALLY HANDICAPPED PROGRAM: THE MEASURABLES AND THE UNMEASURABLES AFTER TWO YEARS

Mary Meeker, Ed. D.,
Educational Psychology Consultant to Schools,
Lecturer, University of Southern California,
Los Angeles, California

MARY MEEKER, Ed. D.

Because of California's tremendous population growth, special education classes have steadily increased. Independent districts and counties were early authorized by the state to provide programs for physically handicapped, mentally retarded, and gifted. In 1963, following many comprehensive studies (Bower, 1958, Lambert, 1963, Keuffer, 1963; Jackson, 1962; Howe, 1963; et al*) provision for a new kind of special program, the Educationally Handicapped, was legislated into the state education code, A.B. 464; Chapter 7.1; Chapter 6.

The Educationally Handicapped pupil was defined as a "minor whose learning problems are associated with a behavioral disorder, or a neurological handicap, or a combination thereof, and who exhibits a significant discrepancy between ability and achievement." To qualify for inclusion in this special program, a student's behavioral or neurological problems must be associated with a learning problem which prevents him from learning and performing in an ordinary classroom in accordance with his tested ability. The law specifies that the individual identification of a child as educationally handicapped is the

*Bower, E.M. A PROCESS FOR EARLY IDENTIFICATION OF EMOTIONALLY DISTURBED CHILDREN. Sacramento: California State Department of Education, 1958.

*Howe, John W. AN EXPLORATORY STUDY OF CHILDREN WITH NEUROLOGICAL HANDICAPS IN SCHOOL DISTRICTS OF LOS ANGELES COUNTY. Los Angeles County Superintendent of Schools Office, 1963.

*Jackson, E.H. "A Four-Year Project in the Elementary School for Emotionally Handicapped Children." Unpublished dissertation, The University of Southern California, Los Angeles, 1962.

*Keuffer, E.A. "A Guide for Screening Applicants to Special Programs for Educationally Handicapped Children." California: San Mateo County Superintendent of Schols, 1964. (Ditto copy.)

*Lambert, N. THE DEVELOPMENT AND VALIDATION OF A PROCESS FOR SCREENING EMOTIONALLY HANDICAPPED CHILDREN IN SCHOOL. Sacramento: California State Department of Education, 1963.

*Meeker, M.N. "An Evaluation of a High School Educationally Handicapped Program after One Year." WPA, 1966.

responsibility of: 1) A certified employee (teacher, supervisor, or administrator); 2) A credentialed school psychologist and 3) One or more licensed physicians with experience in working with children who represents such fields as pediatrics, neurology, psychiatry or other specialty which the problems of the individual child may make necessary.

For all practical purposes, then the term, Educationally Handicapped (EH) may refer to a student who is **Environmentally, Emotionally, Educationally** unable to learn curriculum when it is taught in the traditional manner. The first two categories may or may not be inclusive of the neurologically handicapped (by medical diagnosis), but certainly the latter category will include those who are achieving 2 to 5 years below grade level. Although the curriculum content for pupils in the EH programs is based upon the course of study outlined by the county, local or state requirements, emphasis is placed on fundamental school subjects with adaptations in courses which may be necessary according to the learning characteristics of the pupil. Since there are special classes for the physically handicapped and mentally retarded, those students are precluded from admission to the EH program.*

For each student placed into the EH program, the state allocates a sum of $910.00 to include costs of identification, consultants, materials, teachers and classrooms. Schools may institute EH classes at each grade level through tenth grade; no more than two per cent of the district school population may be enrolled with a limit of eleven students in the primary and elementary and junior high schools unless more than three chronological years separate the students, then the enrollment becomes a maximum of nine. At the high school level, the maximum is twelve pupils unless the age spread is greater than three years, and then the maximum enrollment shall be ten.

The first evaluation of an EH program was made in a paper to Western Psychology Association, 1966. (Meeker, 1966)** It was a report on a high school program which had been instituted a year previously. The following report is an evaluation of the same program after two years in progress.

As more and more evaluations are made, there will be an unmistakable indication that, at least in California, the introduction of this special program will literally explode the few assumptions that education is predicated upon — that given a normal IQ score, all children can learn to read, write and spell.

*For a complete explanation of the legislation, descriptions of procedures and materials, and a complete bibliography, the reader is referred to the Secretary, California State Association of School Psychologists and Psychometrists, 6917 Briggs Drive, Sacramento, California 95828.

** Meeker, M. N. AN EVALUATION OF A HIGH SCHOOL EDUCATIONALLY HANDICAPPED PROGRAM AFTER ONE YEAR. WPA, 1966.

Psychologists and administrators have been forced to look at "methods", at differential abilities of children, at motivation of teachers and children. Many theoretically sound notions have been experimented with—operant conditioning, teaching machines, matching personality needs of teacher and child; and other theoretical notions will prove useful. The important thing is that the EH funds have allowed experimentation and application of heretofore untested but recommended techniques for teaching; new methods of diagnoses and identification have risen.

Regardless of the technique employed for teaching these children, the content of the subject matter is often prescribed by law. In the following study, the content of this subject matter has been reorganized according to a theory of intellectual functioning (structure of intellect, SOI, a factor analytic model of intellectual abilities by J.P. Guilford) as a method of filling the prescription for the individuals placed in that educationally handicapped program. Under the direction of Jim Gladhill and Harry McKee, the Redondo Beach Elementary School District has adopted the SOI approach to individualized instruction for their twelve classes of educationally handicapped children.

The role of the educational psychologist and his practice within the school systems is still currently being defined. He is a newcomer to the schools. He is neither an orthodox clinician nor a pure education methods specialist—he is a child development psychologist whose knowledge is permeated with learning theory, education practices, and sociological principles.

The school psychologist is a type of educational psychologist. At present his primary function is the identification of sources of learning and behavior problems which handicap the students who are referred to him. He must use individual methods of appraisal to determine the student's needs; he must determine how these needs can be met within the school environment with whatever school capacities are available. The new legislation in California for establishing Educationally Handicapped classes has allowed the psychologists to use more than his skill to test. But it has also presented him with many students whose problems are not clear.

Sometimes the problems are such that outside referral is the only answer. Sometimes, however, the problems stem from cognitive deficits such as a poor memory, inability to see relations, poor units discrimination, and others, and for these deficits, the resolution of the learning or behavior problems must be found by making appropriate modifications of curriculum practices. This means that a hygienic or therapeutic approach to solving individual problems which stem from cognitive disabilities can then be achieved within the school environment by changing not the subject matter, nor the method, but the task.

Curriculum has never been developed within a theory of intellectual functioning of human abilities. It has grown with tradition as a father and experts as mother-come-lately. And it has never been developed according to individual, differentiated abilities. There is, however, abundant information available today which seems to be useful for the purpose of organizing curriculum experiences around a theory or model of intellectual abilities — Guilford's structure of intellect (Guilford, 1959).

When the first high-school program for educationally handicapped students was to be organized in a lower middle class area, the author, as consulting psychologist for that purpose, made the assumption that given average potential, the students' cognitive disabilities should serve as the primary basis for their teaching.

METHOD

All ninth-grade students and tenth-grade students who scored 90 on the CTMM (Form J, 1957) whose achievement in reading and arithmetic were at least three years retarded by group tests (CAT) were screened for the EH program. Screening consisted of interviews, Bender-Gestalts, WRAT, Stanford-Binet LM, and if necessary the Kohs blocks from the WISC.

All Binet responses of those students selected for the program were placed into individual graph profiles of the structure of intellect (SOI) by means of templates designed for that purpose (Meeker, 1965).

Three classes, 12 in each, were begun. Individual programs were designed to meet each student's needs based on four categories: cognitive, emotional, physiological, and academic.

Cognitive needs were determined by the structure-of-intellect profile and specific recommendations for their deficits and strengths were made. The teachers were instructed in means of organizing their curriculum subject matter according to the SOI model. Figure 1 is an example outlining the Binet responses available to them.

Emotional needs were determined by psychometric and interview material, and were met by consideration of teacher placement both in the EH classes and in their other regular classes. Aspects of the interpersonal relationships to be established such as sex of teacher, type (authoritarian, permissive, pressure, accepting, standards and values, etc.) of teacher were considered in each placement. These teachers were then contacted and after students were placed, each teacher was given information as to pupil needs both academic and emotional. These discussions were informally carried on in the teacher's room with the psychologist and head counselor and sometimes the nurse.

AGE	ITEM	CELL	COGNITION	MEMORY	EVALUATION	CONVERGENT PRODUCTION	DIVERGENT PRODUCTION	DEFINITION	CELL
AA	1	CMU						Is aware of meanings of words or ideas	CMU
	2	CSC						Sees common features in numbers	CSC
		NSI						Substitutes or derives symbols	NSI
	3	DFT						Changes set to meet new structural requirement	DFT
		CMU						Is aware of meanings of words or ideas	CMU
		CMT						Sees several meanings to a word or expression	CMT
	4	EMU						Ability to apply varied word meanings	EMU
		CMS						Ability to comprehend or structure problems in preparation for solving then	CMS
		MSI						Memory for well-practiced number operations	MSI
	5	CMU						Is aware of meanings of words or ideas	CMU
		NSS						States the order of symbolic systems from start to goal	NSS
		CMU						Is aware of meanings of words or ideas	CMU
		NMT						Shifts function of object, or part, to use in a new way	NMT
	6	DMS						Produces and organizes phrases and sentences	DMS
		CFT						Manipulates or transforms objects into another visual arrangement	CFT
		IFS						Recalls arrangement of objects previously presented	IFS
		CFS						Perceives spatial patterns and maintains orientation	CFS
	7	CMT						Sees several meanings to a word or expression	CMT
		CMU						Is aware of meanings of words or ideas	CMU
	8	EMU						Ability to apply varied word meanings	EMU
		CMU						Is aware of meanings of words or ideas	CMU
M	Alt.	CFT						Manipulates or transforms objects into another visual arrangement	CFT
		ESR						Decides which symbol relations are consistent with others	ESR

FIGURE 1

Score Sheet, Stanford-Binet Form L-M, for Age AA.

The teacher was made aware of the student's academic level in each subject tested, his cognitive strengths and weaknesses according to the SOI analysis; he was asked to attempt to have two standards of grading and conduct in his room—his customary one, and another considering the child's needs. Since this was a new program, teachers needed such training and understanding. For the most part, their flexibility and carry-through were excellent. A few were not flexible to carry through even though they knew the program was attempting to keep these students from being drop-outs. Most teachers came from middle-class environments and were shocked at the home conditions common to the type of students they were teaching. (This high school had a population of over 2600 and served the upper-lower, lower middle Caucasian community.)

Academic needs were based on group tests of achievement. Teachers were selected as above and instructed similarly. Since the students were to spend a block of two hours for English and science/or history with their EH teacher, the rest of their school time would be spent in regular classes to fill the state requirements (California) for each grade level.

Physiological needs here are not easily generalized. These sorts of things were considered to be physiologically based: refusal to undress for gym because of immaturity, indications that the child was a motor learner, perceptual dysfunctioning as shown by Benders, medical findings such as asthma, abnormal EEG's, psycho-sexual trauma, and others. After consultation with the physician and other members of the staff, it was decided upon to regard these as symptomatic; there were no facilities for etiological erasure medically or with psychotherapy. The staff recognized the limitations imposed upon school personnel when dealing with certain problems.

PROCEDURE

Soon after placement, when scheduling problems were over, the Nelson Reading Test (Silent Paragraph) was administered to all students. Table 1 shows the results for the ninth-grade students upon leaving the program after two years along with interim scores.

Of the 36 students placed, 24 were ninth graders. Their scores are shown in Table 1. Of the 24 originally placed, 18 finished the two years. The losses were due to moving, pregnancy, and marriage.

It was apparent at the beginning of placement that most of these students had begun their first year of school "young for their grade" with birthdates in August, September, October, November, and December.

The scores in Table 1 were obtained from the Reading Laboratory. Each student in this

TABLE 1

**The Nelson-Denny Reading Scores for EH Students During
Two Years of Placement**

Student	Sex	Binet IQ	Binet Age	Binet Vocab.	Date of Testing 4-65	10-65	4-66	10-66
SM	F	85	14.4	15	5.0	5.2	5.1	7.9
CA	F	123	14.6	23	4.9	5.7	5.5	7.8
SC	F	98	14.3	17	6.5	7.1	9.2	12.4
DJ	F	103	14.5	12	3.3	3.6	3.9	8.6
SM	F	123	14.9	15	5.6	6.1	7.1	9.7
CH	F	105	14.6	20	5.5	6.5	6.5	8.3
RR	F	95	14.5	15	4.9	5.6	5.9	7.9
WT	F	97	14.11	19	4.6	4.4	4.8	7.3
DJ	F	96	14.6	18	5.0	5.3	5.5	8.1
DM	M	89	14.4	15	3.9	4.3	4.0	7.8
JJ	M	94	15.3	20	6.0	6.1	6.7	10.1
JD	M	90	15.8	17	5.3	5.0	6.1	7.9
DJ	M	116	15.3	16	7.0	7.3	7.3	9.7
OG	M	107	14.5	16	6.5	6.3	6.4	9.9
RV	M	103	14.3	17	3.7	4.2	4.8	6.8
KJ	M	116	14.8	20	5.4	5.6	6.3	7.3
RC	M	92	14.5	12	3.7	4.5	5.3	5.9
JA	M	110	15.7	20	7.1	7.2	7.6	10.6

n=18

high school goes through the Reading Laboratory as part of his English course each year. The EH students were programmed for the regular reading lab in their turn but were also given a second run through at the end of the year and results were given to the EH teacher for remedial purposes. It was apparent, too, from the Binet vocabulary as well as the WRAT that reading was a major academic problem for the group; therefore the teacher incorporated more reading than "English" and various machines were purchased for that purpose.

Results after the first year were discouraging and both teachers found them hard to accept.

Each teacher used a card system for daily assignments; the student worked at his own pace on these although he was also responsible for weekly class assignments and was graded accordingly.

PHYSICAL SETUP

The class is housed in the large home economics room with all cooking facilities open to students for special occasions. Frequent breakfasts were held. The physical academic set-up was structured according to the same plan used by Frank Hewitt at the Neuropsychiatric Institute clinic school in the medical facilities at UCLA, Westwood. Work centers were assigned to each student; this consisted of a large storage cabinet partitioned for each student. Group work centers were physically separated by tables with freedom of movement from one to the other at any time except when class assignments or tests were being worked upon. At no time were the individual centers used as punitive measures (although one teacher often said she wished she could, and "put a thick door on it!"), and since these were adolescents, many preferred spending most of their time in groups.

Thus their room was very structured with freedom of movement between centers allowed, and their academic and curricular work was equally structured and tailored to the individual by means of SOI findings. One reading center consisted of a tachistoscope, language master, SRA materials; another consisted of many paperback novels (no sign-in or-out system, no report system—freedom of choice in reading).

Another center consisted of Piagetian materials for the experiencing of space and volume conservation principles. Two tape recorders with headphones were available for private use. A TV center with comfortable lounge chairs was used when something interesting was on. A blackboard and writing center for those students with encoding problems was used most frequently. A small sitting room off to one side either for group working or for resting was also available.

WORK MATERIALS

Nearly all students showed deficits in the immediate memory area as well as in the divergent area, and almost all showed weakness at the units level across all operations. Unexpectedly, almost all showed strength in the Evaluation operation. Exceptions to this were found among those who had been judged as delinquents. Some of Guilford's tests were used as models for instructional materials, and a scaled-down version of Upton's CREATIVE ANALYSIS was devised by the teachers using their own curriculum course of study. Students were given innumerable cards on which were pictures and were told to classify them as many different ways as they could. This was an attempt to provide them experience in cognition of units, evaluation of relations, convergent reproduction of a system. As often as possible the teachers improvised memory exercises in auditory, visual, and motor areas. Such materials were used for 20-minute segments of time and were aimed at individual deficits. As mentioned previously, recorders, tachistoscopes, language masters, and other machines were used.

MAKEUP OF THE CLASSES

All but a few had Binet scores over 90 with a top of 123 and a mean of 102. The two with 85 and 89 IQ's were placed because tests indicated that their problems were encoding rather than decoding or comprehension. This clinical impression was backed up with SOI profiles indicating that Evaluation was good, Cognition was good, but Convergent Production was deficient (see Fig. 2).

Figure 2 shows a profile of structure-of-intellect failures and successes in the Stanford-Binet of an 85-IQ student. Memory is characterized by failures on immediate memory items, Cognition is quite good, Units are poor in every major operation, and the abilities to reproduce (encoding) are very poor except where transformation was called for. Transformation is defined as making changes of various kinds (redefinition, shifts, or modification) of existing information or in its function. Thus one might conclude that the student here was not having cognitive problems in comprehending, but in showing that he had comprehended, not decoding, but encoding material.

Figure 3 shows a typical EH profile where Memory is poor, Evaluation is good, and Units discrimination in any one of the major kinds of abilities is weak. The CMU cell (Cognition of Semantic Units) is vocabulary and accounts for only one of the factors or cells in the total structure of intelligence in the SOI. This student's IQ, hardly a standard error more than the one in Figure 2, shows quite a different pattern of abilities. Unquestionably, the Memory domain is weak and one could hardly expect success in school work with this kind of memory. Yet Evaluation is strong and Cognition shows strength. Of real interest in this pattern is the strength in Figural (column under F in each of the give major abilities) dimensions. If one wanted to teach to this child's strengths, figural materials would be the easiest to use in teaching any concept—or to concrete-ize curriculum materials. The ability to evaluate is also strong. A general weakness prevails in understanding semantics as shown under Cognition M and both Divergent and Convergent Production M columns. Abilities to see Relations is another strength across the major abilities (see R rows).

It is important to keep in mind that the structure of intellect analysis of the Binet is only as good as the Binet itself in that it attempts to capitalize upon the reliability and validity of the Stanford Binet. Theoretically, one might question the value or weight of any sub-item at any year level and rightly so, but this does point up the weaknesses of making judgments based on the scoring system of any test.

Three students had EEG's indicating abnormal wave patterns, and two of these had been home bound for the two previous years, unable to stay in a classroom. Nearly all had very poor Benders. Four were very obese; many had visual misperceptions which were

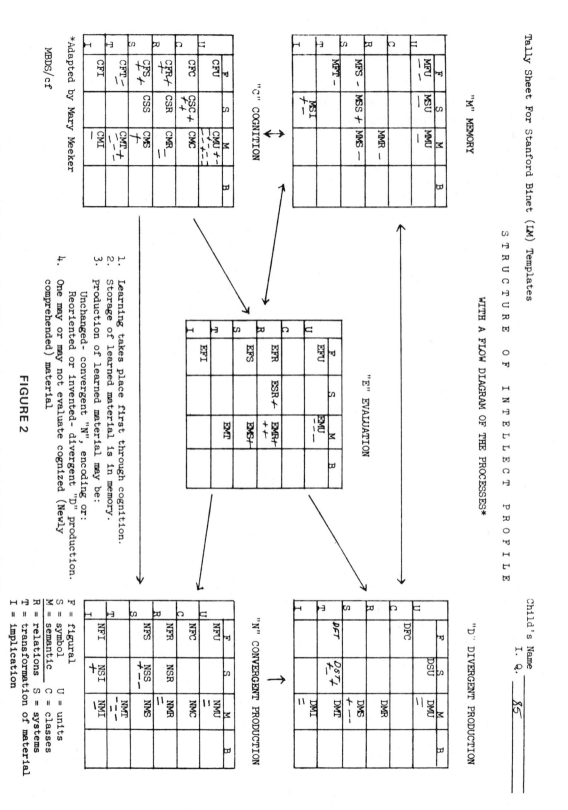

Tally Sheet For Stanford Binet (LM) Templates

STRUCTURE OF INTELLECT PROFILE

WITH A FLOW DIAGRAM OF THE PROCESSES*

FIGURE 2

Structure-of-intellect profile of failures and successes in the Stanford-Binet of an 85-IQ student.

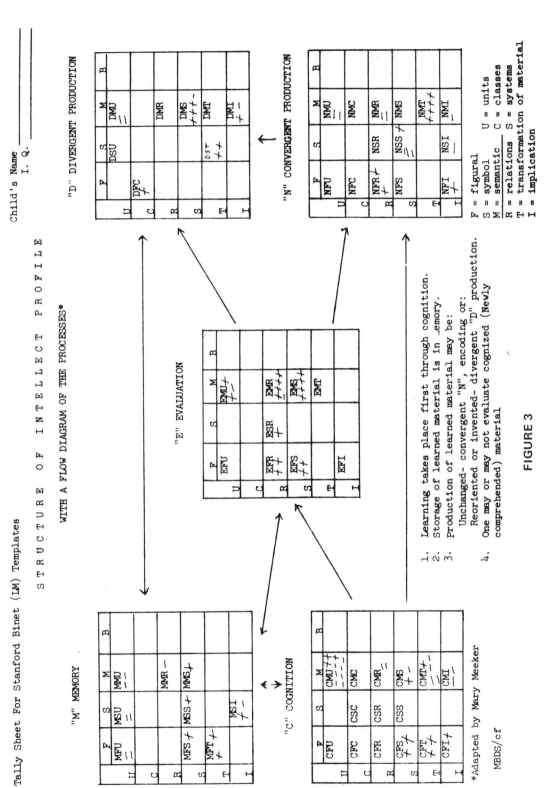

Typical EH structure-of-intellect profile of failures and successes in the Stanford-Binet of a 103-IQ student.

FIGURE 3

not found on any physical examination or neurological examinations of the superficial kind. Several of these could see that the BG was different but could not reproduce figures correctly.

Some (Mexican, Negro) had family and subcultural values which caused social problems. Scanty case history on prenatal, perinatal, and later illnesses gave some indication of positive etiology in these areas, but the medical doctor and the psychologist had to work with "what was" rather than with "why." If medication was indicated, the family doctor was contacted and the recommendation made.

In each case there was a long history of academic failure involved in most subjects. It was decided to look upon the varied wealth of individual problems as being reflected currently in poor communication skills, with reading the most serious. The two teachers were a Negro and a Caucasian; they were volunteers from the regular staff. They had no special training. One was strict, letting not the slightest social infringement go uncorrected, but was unbelievably flexible. The other was gentle, permissive, non-pressuring. Both were inordinately sympathetic, and identified closely with their students. Both were service oriented and willing to experiment.

RESULTS

After one school year no academic test showed any significant gain in score. However, remarkable improvement showed up in social gains. The groups became tight groups. One girl won vice-presidency of the ninth grade for the school. Two of the obese lost weight. One Negro girl who had been so hostile she was unapproachable became "integrated" when the class refused to go to a pep rally because she managed at last to express her fear of rejection due to race. Another girl became a majorette. One girl who had been physically assaulted as a youngster spent the entire year talking into a tape recorder every moment she got the chance but never played it back—she never turned in assignments; she sat. At the end of the first year she began to do assignments. The NH students remained in school after being homebound previously. One boy who had been severely beaten and scarred when he was younger made tremendous gains in social skills and became one of the most popular boys on campus and one whom everyone spoke to. Three boys who had refused to undress for gym (undescended testicles) stayed in physical education for the entire year without being thrown out. Two severe asthmatics were able to keep up grades although absences and incidences of asthma continued to reflect pollen and bacterial conditions. Their relief from fears of failing due to absence could not be measured.

By the end of the first quarter most of the students were discussing their personal problems. One of these for the group was the stigma of being in the EH class. At the beginning of the year they had dubbed it the "nut class." At the end of the year they started a club for the next year in case they would not be put back in the EH class; they called their club the "Door in the Wall" Club. In one discussion they decided that was what being there in the EH class was like — like someone had opened a door in a wall. They planned not to separate during the summer, to work and save money in the class kitty so that when the legislature convened they could charter a plane to Sacramento to talk to the men who legislated the EH program. They wanted to inform the men that the class was a good idea, but that the name was hard to explain to others and made them ashamed to be in the class — could the name be changed?

DISCUSSION

Obviously such changes in feelings of human worth cannot be fully reported, nor can they be measured, for such social-human changes would suffer by measurement due to the vagaries of statistical instruments or means which would be employed.

The staff began to wonder if perhaps, at a time in adolescent development when an individual concept of self is non-existent, it is possible to develop a group-concept which can successfully replace a self-concept.

Two failures were apparent in the unmeasurables. Boys who already had juvenile records and who were also completely unmotivated to stay in school could not be retained. Their crimes continued and each one eventually got into trouble which took him out of the school. These students, unlike the others, did not have memory deficits in the structure of intellect. They did show Evaluation deficits.

The other failure occurred in the first-generation Mexican girls whose education was being tolerated by their parents who really felt that their daughters should be getting married and having babies. This did happen to two girls who fit this category.

As Table 1 indicates, after two school years academic tests gains caught up with social gains and students made from six to three years gains. Most of them were either at grade level or comparable to the level of their classmates who were in regular classes and had been. (The average ninth grader in this school scores about a year and a half or more below grade level.) The encoding problems did not make such high gains, and they have been retained at extra expense in the program for another year, for their progress, though cumulative, is slower.

All two-year EH students who remained except for the encoding problems were returned to full-time regular classes as 11th graders. They are checked weekly on a volunteer basis. Not only have social gains been retained, but on the whole the individuals can honestly be described by present teachers as more mature than their classmates.

At present, the consensus of opinion among staff is that personality growth can occur in a class where teacher-pupil relationships are planned and controlled, and that academic progress is well implemented when curriculum is not only individually designed within a theory of intellectual functioning such as the SOI but is taught specifically for so many minutes at a time. The security gained on the part of the students with structured work on their own deficits in intellectual factors seems to alleviate their fear of failure; this allows both cognitive growth and personality growth to occur. It seems advantageous to plan curriculum so that it is rooted in a theory of human intelligence capabilities rather than based on tradition.

SUMMARY

A total program for educationally handicapped students at the high-school level was organized whereby curriculum was developed on an individual basis for each student. In a sense, a tri-part approach design for overall improvement in achievement was used.

First, it was assumed that for many of the students, emotional problems were overlays of cognitive deficiencies and/or neurologically undetectable dysfunctioning. Their successes and failures on the Stanford-Binet LM were placed into the structure of intellect so that an individual profile of their separate deficiencies and strengths was rooted in a theory of human intelligence. Secondly, student placement was made on the basis of teacher-student interpersonal relationships according to student needs, at least as best could be determined. Thirdly, individual curriculum was "taught" during controlled time with the utilization of psychological information and teacher and machine efforts.

The results indicate that growth and improvement in measurable achievement tests did not show up the first year, but by the end of two years significant gains were made.

However, social gains were obvious by the end of the first semester and were even greater by the end of one year and two years. These students are being watched this, the third year, to see whether gains are held or where regression occurs since they have now been returned to a full, regular high-school schedule. It is felt that maturational gains based on time alone could not have accounted for the increase in improvement.

References

1. Guilford, J. P. THREE FACES OF INTELLECT. American Psychologist, 1959, 14, 46-79.

2. Hewitt, Frank. EDUCATIONAL ENGINEERING WITH EMOTIONALLY DISTURBED CHIL-DREN. Paper presented at Western Psychological Association, April 1966, Long Beach.

3. Los Angles County, Office of the Superintendent, Division of Research and Guidance. STRUCTURE OF INTELLECT COMPONENTS IN THE STANFORD-BINET, FORM L-M, Bon-sall, M., & Meeker, M., Programs for the Gifted.

4. Meeker, Mary. A PROCEDURE FOR RELATING STANFORD-BINET BEHAVIOR SAMP-LINGS TO GUILFORD'S STRUCTURE OF THE INTELLECT. Journal of School Psychology, 1965, 3, No. 3, 26-36.

5. Upton, A. and Samson R. CREATIVE ANALYSIS, Dutton and Co. New York, 1963.

INDEX

VOLUME 1
and
VOLUME 2

Affective abilities 157,
Agencies and services 37
  Legal 39-40
  Medical 37-39, 305
  "Mental Retardation Services
    Board" (Los Angeles County)
    441-442, 447, 452-454
  "Pediatrics Outpatient
    Clinic" (University of
    California) 57, 76, 90, 97,
    100
  "Psychological Associates"
    459-463
  "Short-Doyle Clinics"
    (California) 443-444, 449
  Social Welfare 37-38
Alphabet see: Symbolization
Anxiety 141-142, 144, 148,
  323-324, 363
Arts and Crafts 23, 150-151,
  325
Associations and societies
  292, 442

Behavior, deviant
  Definitions 39-46
  Etiology 38, 89, 212-214,
    305
  Juvenile delinquency 39-40,
    42, 429, 436
  Treatment 37-39
  Types 46, 81, 89-90, 96,
    214, 281, 323-324, 357,
    429, 436
  see also: Disturbed child;
    Emotional disturbance
Behavioral description
  225-227, 229-238
Behavioral modification
  goals 21, 240
  Model 17, 2021, 225-248
  Techniques 241-245, 248
  see also: Tests, diagnostic
Disabled child 35
  Blind 40
  Deaf 210-211
  Handicapped 84, 97
  Teaching of 34-36, 38
  see also: Visual problems;
    Hearing problems
Disturbed child 64-76, 98-99
  Autistic child 16, 25,
    334-338
  Behaviors and disabilities
    81, 141-142, 144, 178,
    185-192, 210-211, 214,
    216-217, 281, 323-324
  Definitions 47, 121, 123,
    209, 210
  Etiology 212-214
  Neurotic child 141

Psychotic child 141
  Schizophrenic child 331-332
  Teaching goals and
    methodology 158-161,
    320-323, 325
  Teaching programs 45-48,
    161-171, 209, 320-338
  Teaching techniques 147-153,
    321-323, 325-334, 341-349
  see also:
    Behavior, deviant;
    Brain-injured child;
    Dyslexic child;
    Emotionally disturbed child
Drama and dramatic play
  23, 152
Dyslexic child
  Behaviors and disabilities
    214-215, 392-393, 396-397
  Diagnosis 398-403
  Etiology 395-397
  Statistics 393, 399, 400
  Teaching goals 463
  Teaching programs 397-398,
    459-463
  Teaching techniques
    404-421, 463-466
  see also:
    Brain-injured child;
    Disturbed child;
    Learning problems and
    disabilities; Reading
    problems and disabilities
Blindness see: Disabled
  child; Visual problems
Body concepts 146, 319,
  322-323, 325-332
Bain see: Central nervous
  system
Brain-injured child
  Associations and societies 292
  Behaviors and disabilities 142, 214-215,
    261-263, 281, 396-397
  Teaching programs 159, 256-257,
    268-271, 276-277, 320-321
  Teaching techniques 263-265, 269-270,
    276, 331
  see also: Central nervous
    system; Disturbed child;
    Dyslexic child

Camps 25
Central nervous system
  Dysfunctions 65-69, 75-76,
    80-81, 89, 211, 214-215,
    321, 396-397
  Role in learning 57-64,
    68, 95, 321-322, 397
Children see under specific
  headings: Brain-injured
  child; Disabled child;
  Disturbed child;
  Dyslexic child;
  Emotionally disturbed
  child: Mentally
  retarded child

Conceptualization 147,
  322-323, 328-330, 341,
  396-397
Curriculum see:
  Special education

Deafness see:
  Disabled child;
  Hearing problems
Diagnosis and evaluation
  Diagnostic labels 210-212,
    393
  Program evaluation
    procedures 258-260,
    274-275, 280-289, 301-302,
    324-325, 356, 357-358, 377,
    398-403, 443-444, 459-462
  Role of 130-131, 158

Education
  Functions and goals
    18, 20, 157-158, 240,
    374-375, 379-380, 427
  Responsibilities
    209, 391, 395
  Validation of procedures
    122, 128-129, 384
  see also:
    Special education;
    Teachers and educators
Ego 319, 321-323, 334, 430
Emotional disturbance
  Etiology 212-214, 299, 301,
    305, 306-308, 361
  Features 141-142, 321
  see also: Behavior, deviant;
    Disturbed child;
    Psychosomatic complaints
Emotionally disturbed child
  Behaviors and disabilities
    21, 210, 357, 362, 429
  Definitions 38, 39-43,
    45-46
  Diagnosis 177
  Statistics 41, 139, 353
  Teaching goals and
    Methodology 299, 301,
    305-309, 313, 353-354,
    427-431, 433
  Teaching programs 36, 39,
    177-180, 209-210, 297-315,
    320-321
  Teaching techniques
    142-143, 145-152, 181,
    183-184, 198-201, 216-221,
    302, 358-366, 431, 433-435
  see also: Disturbed child
Environmental background
  60, 84, 86
  Disadvantaged child 32-33,
    46

Fantasy 145-146, 183-184

Hearing problems 83, 211

Hyperkinetic syndrome 81

see also:
Disturbed child
Hysteria 42

Instinctive drives 142
Intellectual capacities
81-83, 86, 157, 210
Change in 16, 33
Testing 35, 58-59, 99
see also:
Mentally retarded child;
Tests, diagnostic
Language 60-63, 335-336, 397
Bilingual child 66
Tests 65-76, 288, 289, 460
see also: spoken language;
Symbolization;
Written language
Language problems and
disabilities
Effects 213-215
Etiology 211, 214-215, 260
Types 210-211, 260, 405
Laws and legislation
Concerning disturbed
children 37-38, 39-40, 41,
257, 278, 355-356
Concerning mentally retarded
children 447, 449, 453
Learning
Central nervous system in
60-64, 68, 95, 321-322,
396-397, 408-414
Influences on classroom
31, 60, 226-227, 357,
363-364
Motivation in 160-161,
219, 244-245, 398, 431,
434-435
Reinforcement in 160-161,
227-228, 243-244, 248
Stimulus and response in
159, 160-161, 171, 242-245
Learning problems and
disabilities 31-32, 36-37
Central nervous system
dysfunctions 58-59,
63-85, 89-95, 98-104
Diagnosis 80-81, 98-99
Effects 31, 87-96, 213-215
Etiology 84, 86-87, 89,
97, 395-396
Hearing disabilities 83,
260, 323-324
Treatments 33,
459-466
Visual disabilities 260,
323-324
see also: Reading problems
and disabilities;
Written language
Library usage 241

Mathematics see:
Symbolization
Medicine and medical
specialists

Attendant 379-380
Medical examinations
81, 286
Medical model 38-39,
42-45, 305, 396-396
Nurse 97, 379, 448
Pediatrician 211
Physical therapist 269
Physician 55-58,
87-104, 448
Role of 55, 258, 311
Speech pathologist
211, 259-260
Student 55-56, 97
Mental Health Survey of
Los Angeles County 442-446
Mental Hygiene Movement 305
Mental illness 42-44, 209
see also:
Disturbed child;
Emotionally disturbed child
Mentally retarded child
Associations and societies
442
Definitions 38, 46, 442
Etiology 450
Statistics 378, 441
Teaching goals and
methodology 159-163, 169,
170, 373-378
Teaching programs 35-36,
375-382, 443-450
Teaching techniques 16,
160, 161-171, 248,
376-377, 381-382
Welfare programs 441-454
Models and philosophies 17
Behavioral modification
model 17, 20-21, 225-248
Medical 38-39, 42-45, 305,
395-396
Neuro-physiological
24-25, 319-338
Psychiatric 213-215,
299, 395-396
Psychopedagogical or
Orthopedagogical model
22-24
Social Competence model
19-20, 297-315
Special milieu model
24-25
Motor abilities
and disabilities
Graphomotor difficulties
66, 80, 148
Psychomotor seizures 84
Role in learning 157
Teaching of skills 319,
322-323, 328, 330, 465
Tests 287-288
Music 151, 337

Newspaper 166-168
Nonverbal disabilities
see under specific headings:
Body concepts; Motor

abilities and disabilities;
Self-concepts
Norms and values 46
Middle-class values 33,
43-44
Norm violation 35 41
Teaching of 161, 162
see also: Behavior, deviant

Parents
Counseling 87-96, 180,
268, 270, 274, 324-325,
463
Reactions to child's
learning problems 87-96
Role in teaching programs
166, 169, 357, 463
Perception 125, 397
see also:
Sensory stimulation
Perceptual training see:
Perception; Special
education programs
Personal identity see:
Self-concepts
Physical education 23, 152,
325-332, 435-436
Therapist 269
Psychiatry and psychiatrists
Concern of 38, 42
Psychiatric model 213-215,
299, 395-396
Responsibilities 40, 209
Role in teaching 211, 269,
311
see also: Psychotherapy
and psychotherapists
Psychology and psychologists
Role in teaching 17,
258-259, 311
Training 278, 448
View of dyslexia 395-396
Psychosomatic complaints 83,
90, 96
Psychotherapy and
psychotherapists 23, 212,
437
Group therapy 23, 141,
463
Limitations 44, 87
Uses of 178, 180, 459-460
Puzzles 163, 164

Reading 147-148
Learning 60-63, 95
Teaching 336, 358-359, 410-417
Tests 67-76, 288
see also: Symbolization;
Written language
Reading problems and
disabilities 391
Diagnosis 57-81
Effects 57
Etiology 83-84, 395-397
Therapy 100-104, 362-363,
410-421

Types 60-69, 95, 362, 392
see also: Dyslexic child;
Learning problems and
disabilities
Research 112-117, 384

School failure 56, 57, 96
Schools *see:* Special
education programs and
schools
Science teaching 149-150, 377
Seizures *see:* 193, 216, 303
Self-concepts
Development 220, 323, 357
Teaching 146-147, 334-336
see also: Ego sensory stimulation 25,
Sensory stimulation 25,
143-144, 171, 214, 241,
323-324
Social adjustment 180-181,
315
Development 23, 147, 165,
313-314, 336-337
Effects 306-308
Goals in teaching 161,
162, 308
Skills needed for
302-303, 430-431
Social competence model
17, 19-20, 297-314
Teaching techniques 166,
200-201, 216-218, 299,
332-334, 360
Social studies teaching
148-149
Social workers 445
Role 211, 309-310
Training 127, 448
Space
Classroom use of 144,
166, 181, 276
Orientation in 147,
325-328
Special education 34-36,
122-125
Curriculum 124-125,
145-152, 161-171, 178,
218-221, 226-117, 319,
325, 358-366, 433
"Educational therapy" 34,
130-136, 319
Functions 31, 34-37, 121,
124-125,
157-159, 321-323,
373-374, 427-429, 432
Goals 160-163, 169, 201,
218, 220, 229, 235,
240-241, 256, 270, 274, 306,
308, 325, 356, 463
Interdisciplinary aspects
125, 127, 139-140,
178-180, 211-212, 258-261,
308-311, 360-362, 379-381,
437
Methodologies 37-39,
42-45, 126-127, 159-161,

170, 263-264, 299, 301,
305-308, 320-323, 353, 354,
375-378, 430-431
Responsibilities 45-48, 157-158, 209
Services 44-45, 125
Teachers 125, 184-198,
219-220, 364, 436
"Therapeutic instruction"
130-131, 139-140
Training for 125-130,
132-135
see also: Education
Special education programs
and schools 23
Columbia University
161-171
Cumberland House
Elementary School
298-299, 313-314
Day Schools 35, 178-206,
209-221, 319-320, 324-338
Denton State School 381-382
Devereux Foundation
432-437
Dubnoff School 319-338
European programs 47, 298
For mentally retarded
376-378, 443-450
League School 209-221
Livonia Public Schools
357-366
Mansfield Training School
381-382
"Perceptual Development
Program" 255-278
"Project Re-Ed" 297-315
Psychological Associates
459-463
Public schools 46, 209,
255-257, 268-278, 353-366,
391, 395, 431, 459-463
Residential schools 35,
46-47, 177-178, 295-314,
373-385. 427-437
"SLD Preventive Program"
397-398, 404-422
"Therapeutic Preschool
Project" 181-206
Training schools
(reformatories) 47,
427-437
University of Washington
229-248
Wright School 298-299
Special education techniques
16, 125, 264-265, 334-338,
359-360
Audio-visual aids 377
Control of environment
21, 181, 199, 270, 276,
333-334
Curriculum modification
124-125, 142-147
Exercises 341-342,
404-421, 463-466
Grading 228, 431, 434-435

Group projects 199-201,
216-218
Grouping 269-270, 276,
302, 333
Programming and sequencing
of activities 169-170,
240-244, 325-332, 377,
404-419, 433
Reinforcement 227-228,
248
Routine 143, 198-199
Stimulus control 143-144,
171, 241
Structuring of activities
166, 169-171, 198-199,
212-213, 220, 334,
363-364, 412-421.
Team-teaching 183-184,
308-309
Timing and pacing of
activities 142-143, 198,
241, 364-365, 433-434
Validation of 122, 221
Specific language
disability *see:* Dyslexic child
Spelling *see:* Written
language
Spoken language 411, 413
Problems and disabilities
66, 80, 260, 392-393, 466
Speech pathologist 211,
259-260
Statistics
Dropouts 57
Dyslexic children 393,
399, 400
Emotionally disturbed
children 41, 139, 353
Mentally retarded children
378, 441
Symbolization 60-63, 68
76, 95
Alphabet 75-76, 404-408
Mathematics 148, 242, 289,
336, 359

Teachers and educators
297, 311
Professional exchanges
383-384
Recruiting 269, 384, 445,
447-448
Roles 20, 96-97, 125,
220-201, 212, 218-220,
226-228, 260, 368, 299,
302-311, 360-362, 364, 379
Skills needed by 131-132,
184-198, 219, 260
Teacher-student relation
23, 184-198, 248, 436
Training 122, 127-129,
134-135, 238-240, 257-261,
277-278, 298, 303-305,
395-397, 445-446, 448-449
Tests, diagnostic 64, 95,
106, 260, 284-285, 402,
403, 460-467 passim

"Bender Visual Motor
Gestaly" 68-69, 100-101,
459
"Benton Test of Visual
Retention" 75-80, 100
"Durrell Analysis of
Reading Difficulty" 102
"Frostig Developmental
Test of Visual Perception"
69, 71-74, 95, 266, 461,
464
"Gilmore Oral Reading Test"
91
"Illinois Test of
Psycho-linguistic
Abilities" 460, 461, 464,
467
"Screening Test for
Identifying Children with
SLD" 401-403
"Stanford-Binet" 58, 66
"Wechsler Intelligence
Scale for Children" (WISC)
59, 64-68, 90-91, 99-100,
461
"Wepman Auditory
Discrimination Test" 461,
464
"Wide-Range Achievement
Test" (WRAT) 65-66, 91,
102
see also: Intellectual
capacities; Medicine and
medical specialists
Therapies see under the
specific heading: Arts
and crafts; Drama and dramatic
play; Music; Physical
education; Psychotherapy and
psychotherapists;
Vocational training
Thesis 112
Time 146-147, 166
"Trivsel" 18

United States
Office of Economic
Opportunity 33
Public Health Service
379-380, 382

Values see: Norms and values
Visual problems 83-84,
465-466
see also: Disabled child
Vocational training 376-377,
381-382, 445, 449-450

Written language
Learning 59-63, 68, 76, 95
Spelling problems and
disabilities 76-80, 392
Teaching 148, 404-412,
418-421
Tests 65-76, 288

Alphabet *see* Symbolization
Anxiety 178-80
Automation 51

Behavior, deviant
  In learning problems 179-80
  See also: Disturbed child;
  Emotionally disturbed child
Brain-injured child 278, 471-72
  Doman-Delacato treatment 327-30
  Sidedness 344
  Testing 326-27
  See also Mentally retarded child

Communication 82
  See also Linguistic skills
Computers 35-38, 44-45, 51
Curriculum *see* Special education
Cybernation 45-46, 57
  In vocational rehabilitation 62-68

Development
  Laterality 336
  Ontogenetic 331
  Sequential 332-34
Disadvantaged child
  Language development programs
    155ff, 162-65
Disturbed child
  Autistic child 438
  Behavior and disabilities 416
  Control of environment 315-16
  Neurotic child 438
  Phobic child 438, 439
  Psychotic child 438, 439
  Schizoid child 438
  Teaching goals and methodologies
    443
  Teaching programs 313, 415, 436
  Teaching techniques 440-41,
    442-43, 443-57
  Therapeutic tutoring 175
  See also Emotionally disturbed
    child
Doman-Delacato
  Critique of 330-32, 334-36, 339-46
  Experiments cited 347-69
  Reaction to 328-30
  Theory of neurological organization
    324, 331-34, 336-39
  Treatment rationale 326

Educable child 81
  See Mentally retarded child
Educationally handicapped 481
Emotionally disturbed child 435
  Academic potentials 243, 246-47
  Behavior and learning 220-21
  Behaviors and disabilities 213-19,
    398-99, 401
  Classroom remediation 234-42

Communication skills and learning
  223-42
Definitions 216-217
Educational diagnosis 212-13. 215.
  220-21, 437
Environmental controls 221
Intellectual capacities 243-45
Learning problems of 180, 186,
  438-39
Number concepts 190-91
Public school programs 270-72
Reading 186-90, 248-69
Teaching relationship 393-400
Teaching goals and methodologies
  214-15, 219, 243, 247-48,
  393-99, 399
Teaching programs 215ff, 313-19,
  393, 436
Teaching techniques 401-06, 443,
  455-60
Tests 223-33
Therapeutic tutoring 175

Fantasy in learning 183-84, 188

Institutes for the Achievement of
  Human Potential 324, 325
Intellectual capacities 81, 243-45
  See also Mentally retarded child
International Teaching Alphabet
  (ITA) 201

Language problems and disabilities
  465, 467
  Mentally retarded 470
  Peabody Oral Language Develop-
    ment Kits 155-68
Laterality
  Aphasia 343
  Cerebral dominance 337
  Concept of 337-38
  Decussation 337
  Eye dominance 344
  Reading 340, 341-42
  Sensitivity 340
  Speech 338, 340, 341, 342-44, 345
  Tonality 339, 341, 345
Learning
  Motivation in 175
  Reinforcement in 156
Learning problems and disabilities
  473-74, 481
  Causes 181-82
  Communication skills 223
  Described 185
  Developmental lags 416-17
  Emotionally disturbed child 212ff
  Psychogenic 176
  Visual 89-91, 278-80
Linguistic skills and learning 223-42

Mathematic
  See Symbolization
Mentally retarded child
  Behavior 474-75
  Cognitive abilities 472-73
  Cultural factors 467-68

Definitions 277
Diagnosis 469-70, 471-72
Emotional factors 466-67
Frostig-Horne training program
  89ff
Language development programs
  155ff, 165
Learning patterns 473-74
Motivation 468
Multiply handicapped 471
Perception 473
Programmed learning 475-76
Reading experiment 361
Research in educating 465ff
School role-learning 83
Stimuli in learning 780
Teaching programs 89-90, 108-09,
  280ff, 313-19
Tests 90-108, 108-13, 117-19, 227,
  278, 280, 283-85
Visual perception in learning
  89-108
Visual training 289-96
Motor abilities and disabilities
  Role in learning 91ff, 472
  Tests 90-108
Music, tonality in 339

Neurological organization, theory of
  323, 324-26, 330, 331
  Doman-Delacato rationale 326-28
  Laterality 336-48
  Reading 347-69

Ontogeny
  Recapitulation theory 324, 325-26,
    331

Parents
  Counseling 408-09
  Reactions to child's learning prob-
    lems 316, 318
Perception in learning 199-200
Piaget, perceptual theory 198
Psychologists, role in schools 483

Reading
  Difficulties 186-90
  Initial Teaching Alphabet 201-02
  Neurological organization theory
    340
  Perceptual aspects 197-206
  Remediation experiments 347-69
  Tests 350-69
Reading problems and disabilities
  Remediation 257-69
  Systems approach 52-53
  Therapy 449-51
Rehabilitation Center 324
Research
  Role in schools, 17-21
  Validity of 347-48, 350-69

Schools *see:* Special education pro-
  grams and schools
Sensory stimulation 89, 278-80
Spatial relations 90-91, 101, 103, 116

Special education
  Curriculum 81-85, 489, 495
  Educational therapy 280-82,
    313-19, 415-16
  Failures, reasons for 415
  Goals 57-62, 211
  Language development 155
  Materials 15, 21, 22, 184-85
  Methodologies 282-83, 484-89
  Programming 51, 54-57
  Reading 197-206
  Speech therapy 155
  Teachers 211
  Technological changes 35
  Therapeutic instruction 28, 175
Special education programs and
  schools
  California Educationally Handi-
    capped Program 481
  Delacato Studies in 350-69
  Elgin Public Schools 215-72
  For emotionally disturbed 393,
    406-09
  Hope School for Mentally Retarded
    Children 108
  Institues for the Achievement of
    Human Potential 324ff
  Junior Guidance Classes Program
    313-19
  Language development 161
  Manhattanville Community Centers
    313
  Materials 21ff
  For mentally retarded 108
  Palolo (Hawaii) School District 436
  Problems in 18-19
  Redondo Beach Elementary School
    District 483
  Santa Monica Unified Schools 436
  Social worker in 393
  Tulare County (Calif.) 436
  Vanguard School Career Guidance
    Center 41ff
Special education techniques
  Control of environment 215-16,
    221-23, 315-16, 418-19, 442-43,
    444, 489
  Engineered classroom 436ff
  Evaluation of 24, 419-26
  Grading 445-48
  Language development 155-68
  Materials used in 184-85
  Remediation 234-42, 257-69
  Structuring of activities 63-66,
    449-54
  Teachers 416-19
  Team-teaching 314, 317-18
  Testing 225-33
  Therapeutic tutoring 175, 424
  See also: Linguistic skills;
    Reading disabilities
Speech development and neurological
  organization theory 338, 340
Symbolization
  Alphabet 201
  Mathematics 451

Teachers and educators
  Goals 394
  Roles 53- 54, 211, 399-406
  Skills needed by 317
  Teacher-student relations 393-99,
    417. 443
  Teaching experiment, role in
    158-59
  Training in research methods 20-21
Teaching materials, 21ff
  Neurotic child 184-85
  See also Special education
Tests
  Assessment of 381-84
  Auditory-Vocal Association Test
    166, 167
  Bender-Gestalt 484
  California Achievement Test 484
  California Reading Test 362
  California Test of Mental Maturity
    484
  Cattell Infant Intelligence Scale 277
  Columbia Mental Maturity Scale
    281
  Conceptual Styles Test 404
  Developing 384-87
  Diagnostic 489-93
  Doman-Delacato Developmental
    Profile 326-27
  Examiner 385
  Gates Basic Reading Test 350-52
  Goals 387-89
  Gray Oral Reading Paragraphs Test
    358, 360
  Harris Tests of Lateral Dominance
    342
  Harrison-Stroud Reading Readiness
    Test 356
  Illinois Test of Psycholinguistic
    Abilities (ITPA) 161, 223, 294,
    404, 416, 419, 430
  Iowa Silent Reading Test 361
  Iowa Test of Basic Skills 365-66
  Frostig Developmental Test of
    Visual Preception 90-108,
    121-52, 416, 419, 430
  Keystone Visual Survey Test 364
  Kuhlmann-Anderson IQ 362
  Large-Thorndike Intelligence Test
    364
  Leiter International Scale 282
  Metropolitan Achievement Test
    162
  Metropolitan Readiness Test 166
  Metropolitan Reading Test 359-60
  Nelson Reading Test 486
  Peabody Language Development
    program 156
  Peabody Language Production In-
    ventory 162
  Peabody Picture Vocabulary Test
    161
  Preschool 385
  Primary Mental Abilities Test 162
  Scheffe's Test of Multiple Compari-
    son 288
  Scholastic Aptitude Test 354-56

Stanford-Binet LM 484
Stanford-Binet Intelligence Scale
  162; revised 278, 280
Stanford Reading Achievement
  Test 360, 361-62, 363, 364
Vocal Encoding Test 166, 167
Wechsler Intelligence Scale for
  Children (WISC) 162, 278, 416,
  419, 431, 484
Wepman Test of Auditory Dis-
  crimination 416, 419, 431
Wide Range Achievement Test 162,
  484

Visual Preception
  Tests in 90-108
  Frostig-Horne training program
    89ff
Visual problems
  Mentally retarded child 278-79
    289-96
Vocational rehabilitation 39, 43
  Audio-visual aids 64
  Curriculum modification 48-49
  Goals in 57-62
  Structuring of activities 63-66
  Systems approach 51, 63; see also
    Computers
  Teaching techniques 59, 63-66
  Vanguard School Career Guidance
    Center 41-43, 46ff